Place-Based Education in the Global Age

in the Global Age

Local Diversity

Place-Based Education in the Global Age

Local Diversity

Edited by

David A. Gruenewald
Gregory A. Smith

Routledge
Taylor & Francis Group
New York   London

First published by Lawrence Erlbaum Associates, Inc., Publishers
10 Industrial Avenue
Mahwah, New Jersey 07430

Transferred to digital printing 2010 by Routledge

Routledge

270 Madison Avenue
New York, NY 10016

2 Park Square, Milton Park
Abingdon, Oxon OX14 4RN, UK

10 9 8 7 6 5 4 3 2

International Standard Book Number-13: 978-0-8058-5864-8 (Softcover) 978-0-8058-5863-1 (Hardcover)

Library of Congress Cataloging-in-Publication Data

Place-based education in the global age : local diversity / author/editor(s) David A. Gruenewald and Gregory Alan Smith.
   p. cm.
Includes bibliographical references and index.
ISBN-13: 978-0-8058-5864-8 (alk. paper)
ISBN-10: 0-8058-5864-4 (alk. paper)
   1. Place-based education. 2. Community and school. I. Gruenewald, David A. II. Smith, Gregory A., 1948-

LC239.P527 2007
370.11'5--dc22   2007014374

Visit the Taylor & Francis Web site at
http://www.taylorandfrancis.com

CONTENTS

PREFACE

The idea for this book emerged in an unusual place: the basement of the public library in Hermiston, Oregon. Both of us drove 3 hours to meet there one January morning, David from Pullman, Washington, and Greg from Portland. David would have been deterred by snow and postponed this meeting if Greg had left a little later, but absent the chance of getting through to him by phone, David crossed the wintry Palouse west to Walla Walla, and then drove down into the Columbia Gorge. After meeting the spring before in Chicago at the 2003 American Educational Research Association Annual Meeting, we had decided that more conversations, if not some joint project, were in order.

In our work as teachers and researchers, we have long been concerned about the division between environmental educators and those who direct their attention to matters of social justice and equity. We are convinced that human welfare will depend on the ability to reconcile these two domains in the coming decades, yet the impacts of industrial activities, human numbers, and consumption are rarely acknowledged by educational researchers or faculty members in schools of education. We hoped that a book that conjoined the human and the more-than-human worlds might stimulate some needed dialogue.

Our previous work on place-based education (see Preface references) and the larger tensions between environment, culture, and education gave us a framework for this dialogue. For about 10 years, place-based education has been developing as a significant educational movement, and many of the major figures in this movement tell their stories in this book. Along with others working the terrain between environment and culture, we suggest that reversing a slide into social and environmental degradation will require a heightened awareness of place. Sometimes this awareness leads to a process of decolonization, that is, coming to understand and resist the ideas and forces that allow for the privileging of some people and the oppression of others—human and other-than-human. At other times, place-consciousness means learning how to reinhabit our communities and regions in ways that allow for more sustainable relationships now and in the long run.

This book is an effort to explore what an educational process that supports decolonization and reinhabitation might look like. We contacted colleagues from North America, Australia, and the Middle East to describe work they are engaged in that addresses, in one way or another, these issues. Not everyone shares our perspective about the need to confront oppressive institutions, but all of the contributors in this volume demonstrate a commitment to finding ways to more deeply connect children and young people to the places where they live. From that connection can emerge the caring, knowledge, responsibility, and skill required to make those places healthy and humane.

At base, it is this vision of health, bio- and cultural diversity, humanity, and beauty that drives us forward, and this is what we feel is so imperiled by the global economic forces currently overdetermining the character of so many of the planet's places. An educational process grounded in place will admittedly be insufficient to counter the power of transnational giants, but growing numbers of young people who grasp the nature of their situation and possess the skills and understandings required to live well in place, may possess the combination of determination and intelligence required to construct something different.

Many people helped to bring this book into being. We wish to express our thanks to all of the contributors for the work that they describe and for their willingness to participate in this project and to respond to, sometimes, several requests for rethinking and revision. Their good humor and cooperation made the process of pulling this volume together more a pleasure than a chore.

We also wish to thank our editors at Erlbaum, Naomi Silverman and Erika Kica, for their encouragement of this project and steady support as they midwifed it through the stages of production.

Finally, we thank our wives, Jill and Becky, for the time and support they have provided to us to write and edit what has become a substantial volume. They share our hope in the possibilities of place, a hope that keeps us going as we watch our children grow through childhood or into adulthood. We dedicate this volume to them.

OVERVIEW OF THIS VOLUME

Place-Based Education in the Global Age: Local Diversity is organized into three sections; each section begins with a brief introduction by the editors. The first section, Models for Place-Based Learning, is a collection of success stories from around the United States. Here, practitioners in diverse rural, suburban, and urban environments tell how a focus on place contributes to everyone's learning while supporting the larger goal of democratic participation for the public good. Reclaiming Broader Meanings of Education, Section II, explores some of the reasons for pursuing place-based education. The authors argue that if educators are concerned about the well-being of diverse communities, they need to begin paying more attention to the relationship between community well-being and the process of schooling. The last section, Global Visions of the Local in Higher Education, shows how educators from such diverse places as New Mexico, Israel, Sydney, and New England are using place as a focal point for developing community leaders, understanding the tensions between Israel and Palestine, fostering connection and consciousness-raising in the bush and in the city, and for showing future teachers the power of place-based learning.

REFERENCES

Gruenewald, D. (2003a). The best of both worlds: A critical pedagogy of place. *Educational Researcher, 32*(4), 3–12.

Gruenewald, D. (2003b). Foundations of place: A multidisciplinary framework for place-conscious education. *American Educational Research Journal, 40*(3), 619–654.

Gruenewald, D. (2005). Accountability and collaboration: Institutional barriers and strategic pathways for place-based education. *Ethics, Place and Environment: A Journal of Philosophy and Geography, 8*(3), 261–283.

Smith, G. (1998). Rooting children in place. *Encounter, 11*(4), 13–24.

Smith, G. (2002). Going local. *Educational Leadership, 60*(1), 30–33.

Smith, G. (2002). Place-based education: Learning to be where we are. *Phi Delta Kappan, 83*, 584–594.

Ray Barnhardt
Co-Director, Alaska Rural
   Systemic Initiative
University of Alaska
Fairbanks, AK

Julie Bartsch
The Rural School and
   Community Trust
Bolton, MA

John I. Cameron
Place Research Centre
University of Tasmania
Tasmania, Australia

Matt Dubel
Greenfield Center School
Greenfield, MA

Freema Elbaz-Luwisch
Department of Education
University of Haifa
Mount Carmel, Haifa, Israel

Mark Graham
Visual Arts Department
Brigham Young University
Provo, UT

David A. Gruenewald
College of Education
Washington State University
Pullman, WA

Clifford E. Knapp
College of Education, Emeritus
Northern Illinois University
DeKalb, IL

Michael Malahy Morris
College of Education
University of New Mexico
Albuquerque, NM

Robert Michael Pyle
Independent scholar and writer
Grays River, WA

Elaine Senechal
Science Department
Tewksbury Memorial High School
Tewksbury, MA

John Siskar
School of Arts and Humanities
Buffalo State College
Buffalo, NY

Gregory A. Smith
Graduate School of Education
    and Counseling
Lewis & Clark College
Portland, OR

David Sobel
Department of Education
Antioch New England Graduate
    School
Keene, NH

Mark Sorensen
STAR School
Leupp, AZ

Paul Theobald
Center for Excellence in Urban
    Education
Buffalo State College
Buffalo, NY

Rachel Tompkins
The Rural School and
    Community Trust
Arlington, VA

Making Room for the Local

David Gruenewald
Gregory Smith

This volume has two major purposes. First, we wish to contribute to the theory and practice of place-based or place-conscious education by collecting instructive and inspiring stories that can serve as exemplars for this exciting, burgeoning field. Second, we want to make the case through these stories of collaboration that place-based education can be viewed as the educational counterpart of a broader movement toward reclaiming the significance of the local in the global age.

This broader social movement, sometimes called "the new localism," has emerged in part as a response to patterns of economic development that disrupt, rather than cultivate, community life. Many communities across the nation and across the globe recognize that economic globalization, however inevitable and beneficial it may be to some, is far from the unconditional good it is often claimed to be (Korten, 2001; Mander & Goldsmith, 1996). As multinational corporations constantly relocate in search of cheaper labor and production costs, communities in the United States are left with high rates of under- and unemployment, a shrinking tax base, and, often, environmental decay. Wal-Mart and other superstores continue to displace local businesses and depress wages; the pressure to keep prices down leads to a downward spiral of more downsizing, outsourcing, and fewer economic opportunities for struggling communities. In short, the new localism recognizes that economic globalization under corporate capitalism is, potentially, economically devastating, culturally homogenizing, and ecologically destructive to local communities. Efforts to reclaim the local, however, are not based on a blanket rejection of capitalism or of a market economy. Instead, the new localism embraces a kind of place-conscious economic development that will benefit the inhabitants of local communities today and for the long term (Shuman, 1998).

Just as local communities often suffer the negative impacts of globalization, so do children and adults at all levels of schooling. The process of formal education in schools and universities is often totally isolated from the immediate context of community life. Interaction with the wider community and all the learning opportunities these could afford is overlooked in the push for each student to meet prescribed content area standards through decontextualized classroom instruction. Furthermore, education is explicitly linked in policy and practice to the narrative of economic globalization. Today, the seldom-questioned, underlying assumption about the purpose of schooling is to prepare the next generation to compete and succeed in the global economy (For a recent iteration of this position, see Friedman, 2005). In many respects, public education has become the business of training children and youth to enter the global marketplace as consumers and workers. This is not a new story. Since the inception of mass schooling or "industrial education," the central purpose of education in the United States has been to promote nationalism while providing big businesses with a compliant and skilled labor force. However, what is new today is a growing skepticism among diverse constituencies within civil society regarding the intentions of powerful corporations and the impacts of their self-serving actions. Around the country and around the world, citizens are becoming aware of the need to take responsibility for mediating the impacts of globalization on local cultures and ecosystems. Although there is a growing political, economic, and cultural literature describing how reclaiming the local might mitigate against the potentially harmful effects of globalization, little writing exists on the role of education in this process.

Part of the reason that the narrative of globalization remains largely unquestioned in schooling (despite the fact that communities everywhere are beginning to question it) is that the link between corporate capitalism and schooling has never been stronger. Shrinking public expenditures are coupled with a growing corporate presence on public school and university campuses. Programs deemed superfluous to basic skills or job training are being cut, and entire schools are being eliminated as colleges and universities experience the educational equivalent of downsizing. Since the early 1980s and the publication of *A Nation at Risk* (National Commision on Excellence in Education, 2003), trends toward standardization and accountability have been linked to the perceived need to keep pace with other nations in the global economic competition. More recently, the discourse of standards, accountability, and excellence has been linked to efforts to close the historic achievement gaps between different racial, cultural, and economic groups. Thus, the No Child Left Behind Act of 2001 is invoked at once as legislation aimed at ending inequality of educational opportunity and at strengthening the economic advantage of the entire nation. When the narrative of globalization becomes effectively linked to the narrative of social justice and equity, globalization becomes increasingly difficult to challenge. Meanwhile, efforts to close the achievement gap or the "digital divide" are often sponsored by corporations that bait schools and universities with consumer technologies that only reinforce the narrative of globalization by distracting educators and students from the educational possibilities and needs of local communities (Bowers, 2000).

Contributing to the educational and economic narratives that keep the attention of educators and learners focused away from their own communities is the power of corporate-sponsored media. Few people would argue that first television and now the Internet and their associated technologies and products help to choreograph youth and consumer cultures based on the commercial values that benefit corporate media sponsors. The entertainment-style technology–industrial complex reinforces the narrative of economic globalization by constructing children and youth around the world as hi-tech consumers rather than citizens. A youth culture based on commodification of experience through product identification intensifies alienation from community and from the intergenerational relationships necessary to strengthening community ties. Furthermore, a technologized consumer culture reinforces a brand of competitive individualism familiar now to both school and work environments. Corporate-sponsored media constantly teach that participation in the global economy through the consumption of ever-new products (made from cheap labor in deregulated environments around the globe) is a right as well as a measure of success and self-worth. Thus, in tandem with schooling and the narrative of globalization, corporate media distort what it means to be a person, a learner, and a member of a local community.

In fact, in many places, a case can be made that the process of schooling actually encourages many youth to reject their home communities and to look elsewhere for the good life depicted by media advertisers and the entertainment industry. For many people, the ability to earn a decent living means having to move great distances from their families, and to move again and again as directed by the job market. This pattern of uprooting means that many people simply do not live long enough in one place to develop intimate relationships to places. Instead of what Orr (1992) calls "inhabiting" a place, many people only "reside" where they live, and develop no particular connection to their human and non-human environments. This phenomenon of "placelessness" is associated with alienation from others and a lack of participation in the social and political life of communities. However, many people, families, and communities are resisting the experience and cultural trends of alienation and rootlessness by consciously deciding to stay put, dig in, and become long-term inhabitants of a place. The new localism is not only about creating the economic conditions that make staying put possible; it is also about conserving and creating patterns of connectedness and mutuality that are the foundation of community well-being.

PLACE-BASED PRACTICES IN DIVERSE CONTEXTS

Just as the new localism can be understood as diverse acts of resistance against the ravages of globalization and rootlessness, place-based education can be understood as a community-based effort to reconnect the process of education, enculturation, and human development to the well-being of community life. Place-based or place-conscious education introduces children and youth to the skills and dispositions needed to regenerate and sustain communities. It achieves this end by drawing on local phenomena as the source of at least a share of children's learning experiences, helping them to understand the processes that underlie the health of natural and social systems essential to human welfare. In contrast to conventional schooling with its focus on distant events and standardized knowledge, education conscious of place systematically inducts students into the knowledge and patterns of behavior associated with responsible community engagement. What does this look like?

High school students in the coastal community of Seaside, Oregon, have played a central role in the collection and presentation of data associated with the writing of an urban renewal grant sought by the city to purchase and restore a former mill site only a few blocks from the city's central business district. The city hoped to turn this site into a park and nature center at which local residents and tourists can enjoy both recreational and educational experiences. At the outset, students in science classes helped catalog natural features and gathered information required by the grant application. After the grant was awarded, other students went on to conduct more specific inventories of habitat used by birds, mammals, and fish in an effort to determine where buildings, paths, and other developments could be introduced with a minimum effect on the site's nonhuman inhabitants. In this process they learned how to use global positioning technologies to develop finely detailed maps that could then be used by the city's planners. Throughout this project, students served as intellectual resources for their community, gathering and processing data that would have been prohibitively expensive for public employees to collect. Their labor contributed significantly to a successful outcome for the city and its residents. This experience demonstrated to young people the way that collective action can lead to desired results.

Students in another coastal community on the opposite side of the continent encountered a similar lesson, in this case one about economic development. Lubec, Maine, is located on Cobscook Bay just south of the Canadian border (Hynes, 2003). Once home to a community of north Atlantic fishermen and their families, it has experienced the severe economic repercussions associated with the decline of this region's ocean fisheries. Parents are painfully aware that a way of life that had supported people for generations is now threatened. Like families in many rural communities dependent on extractive industries, they had resigned themselves to the exodus of their sons and daughters, forced to leave in pursuit of viable economic opportunities elsewhere. A young science teacher at the local high school decided to take on this issue and explore the possibilities of aquaculture. If the resource could no longer be found in the oceans, perhaps people could farm the sea in ways that would provide living wages for those who wished to remain in Lubec. With help from the community and a handful of external funders, this teacher and her students began a pilot project raising mussels, trout, tilapia, and sea urchins whose roe is considered a delicacy by the Japanese. Students have contributed their physical labor to the construction of a dock and the retrofitting of a water treatment facility for mussel and tilapia farming. They have contributed their intellectual labor to an investigation of the kinds of feed most likely to result in roe of the color most desired in Japan. Like their counterparts in Seaside, students in Lubec have become intellectual resources for their town, engaged in learning activities that promise to benefit both themselves and their elders. Together, they are collectively creating a future for themselves that otherwise would not exist.

A few hundred miles south in Boston, students at the Greater Egleston Community High School are helping to regenerate an urban environment. Their work is described at length by Elaine Senechal later in this volume. As young people in Seaside are restoring a former mill site and those in Lubec a decimated economy, adolescents in this Roxbury neighborhood are attempting to restore the quality of the air. Roxbury is crossed by a number of major thoroughfares and is the site of the bus lot for the Massachusetts Bay Transit Authority; the result is high levels of air pollution and rates of asthma among its primarily ethnically diverse, poor, and working-class residents. In conjunction with Alternatives for Community & Environment (ACE), a nonprofit organization committed to addressing instances of environmental injustice, students have been instrumental in pressuring local public health agencies to monitor air quality with a level of attentiveness that did not exist before they became involved. They have also taken the lead in presenting this issue to the public, developing a system utilizing different flags to alert their neighbors about air quality, lobbying state officials to pass legislation guaranteeing to people the same protections as endangered species, and encouraging the enforcement of state anti-idling regulations. Through their work to enhance the physical environment in which they and their relatives and neighbors live, students at the Greater Egleston Community High School are learning leadership and negotiation skills essential to community organizing and development.

In each of these three communities—urban, rural, White, and non-White—students are encountering learning experiences that arise from local contexts. They are, furthermore, learning that they have the capacity to use their minds and energy to make contributions to their communities that are valued by others and that promise to improve people's lives. Formal education in these circumstances becomes meaningful and a source of communal connection. Too often high school education, in particular, can act as a source of alienation, especially for students who may not be academically inclined. When course work is conjoined to the life of the broader community in the way it has been in Seaside, Lubec, and Egleston, students grasp the power that comes when knowledge and collective endeavors are linked in this way. In such settings students do not need to ask why they are learning; they know the answer to that question as they work on tasks that benefit others.

In the face of the economic, social, and environmental dilemmas associated with the globalization of industrial civilization, the lessons these students encounter may well be essential. Much of the success of the human species can be ascribed to our adaptability, a characteristic predicated on people's ability to respond collectively and over time to the conditions encountered in specific places. Diverse cultures across the planet have arisen because of this capacity. Human adaptability, however, is being diminished, and traditions of successful adaptation are being disrupted and destroyed, by the imposition of a single set of understandings and a single way of life on all people everywhere. Patterns of self- and community-reliance have been replaced by dependence on increasingly centralized institutions that have diminished the importance of more localized responses as they impose the logic and efficiencies of a market economy. This process is unraveling both the natural and social systems that underlie our species' health and security. If not altered, the severe environmental breakdown, political instability, and human misery encountered in places like Haiti could become the norm rather than an unfortunate exception.

CORE THEMES IN PLACE-BASED EDUCATION

In *Becoming Native to a Place*, Jackson (1994) argues that either all places are holy, or none of them are. All places, in other words, are deserving of our attention, respect, and care. The questions that lie at the core of this volume are: What educational forms promote care for places? What does it take to conserve, restore, and create ways of being that serve people and places? What does it take to transform those ways of being that harm people and places? Given the degree to which global elites benefit from current institutional arrangements, it seems unlikely that more than a few of the privileged members of industrial and postindustrial societies will sponsor the needed initiatives. The international impasse over carbon emissions is indicative of the dilemma faced by those who hope to marshal change at this level. Globally, however, initiatives at the local level are now demonstrating the real possibility of change. Suzuki and Dressel's 2003 volume, *Good News for a Change*, describes efforts set in motion by ordinary people across the planet. Committed to particular places, individuals and groups of individuals have embarked on projects that are protecting natural resources, creating sustainable economic opportunities, and preserving the integrity of established human communities despite the stasis encountered in most transnational organizations. As Esteva and Prakash (1998) assert in *Grassroots Postmodernism*, it may be with these people on the margins of industrial society that the foundation for a hopeful and humane future is being laid. The stories told in the following pages illustrate the widespread growth of grassroots movements, and the vitality of those who live and work in the margins.

We believe that an education that orients children and adults to the values and opportunities that inhere in the places where they live could provide the dispositions, understandings, and skills required to restore and democratize humanity's adaptive capabilities in ways undreamed of by the insulated elites who populate emerging global cities like Chicago or Mumbai or Tokyo. That education must first lead children to recognize the assets found in the human and natural environments closest to them, including understandings drawn from traditional cultural practices that emphasize restraint in the use of natural resources and support for social practices informed by mutuality (Bowers, 2005). At its most fundamental level, place-based education must overcome the traditional isolation of schooling from community life. The walls of the school must become more permeable, and local collaboratives and support structures must be built and maintained so that education truly becomes a larger community effort. This education in connection to place must also inspire in learners an appreciation of beauty and wonder, for it is through the experience of beauty and wonder that we risk opening ourselves to others and the world. By connecting to and appreciating places, children and youth begin to understand and question the forces that shape places; they develop a readiness for social action, and, with the proper adult guidance, the skills needed for effective democratic participation.

Democracy has always been a struggle for meaning and for change, and place-based education must demonstrate to students the challenges and potentialities of collective effort. For most people living today, the promise of individual economic mobility is a cruel illusion; their wealth and security must instead be found in the care and imagination of others close to home. Only as members of mutually supportive social groups have human beings, for all but the past half millennium, been able to assure their own survival. Current population trends and declining natural resources including water, land, and fish as well as easily extractable fossil fuel suggest that even with the benefits of science, future circumstances will not be that different from those faced by our ancestors in earlier eras. The ability to work with others toward commonly defined and enacted goals will be essential. Rather than relying on distant rulers to make things right at the local level, people need to learn how to make things right on their own. Individually, this will almost certainly prove to be impossible. A review of the achievements of past and present preindustrial societies, however, provides ample proof of what small groups of people acting collectively can accomplish. This should not be interpreted as a rejection of the benefits of science and technology but rather a reassertion of our species' remarkable capabilities even when stripped of the powers afforded us by modernity.

An education in place must also acquaint students with the way that their own health and security are codependent on the health and security of everyone and everything around them. This knowledge of interdependence must have emerged over time through painful experiences for our predecessors and remains embedded in the language and culture of Native peoples on all continents. Knowledge of interdependence, now reemerging in societies across the globe, must come to inform all human decisions if people currently alive hope to pass down to their offspring places worthy of inhabitation. Interdependence is not an abstract idea, but a lived experience of all people in all places, best understood though the study of the commons that we share with human and nonhuman others. Bowers (2005) describes *the commons* as those relationships and systems that contribute to the well-being of a community and that have not been commodified by the capitalist–industrial system. These include natural systems such as air, water, and forests; cultural systems such as public spaces and the legal protections that keep them public; and civic associations found in mentoring and intergenerational relationships. Through an education in place that connects teachers and learners to the life of the wider community, these ecological and cultural commons must be identified, conserved, and restored.

In addition, an education in place must not be tuned to nostalgic or homogenous images of the local, but to local diversity, the diversity within places and the diversity between places. Place-conscious education challenges conventional notions of diversity in education, of multiculturalism or culturally responsive teaching, which too often take for granted the legitimacy and value of an education that disregards places in all their particularity and uniqueness. Critical issues of race, class, gender, and other aspects of culture can become abstractions unless these issues are grounded in concrete experience, experience that always takes place somewhere. Place-consciousness toward diversity and multiculturalism means reconnecting these themes with the rooted experience of people in their total environments, including the ecological. This rooted experience has both a spatial and temporal dimension; place-consciousness, therefore, must also include consciousness of the historical memory of a place, and the traditions that emerged there, whether these have been disrupted or conserved.

Finally, an education in place must be an education in ethics. People need to be aware of that which fosters wholeness and life and that which fosters division and harm. As the Amish make decisions about which technologies to accept or reject on the basis of their communal consequences, so do all people need to begin accepting or rejecting the products of human imagination and inventiveness according to their impact on the welfare of other humans and other beings and the vast natural systems that support life. Grounded in such understanding, children will be in a better position to determine which of the aspects of the emerging global civilization are worth preserving and which would be best to abandon.

AN EDUCATION FOR THE FUTURE OF PLACES

From its inception, one of the driving forces behind modernity has been the desire on the part of human beings to gain and assert increasing control over phenomena that affect their lives. To some extent, humanity's growing understanding of the natural world has allowed people to believe that such control is indeed achievable. One of the central flaws in the drive to globalize the economy and culture, however, lies in the illusion that the economic and political managers of the massive, centralized systems that now govern the lives of most people are in fact able to predict and control events outside their immediate domain. The political chaos in Iraq following U.S. military intervention and growing climate instability linked to the burning of fossil fuels demonstrate the degree to which both social and natural forces defy the will of even the most powerful human beings.

The beginning years of the 21st century are serving as an object lesson in humility and the dangers of hubris. The complexities of the planet and humanity in all its diversity will elude our species' capacity to understand and manage; furthermore, any effort to assert human will on this scale will almost certainly have results not dissimilar from what is occurring in the Middle East and the skies above us. Margaret Thatcher's assertion that there is no alternative to globalization must be replaced by a reinvestment of faith and energy in the capacity of people in local and regional settings to make decisions and adapt to changing conditions in ways that will benefit both them and their descendants over the long term.

Place-conscious education provides one strategy for developing in people the capacity to reclaim the inventiveness, imagination, and courage that over millennia allowed our predecessors to make use of the possibilities provided by the planet wherever they found themselves. They aligned themselves with no universal ideology or set of understandings. They instead relied on their own intelligence and ability to collaborate with others to create cultures and social conditions that allowed for their survival and enough security to pass down their understandings and traditions from one generation to the next. They were able to do this not by controlling phenomena but by interacting with the world around them in ways that truly fit the conditions they encountered. This is what our ancestors throughout time have done to make this planet their home. It is what we and our descendants must do, as well.

REFERENCES

Bowers, C. A. (2000). *Let them eat data: How computers affect education, cultural diversity, and the prospects of ecological sustainability.* Athens: University of Georgia Press.

Bowers, C. A. (2005). *Revitalizing the commons; Cultural and educational sites of resistance and affirmation.* Lexington, MA: Lexington Books.

Esteva, G., & Prakash, M. (1998). *Grassroots postmodernism.* London: Zed Books.

Friedman, T. (2005). *The world is flat: A brief history of the twenty-first century.* New York: Farrar, Straus, & Giroux.

Hynes, M. (2003). *Revitalizing economics around Cobscook Bay.* Washington, DC: Rural School and Community Trust.

Jackson, W. (1994). *Becoming native to a place.* Lexington: University of Kentucky Press.

Korten, D. (2001). *When corporations rule the world.* San Francisco: Berrett-Koehler Publishers; Bloomfield, CT: Kumarian Press.

Mander, J., & Goldsmith, E. (Eds.). (1996). *The case against the global economy: And for a turn toward the local.* San Francisco: Sierra Club Books.

National Commission on Excellence in Education. (1983). *A nation at risk: The imperative for educational reform.* A report to the nation and the Secretary of Education. United States Department of Education. Washington, DC: The Commission.

Orr, D. (1992*). Ecological literacy: Education and the transition to a postmodern world.* Albany, NY: State University of New York Press.

Shuman, M. (1998). *Going local: Creating self-reliant communities in a global era.* New York: Free Press.

Suzuki, D., & Dressel, H. (2002). *Good news for a change.* Toronto: Stoddart.

I

Models for Place-Based Learning

Place-based education is both an old and a new phenomenon. All education prior to the invention of the common school was place-based. It is education as practiced in modern societies that has cut its ties to the local. Reformers such as John Dewey and William Heard Kilpatrick in the early 20th century spoke to the importance of incorporating students' experience of particular communities and places into their formal education, but the tendency toward centralization and standardization in the broader society marginalized their perspective and the practices they advocated. Although the press toward standardization remains as strong or stronger than ever, educators in a variety of locales are developing approaches to teaching and learning that redirect students to the value of the local. In doing so, they have inspired a rebirth of interest in the potentialities of the unique knowledge and experience encountered in the multiplicity of cultures and subcultures that make up our increasingly global society. The chapters in this section describe possibilities that have emerged when people in schools link learning with phenomena immediately available to their senses and lives.

Clifford Knapp is one of the elders of the environmental education movement. His efforts, however, have never been focused entirely on natural phenomena. In Knapp's chapter, he describes a range of different contemporary models of education that have sought to bridge the gap between students' lives outside of school and what they encounter in classrooms. From the cultural journalism characteristic of the Foxfire program to real-world problem solving, these innovative approaches have offered practitioners a way to revitalize students' interest in learning and not infrequently reenergized teachers themselves. Knapp provides a useful overview of possibilities that can arise as people in particular places direct their intelligence and imagination to what is close at hand.

This is exactly what art educator Mark Graham did with his students when he taught in a school located on Long Island, New York. Demonstrating the way that place-based education is as relevant to urban as well as rural students, Graham describes a course that introduced young people to place through art and art making. In an attempt to develop a way of looking at the world that was not dominated by the mass media, he encouraged students to examine and portray aspects of their own world left out of the images encountered on television and contemporary films. Drawing on history and art produced in earlier eras, the course sought to stimulate in students a way of seeing the world that focused less on the conquest and consumption of places than on the building of relationship and personal meaning. Graham's work provides an example of the way teachers can help cultivate in their students the sense of connectedness that underlies the forms of caring and stewardship essential to the maintenance of sustainable relationships between humans and the places where they live.

The next three chapters show how schools that attend to what is close at hand can lead to a transformation of communities and places. Educational leader and teacher Mark Sorensen describes the STAR School in northern Arizona and its work with students who are primarily of Navajo origin. Located just off the reservation, this small charter school aims to develop in its students a deep sense of kinship to other people and all things. The acronym that composes the school's name, *Service To All Relations*, captures that purpose. Much of the school's service to others can be seen in the way that students participate in activities that benefit their communities and the Earth. But another component can be seen in the way that the school itself seeks to model patterns of behavior aimed at showing local residents how they might shape new institutions, adopt innovative strategies for generating power or growing plants, or embrace less conflictual and more empowering patterns of communication and human interaction. At the intersection of many cultures, the STAR School seeks to affirm the local at the same time that it spurs its low-income and often disenfranchised supporters to imagine and make real more fulfilling lives for themselves and their children.

Julie Bartsch, a writer and activist employed by the Rural School and Community Trust, has been intimately involved with some of the educational and community development efforts described in Chapter 9 by Rachel Tompkins. Like the Navajo Reservation, rural communities in the Northeast corner of the United States are the victims of poverty and abandonment. Left on the margins of industrial society, small communities whose members once supported themselves by fishing and logging are faced with the out-migration of young people confounded by limited employment opportunities. The long-term health of these communities rests on their ability to revitalize their economies and cultures so that they can both support and attract the young. Place-based educational efforts, in part underwritten by the Rural Trust, exemplify what the convergence of schools and community development can accomplish.

Elaine Senechal recounts her experience as a science teacher in an inner-city Boston community that has been similarly abandoned by an economy and political trends that disregard the poor and people of color. As mentioned earlier, Senechal and her students at the Greater Egleston Community High School were faced with a rising incidence of asthma associated with traffic-caused air pollution. Basing their advocacy efforts on a state anti-idling law, students' political efforts over a number of years led to a legal judgment against Boston's transit authority that will result in the replacement of most its fleet of diesel busses with cleaner natural gas busses. As with the place-based educational efforts described in Sorensen's and Bartsch's chapters, a focus on local issues is linking students with their communities in ways that are improving the lives of their families and neighbors.

The final chapter in this section is written by Ray Barnhardt, a long-time advocate for Alaska Natives and other indigenous peoples. Barnhardt describes a statewide effort to integrate non-Western knowledge systems and cultural practices into Alaska's public educational system. With sizeable grants from the National Science Foundation and the Annenberg Rural Challenge, the Alaska Native Knowledge Network (ANKN) started by Barnhardt and others has for over a decade been developing an approach to culturally responsive education that is now being adopted and modified by indigenous groups around the world. The ANKN demonstrates a systematic process for ensuring that local cultural knowledge systems are given a place in the education of children who are members of non-Western cultures. This approach validates cultural diversity by affirming not only the history and festivals of specific ethnic groups, but also the way in which these groups have constructed their understanding of the world and peoples' relationship to it. These understandings are often disregarded or viewed as inferior to the Euro-American perspectives that dominate most school curricula. Barnhardt's efforts demonstrate how parity between perspectives and practices can support the perpetuation of cultural traditions that have proven their appropriateness for the regions in which they have emerged. The Alaska Native Knowledge Network exemplifies a way to protect local cultures from the homogenizing effect of globalization, reminding us of the close link between diversity and locality.

By its very nature, place-based education is not something that can be packaged and then disseminated. It depends on the creative interaction between learners and the possibilities and requirements of specific places. What the models presented in this section provide is a sense of what can be accomplished when educators direct their attention to local phenomena. They should be seen, however, more as sources of inspiration than as recipes to be followed. Furthermore, these examples show that even within the context of highly bureaucratized and standardized educational systems, innovative teachers and activists are finding spaces within which to create learning opportunities that strengthen and extend students' relationship to particular communities and places. In this process, many of these approaches to teaching and learning are contributing not only to the education of children but to the enhancement of the social and natural environments in which they live.

CHAPTER 1

Place-Based Curricular and Pedagogical Models
My Adventures in Teaching Through Community Contexts

Clifford E. Knapp

A place is a piece of the whole environment which has been claimed by feelings.

—Alan Gussow, Artist-in-Residence for Mother Nature (1974)

INTRODUCTION

I first started to think about the power of a place-based pedagogy in the early 1970s when I heard artist Alan Gussow speak about "a sense of place" at an outdoor education conference in New York. When he referred to "place" as a piece of the environment claimed by feelings, I understood why this idea captured my attention. Having grown up in a New Jersey suburb across the river from New York City in the 1940s and 1950s, I recalled the pleasant memories of exploring the vacant woodlots and blackberry fields near home and fishing in the nearby waters (Knapp, 1999). A summer camp counselor job while in college was my introduction to teaching others about nature and human nature in places I then considered to be wilderness. I later pursued a career in outdoor and environmental education and taught at the elementary, junior and senior high, and university levels for over 40 years. My positive feelings about outdoor places were claimed early in life by my surroundings, including the people in them, and eventually I earned a living by "taking people for walks in the woods and fields."

Today the field of place-based education has established a paper trail of thousands of pages in its young life as an educational movement. This doesn't mean that place-based education has never before been tried in schools and other educational institutions. In fact the idea of learning from the local surroundings predates the formation of formal schooling; it was simply labeled differently or not labeled at all and implemented in a variety of ways. Several authors (Gruenewald, 2003; Powers, 2004; Smith, 2002; Sobel, 2004; Woodhouse & Knapp, 2000) acknowledge a variety of other descriptive names to indicate the linking of local places to the formal educational process. For example, the following terms have been used to describe forms of place-based education: community-based learning, service-learning, environment as an integrating concept, environment-based education, outdoor education, bioregional education, ecological education, sustainable-development education, cultural journalism, nature studies, real-world problem solving, and many others. A few researchers (e.g., Hug, 1998), believe that place-based education is a unique descriptor emerging as a result of an evolution of historical terminology and practice. From the late 1800s to the present time, several movements in schools have promoted the educational use of local areas as integral parts of the curriculum: nature study, conservation education, outdoor education, environmental education, and more recently, place-based education. Both viewpoints about terminology illustrate how educational movements take on various labels depending on who conceives of and writes about them.

An article by Newmann and Oliver appearing in the *Harvard Educational Review* in 1967 describes their idea of place-based education as " a proposal for education in community" (pp. 95–101). They recommended that learning should be pursued in three different contexts: the school, the laboratory-studio-work, and the community seminar. In the school context, they recognize the need for systematic, preplanned, and formalized instruction in basic literacy skills, health and hygiene, and the like. In this context the teacher has clear objectives with terminal student behaviors in mind. They recommend that school learning should be problem-centered and exciting and should constantly consider reorganizing basic content leading to insights and understandings. They see this kind of learning as only one of three types that should occur during the educational process. In the second context, labeled "laboratory-studio-work," the completion of tasks is the major objective. Laboratories could be factories, art studios, hospitals, libraries, or political headquarters. Student activity would be governed by the developing nature of the selected problem or task. In these types of laboratories, learning should occur as a by-product of genuine participation in the activities. In the third context, community seminar, the purpose would be to reflectively explore community issues and meanings. Leaders of these seminars could be teachers hired by the school or any other qualified community expert. The major purpose of the seminars would be reflection and deliberation on the actions stimulated by the laboratory context. Again, learning in the seminars should not be preplanned, nor would there be specific tasks or problems to solve. Newman and Oliver thoroughly outlined an educational plan that linked formal schooling with the community context without inventing a specific label for it.

For purposes of this chapter, Sobel's (2004, p. 7) broad definition of place-based education was chosen:

> The process of using the local community and environment as a starting point to teach concepts in language arts, mathematics, social studies, science, and other subjects across the curriculum. Emphasizing hands-on, real-world learning experiences, this approach to education increases academic achievement, helps students develop stronger ties to their community, enhances students' appreciation for the natural world, and creates a heightened commitment to serving as active, contributing citizens. Community vitality and environmental quality are improved through the active engagement of local citizens, community organizations, and environmental resources in the life of the school.

For those seeking other definitions of the term, the references at the end of the chapter provide other variations on this major theme. Kehrberg (n.d., pp. 1–2) at the University of Montana, writes: "Place-based education is a broad term that not only refers to a method of teaching, but a growing movement to redefine schooling, and a theory about how we should ultimately view education. Therefore, developing one simple definition for this term proves difficult."

This chapter deals mainly with what I learned from teaching 12 semesters of a graduate course in place-based education at Northern Illinois University. It describes the curricular and pedagogical models I used in designing this course titled, "Integrating Community Resources Into Curriculum and Instruction." I taught the first of these 12 courses in 1991 and the last in 2004. In 1992 I published an article (Knapp) describing my responses to teaching the course for the first time. Then I had many more questions than answers about how this learner-centered style of teaching was supposed to work. Obviously I had enough confidence in the approach and in myself to continue teaching in that way for another 11 courses. The more I taught the course, the more I was convinced that I was doing something important and that my students were learning about place-based education and other needed skills and concepts. This chapter also provides an outline of my educational philosophy and how it was applied to the implementation of the course.

SHARING EXCERPTS FROM MY EDUCATIONAL PHILOSOPHY

I believe firmly in sharing my educational philosophy with my students during the first few meetings of the class. This is important because everything that we will do together is derived directly from this worldview of teaching and learning. Each time I redesigned and taught the course, I attempted to make my course syllabus align more consistently with my developing educational philosophy. Just as the design of the course changed slightly each time after teaching it, my educational philosophy also changed in some ways.

The acts of teaching and learning have dominated my adult life. I learned so that I could teach and I taught so that I could learn. Teaching and learning are inextricably connected and both have been important to me. Now, I don't do one without being aware of the other.

Teaching is a process of creating climates and conditions that engage students in learning with others. My primary role as designated leader is to structure course experiences rich in potential learning opportunities for as many students as possible. This structure must provide students with choices of their pathways to knowledge based on their needs, interests, and preferred learning styles. I can only invite learners to participate in the learning process. Education is largely a do-it-yourself enterprise after the teacher's job is finished.

I view teaching as an ongoing experiment. The question, "If I as teacher create a certain environment, what, if anything, will my students learn?" has guided my practice. I use a Socratic questioning approach in much of my teaching, under the assumption that collectively my students already know many of the answers. I sometimes ask questions when I don't know their answers. I will not restrict my students' learning because of the limits of my knowledge. I often learn something from teaching that changes my way of thinking about my next course. Because teaching involves such a complex array of human interactions with people and places, I have never felt that I had mastered the art and science of teaching.

Teaching depends on establishing a person-to-person relationship with my students. I show my human side to my students and try to find out about their human sides outside of class. Then we can all connect as human beings on the same learning quest. I attempt to create norms that assure everyone that we will support each other's attempts to navigate the sometimes frightening and often exciting waters of learning. I build as many bridges as possible between my students and me, and we cross them together as we learn about each other and the course content.

Teaching involves a mandate to challenge students to think reflectively. Thinking deeply about how learning is taking place and how knowledge will be applied to life is an important path to knowledge. My role is to design situations in which students experience dilemmas in the realm of knowing and feeling. When I help create meaningful and engaging problems in their lives and assist them in resolving some of this turmoil, I feel that I am truly teaching.

Teaching means extending the classroom beyond the four walls of the classroom and the two covers of books. It means immersing students in direct experiences with people and places in order to learn in the context of realistic community situations. My classrooms become the natural and built environments surrounding the indoor classroom of the university. Contextual learning becomes the vehicle for creating meaningful curriculum and instruction. I constantly ask myself, "Where is the best laboratory for learning and what experiences will help my students find the knowledge they want and need?" We enter the experiential learning cycle together at the point of action and then proceed through the stages of reflection, conceptualization, skill development, value formation, application, and then return to further action informed by acquired knowledge.

Teaching is guiding students on adventures into partially unknown territory. Although the purpose and objectives for my courses were always clear, some of the curriculum content springing from the needs and interests of my students was not. Because of my background as a questioner and explorer of places, I am able to create and interpret the course maps that we create together. By using my knowledge compass, I can help students navigate over much of the terrain outlined in the syllabus. I never will have complete and accurate maps nor will know all of the course territory. Sometimes my students show me new places that don't appear on the course map. When this happens, we explore together. With each trek into the subject matter, I feel more confident on the journey. At the same time, I realize that knowledge is always growing and changing, and I can never rest on the past for very long. When my students gain enough knowledge and confidence to lead, I step aside and become a learner with them.

Teaching can lead to lifelong friendships and professional contacts. I am still in touch with some students from past courses. Even when we are not connected in reality, we are linked through memories. As I reflect on my own education, I remember the junior high physical education teacher who told me the best way to dry myself after showering; the teacher who asked me to carefully consider what's worth teaching; the teacher who modeled a warm personality and, at the same time, demanded academic excellence; the teacher who respected my work ethic and hired me to help him after school; and the teacher who paid me a compliment by selecting a line from an Oliver Goldsmith poem for my autograph book: "And still they gazed and still their wonder grew, that one small head could carry all he knew." Those teachers and others noticed and accepted me as a person, despite my limited knowledge of their disciplines. They gave me gifts of caring and concern, and I attempt to return these gifts to my students when we share time in class.

I teach to create a friendlier and more peaceful world community. My goal is to achieve more harmony both among the earth's human inhabitants and among other beings and ecosystems. I believe that our survival and quality of life depend on developing an environmental ethic that honors and cares for the planet. Being earth friendly is not only my goal as a teacher; it is a value applied to my personal life. I strive to reconnect others and myself to life-sustaining nature. In nature lies the "greenprint" for a higher quality life.

Learning rarely involves only a single destination. It is also a continuing process with many variations. Learning should lead to further questioning and eventually to more learning and other questions. My aim is to help students investigate problems on their own and with the help of others. Learning shouldn't be a lonely endeavor. Teaching means that I should model being an active, engaged learner. I am still excited about learning and my students need to see that. Through freely sharing my ongoing adventures in seeking knowledge, I can inspire my students. I must clearly demonstrate what I expect from my students and share verbally how this happens in me.

To summarize my philosophy of education, I believe that teaching and learning are firmly linked. Teaching involves creating environments that are emotionally and physically safe while retaining elements of risk and adventure; are structured and organized while remaining flexible and full of choices; are stable and predictable, yet experimental; are friendly and caring, yet formal and disciplined; and are intellectually challenging without being stressful and tedious. Whenever possible, I provide direct experiences in realistic contexts in order to stimulate learning. I serve as a guide on explorations of the unknown and gradually transfer leadership to my students as they gain confidence and skills. I seek lifelong friendships and professional contacts from my students and teach to make the world a better place. I am a student-centered teacher following a self-imposed mandate to view teaching and learning as a joyful adventure. I cannot separate the connections between them.

DESIGNING THE COURSE

Before I could teach the course, "Integrating Community Resources in Curriculum and Instruction," I had to wait until two senior faculty members retired. Finally, when they did, I was offered the opportunity. I was quick to accept because I had always eyed the course with great interest. The former professors had established the format of students investigating a place or person, gathering information by interviewing others, and writing chapters in a published manuscript. I liked this final book product as a way of motivating the students to explore their interests as well as aspects of the local area. Every student's writing skills were not strong, but the exercise of writing promoted thinking and most students experienced success by improving their skills.

I designed the course with five major student goals in mind:

- To explore and apply the theories and practices of experiential education and place-based education.
- To increase skills and attitudes in group dynamics, human relations, and community building.
- To investigate local instructional resources (people and places) using experiential learning methods.
- To design and implement a cooperative book-writing project using techniques of cultural journalism.
- To expand knowledge about available community study instructional resources (e.g., books, periodicals, Web sites).

In addition to these broad goals, about a dozen more specific student outcomes were listed. These included: writing entries in a learning log (journal); constructing interview questions, interviewing a person, transcribing the text, and incorporating the information into a 1,500–2,000 word article for publication; analyzing the dynamics of the ongoing group process; viewing the local area through the lens of a teacher planning a field trip; teaching a needed skill or topic to others in the class (e.g., following the required writing style format or sharing a valuable written resource); applying teaching approaches from various place-based educational models; preparing an assessment portfolio consisting of selected examples of their written work; assuming a leadership role in the school to help other teachers use community resources; and participating fully in a learner-centered, democratic classroom.

Despite a number of structured assignments, students always had a great deal of autonomy in making many choices. For example, these choices included selecting the content for their articles, designing the book and other instructional aides, deciding on a book title and theme, selecting some of the class content and time allocations based on project needs, and deciding on the format for their learning logs. Based on constructivist learning theory, my strategy was to structure most of the class activities in the beginning of the semester and gradually assume less control as the students' skills and understandings of the tasks ahead became clearer. This approach could be described as sharing leadership responsibility. I led the activities until my students were able to assume leadership on their own. Constructivists sometimes refer to this method of guiding student learning as scaffolding:

> As a classroom practice, scaffolding involves having the teacher provide a great deal of structure when children are first introduced to new material and then gradually turn more and more of the responsibility for learning over to the students as they become more competent and confident in the process. (Danker, 2005, pp. 22–23)

When I began to teach this course, I selected Wigginton's book, *Sometimes a Shining Moment: The Foxfire Experience* (1985), as the major text. In the mid-1990s I used Osborn's book, *Using Community Resources* (1994) as a supplementary text to the many handouts gathered from a variety of sources. As I discovered new articles and wrote more of my own, I moved toward a text consisting of collected readings that were targeted more closely on the course design.

EXPLORING THEORY AND PRACTICE FROM EXPERIENTIAL AND PLACE-BASED EDUCATION

There has never been a shortage of terminology used to describe various approaches to exploring the environment from an educational perspective. To illustrate this, I distribute a collection of 78 different terms to

"...describe the fields of education in, about, and for the environment" (Knapp, n.d.). In this course we focused mainly on two of the labels: experiential education and place-based education.

In November 1994 the Board of Directors of the Association for Experiential Education approved a definition and principles of experiential education for the first time. This brief definition and 12 principles of practice were useful to explain the theory underlying how the course was designed: "Experiential education is a process through which a learner constructs knowledge, skill, and value from direct experiences" (Proudman, 1995, pp. 1–2). The principles outline the importance of being aware of a learning cycle composed of reflection, critical analysis, and synthesis. Learners are characterized by taking initiative, making decisions, being held accountable for the results, posing questions, experimenting, solving problems, and constructing meaning from experience. They are engaged intellectually, emotionally, socially, soulfully, and/or physically in authentic learning tasks as human relationships are nurtured. Risk-taking and uncertainty are a part of sometimes-unpredictable experiences. The educator's primary roles include structuring suitable experiences, posing problems, setting boundaries, ensuring safety, and facilitating learning. Unplanned, spontaneous opportunities for learning are encouraged whenever appropriate. Experiential education capitalizes on the natural consequences resulting from both unplanned and planned activities. These characteristics of experiential education are exemplified in the course syllabus and serve to explain to my students "why I do what I do."

Place-based education shares most of these characteristics and also provides more specificity and guidance for my students. Knapp and Woodhouse (2003, p. 242) list 10 characteristics of this educational approach including: The surrounding phenomena provide the foundation for interdisciplinary curriculum development and contain ecological, multigenerational, and multicultural dimensions. Students and teachers are encouraged to cross the boundaries between the school and the community and become involved in a variety of constructive ways. Learners are expected to become creators of knowledge as well as consumers of knowledge, and their questions and concerns play central roles in this process. They are assessed on the basis of how this knowledge contributes to the community's well-being and sustainability, not just on how well they are prepared to earn a living. These principles of experiential education and characteristics of place-based education are often demonstrated throughout the semester and noted by reflecting on the various experiences we share.

UNDERSTANDING GROUP DYNAMICS, HUMAN RELATIONS, AND COMMUNITY BUILDING

After meeting a group of new students and explaining the goals, outcomes, assignments, texts, and other details of the course syllabus, I began the process of building the learning community. This took parts of several class meetings and only succeeded when the students understood the purpose of the community-building exercises and accepted the idea. These exercises consisted of various structured activities, including what are commonly called initiative challenges; for example, rapidly passing a hula hoop around a circle of people standing with their hands clasped. In addition to these physically oriented activities, I used interpersonal exercises designed to encourage the sharing of information about each student. The underlying assumption in doing this was that the more we know about each other, the more likely we will discover commonalities and develop a caring and concerned relationship. For example, I invited students to bring in one special object from home to share with the class. I also distributed 5" × 8" file cards to the students in order to create name placards for their desks. I tried to learn their names as soon as possible because that communicates that I value them as persons. These name cards also became a weekly bridge between my students and me when they wrote about a joy or concern and handed the card to me at the end of class. I read each one and responded as a way of showing them that I cared about them and their lives outside of class. Another one of my favorite human relations activities, drawn from the Foxfire approach (Wigginton, 1985), consisted of the students sharing the most memorable experiences from their early schooling. In addition to giving them opportunities to speak to the rest of the group and reveal something about themselves, this activity illustrated the power of certain experiences that became etched in memory. Many of these memorable experiences did not relate directly to the formal "academic" curriculum but were steeped in emotionally impactful occurrences such as seeing a teacher cry, taking an outdoor field trip, or making jelly. Analysis of these memorable experiences revealed that many of them contain emotional impacts related to feeling success, pride, shock, or surprise. This activity illustrated the importance of experiential learning (an emphasis in the course) at the same time it helped to bond the members of the class.

Some of the early group initiatives (challenges) were contrived (i.e., passing a hula hoop around a circle), but many later activities were grounded in the necessary tasks needed to cooperatively complete our projects (i.e., brainstorming the title and format of the book or doing peer editing of the manuscripts). These community-building activities contributed directly to cooperative decision making and group tasks later in our course. Critics who say that these activities are a waste of valuable class time are more likely to view the teaching role as mainly conveying content (known as professing at the university level) and may not share many of the beliefs expressed in my educational philosophy.

The reading collection contained several articles and checklists to help the students understand group dynamics and some of the techniques used for building student-centered learning climates. For example, the students read "Guidelines for Creating Student-Centered Learning Communities" (Knapp, 1996, pp. 95–98). This document suggests student and teacher roles, curriculum and instruction theory, classroom culture, the role of the surrounding community, and suggestions for reflection, assessment, and evaluation. The more the students understand the background for the community-building activities, the more likely they will accept them as meaningful and participate actively in them.

INVESTIGATING LOCAL INSTRUCTIONAL RESOURCES

One important goal of the course was to help educators become aware of the learning potentials of local areas for their students. In other words, I wanted them to become enthusiastic about taking their students to surrounding places and meeting resource people as a part of the regular curriculum and to view the community through the lens of place-based education. Early in the course we took a field trip to reveal the learning potential of the site and personnel at that place. For example, I planned a visit to a local bookstore. Through the use of a guide sheet consisting of 19 questions, the students investigated the teaching/learning potential of that location. They were allotted one hour to find as many answers to the questions as possible, although I stressed that they could spend all the time on only one question if it captivated their interest. The students worked in groups of three to practice cooperating to complete a task. There would be many other group projects to follow that required levels of trust, leadership, follower-ship, and cooperation. This activity also modeled how they could learn from a community resource that later served to guide the writing of a chapter in our book.

Following the bookstore trip, I designed a reflection sheet consisting of 11 deep understandings (big ideas) and 10 core concepts that I hoped that they learned from the experience. I'm sure that the students learned more than these 21 ideas, but hopefully I was adding to what they learned by listing them. Reflection during or after an experience is a common practice in experiential education, and I believe that usually a reflection session expands the learning for the whole class. This extended learning occurred because the reflection was done publicly in a group, and when an individual expressed an insight, others could learn from that comment. I recognized that what the students learned from the bookstore experience was based, in part, on the prior information they had about how bookstores functioned. By listing some of the deep understandings (e.g., "The field trip should provide a model or template to help teachers plan similar field trips for their students.") and some of the core concepts (e.g., "The Foxfire Fund, Inc., has produced a variety of books written by high schoolers."), I attempted to communicate more of my rationale for taking the trip. I figured that if my students (who were educators) came away from this experience with an attitude of excitement about the learning potentials of a bookstore for themselves, they would more likely plan a similar trip into the community for their students. The bookstore field trip prompted my students to view an ordinary community place as an extraordinary learning site and a source of interesting people who could teach them important things. For example, over the years, my students chose a variety of places to write about including: a recycling center, water-treatment plant, butterfly garden, courthouse, fen, cave, skating rink, bird-banding station, beauty salon, flower shop, sculpture, factory, hospital, investment company, auto-body shop, correctional center, and morgue.

During the reflection session, I asked a series of questions about the experience and waited for their responses. For example, I asked: Was this an engaging and memorable experience? If so, why? What question on the guide sheet was the most interesting? Why? Did you devise a good plan for your small group to maximize the use of the hour investigation? How could you improve your plan the next time you go? Can you name the members of your trio? If not, why not? Did you experience any conflict? If so, how did you resolve it? How was this field trip the same and different from those you plan as a teacher? Did you find any surprises at the bookstore? How would you improve this lesson for your students? These kinds of questions following any experience, both indoor or outdoor, can be helpful in meeting the course goals and outcomes. During the course, I planned other out-of-classroom excursions to the campus grounds and the computer laboratory. I also brought in a resource person and structured an activity designed to help them discover more about the surrounding university property. For anyone who has limited experiences with leaving the security and comfort of the four walls of the classroom, it is important to model several ways to integrate community resources into curriculum and instruction.

DESIGNING AND IMPLEMENTING A
COOPERATIVE BOOK WRITING PROJECT

Clear writing is an indicator of clear thinking and a vehicle for clear communication. Some people write well and easily, and others write poorly and with painful plodding. Teachers are no exception to these generalizations. Writing was encouraged through various assignments, the main one being a university-published book consisting of several drafts of a place-based education article from each person in the class, including me. Other ways to encourage the expression of ideas through writing included a weekly communication card, a learning log or journal, course notes, and a portfolio containing any additional writings completed as part of the class.

Whenever possible, I attempted to model how to write by sharing my published and unpublished articles with the students. I also demonstrated how I edit a piece of writing by showing a selection on a screen using the overhead projector or preparing a handout that provided them with a lesson on how to edit. I also shared some protocols that I used when reviewing articles for publication in professional journals. These activities helped to prepare them for the job of peer editing their classmates' writings. This was done in small groups of four or five after establishing some ground rules for how to edit in a caring way. Based on comments I have heard or read from my students, these peer editing sessions proved to be very helpful and less stressful than handing their papers to me. Despite the increased stress levels produced by my editing their papers, I asked for at least three drafts of their article throughout the semester. Not all of the students complied, but most did.

I encouraged the students to read the collection of articles about writing I compiled into a textbook. For many of the students, this was the first time they had been asked to write more than a short note since they graduated from college with their bachelor's degrees.

The writing process involved more than just following the procedures outlined in the American Psychological Association's (APA) publication manual (2001). The students selected their place to write about and the resource person to interview for information about that place or topic. At first some of the students threw up their hands in frustration and asked in a panic-stricken voice, "What should I write about?" Of course, I never told them. That was not my role in this instance. Part of the challenge of the assignment was for them to make this and many other decisions on their own or in cooperation with the whole class. At this point in the course, I took more of an advisor role, rather than to provide information. I gradually released my leadership role to the students as they became more prepared to handle that responsibility. For example, when I discovered that one of the students was familiar with the APA publication manual, I asked him if he would prepare a handout and teach a lesson on that topic. He did so, and became the class expert to the point of proofreading all of the manuscripts before publication. When it came time to lay out and produce the book, other students stepped up and either taught lessons or headed committees responsible for those tasks. Committees had to compile biographical sketches, write a list of field trip tips, compile a table of contents, collect additional appendices, select visual images, edit final copy, design the cover, and conduct the computer technology functions necessary to produce the book. The last time I taught this course, a committee chose to place the entire text of the book with added resource information about the sites on CD-ROM. This decision was their choice because one of the students who had the skills volunteered to head that committee. I had no expertise to lead this project. I was usually asked each semester if I would write the foreword or afterword for the book, and I always shared my written drafts with the class so they could edit them. The day we transferred the finished articles to a disk for delivery to the university printing services, the students knew their roles and worked feverishly to meet the established deadline. Although the work was hard and the stress level considerable, we were elated when the boxes of books were unpacked and distributed to everyone on the last day of class. Each student received at least five copies of our book. As they browsed through the pages, I'm sure that most of them turned to their article first and feasted on the sight of their accomplishment.

EXPANDING KNOWLEDGE ABOUT COMMUNITY STUDY INSTRUCTIONAL RESOURCES

I wanted my students to leave this class with an array of ideas about how to use community resources in their teaching as well as know where to locate other instructional materials for further reference. Their collected readings provided more "food for thought" than we had time to discuss in class. I designed the course using five place-based educational approaches: Foxfire, Expeditionary Learning, Environment as an Integrating Context For Learning, Problem-Based Learning, and Contextual Teaching and Learning. Each of these programs or approaches has produced a body of literature that is readily available for study. These five models share some common characteristics. They can be applied in settings that include K–12 grade levels as well as undergraduate and graduate education. They are interdisciplinary, learner-centered, hands-on, project- or problem-centered, and cooperative learning oriented. They also advocate authentic assessment experiences in the local community and encourage higher-level thinking skills. Despite these common characteristics, they also have distinct implementation histories and take on separate identities.

I could have chosen other programs to guide the curriculum and pedagogy used in this course. Other fine programs exist and are currently in use in various places. In the August/November 2001 issue of the journal *Thresholds in Education,* I compiled a list of 17 selected place-based curricular programs along with information about how to access their Web sites (Knapp, 2001, p. 56). Powers (2004), cofounder of Program Evaluation and Educational Research Associates, evaluated and reported two aspects of four place-based education programs. She examined the strengths and challenges (weaknesses) of the programs and trends in teacher practice change across those programs. Fortunately, there are many models for educators to examine if they would like to learn more about this growing field.

In order to understand more fully how I used the five models in designing the course in community investigations, next I briefly summarize their purposes and some of their useful curricular and pedagogical ideas.

Foxfire

The most succinct description of Foxfire appeared in a recent book by Hatton (2005):

> Foxfire is a not-for-profit, educational, and literary organization based in Rabun County, Georgia. Foxfire's learner-centered, community-based educational approach is advocated through both a regional demonstration site grounded in Southern Appalachian culture that gave rise to Foxfire, and a national program of teacher training and support that promotes a sense of place and

appreciation of local people, community, and culture as essential educational tools. (p. vi)

One of the most useful Foxfire contributions has been the development of a list of 11 core practices or tenets of effective instruction to describe this approach to teaching and learning. These practices have been tested by thousands of teachers for over 40 years since the founder of Foxfire, Eliot Wigginton, began to write a set of guiding "truths" for teachers in 1966. Hatton (2005) suggests that the core practices should be applied as *a way of thinking* rather than *a way of doing*—in other words, as a philosophy of education that informs practice. Practically all of the 11 core practices are reflected in my previously stated philosophy of education. Some of Foxfire's strengths include: capitalizing on student concerns, increasing student choices, encouraging reflection on experiences, linking required content to life situations and other disciplines, promoting student action and involvement, emphasizing teamwork in small and large groups, and connecting the school and community in meaningful ways.

Foxfire stresses the importance of capturing the wisdom of local people through interviews. If some of the students in Rabun County, Georgia, had not talked to many of the Appalachian elders and transcribed this information into newsletter and book form, much of it would be now lost. The Foxfire approach honors student intelligence and experience by involving them in the process of choosing some curricular content and method within the limitations of the prescribed school and state standards. Eleanor Duckworth describes this respect for student input as "...trying to engage learners with their own ideas" (quoted in Hatton, 2005, p. 7).

Expeditionary Learning (EL)

Expeditionary Learning (EL) is a nonprofit school improvement and teacher development organization with a growing national network of 136 schools reaching almost 50,000 students in 27 states, the District of Columbia, and Puerto Rico. EL has a research-based design built around learning expeditions, other active forms of teaching and learning, and a challenging and supportive school culture. The design emphasizes high achievement, character growth, and high expectations. (More information about Expeditionary Learning can be found at the organization's website: http://www.elob.org/design/who.html.)

The program is based on the educational philosophies of Kurt Hahn, Outward Bound's founder, and other educational leaders, including John Dewey, Paul Ylvisaker, Harold Howe, Ted Sizer, Eleanor Duckworth, Howard Gardner, Debbie Meier, and Tom James. In 1992 Outward Bound, originally a wilderness-based experiential program, received a grant from the New American Schools Development Corporation for a 5-year experiment applied to urban schools in five cities. Since the funds have ceased, EL has become self-supporting and continues to operate nationally. The list of 10 design principles they developed includes the following important guidelines: basing a curriculum on the students' curiosities, promoting self-directed learners, capitalizing on student successes and failures by learning from them, learning in diverse groups, contacting the natural world, using reflection, and participating in service projects to help others (Campbell, Liebowitz, Mednick, & Rugen, 1998).

EL stresses in-depth investigations of topics through curricular designs labeled "learning expeditions." These expeditions are metaphors for the ways in which wilderness trips may unfold. All of the difficulties and unpredictable events cannot be anticipated as students and teachers explore unknown territory and seek knowledge. One valuable aspect to EL lessons is the guiding questions that serve to spark student interest and curiosity. These guiding questions often "invite" students to do fieldwork outside the school to get their answers. Another feature of EL is the emphasis on an ethic and practice of service to and compassion for others. Many of the EL expeditions have built-in relationships to character development and community service. To help the EL practitioner, a newsletter, *Fieldwork*, describes ongoing best practices based on classroom experiences.

Environment as an Integrating Context For Learning (EIC)

Environment as an Integrating Context for learning (EIC) designates pedagogy that employs natural and sociocultural environments as the context for learning while taking into account the "best practices" of successful educators. It combines these approaches in a way that: breaks down traditional boundaries between disciplines; provides hands-on learning experiences, often through problem-solving and project-based activities; relies on team-teaching; adapts to individual students and their unique skills and abilities; and develops knowledge, understanding, and appreciation for the environment—community and natural surroundings. (Lieberman & Hoody, 1998)

Lieberman and Hoody (1998) conducted a 3-year qualitative study funded by a grant from the Pew Charitable Trusts. Representatives from 12 states convened to design and implement the examination of K–12 schools that met their requirements for innovations using the environment as an integrating context for learning. One valuable contribution is the research-based approach focused on examining evidence gathered from the 40 study schools. This effort investigated the results of applying a set of best practices, including striving for higher-order thinking skills, promoting self-motivated learners, appreciating the local environment, and adapting to individual learning abilities.

One feature of EIC schools was the emphasis on collaborative teaching teams composed of other school subject-matter teachers and specialists, as well as experts from the community. Researchers found that many EIC teachers felt revitalized as a result of using the school's surroundings and the larger community as a way to organize instruction. The study pointed to several benefits of organizing learning around natural and sociocultural environments including: better performance on standardized achievement tests in reading, writing, math, science, and social studies; reduced classroom management problems; increased student engagement and enthusiasm for learning; and greater student pride and ownership in accomplishments (Lieberman & Hoody, 1998, p. 22).

Problem-Based Learning (PBL)

Problem-based learning is focused, experiential learning (minds-on, hands-on) organized around the investigation and resolution of messy, real-world problems. It is both a curriculum organizer and instructional strategy, two complementary processes. PBL includes three main characteristics: engages students as stakeholders in a problem situation; organizes curriculum around this holistic problem, enabling student learning in relevant and connected ways; and creates a learning environment in which teachers coach student thinking and guide student inquiry, facilitating deeper levels of understanding. (Torp & Sage, 1998, p. 14)

The characteristics of starting with a well-selected and ill-structured problem, focusing on in-depth learning of a particular topic, encouraging students to "invest" in the problem solution, drawing on several curriculum areas, and teaching specific concepts and skills at critical points when the need arises, all contribute to the program's success. The fact that PBL often promotes a high degree of ownership of the problem and creates a personal investment in the solution contributes to the relevancy of the knowledge gained. If students can become actively engaged in the process of discovery and they see what they learn as meaningful and related to real-world issues, they will enjoy learning and continue to seek more knowledge in the future. This idea is the basis for the constructivist educational theory that is valued by many educators today.

Contextual Teaching and Learning (CTL)

> The general principles and primary characteristics of contextual teaching and learning . . . include: developing self-regulated learners, anchoring teaching and learning in students' life contexts, teaching and learning in multiple contexts, using problem-based learning, using interdependent learning groups, and assessing students' progress through authentic assessments. (Sears, 2002, p. 5)

I most value relating subjects to real-world situations, connecting knowledge to its applications in society, using multiple instructional contexts, and using interdependent learning groups to solve problems. In many ways, contextual teaching and learning summarize and encapsulate most of the educational principles and characteristics described in the other model programs. "Contextual teaching and learning (CTL) is a concept that helps teachers relate subject matter to real-world situations" (Sears, 2002, p. 5). It stresses the importance of *how* and *where* a person learns and the fundamental connection of both to what a person learns.

The examination of these examples of place-based educational programs and approaches provided my students with a variety of references written by diverse authors. Perhaps this variety presented a more convincing case for incorporating some of the characteristics of these programs into their own personal educational philosophies. If leading educators thought that community study was important, maybe my students would pay more attention to the idea. Another reason to offer a variety of models for place-based education was the hope that at least one type of program would spark an interest and would encourage teachers to implement this way of teaching.

WHAT HAVE I LEARNED FROM TEACHING THIS COURSE?

The lessons I've learned have been many and powerful over the 12 semesters I taught the community studies course. Most of the memorable ones have been described in this chapter. In the course, I helped to create a place of safety and adventure that claimed many of my students' feelings. I am convinced of the soundness of my educational philosophy through years of field-testing and adapting my approach. Although I would never say that I have mastered the art and science of teaching, I have come a long way since I first started. I have fewer questions about what will happen when I apply the pedagogies described in this chapter. I trust the cooperative and democratic group processes more than ever and believe that most of my students will succeed using these methods. I also realize that my teaching methods are not for everyone and that in some students, I stimulate levels of anxiety by using these practices. Some learners expect their teachers to define every parameter of the course in specific fashion. I never did in this course. Some teaching styles do not match perfectly with some preferred learning styles. I also cautioned my students that they didn't need to incorporate the full place-based model presented in class when they taught. They could take small steps by using selected activities before learning to run at full speed with this approach to teaching and learning. By teaching in this way, I could never accurately predict how my students would respond to the responsibilities of being self-directed and cooperative learners. I realize I can never know all of the course content before I launch my teaching/learning journey. By using this instructional approach, I am constantly reminded of the explicit interrelatedness of teaching and learning. I am convinced that today's teachers need to learn more about their communities and incorporate the instructional resources of people and places into their teaching. Place-based education is growing in importance as well as popularity. As more of the positive impacts of place-based education become known, I believe that educators will see improvement in their students' learning abilities and joy of learning.

WHAT A FEW PAST STUDENTS REMEMBER FROM THE COURSE

I was curious about the long-term impact of this course in integrating communities into curriculum and instruction, so I contacted a handful of past students. This effort was not a scientific poll because I just called several people who I knew were employed nearby. I asked them to tell me what they remembered from taking the course and how they might be using some of those ideas in their work as educators.

Aaron was most impressed with the "marrying" of the process and product in the course. He viewed the methodology we used as a metaphor for the course content. He wrote, "The content of what we usually teach and the methods we use to teach that content are often separated by a huge gulf." In this case, the course combined the process of working as a team with the knowledge of community resources in a way that led him to design a high school course about Native Americans by creating a tribe in order to study tribes. Aaron learned that the process involved in learning a body of content could be blended with what he wanted his students to know and do.

Rhodora remembered the community-building process that preceded the book writing. She mentioned the importance of listening to others and expressing her own needs to the class. She recalled how creating a safe learning environment enabled "even the shyest class members to speak without fear of their ideas not being taken seriously." She thought the structured team-building process helped to create a sense of group unity and history by allowing the students to get to know each other.

Debra grasped the importance of helping students develop a sense of place in their communities. She thought that her students' intimate associations with the land were continually being assaulted by modern-day progress and the consumer-driven demands of our society. She asked, "If we cannot relate to the land, how can we save it?" Her work as an arboretum education specialist provided ample opportunities to give others the direct, sensory contacts with the earth necessary to build their sense of place.

Deb J. and Dana emphasized the importance of journaling and reflecting on the course experiences after we did them. They valued the collaborative learning that occurred and believed that seeking, knowing, and utilizing community resources should be a fundamental component of a good education. They believed that this type of learning would lead to a more responsible citizenry.

Ann was convinced that students should explore and find meaningful experiences within the community. As a biology teacher, she mentioned taking field trips to the zoo, cooperating with a local anatomy laboratory to study a human cadaver, and inviting guest speakers from the community to address their careers and special projects. Her service-learning group organized a walk-a-thon to raise money to support an African culture they had studied.

Maureen used what she learned about investigating a community in a personal way when she moved out-of-state to teach. As a teacher, one of her first projects with her students was to have them write a book and make a video based on a class field trip to study a bison hunt. Then her students presented what they learned to other classes at the school. She said, "The learning just multiplies when they do something and explain it to others. My students like to do these projects rather than only read about them."

Bob recalled that the course sharpened his awareness of opportunities to teach about the resources of the community and noted how the members of our class felt a sense of empowerment and camaraderie as they worked as a team to plan, write, and produce a document that celebrated the value of place-based education.

Did this small sample of past students grasp some of the objectives I established in the course? Without a doubt, they did. Others who I didn't contact also may have gained some of these same benefits. Although they mentioned a variety of highlights, they all achieved some of what I'd hoped for. Some remembered the process of building a unified and caring team to make better group decisions tied into the creation of a final written project. Others remembered the importance of instilling a community sense of place in their students. A few put the process and product together and used the community as a learning laboratory to inform themselves and their students. In the communities course, the process of learning about how a community works and producing concrete evidence of this knowledge became the course content.

My hope is that this chapter has provided you with enough ideas to promote, plan, and teach a similar course in place-based education. I also hope this chapter has opened some new doors for you. If it has done this, perhaps you can exit those doors and go out with your students to explore the places around you to enrich their lives so that they can claim feelings of joy, success, and accomplishment, too.

REFERENCES

American Psychological Association. (2001). *Publication manual of the American Psychological Association* (5th ed.). Washington, DC: Author.

Campbell, M., Liebowitz, M., Mednick, A., & Rugen, L. (1998). *Guide for planning a learning expedition*. Dubuque, IA: Kendall/Hunt.

Danker, A. C. (2005). *Multicultural social studies: Using local history in the classroom*. New York: Teachers College Press.

Expeditionary Learning. Who we are: Our principles, practices and schools. Retrieved March 25, 2005 at http://www.elob.org/design/who.html

Gruenewald, D. A. (2003). The best of both worlds: A critical pedagogy of place. *Educational Researcher, 32*(4), 3–12.

Gussow, A. (1974). *A sense of place*. New York: Seabury Press.

Hatton, S. D. (2005). *Teaching by heart: The Foxfire interviews*. New York: Teachers College Press.

Hug, J. W. (1998). *Learning and teaching for an ecological sense of place: Toward environmental/science education praxis.* Unpublished doctoral dissertation, Pennsylvania State University, State College.

Kehrberg, G. A. (n.d.). *Place-based education: An annotated bibliography.* Unpublished manuscript, University of Montana, Missoula, MT.

Knapp, C. E. (n.d.). *Some terms to describe the fields of education in, about, and for the environment.* Unpublished manuscript, Oregon, IL.

Knapp, C. E. (1992). Putting principles into practice: Traveling the Foxfire trail in graduate school. *Journal of Experiential Education, 15*(2), 36–39.

Knapp, C. E. (1996). *Just beyond the classroom: Community adventures for interdisciplinary learning.* Charleston, WV: ERIC Clearinghouse on Rural and Small Schools.

Knapp, C. E. (1999). *In accord with nature: Helping students form an environmental ethic using outdoor experience and reflection.* Charleston, WV: ERIC Clearinghouse on Rural and Small Schools.

Knapp, C. E. (2001). Selected place-based curricular programs. *Thresholds in Education, 27*(3 & 4), 56.

Knapp, C. E., & Woodhouse, J. L. (2003, June 27–29). *Place-based pedagogy: Experiential learning for culturally and ecologically sustainable communities.* Conference Proceedings, Glasgow Caledonian University, Glasgow, Scotland.

Lieberman, G. A., & Hoody, L. L. (1998). *Closing the achievement gap: Using the environment as an integrating context for learning.* San Diego, CA: State Education and Environment Roundtable.

Newmann, F. M., & Oliver, D. W. (1967). Education and community. *Harvard Educational Review, 37*(1), 61–106.

Osborn, N. A. (1994). *Using community resources.* Dubuque, IA: Kendall/Hunt.

Powers, A. L. (2004). An evaluation of four place-based education programs. *Journal of Environmental Education, 35*(4), 17–32.

Proudman, B. (1995, February). AEE adopts definition. *The AEE Horizon: Newsletter of the Association for Experiential Education.* Boulder, CO: Association for Experiential Education, 15, 1–21.

Sears, S. (2002). *Contextual teaching and learning: A primer for effective instruction.* Bloomington, IN: Phi Delta Kappa Educational Foundation.

Smith, G. A. (2002). Place-based education: Learning to be where we are. *Phi Delta Kappan, 83*(8), 584–594.

Sobel, D. (2004). *Place-based education: Connecting classrooms & communities.* Great Barrington, MA: The Orion Society.

Torp, L., & Sage, S. (1998). *Problems as possibilities: Problem-based learning for K–12 education.* Alexandria, VA: Association for Supervision and Curriculum Development.

Wigginton, E. (1985). *Sometimes a shining moment: The Foxfire experience.* New York: Anchor Books.

Woodhouse, J. L., & Knapp, C. E. (2000). *Place-based curriculum and instruction: Outdoor and environmental education approaches.* Charleston, WV (ERIC document Reproduction Service No. EDO-RC-00-6).

CHAPTER 2

The Fringe of Nirvana
Aesthetic Places and the Art Classroom

Mark Graham

INTRODUCTION

Ever since I crouched behind my father in the cold dawn, trying to take pictures of beavers on the edge of an old pond in the Uintah Mountains, the wilderness has always felt sacred. My father and I walked for miles to distant lakes along rocky ridges. I learned to prize the quiet, the deep forest, the narrow path. Like Thoreau, I want to speak a word for wildness. "Give me the ocean, the desert or the wilderness!" (Thoreau, 1862, p. 481).

But, unlike Thoreau, I drive a car and live in a suburb of New York City on the edge of Long Island Sound, where the desert wilderness of my youth is a distant echo. Walking, paradoxically, is now the domain of the city dweller, where a car is superfluous. But even here, in New York City, as I set up my easel to paint the skyline above the trees in Central Park, the majesty of light and breeze thrills me, just as if I were perched on a rock below Mount Moran.

I am an artist and a teacher. I work with high school students. They are maddeningly self-absorbed, but idealistic. They can be selfish and apathetic and yet generous and passionate in their caring. Their artistic horizons are narrow, their senses and desires bullied by an insistent media. Often, their lack of connection to their own community attracts them to the aesthetics of alienation and dissonance. Too often, reverence for anything is replaced by cynicism about everything.

This chapter is about one of my teaching experiments. It is about the artist in the classroom and the aesthetic experience. It is about defining a sacred space and learning to experience and even reverence the wildness close to home, and the possibilities of community in the context of a high school art class. It is about creating images in line and paint and seeing things in new and unexpected ways. This chapter describes our work in a classroom and our efforts to weave new meaning into our lives outside the classroom. It explores our attempt to sparkle at the intersection of culture, the aesthetic experience, the search for the sacred, and the kind of wildness Thoreau described. It is the record of our endeavors to understand who we are and our glimpses of an education that honors the places where we live and the many communities woven into our lives.

CONTEMPORARY ARTISTS

The model for the contemporary artist is often based on isolated individualism. Artists are cultivated like hothouse flowers in graduate schools where they work in isolated studios and dream of gallery openings. The art world is defined by who is selling and who is showing. Art becomes a collection of precious objects, another commodity disconnected from everyday life. The story of the lonely genius, isolated from society and relieved of social responsibility, is a persistent theme in the art world.

However, for some artists, vision is a social practice, and art is a means to heal soulless approaches to the world. Art making can be rooted in holistic concerns, not the fruit of a disembodied, factual eye (Gablik, 2004). Among these artists there is the possibility of meaningful iconography about the earth and the places to which we belong. Art becomes more than individual self-expression practiced by the strange and gifted. It becomes a language for a conversation about experience, a way to inquire about the world, even a way to change how we see the world and our relationship to it.

The story of my journey as an artist may as well begin at the Art Student's League of New York. The League was organized in the late-19th century by a group of artists as a kind of American art student academy. Through the 20th century, it continued as a link to artistic tradition, and many artists stopped there to study. I did not know any of this when I entered its doors; I was just looking for a place to paint. I did not imagine I would meet Frank Mason.

In the quiet winter afternoon at the League, the smell of linseed oil and turpentine cast a spell on the senses as the shadows settled on the casts of Phideas and Donatello. But when Frank Mason thundered down the fourth-floor wooden hallway, palette cups rattled and students trembled. Entering the studio, wrapped in an immense black cloak of a paint smock, he had the wrinkled countenance of a roaring, laughing lion. It was frightening and exciting; he seemed to bend space, and things began to look different. Frank Mason lives in a world of giants: Rubens, Rembrandt, Beethoven. They are the landscape behind his huge opinions.

To set the stage, he told a story: The brave and daring, but poor, artist who loves beauty awakes to the noise of the fireman breaking down the door with the rent notice; "Now we shall see what will become of his dreams" (Genesis 37:20). Beauty, craft, and the great music of painting are threatened by ignorance and materialism. But somehow, the artist escapes, and the painting begins.

This was a quiet drama watched attentively by a circle of students. If you observe closely, you might have caught a glimpse of the ideals of Phideas, the light of Rembrandt, or the energy of Rubens on the little square of linen. We were invited into a community of great artists and big ideas. "The music doesn't belong to anyone; it is too big for that," we are reminded. Even after he left, after our minds settled down, after we stood around the swirling river left on the canvas, the world no longer looked the same. It was transformed; it was bigger, richer, full of nobility and pathos and light and atmosphere.

For me, Frank Mason was a link to a tradition of painting, a link to craft, and even more, a link to profound expressions of the human spirit. His power was "in the capacity to awaken a truth within us" (Palmer, 1998, p. 21). We knew there was a great thing in our midst. The quiet of the gray studio and the excitement of these ideas led naturally to the quiet of a museum. Like the forest, these places invited listening, reflection, and seeing the world in new ways.

And so I learned to paint. Painting is like going for a walk. I have the paint box in one hand, the easel in the other. I step through a break in the fence and the branches of the trees close around me. The taken-for-granted world is left behind. The rush of imposed desire and artificial purpose begin to fade as I walk down the grassy path into the clearing. Slowly, with deliberate ritual, the easel is assembled, the paintbrushes ordered, and a deeply felt place is summoned. I begin to paint the mountain. It is all there in the first few brushstrokes, the violet quiet air, the light, the long white grass.

I am thinking of *Henderson the Rain King*. When Henderson was in Africa, he awoke and contemplated the morning light on the white clay wall of his hut:

At once I recognized the importance of this, as throughout my life I had known these moments when the dumb begins to speak, when I hear the voices of objects and colors.... My soul was in quite a condition...it was a state as mild as the color itself. I said to my self, "I knew this place was of old." Meaning, I had sensed from the first that I might find things here which were of old, which I saw when I was still innocent and longed for ever since, for all my life—and without which I could not make it. My spirit was not sleeping then, I can tell you, but was saying, Oh, ho, ho ho ho ho ho! (Bellow, 1978, p. 46)

Like the fringe of Nirvana, he thought. And like Henderson, I am wondering, How do I break the spirit's sleep and enter this place?

THE ARTIST IN THE CLASSROOM

Greene (1978) said that if we lose sight of our aesthetic perceptions, we deprive our students of possibilities: "We may leave them buried in cotton wool, in fact, and passive under the hammer blows of the fragmented, objective world" (p. 186). Yet, "Were we to succeed in making the artistic-aesthetic central to the educational undertaking, we would be committing ourselves to the expansion of the individual, human part of those we teach" (p. 188).

The artist in the classroom confronts the deep reasons for school. The artist questions the isolation of the classroom from the community. The hypnotic, insistent allure of commercial media is questioned and a more authentic experience is sought. The painting, the poem, the drawing is a catalyst for this experience.

As education is turned toward predication, mechanistic rationality, and measurement, the exploratory vision of art education becomes more vital. The art teacher embraces ambiguity, surprise, imagination, and idiosyncratic outcomes. The artist teacher is looking for an occasion to disrupt the superficial topic, to connect learning to the lives of students.

In school we like to outline, explain, label, and classify. We strive to cover the material, wrap things up, and get to the conclusion. Heaven forbid our objectives are not clear and all outcomes anticipated. Standardization is the goal. Knowledge is packaged, taken out of context, and then memorized. Something else is needed. Greene (1978) suggests that the aesthetic experience "provides a ground for the questioning that launches sensemaking and the understanding of what it means to exist in the world" (p. 86). Or what we exist for.

EDUCATION, TEACHING, AND SACRED PLACES

"Life is not possible without an opening toward the transcendent" (Eliade, 1959, p. 34). Did archaic, religious man really consider the world a sacred place, as Eliade suggests? "Religious man thirsts for the real. By every means at his disposal, he seeks to reside at the very source of primordial reality, when the world was in the state of being newly born" (Eliade, 1959, p. 43).

The sacred mountain, the ladder, the temple all point toward a transcendent reality and relief from chaos. The sacred stone, the oak tree, the column connecting heaven and earth, the white whale, the velveteen rabbit all contain a glimpse of the dramatic irruption of the sacred into the mundane world.

The habitation of the archaic innocent is symbolically situated at the center of the world. According to Eliade (1959), "The house is not an object, a machine to live in; it is the universe that man constructs for himself by imitating the paradigmatic creation of the gods, the cosmogony" (p. 74). So much for the house. Maybe school is more than a factory, too.

In contemporary life and school, the world is taken for granted, community is often fractured, and children can feel more connected to television characters than to their own families. Schools can feel like factories, places to prepare standardized products for competition in the global economy. In this world, the notion of sacred is strange, and rarely encountered. The world is depicted as an object of consumption. Places are owned, measured, used up, and thrown aside.

But the art classroom defines a space that is different from the rest of school. It is a hospitable place, inviting, safe, and interesting. Perhaps the artist's studio holds clues to an education that is more transcendent and yet less isolated from the context of students' lives. Perhaps the artist in the classroom can create possibilities for a form of learning that cultivates awareness and care for place. Dewey (1954) said, "The function of art has always been to break through the crust of conventionalized and routine consciousness" (p. 183). Artistic creation "rejects the world on account of what it lacks and in the name of what it sometimes is" (Greene, 1978, p. 92).

The history of art is filled with sacred objects and images of sacred people and sacred places. Even paintings without a religious context often reflect an intent to give the world a lasting, sacred quality. Cézanne's painting of Mont Sainte-Victoire or Asher Durand's paintings of the American landscape reflect an interest in the transcendent and a certain reverence for the earth. Artists often attach themselves to places, carving out sacred spaces, creating personal mythologies, and attending to the details of their specific location. Think of Christo and Jean Claude's gates, Albert Bierstadt's Mount Moran, Thomas Moran's Grand Canyon, Chagall's village, or Georgia O'Keeffe's desert.

Many contemporary artists are making the ecology of place the primary subject of their work. Learning to see, becoming aware of the beauty of the natural world, of the possibility of defining sacred place, is an essential step toward ecological responsibility. "Without a fascination and reverence for the grandeur of the earth, the energy needed for its preservation will never be developed" (Gablik, 2004, p. 77). For example, in the art of Andy Goldsworthy, nature is the subject, not just the background for his work. His approach is based on respect, thoughtful reverence, and personal dialogue rather than domination. "When I'm working with material, it's not just the leaf or the stone...that I am trying to understand, not a single isolated object, but nature as a whole...." (Goldsworthy, cited in Gablik, 2004, p. 91).

It was the cultivation of this attitude of reverence and personal dialogue with the natural community that was the motivating idea behind my teaching experiments that attempted to weave drawing, painting, photography, and walking into our classroom:

> Some place. Any place. No place. What is a place? Is it geographical or psychological? Real or imagined? A sense of place vitally shapes our being, our identity....It refers not simply to location but, at a deeper level to home, departure, arrival, and destiny.... It is what connects us to our community and what divides us from others. (Golden, 2001, p. 20)

THE PROJECT

I love teaching because of the unexpected surprises that my students give me and the conversations about ideas that develop during our work together. I often start with a question that is also part of the artistic process I am engaged in at the time. As a painter, I was searching for an artistic language to convey the ineffable sense of place I often feel. I wanted to continue this quest in my classroom.

I can never predict where students might take the ideas we will explore. In our classroom, personal experience is valued, experiments are encouraged, and mistakes are viewed as important parts of learning. Conversation about the work is encouraged and is part of our daily routine. I know that I am succeeding when students bring their lunch and stay after class to continue talking and working.

One of the recurring themes in my own work is the notion of landscape as sacred geography and the painted picture as a metaphorical construction of meaningful connections to specific places. My paintings are about atmosphere, light, sky, and the view from a small trail. Even when I paint the city wall graffiti, the place speaks about myths and symbols and paths through the woods. It was this theme of landscape, wildness, personal dialogue with nature, and our connections to the community that I set out to explore with my students. The idea was to cultivate awareness, thoughtfulness, and a sense of discovery, even a sense of reverence and belonging to place among my high school students. I wanted them to awaken, to consider questions about the meaning of the sacred in the context of their own lives. I wanted them to define, in drawings and paintings, places to which they were connected. I wanted them to study the landscape and appreciate its beauty, to appreciate nature's resistance against concrete. I wanted them to articulate in words some of their experiences and communicate the evolution of their thinking in a public exhibition, among their peers, their parents, and others in the community. Our investigation began with the complex landscape of the Long Island community we shared with the ocean, birds, animals, and trees and extended to the bridges and streets of the great city to the west.

We began by looking at many kinds of sacred places in art and culture: the wild landscape, sacred because of its transcendent clothing by the unseen hand of deity; buildings and rooms, deemed sacred as places that house deity; iconic images that reflect a divine presence by depicting the invisible made visible. Students were asked, How is this sacred space defined? Who defines it? How do we recognize it? Have you ever experienced it? Where are the places you go for refuge? How does a place become sacred? What is your sacred geography?

Their answers were often poignant and unexpected: *My backyard garden. My bedroom. The ocean. Camp. Inside a book. I don't have any special places, I left them all in Kansas. My magical places are in Japan. In the apartment where I grew up. In the tree. My place of refuge is the pool. My mother. Music. It became sacred because of what we shared there. Because that is where I was the most happy. It was the last time we were all together.* Each question was the catalyst for a drawing. Drawing became a meditation on the special places in our lives.

It is impossible to explore these ideas without referring to the context of culture and art. For example, we explored American 19th-entury landscape painters like Thomas Moran, whose paintings of the Western landscape were instrumental in establishing our national parks, promoting the idea of wilderness as sacred place (Goetzman & Goetzman, 1986). Moran's work echoed the sentiments of other American luminist artists who painted the natural landscape as an exploration of sacred earth. We looked at nature photography that in many instances conveys a vision of nature as Eden or Paradise, completely separate from man, history, or utility (Solnit, 2002). We discussed the relationship between artist and various ideas about nature and wilderness. We explored our restless natures and the mosaic of places around us that reflect the disparate roots of our wanderings. We examined the ways that contemporary materialistic, consumer culture seeks to erase the metaphysical and eradicate all reverence for nature. We tried to break down the insistent images encouraging us to see the world merely as an object for consumption.

We explored the barely visible natural histories of our island home, the 18th-century graveyard that touches the school grounds, the estates turned into parkland, the old natural economies of the place, the cavities left from sand excavation for New York City skyscrapers, the shoreline. We observed and inventoried the signs of civilization washed up onto the rocks and recorded in our sketches the humid ocean atmosphere filled with light. Some students explored the city itself and our relationship to it.

Our classroom activities included the careful cultivation of craft. Small drawing exercises based on the work of other artists helped us to see simply, to get the big relationships before the details. We struggled to see with the artist part of our minds that doesn't have names for things. We learned to take our images apart and reassemble them in new ways. The carefully scripted development of skill, vision, and thinking slowly built our classroom community as we shared our personal visions. A necessary prelude to our great project was the many small exercises needed to learn the artistic language and skills of medium required to say something. Leave these small steps out, and thought becomes hidden in ineptitude.

Students were sent out with sketchbooks and cameras to define a sacred place, to find the beautiful spot, to find the ugly spot, to find the crimes against nature, to record nature's resistance against stone and concrete. It was an exercise in walking and looking and questioning. It was an exercise in defining a sacred geography and considering our place in it. It was a reflection about what is important in our lives and our connections to places. Many conversations about ideas and images took place over the patches of color taking shape. The sharing of personal experiences in drawings and photographs became a deeply interesting experience for students. They came back to the classroom each Monday with a collection of images they had gathered, and stories to go with them.

These photographs and sketches gradually became paintings. But now, through conversations about what is sacred, the paintings came alive with new thoughts; the rocks and ocean, the trees and street took on new meanings. The ocean shore was no longer scenery but an expression of a longing for what yet had no name. The backyard garden came to represent childhood hope and innocence. The city bridge became a metaphor for a personal journey. We were sometimes troubled by what we had found and sometimes thrilled to once again belong to a place. For example, a foray to capture the sunset at the end of the island also produced a photographic essay on the flotsam that had been thrown into the bay. This collection of castoffs from consumer culture led to a discussion about garbage and its effect on animal life in the bay. We realized we had become numbed by the incessant glare of visual culture when Jolie's photographic collages (Figures 2.1 and 2.2) reminded us that Main Street is also a charming panorama of architecture, trees, and water.

Amelia often left the classroom to create drawings of the school as seen from the forest's point of view. Her graphic reports of glass, refuse,

Figure 2.1   Jolie's street collage.

Figure 2.2   Jolie's street collage 2.

and graffiti on trees made us ponder the school's impact on nature. Josh's photographs of graffiti in the city made us reconsider graffiti and its meaning and function as art or as signs. The paintings, and the journey to make the paintings, became a conversation about personal geography and our relationship to our island home, the homes we had left, and the homes we hoped to find.

Our school has many students from other places who have taken up residency in our community. Borders and displacement are often the themes of their artistry. For these students, the theme of connection to places is intimately connected to the theme of displacement. For example, Josselyn, from El Salvador, created a series of drawings and paintings of a bench next to the beach at the edge of her neighborhood. They began as a collage of photographs and cut paper, sunset and sky and ocean. A wistful romantic image was the result, a theme of contemplation, she claimed. A place where she could think about her journey and her destination. Her community is defined by borders of language and shared traditions. As she thought about carving a special place, far away from the land she was used to, she created a drawing of her porch leading into the street as seen from her window, a simple image that evoked the threshold of home and the entrance to a foreign world. As she gained confidence, she began to include members of her family in her drawings as part of the landscape. These paintings later evolved into a series of family portraits, framed in the interior windows or yard surrounding her home. She set her father in a Salvadorian landscape, and her brother and sister in the window looking out into the street of her new home. As her work was recognized and her artistic voice was given credence by her peers, her thinking evolved from being an outsider in a strange and sometimes beautiful landscape, to feeling that she belonged.

This merging of craft, experience, and connection to our environments unfolded every week when we gathered to share our drawings and photographs and talk about our artistic attempts to define sacred places. Students reflected on their experiences in the sketchbook journals. Jessica wrote about the subway and her experiences in the city: "You exit the subway and drop your Metrocard. As you go to pick it up, your eyes scan the dirty floor covered in graffiti. Your eyes continue on this path until they reach a man and boy sitting huddling in the corner.... This is their home." Like Amelia's discovery of the desecrated trees in our midst, Jessica's questions about home and homelessness engendered conversations about our own place in the world and our responsibility to others.

Questions were a catalyst for the journal entries. For example, What are some of the borders in your life? Where do you find refuge? What defines home for you? Often, issues of migration and dislocation from places emerged. Stephanie wrote at length about her difficulties in moving from Japan to New York, Jamie about the struggle to feel at home after moving from Kansas, Josh about his feelings of nostalgia for New York City. Sometimes these reflections were about the history of the places that surround us, and the struggle for belonging. Anka wrote about the places in school where she felt alone, different, or awkward. The result was a sense of recapturing a measure of significance in the ordinary moment. Through a new sense of connection to places, the places became charmed.

I was asking the same questions about places that I posed to my students. They were the kind of questions that created more questions. And I was painting. I made a painting by flashlight from my attic window of a house across the street that became magical in my imagination, a fairy house. It was lit by streetlights, and the memories of stories I told my children at night in the attic bedroom where they slept. The old cemetery at the edge of school became a painting of a child's Halloween walk populated by children, sorcerers, and black cats. I began to appreciate in a new way the potential for poetry in the familiar road to school. Like my students, I was seeing familiar places in new ways and seeing other places that were once invisible.

The recognition and appreciation for our personal journeys grew as we gathered to share our work and talk about our experiences in working out our connections to the place where we lived. Students who were once invisible gradually emerged from obscurity. During one of the first critiques, Josselyn brought in a painting of the bench next to the beach that had become a metaphor for her search for solitude and quiet. It was difficult for her to find words in English, but the class greeted her idea and her painting with warm enthusiasm. Her countenance brightened as she realized that her experience and her work were being taken seriously.

Jolie thought of herself as the radical free thinker among us. She listened to unusual music, belonged to Amnesty International and the Gay–Straight Alliance, and dreamed of going to Oberlin College. She created a montage of the street, with lights, skies, her own feet, and her friend coming to meet her. Her images contained the sophistication of adolescent conversation, including complex allusions to music, fashion, and identity. She wanted to show us Main Street as if it were as new and exciting as a conversation after school was over. Her sense of place was defined by relationships, sociality, ideas of social justice, and changing the world. She wanted to experiment, to do paintings on old fences, to create billboards for people to see. It was appropriate that she chose to focus on the street, the swift car, the stripe, the red light, a hint of graffiti, and the feet and smiling face.

The conversation in Jolie's painting was mirrored by the conversation in the art room. Students worked in groups and talked about their images, seeking approval, opinions, and perspective from each other. The work evolved slowly as they talked together and as we talked as a group. Often, some part of the piece would seem to work, and this piece would point the way to how the whole painting should come together. Our appreciation of the place where we lived grew as we heard the stories and saw the images of other students.

As the students worked and began to gain momentum, I tried to stay out of things, to let them take their ideas to their own destinations. And so I worked on my own painting of the classroom. For me, the art studio was a magical place full of adventure and mystery. And so I painted the tables spread with papers, the colorful chairs, and fleeting impressions of the students about their work.

Like Jolie, Amelia is a dreamer. She started working with rooftops and trees, with a ladder leading suggestively to the roof. It made the view more rural than seemed possible in the suburb. This was a view from a high window in her house. Later, she focused on drawing and painting around where she lived, especially her home. For her, the sacred was in the familiar and the connection to childhood memories. Her poetry described her childhood games and creation of an imaginary town inside her living room. She called it bedsheet town. She drew a stairway leading to her backyard, and then developed a painting called "Lot of 40 X 100 X up Safe" (Figure 2.3). In the margins, 40X100X UP was written in blue, with SAFE written in the corner.

Over the course of the semester, Amelia's interest in environmental issues grew. She created a series of drawings about the places around the school, including views of the school from the surrounding forest. As mentioned earlier, her writing pondered the graffiti written on trees and the evident carelessness of her peers toward the forest. Her interest in the natural habitat of the school led her to imagine a garden of indigenous plants in the dusty courtyard between school wings. She sketched the courtyard during her science class, and turned her idea into a grant proposal that eventually funded her dream garden. It was a curious juxtaposition, to see Amelia imagine a garden in the desert of adult and adolescent indifference. We had not considered the plight of the trees around the school until Amelia illustrated their condition. Nor had we

Figure 2.3 Amelia's painting of her backyard.

considered the possibilities for new growth within the school boundaries until we saw her sketches of the place restored.

Our method was not just the snapshot or the painting of the scene, but working from multiple images to create a collage of the complexities of our places. Kimberly created a forest eclipsed by the silver straight lines of the Long Island Railroad. I would like to think that everyone gained a new appreciation of where they lived and the community to which they belonged. Her trains moved off into the distance, signs of commerce, concrete and metal, trees and flowers. Kimberly defined for us the obvious connection of our community to the great city. Many of the residents left on that train every morning, and returned late in the evening. It was, to some extent, the reason for the town; it was the conduit to economic life. We accepted this, and why not? We all took the train to the subway, to Central Park, and to the museum to consider how others had defined the sacred and the place. In her own mind, Kimberly was already on her way to the city; her eyes were on the distant horizon of the city and her future life. It was appropriate that her work featured the Long Island Railroad, which in many ways defined our town.

Josh took this interest in things urban another step and did a series of drawings and paintings based on the city, especially the bridges to the city (Figure 2.4).

He had been born in New York and felt a nostalgic sense of belonging to it. His silhouettes of bridges and skylines conveyed a sense of the dreams and desires that the city evokes among those who live in the city or live around it. It is a place where anything can happen, where possibilities of rapture, disappointment, and fulfillment abound. His images evolved from bridges to scenes of particular streets and walls etched with graffiti's secret language. His images provoked discussions about the language of graffiti and the borders it created, about property and the signs that assail our lives. Some argued that graffiti cluttered our minds and desecrated our views. Others argued that billboards and their messages were every bit as damaging to our mental landscape.

Figure 2.4   Josh's city bridge painting.

Anka chose to describe her interior, personal worlds. Her place of refuge was her desktop, including her lamp, notes, pieces of papers, pens, meticulously rendered in colored pencil, and it was this that she drew (Figure 2.5).

Her drawing included surreal, dreamlike reflections in the glass and metallic surfaces and complex patterns of wrappers she had saved and glued to the wall. Shadows of imaginary characters graced the desktop.

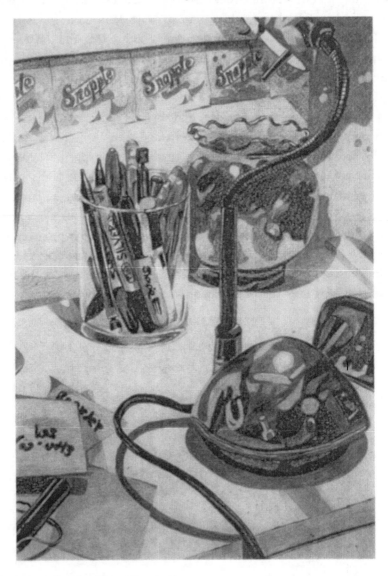

Figure 2.5   Anka's drawing of her desk.

Figure 2.6 Victoria in the tree: collage.

Later, these drawings became a painting that included a window looking out into the unknown jungle foliage of the night landscape.

Like Anka, Victoria chose to stay close to home, creating a self-portrait with her cat, high up in the tree (Figure 2.6). Multiple images were woven together into a complex picture of cat, leaves, branches, and girl. Victoria never got to the painting because she became so absorbed in the puzzle of the collage. But the collage was a masterpiece of invention and multiple viewpoints.

Our conversations and images came together in the final exhibition. The students prepared written commentaries about their work that were displayed next to their images. We had all seen the work before and felt we knew it well, but it was different seeing it all together in the gallery. Each piece was carefully mounted and hung as a sequence, including preliminary plans, sketches, studies, and final paintings. The students spent many hours planning the arrangement and relationships among the images.

The exhibition introduced other members of the community to our newly discovered sense of place. When the biology teacher discovered Amelia's interest in restoring plants, he became the catalyst for her efforts to revitalize the courtyard. Josselyn's parents saw their daughter among her peers with important things to say about their experience. They saw in her work the delicate strands of a bridge to belonging. Jamie, who had left all her special places in Kansas, followed the principal around during the exhibition opening, explaining what it all meant. Josh's paintings of New York City became the heart of his art portfolio and were later published by the Scholastic Art Awards.

The overall effect was a weaving of a rich mosaic of different experiences, held together by a new awareness and sense of belonging. It was not simply an exhibit of landscape scenes, seascapes, streets, or houses. It became an exhibit about home, journeys, nature, dreams, and awareness. The work was moving because both the artist and the audience could share the experience of knowing the places that were depicted. I walked through the exhibition many times during the weeks following the opening feeling a deeply personal connection to the work, understanding in new ways the possibilities of these students and the community that surrounds them.

CONCLUSION

In contemporary art, place has acquired a myriad web of meanings, ranging from landscape to city, from real to imaginary, from concrete to conceptual (Golden, 2001). But history and community endure in places, in the land, and in those who live in it. The conversation about the places where we live goes on because the students have participated in a shared history of the evolution of their small community within the larger culture.

We started with the idea that art making could be a social enterprise, connected to the communities around us with a significant moral dimension. I wanted to move from the traditional, but limited, notion of art being solely about personal expression toward a vision of teaching that could engage students in a reflective and social process with the larger community. As we did this, we became a mirror and inspiration to people around us.

The experience transformed our vision and our awareness. We considered questions that do not have simple answers and engaged in imaginative speculation. We began to understand each other in new and unexpected ways. And we began to appreciate our community as a unique web of history, personal experience, and interaction with nature.

The artwork became a visible signifier of an unseen reality, an icon representing the many realities of our lives. The artwork became beautiful and meaningful as the students and I became conscious of the beauty of the world around us and our connection to it.

Place is latitudinal and longitudinal with the map of a person's life. It is temporal and spatial, personal and political. A layered location replete with human histories and memories, place has width as well as depth, it is about connections, what surrounds it, what formed it, what happened there, and what will happen there (Lippard, 1997).

REFERENCES

Bellow, S. (1978). *Henderson the rain king.* New York: Penguin Books. (Original work published 1959.)

Dewey, J. (1954). *The public and its problems.* Chicago: Swallow Press.

Eliade M. (1959). *The sacred and the profane.* Orlando, FL: Harcourt Brace Jovanovich.

Gablik, S. (1998). The nature of beauty in contemporary art. *New Renaissance, 8*(1). Retrieved December 20, 2005 from http://www.ru.org.

Gablik, S. (2004). *The reenchantment of art.* New York: Thames and Hudson.

Goetzman, W. H., & Goetzman, E. (1986). *The west of the imagination.* New York: W. W. Norton.

Golden, T. (2001). Place, considered. In S. Sollins (Ed.), *Art in the 21st century* (pp. 20–65). New York: Harry Abrams.

Greene, M. (1978). *Landscapes of learning.* New York: Teachers College Press.

Lippard, L. (1997). *The lure of the local: A sense of place in a multicentered society.* New York: New Press.

Palmer, P. J. (1998). *The courage to teach.* San Francisco: Jossey-Bass.

Solnit, R. (2002). *As Eve said to the serpent.* Athens: University of Georgia Press.

Thoreau, H. D. (1991). Walking. In R. Dillman (Ed.), *Essays of Thoreau* (pp. 480–504). Durham: University of North Carolina Press. (Original work published 1862.)

CHAPTER 3

STAR
Service to All Relations

Mark Sorensen

OUR PLACE

This is the story of the STAR (Service to All Relations) School, the values it is built on, and the way it meets the challenge of showing students how to live sustainably and to embrace a lifelong love of learning. The STAR School is an off-the-grid, small, solar-powered K–8 charter school. Located 30 miles northeast of Flagstaff, Arizona, it serves a rural and predominantly (80%) Navajo population. Public services such as paved roads, water lines, and power poles, taken for granted elsewhere, are not available in the area surrounding the school. Nevertheless, our place, on the edge of the Navajo Reservation, is rich in history and culture. The natural beauty that surrounds the campus includes 17 extinct volcanic cones and the red sandstone of the Painted Desert. But like children in many other rural places, students here can fall into the trap of believing that meaningful events are only happening in other places—urban places—and to other people, not to them.

The modern disconnection between children and the land—and the people of the land—is aggravated by the fact that American youth spend more time watching television than in school. This is a challenge shared by many rural American communities, but it is particularly critical in Native American communities. In fact, some Native American researchers have suggested that "...cable television seems to be finishing the work of Custer" (St. Germaine, 2000, p. 3). Nearly all of these Native American communities are rural, and some like ours are extremely rural, with an average of fewer than 10 people per square mile within a 10-mile radius of our school. Unless a small rural school purposely focuses on developing relationships among students at the school and between them and their place and its people, students can easily get sucked into the canned entertainment and definition of what is cool provided by MTV, urban rap music, and video games. Many youth are eager to forget about the value of their own place and the story of their own people. The Rural School and Community Trust, however, has shown that an educational approach tied to local places can help rural schools slow or reverse this process (Colchado et al., 2003).

Founded in 2001, the STAR School provides an example of how one rural school serving Native Americans is creating a deeper bond with and understanding of place through a mission that values "service to all relations." The purpose of this approach is to provide students with both the skills to get along in the world and to develop values that encourage self-confidence and a desire to learn so that young people can create productive lives capable of sustaining themselves and their families and communities. At the STAR School, "sustainability" refers to the relationships and resources that provide for the continuity of people and the environment from generation to generation. Smith and Williams (1999) have described this approach as "ecological education." They state, "The practice of ecological education requires viewing human beings as one part of the natural world and human cultures as an outgrowth of interactions between species and particular places" (p. 3). As students learn about the people and environment of their "place," they will develop relationships with the land and its people. Through building these relationships, they will encounter ideas and approaches that have been generated locally but also shed light on understanding the larger world.

DEVELOPING CURRICULUM BASED ON THE HISTORY OF PEOPLE IN OUR PLACE

To be of service to the land and its people, our students needed to be introduced to the history of human settlement and interaction in the area surrounding the STAR School. A curriculum project during the 2004–2005 academic year provides an example of how this happens. Although nearby Native American ruins reveal more than 1,000 years of human inhabitation, most Navajo youth and the non-Native families who live here struggle to feel that our region has any real heroic history or meaning. In understanding our place, it is important to know that we are located on land that has for a century and a half been a buffer zone between two distinctly different cultures: Anglo-American and Navajo. Although cooperation and positive interaction are increasingly common, a heavy cloud of racism and negative stereotypes by members of both groups toward each other has typified their relations both in the past and present. This conflict was played out in the fall of 2004 through the behavior and language of some students. Because such conflicts are part of the history of the people who live in our place, we sought to integrate this challenge into our approach with the "3 Rs" (Respect, Relationship, and Responsibility) and service that comes from the Navajo principle of K'e (kinship and interrelatedness). We looked to the land and people for examples of guiding principles that could help us find ways to sustain ourselves in the face of historical misunderstanding, distrust, and lack of respect between the two cultures.

When the STAR School received a small grant that year to integrate arts into the curriculum, we chose to focus on an historical event that is part of local lore. The "Incident at Padre Canyon," as it is called, occurred over a century ago within 20 miles of the school. This incident involved a gunfight between a group of Navajo hunters and a group of Anglo cowboys. Men died on both sides, creating a great deal of animosity that could have erupted into a range war if it had not been for the relationship between a White missionary and a Navajo headman. Their relationship was built on mutual trust and was the key to a peaceful resolution of the conflict.

The "Incident at Padre Canyon" provided us with an ideal place-based project that reached across the curriculum, as well as a metaphor for how we might sustain our community even through periods of intense conflict. Because of its power as metaphor, this historical event can be built into the curriculum for many years. Through their investigations of what happened, students are learning that their Navajo community has a rich history and that some of the important players in that history are their ancestors.

In their language arts classes, seventh- and eighth-grade students created a play entitled "Tolchaco" (the Navajo place-name for the canyon) that depicts the incident. Youth in the school who wrote, acted, made scenery, worked on music, and built the outdoor amphitheater where the play was presented were not just passive observers in the ongoing development of community; they became meaning makers for the community. The painful facts of the story as well as the triumph of a few good people, both Navajo and Anglo, gave the school community a chance to talk about issues of injustice and cultural conflict. The story demonstrates how people of good will who keep their word and communicate can resolve situations of misunderstanding back into harmony.

In a school like ours, there are many opportunities to deal with racial misunderstanding or lack of respect when the student population is over 80% Navajo with small percentages of Anglo-American, Hispanic, and Black students, and a few Native Americans from other tribes. In the 4 years since founding the school, I have led several school-wide discussions with students to provide facts and dispel rumors. In one discussion, Native students wanted to know if it was true that head lice like blonde heads more than black-haired heads. Many times when the lack of understanding or sensitivity resulted in hurt from comments that went deep, we utilized a nonviolent communication approach developed by Marshall Rosenberg (1999). This four-step approach allows people involved in a conflict to state what they believe to be the facts and to take responsibility for their own feelings and needs, as well as for listening to others take responsibility for these areas, themselves. This process most often resulted in apologies and forgiveness, and it continues to be a valuable approach to resolving conflict in a sustainable way. Experience with resolving conflicts on a personal level led to better understanding of some of the feelings of the people in the play. To further their learning about how people around the world have successfully dealt with injustice, students investigated the life of Mahatma Gandhi and the role of nonviolence in responding to injustice.

The exploration of the "Incident at Padre Canyon" provided a connection to the community that is not only rich enough to cross the curriculum, but also rich enough to cross grade levels and to involve all staff, not just the classroom teachers, as well as elders from the community. The Facilities Manager and the School Director, for example, worked with some of the students to construct the outdoor amphitheater where the play was performed. The Food Service Manager and her assistant taught some of the students to sew costumes representing the style of dress from that era. Grandparents of students who are themselves descendents of the Navajo hunters and headmen in the story volunteered to come into the school to tell students about the events depicted in the play. The participation of these elders added to the depth of this schoolwide project. In this way, community members became active contributors to the curriculum. Involving members of the community in so many ways kept creating new roles for everyone if they wished to take them on. The writing and production of "Tolchaco" is the latest example of the STAR School's commitment to the development of a place-based curriculum.

BEGINNING THE STAR SCHOOL

My own role in starting the STAR School began 30 years ago as an educator of Native American children. Since that time, I have been continually involved as a leader and administrator in Navajo community-controlled schools, mostly as a school director, sometimes as a principal and sometimes as a superintendent. It has been an honor to work for the Diné people to help create schooling that reflects the values of the people and adds to the survivability of the Navajo culture. Because I love the people I work with and live among, I contribute what I can to the Navajo people, in particular, and Native Americans in general. Over these years I have learned a great deal about what allows a tribe to survive, and I have come to the conclusion that an essential part of that survivability is an effective school serving the local community. Every school year I seek better ways to engage all students in the excitement of learning and in creating the life they want.

However, developing effective schools in Indian country is not just about being successful in providing a Western style of education. With a few notable exceptions, schools serving Native populations have been so spectacularly unsuccessful in empowering their Native students that it is necessary to consider alternative values and learning approaches drawn from traditional indigenous education. Shortly after I came to the reservation, a Navajo family, the Tsosies, took me in. Since then, they have treated me as a member of their family and clan. From them, I came to experience the power of a worldview based on *K'e,* or kinship. Through ceremonies and family gatherings, I learned about what it takes to be a good clan relative. I realized that if the practice of *K'e* were big enough to embrace someone like me, a young doctoral candidate from the Midwest, and help me to become a contributing member of an extended Navajo family, clan, and tribe, it provided a truly impressive power for living well in the world. As I became involved with schools, it became obvious that the values that were the foundation of *K'e* (Respect, Relationships, and Responsibility) should also be the foundation for schools that aim to help their communities become sustainable.

The passage of the charter school law in Arizona in 1994 allowed nonprofits and groups of parents and other interested parties to establish public charter schools. In 1995, I helped establish and then became the superintendent of one of the first charter schools serving Native

American students in the country, Tol Chi Kooh (a Navajo term meaning Red Water Canyon) Charter School. This charter utilized existing facilities of Bureau of Indian Affairs (BIA)-funded schools to enhance educational opportunities and involve parents of Navajo students in our area. Although the school succeeded in involving parents and improving school attendance and achievement, the state legislature objected to the complex funding relationship between the existing BIA-funded, tribally controlled schools and this new charter. After 3 years, the legislature reduced and then virtually eliminated the charter arrangement. It became clear to me that if a charter school in Navajo country were to succeed, it would have to be capable of standing alone and using a separate facility. In 1998, as its Executive Director, I helped the Little Singer Community School, a tribally controlled school that had participated in the Tol Chi Kooh school development, create a charter junior high with its own facility on the Little Singer campus. This school, with its monolithic dome and four classrooms, would supplement an already existing Pre-K through 6 elementary program. The focus of the charter junior high in this remote community was on Navajo language and culture, coupled with the introduction of innovative approaches to food production and health. We utilized elders in the community to share knowledge with the students about ways of observing nature. In return, students grew seedlings of various vegetables native to our area and gave them to local families. The Little Singer Junior High charter program continues to exist today and has been featured in several documentaries about place-based education (Adams, 2000).

Prior to this time, virtually all schools in the area were either created by the federal government and thus tainted with the negative history of Indian boarding schools, or were formed by the state public school system and governed by school boards that included no one from the communities on the reservation. More recently, tribal schools have been established largely as the result of the takeover of existing federal schools by tribal communities as provided by PL 100–297, the Tribally Controlled Schools Act of 1988. Although this act provides a greater degree of local community control than ever existed before, the federal government placed a moratorium on the expansion of schools or grades within reservations more than a decade ago. Now, the growth of locally controlled schools and services rests primarily with charter school development.

With this in mind, my wife, Kate, and I decided in July 2000, to create a new charter closer to our home, located a few miles from the southwest corner of the Navajo Reservation. We saw the charter school as an opportunity to invest in our dream of providing a truly inspiring education for youth in this area. We shared a willingness to take risks with our own resources to accomplish this dream. We were especially motivated because of our own son, Miles, who had been traveling over 90 miles a day to attend the Little Singer School; we also longed to have more of a sense of community in our "edge of the rez" community. The school we envisioned would articulate and honor the experience of interrelatedness that underlies the principle of *K'e* and at the same time honor high expectations for academic learning. We believed it was time to demonstrate to those who lived like us, at the interface of Anglo and Indian rural America, that it was possible to create a school that reflected knowledge from both cultures: solar power and technology from Anglo culture and values and plant knowledge of Navajo culture. By investing in service to our community, we hoped to contribute to the growth of the sense of community we longed for.

With Thomas Walker, Jr., a close friend and leader in the nearby Navajo community of Birdsprings, we applied to the state to start a charter school in 2001. My many years of being the administrator of several community-controlled tribal schools and our experience of starting a nonprofit that helped Navajo families build homes contributed to our belief that we were likely to succeed in starting a new school to serve students in our area. Kate's and my 14 years of living at our ranch gathering water off the roof and generating all our electricity from the sun gave us the confidence that we could, in fact, successfully power the school with solar panels if we built energy conservation into the school's policies. Operating the entire school on solar power also clearly reflected our concern about sustainability and fit into the curriculum we hoped to teach. There were no examples to follow in building our solar-powered school because we were the first solar-powered charter school in the United States. In 2002, the second year of the school's operation, the STAR School was awarded the Governor of Arizona's prize for energy efficiency.

Starting with the assumption that our school needed to be a place that helped our community become sustainable, the founders of the STAR School developed a vision for a school that would produce empowered students. In 2003, the STAR School Board, now including two professors of education from Northern Arizona University, Dr. Elaine Riley-Taylor and Four Arrows (Dr. Don T. Jacobs), refined this vision to state that the school would strive to "...inspire all students to have a life-long love of learning" (STAR School Policy Manual, 2003, p. 1). By this we meant joy in the process of learning as well as the development of skills in reading, math, and technology. Students proficient in these areas can experience pleasure in finding out what they need or want to know. Students who are not competent in these skill areas may receive less information and sometimes feel frustrated by the process of learning rather than feel the joy and self-confidence that can accompany gaining new knowledge.

Unfortunately, the record of existing school programs serving Native American students, in our area and nationwide, is that conventional and tribal schools have failed to provide most Native American students with advanced skills in reading and math. In 2002, third graders in western Navajo schools averaged in the 30th percentile on the Stanford 9 reading subtest. In the same region of the Navajo Nation in 2004, 87% of eighth-graders did not reach the level of Proficiency on the Arizona AIMS math test, and 60% scored Far Below Proficiency (Coconino County School Superintendent Data, 2005). These problems are not limited to elementary education. Only 6% of Native American entering freshmen at a nearby university graduate in 4 years. The percentage of Native Americans who are entering the sciences as a profession is lower than any other ethnic group. Perhaps it is not surprising that unemployment in many Navajo communities hovers around 35%, and in the Navajo community of Leupp, which we serve, the unemployment rate is 28%. Sadly, the data also reflect a despair that afflicts some school-aged youth: Native American teen suicide rates are twice that of the general population, a figure that has changed little in the past two decades (Carmona, 2005). It is clear from this information that, in general, schools serving Native American students in our area have not been effective in empowering their students.

If students, however, are shown how to contribute to the community and value their own work, they can develop confidence and the skills required to deal with problems. Thus, through the service of the school governing board, staff, and students to the community, young people develop knowledge about the community that is deepening relationships within the community. Not only do students become healthier and stronger, the community develops its social capital—and becomes more resilient and therefore a more sustainable environment in which students are more likely to succeed. When students succeed, they provide more resources for the community and fewer liabilities. When a rural school is committed to include service and place-based values in its approach to education, it can begin a cycle of resource development in the community that ultimately benefits students. We must find ways to build effective schools for Native American communities because schools can provide needed contributions to the sustainability of those communities and give the next generation tools to successfully support themselves and their families.

Although educators working with Native American students face daunting challenges, researchers have identified a number of strategies that are successful in kindling native students' love of learning and in applying that learning in ways that help them function in the world (Barnhardt, 2005; Tharp, Estrada, Dalton, & Yamauchi, 2000). We have sought to align our activities with some of their findings. One of the strategies involves recognizing and then using the knowledge of local families and elders about the land, plants, and animals of the place where they and their children live. Another strategy involves drawing on the wisdom of the Native cultures to provide a framework for developing the guiding principles of a school. As indicated earlier, the Navajo practice of *K'e*, as well as the traditional practice of Navajo Peacemaking (*Hozhooji Nahat'aa*), has provided a cultural framework for honoring relationships and promoting harmony. In the process of identifying approaches that work with Native children, other educators and I have found that fundamental values that contribute to social and environmental sustainability are similar across many indigenous cultures; they are simply expressed in different ways (Cajete, 2003). The Native Hawaiian value of *malama*, for example, corresponds well with the Navajo principle of *K'e* (Bluehouse, 1996).

What we have termed the 3 Rs (Respect, Relationships, and Responsibility) for easy reference with students has proven to be helpful for this specific population and may provide the basis for sound educational practice for many other rural communities. Considering how Native American, Alaska Native, and Native Hawaiian cultures still exist in spite of the pressures they face to assimilate and drop their identity, these cultures have proven their sustainability. Every one of them values respect, relationships, and responsibility, and they have endured for centuries. If rural communities in general and Native communities in particular are to continue to exist in the face of increasing urbanization, educational approaches based on these principles could be essential for their survival. Given the fact that students in metropolitan areas can also feel disconnected from their place and people, such principles might also be applicable to urban schools, as well. Small, intensely place-based schools like ours may thus play a role in the broader educational environment as they demonstrate ever more effective ways to school children and help their communities sustain themselves.

SERVICE FOR CARE, CITIZENSHIP, AND SOVEREIGNTY

From the beginning, our school's ability to attract families has depended on our willingness to serve parents as well as their children. We do this by encouraging local families to work at the school when they are qualified and helping them become qualified when they are not. Of our 14 full-time employees, 9 are Native American, and all but 2 of the 17 total employees live in the rural community our school serves. Sometimes service comes in the form of picking up a parent who has no working vehicle to come to the school for a meeting. Sometimes it involves taking our students to visit elders in the community and chopping firewood. Often it simply involves responding with care and concern when any community member is in trouble.

Many schools espouse the value of "good citizenship" for their students. Good citizenship is even included in grades K–8 as an Arizona state standard. But although the goal of good citizenship has commendable performance objectives such as knowing how the electoral college works and the names of the Founding Fathers, good citizenship often seems less than relevant to the lives of students on the reservation. In fact, it is not hard to see how good citizenship can be viewed as an assimilationist approach by Native Americans rather than an empowering stance for young people. The concept of "good citizenship" doesn't seem to be designed to serve the students as much as it seems designed to serve mainstream society. Native students who graduate from our area's schools often feel disempowered by the dominant culture (i.e., the last to be hired and the first to be fired) and disconnected from their own communities.

Recently, I saw one of the Navajo students who had attended the Little Singer School when I was its principal. We crossed paths in a discount store in a small border town. Now high school aged, he said, "They don't want me in school." "So what do you do all day?" I asked. "I walk the streets," he shrugged. I urged him to consider other options such as getting a part-time job and going back to school later. He just looked at me and said, "That's OK. I don't have skills." I was stunned into silence because I realized the educational program in our area, including the Little Singer School, had never given this young man the hope or the skills needed to make his way in the world.

When we started the STAR School, we interviewed junior high students in the community about their expectations for their lives in the future; many indicated they hoped they would find a low-paying job in the neighboring town. Some thought they would be dead. A few thought they would be in the military. A handful believed that they would be able to get "a good-paying job" but that it would be in a city and not in any of our small Navajo communities. The ways they responded convinced me that they believed their voices didn't matter and that they had no incentive to get involved, even within their own community.

This sense of alienation is contrary to *K'e*, which emphasizes the interrelatedness of all beings and the responsibility everyone has to care for each other. Also contrary to *K'e* are disrespectful student behaviors that disrupt the learning of others. Although only 10% of the students at the STAR School during a recent year were referred to the School Director's office for behavior violating our commitment to respect, relationships, and responsibility, nearly 80% of those violations were for cursing or disrespectful language with the teacher or other students, behaviors not in keeping with traditional cultural values. The anger expressed by these young people and their lack of respect for adults or fellow students causes great concern among parents and grandparents in the community. They see this behavior as an indicator of the deterioration of Navajo values. Over the years, these issues have been the subject of many hours of discussion among community leaders, parents, grandparents, teachers, and myself.

In an effort to help students reconnect with their own communities and to learn to apply traditional Navajo values such as *K'e*, we have extended the notion of citizenship to include an extensive program of community service. Guided by the 3 Rs, we invite students to choose activities that will allow them to practice respect, relationship, or responsibility. Some students tutor other students after school. Older students read to younger students. Outside of school, students go to the isolated homes of various elders in the community and help clean up, carry water, and chop firewood. In turn, we invite elders to come into the school to speak to students about Navajo ways of living and to share stories of events that happened in the past. These elders sometimes come just to express their gratitude to students for visiting them and making their lives less lonely. Although at first some students complained about the physical labor involved, other students were moved to tears by the condition they found some of the elders in and demanded to know whom they could contact to provide better services to these members of their community. This allowed teachers to teach students about local and regional government and how to pressure governmental programs to become more responsive to the needs of elders. Others responded by asking their teachers to return to the homes of certain elders so they could help them again. In this way, we shifted away from the idea of teaching "good citizenship" to the concept of demonstrating, with the students' involvement, the values of the 3 Rs and service. This shift seemed to be much more relevant to the students and their understanding of traditional Navajo values. It had the additional effect of empowering students through engaging their desire to act in their own community.

Teaching students the value their service can have for themselves and others has real power in increasing the sustainability of the community. The personal and community sovereignty we all cherish (and that is so important to Native people) is vital to a meaningful life. It is best accomplished by truly caring for the people and the land where we wish to be sovereign and by taking action based on that caring. Sovereignty is about being able to make our own choices. Sovereignty given to us by the government, whether it be tribal, federal, or state, can be taken away. In other words, it is not truly ours. Our willingness to act on our caring through service to the people and to the land cannot be taken away. By caring for and serving our land and our people, we understand them in a much deeper way, and that we see our own health is connected to theirs. It makes us want to do our best to help empower our community. It is in this spirit that the STAR School helps students learn about and care for our "place." By modeling service to our students and blending class projects of service into our curriculum, students become models of service in the community.

This focus on service is not business as usual in public schools, where the pressure of high-stakes testing leads educators away from even having a discussion about the long-term survivability of their communities and the role schools play in that future. The level of service we are working to achieve at the STAR School takes a considerable adjustment for students and parents accustomed to schools that focus primarily or exclusively on academics. It is at these times that the advice of Mahatma Gandhi provides our staff and students with the means to accomplish our goals: "You must be the change you wish to see in the world." A school that decides to focus on service cannot expect to do very well when staff members are reluctant to serve each other and the community. On the other hand, a school that does focus on service with the staff members fully involved can expand students' knowledge of the issues in the community and expand the sovereignty they feel in relationship to their community.

The STAR School's development of the concept of "Sovereignty through Service" is perhaps a more indigenous way of expressing the concept of the "culture of attachment" described by McLaughlin and Blank in their article in *Education Week* in November 2004. McLaughlin and Blank refer to the "community-as-text" approach to teaching and learning and define it as including such arenas as "...service learning, place-based education, civic education, work-based learning, and youth development" (p. 34). For Native American communities, in particular, the "community-as-text" approach is valuable to bridge the gap that so often occurs between the range of academic content that is present in most public schools and the living meaning that is woven into the lives of Native students in the form of extended family relationships and traditional ceremonies led by community elders. If public schools serving Native American students would incorporate Native values into the cultural assumptions that are part of the everyday running of schools, Native values would become more than just a superficial overlay, taking the form of Native American Week or an Indian Princess contest. The "community-as-relationship" and the "community-as text" approach to place-based education can help students and teachers recognize the depth of meaning and the complexity of thought that already exists in the experience of living in rural communities.

Although the emphasis on relationships among staff, faculty, and students is not directly linked to instructional content, it is very much connected to students feeling they are respected and valued. That, in turn, is a strong deterrent to students dropping out of school. Ultimately, building trust and increasing interpersonal contact between staff and students have a high value in keeping at-risk students in school. A 1994 study by the Center for Research on Effective Schooling for Disadvantaged Students found that students who dropped out consistently cited poor relationships with teachers and administrators as more powerful motivators for school dropout than out-of-school factors such as the need for approval from home (McPartland & Jordan, 1994). Deyhle and Swisher (1997) also found that Native American students, in particular, were more likely to stay in school when teachers and administrators showed that they respected and understand students' community and culture.

SERVICE FOR ECOLOGICAL SUSTAINABILITY

Prior to building the STAR School, the campus had been the site of more than a dozen old wrecked vehicles. In other words, it had been a junkyard. The process of reclaiming the land involved a number of opportunities for science activities. All the wrecked cars and trucks were removed prior to students' arrival, but there were still many areas where the earth had been badly treated. Soil reparation was among the first set of science learning activities that students engaged in. This focused instruction on relationship with the earth, recognizing that if we do not listen to and cooperate with the land as a relative whom we love, we are not likely to develop sustainable relations with the place where we live. If we choose to act as if the earth is simply a lump of rock and dirt with which we have no relationship, then it is far easier to abuse it and leave it in worse shape for future generations. However, if we choose to care for the earth because we have a relationship with her, as indigenous peoples around the world continue to teach, then multiple opportunities present themselves to enrich students' care for the land in ways that contribute to life for future generations. For example, by composting scraps from the cafeteria, students created environments outside in which they could raise worms and create rich soil. In 2004, the compost was mixed into the soil around newly planted native plants and fruit trees. Watching rainfall runoff patterns across the campus, students, teachers, and community volunteers created berms to funnel the runoff to the new plants. The system has worked remarkably well for our thriving plants, and students won first prizes in the Navajo Nation Science Fair for their plant-related presentations. Over and beyond this kind of formal recognition, we saw the beauty of the land returning because the students were taking care of it. Students are identifying native plants growing around the campus using a book written by a community volunteer. Another Navajo elder teaches students about the traditional uses of each plant. Students also raise plants from seeds in the greenhouse and pot these plants to bring them home to their parents and grandparents.

Another aspect of our place-based science program centers around our solar panels. These represent another aspect of sustainability. Even with the benefit of a backup propane generator, the school experiences occasional days (usually in winter after extended cloudy periods) when we must severely curtail our power use. All of the staff and students live daily within this solar-powered experiment. The STAR School gives students the opportunity to learn the benefits and limitations of this power source and to discuss and study everything about it, from the flow of electrons in the solar panels to the amount of power used by various appliances. In 2004, seventh-grade students who had done experiments and observations of the school's solar system competed with high school projects from other schools in the area of engineering and came away with the first-place award. All students in the school receive an orientation about the solar power system, and students have, on occasion, been interviewed by local radio stations about their knowledge of solar power and their recommendations to others about its benefits.

PLACE-BASED VALUES FOR EDUCATING THE WHOLE CHILD

Being guided by Navajo values means that our educational efforts at the STAR School need to recognize and help develop the whole child and all aspects of being human: mental, physical, emotional, and spiritual. Mental learning can be seen in students' investigation and application of solar power concepts throughout our solar-powered school. Our place-based approach has contributed to physical learning as we get to know the plants that grow on the school property and serve them better, with richer soil made with our own food scraps. With regard to emotional learning, investigating events for the play, "Tolchaco," helped deepen and broaden students' understanding of the way that violence can arise from a lack of respect; this experience also demonstrated the role mutual trust can play in the restoration of social harmony. Students' spiritual lives have been touched as they learned traditional Navajo approaches to conflict resolution, enhancing the sustainability of our own communities and contributing to our ability to act justly. The more we can investigate with students the various meanings of sustainability through service in our own region, the more prepared they will be to meet the world in a harmonious way, with great curiosity and joy. Perhaps the American poet Ralph Waldo Emerson put it best over 150 years ago when he wrote: "It is one of the most beautiful compensations of this life that no man can sincerely try to help another without helping himself... serve and thou shall be served."

Today, Navajo philosophers, giving English words to the ancient Navajo (Diné) concept of *K'e*, teach that by interacting in the world through the principles of respect, responsibility, and relationships, we come to know who we really are as we serve our people and our land. Is this not "one of the most beautiful compensations of life" that Emerson described? We sustain ourselves through service.

REFERENCES

Adams, J. Q. (2000). *A pedagogy of place: Little Singer Community School, Navajo Nation* (a video production funded by the Illinois Board of Higher Education). Macomb: Illinois Staff and Curriculum Developers.

Barnhardt, R., & Kawagley, A. O. (2005). Indigenous knowledge systems and Alaska Native ways of knowing. *Anthropology and Education Quarterly, 36*(1), 8–23.

Bluehouse, P. (1996). *"Navajo Peacemaking" in Navajo Nation.* Unpublished manuscript.

Cajete, G. (1999). *Igniting the sparkle: An Indigenous science education model.* Skyland, NC: Kivaki.

Carmona, R. (2005, June 15). *Suicide prevention among Native American youth.* Testimony before the Indian Affairs Committee, U.S. Senate.

Coconino County School Superintendent Data. (2005).

Colchado, J., Hobbs, V., Hynes, M., King, J., Newell, M., Parker, S., & Wilson, S. (2003). *Engaged institutions: Impacting vulnerable youth through place-based education.* Washington, DC: Rural School and Community Trust.

Deyhle, D., & Swisher, K. (1997). Research in American Indian and Alaska Native education: From assimilation to self-determination. *Review of Research in Education, 22*, 113–194.

McLaughlin, M., & Blank, M. (2004). Creating a culture of attachment: A community-as-text approach to learning. *Education Week. 24*(11), 34 -35.

McPartland, J., & Jordan, W. (1994). *Essential components of high school dropout prevention reforms.* Baltimore: Johns Hopkins University.

Rosenberg, M. (1999). *Non-violent communication: A language of life.* Del Mar, CA: PuddleDancer Press.

Smith, G. A., & Williams, D. R. (Eds.). (1999). *Ecological education in action: On weaving education, culture, and the environment.* Albany: State University of New York Press.

STAR School. (2003). STAR School Policy Manual. Leopp, AZ: Author.

St. Germaine, R. (2000). *A chance to go full circle: Building on reforms to create effective learning.* Paper presented at the National American Indian and Alaska Native Education Research Agenda Conference, Albuquerque, NM.

Tharp, R. G., Estrada, P., Dalton, S., & Yamauchi, L.A. (2000). *Teaching transformed: Achieving excellence, fairness, inclusion, and harmony.* Boulder, CO: Westview.

CHAPTER 4

Youth as Resources in Revitalizing Communities

Julie Bartsch

Katie Wilber and Seth Bolduc remember interviewing men who worked on the last Kennebec River log drive in 1976, learning how hard it was to bring logs down the river from Moosehead Lake to the mills in Shamut, Maine. Their video can be seen on the student-created Skowhegan Community Website and the Maine Historical Society's Memory Network (see For More Information at the end of this chapter for Website addresses for these and other organizations).

Eric Axelman remembers mobilizing a letter-writing campaign and creating a video documenting the salient qualities of the Skowhegan Grange's architecture and history to help save it from becoming another parking lot as had happened to other historic buildings in the town center. An iMovie was also created documenting changes over time resulting in the loss of many historic landmarks.

Dan Hitchcock and Joey Dufour remember showing their iMovie/documentary on "The Changing Face of Industry in Maine" to former Maine Governor Angus King and Steve Jobs of Apple Computer as evidence of how students are using technology to enhance learning and entrepreneurial thinking. As a result, Apple Computer's support was instrumental in launching Maine's Laptop Technology Initiative, a program to put laptops in the hands of every seventh- and eighth-grade student and teacher in the state.

Mollie Pillsbury, Brittany Frost, and Michelle Tayler will never forget the extensive research they did on Margaret Chase Smith and the McCarthy era to create their documentary. They went on to win at Maine History Day, and their documentary was shown in Washington,

DC, at the National History Day competition. The documentary is on the Skowhegan Community Website.

Rachelle Clukey and Matt Dudley remember e-mailing professors and examining the Lake George/Oak Pond Watershed Report written by Colby College students in order to help create a newsletter for Lake George camp owners and lake users on the hazardous effects of invasive plants, acid rain, erosion, and land-use patterns on the trails and beach-front enjoyed by Skowhegan residents.

These are some of the community-based projects graduating students at Skowhegan High School recall from their middle school history and technology classes 4 years before. In the process of learning important history lessons about their community and state, students remembered the sense of importance they felt in contributing important work to their community and the respect they received from adults. "You learned about the history of our town through the stories of real people.... I remember so much more from those interviews and research projects than from most of the courses I've taken in high school... where we just do work, pass the test, and then forget stuff we supposedly learned," commented one of the students.

Skowhegan, Maine, with a strong history of both agricultural and manufacturing activity, is representative of many communities across the rural landscape facing geographic isolation, loss of traditional economies, out-migration of youth, declining school enrollments, and persistently fewer students continuing their education beyond high school. Schools have become vehicles for educating young people to leave, fulfilling the prophecy that these places are doomed to poverty and decline. For those young people who stay, limited local career paths reinforce a perception that there is no sense in trying to succeed.

The state of Maine—faced with high out-migration of youth (27,000 young people left Maine in the 1990s) and continued loss of jobs in resource-based industries such as fishing, farming, and forestry—is endeavoring to reverse these trends by transforming the relationship between schools and communities. Just as there is an immediate need to address issues of student achievement, out-migration, and employment in Maine, there is a parallel need to bring new and increased resources to bear on the reinvention of local economies and innovations to community development. A number of Maine communities are recognizing the powerful synergy created when the resources of community-based organizations are brought into the heart of the learning process, and the energy and skills of young people are directed toward important economic, cultural, environmental, and social issues. In some communities like Skowhegan, it is 12- and 13-year-olds who have captured the attention of town officials as they attempt to find new and innovative ways to address the challenges facing the future of their town.

This chapter looks in depth at how and why Maine is focusing on involving young people in simultaneously addressing the interconnected agendas of school improvement and community revitalization. From statehouse to schoolhouse, Maine's leadership sees the future of its small towns as dependent on the identification and mobilization of internal assets, including schools and young people.

The Rural School and Community Trust (Rural Trust) has invested significant resources in Maine over the past 10 years in support of their integrated effort to improve schools and rebuild healthy and sustainable communities. Believing in the crucial relationship between good schools and thriving rural communities, the Rural Trust provides technical assistance, research, and connections to other rural communities attempting similar efforts; processes for evaluating outcomes; and funding for programs. As the state that ranks highest in the country in terms of the importance of rural education—53% of its students are enrolled in rural schools and more than 60% of the schools are in rural areas (Johnson & Strange, 2005)—the Trust believes Maine could be a national model for connecting the important agendas of school improvement and community revitalization.

THE RATIONALE FOR YOUTH AS COMMUNITY RESOURCES
Reverse Out-Migration of Young People
Like many rural states across the nation, Maine is witnessing a growing out-migration of young people. Research shows that the number of people aged 65 and older has grown three times faster in Maine than the overall population growth, increasing by 20,000 residents in each decade since 1980. In addition, the loss of traditional economies—textile and timber, family farms, fishing—has shaken the economic underpinnings in communities across the state. Military base closings and mergers within the data processing/credit card industry could result in even fewer jobs. The exodus of young people from rural communities has diverse ramifications on a community's demographics and local economy, as well as the relationships rural youth have with their communities. As the average age of residents increases, older members of the community are often less likely "to attend to the needs of their young people" (Innovation Center for Community and Youth Development, 1999, p. 8).

Responding to these complex challenges requires an integrated and creative approach that cuts across traditional sector boundaries, empowers local people, and utilizes youth as a viable source of social capital. If rural communities are to remain viable, they cannot continue to export all their youth. Pam Fisher, co-author of Maine's Commission on Secondary Education report to improve learning in Maine's secondary schools, *Promising Futures* (1998), and Director of the Great Maine Schools Project says:

> If kids could see themselves as viable citizens solving real problems in their communities, then they would have, upon leaving these communities, a clearer understanding of not only their sense of place but how they could improve their communities, work in their communities, or live in their communities as adult citizens. And that is a very real issue for the state of Maine. Kids leave here. We've lost 27,000 students in the last ten years in the state of Maine.... We have retirees moving in and young kids moving out. We're losing our students. (personal communication, 2006)

Maine's Governor Baldacci raised his concerns about these changes in Maine's demographics in his 2003 inaugural address and pledged his commitment to pull together Maine's young adults to learn more about the conditions leading to the migration of this population. Believing that young people may prove to be one of Maine's most important community and economic development resources, Baldacci convened a "Summit on Youth Migration" in July 2005. Over 200 young people, ages 25 to 34, discussed what it would take to make Maine an attractive place for young people under the age of 35 to live, work, thrive, and prosper. "Gathered here are hundreds of potential solutions to unlocking the door to Maine's next renewal," stated the Governor in his welcome. "Those solutions are represented by each of you here and joining through the Internet. This initiative brings young people together to generate ideas, realize opportunities, and achieve sustainable solutions for vibrant communities, quality of life, and the economy of Maine." The governor and attendees have launched a Web site to continue to share ideas and possible solutions to keep young adults in Maine or bring young adults to Maine.

Identify Youth as a Source of Social Capital

Harvard Professor Robert D. Putnam, author of *Bowling Alone* (2000) and *Better Together* (2003), refers to youth as a source of a community's "social capital." The central premise of social capital is that social networks have value. Social capital refers to the collective value of all "social networks" (who people know) and the inclinations that arise from these networks to do things for each other ("norms of reciprocity"). Putnam uses an observation about the decline in bowling leagues in the United States as a metaphor to describe the increasing alienation of Americans from their families and communities as well as the political process. He warns that our stock of social capital has plummeted, impoverishing our lives and communities, and believes that "the generations coming of age in the last 30 years (especially in the '80s and '90s) are generally less engaged than their predecessors" in their communities (Putnam, 2000, p. 25).

The Rural Trust, however, has found that when students' academic work is linked to the needs, issues, and community development imperatives of the local community, their level of engagement in both academics and community increases. Similarly, students become important sources of social capital and potential assets for innovative community development projects. Their ideas and energy often serve as a key point of connection between the school and the community. Young people can change the way a whole town operates.

Community revitalization efforts supported by the Rural Trust demonstrate that just as there is an immediate need to address issues of student achievement and engagement, there is a parallel need to bring new and increased resources to bear on innovative community development projects. These resources need to come from within the community. Rural communities often focus on their deficiencies, seeing themselves as people with special needs that can only be met by outsiders, instead of identifying their internal capacities and assets. Kretzman and McKnight (1993) talk about the need for communities to see themselves as "producers of services rather than just consumers." Once these services are identified, however, there is often a shortage of money and capacity to implement these projects. Local students represent an underutilized resource.

Bruce Hazard, president of Mountain Counties Heritage, Inc. (MCH), echoes Putnam's belief that students and schools in Maine's western mountain region are important untapped social capital. Over the past 5 years, MCH has worked with a broad association of businesses, nonprofits, and government agencies (called the Maine Mountain Heritage Network) to find creative ways to use the region's heritage and natural resources to help meet emerging economic challenges. The Maine Mountain Heritage Area includes 11,000 square miles of forestland, all of Maine's peaks over 4,000 feet, the headwaters of most of the state's major river systems, and over 1,000 lakes and ponds. Hazard and his colleagues see teachers and students as potential collaborators in identifying ways these resources can be used in a regional development effort. Hazard observes:

> The basic idea is that we can build stronger communities and local economies on a base of better working knowledge of our region's resources. That's where the student contribution can begin, helping us to build that knowledge base. As projects develop, there are countless opportunities to participate in other ways—as trail builders, tour guides, local historians, and web site designers. In our communities, we need help in every department. (personal communication, 2005)

The Maine Mountain Counties Heritage Network (MCHN) communities are launching projects in a number of program areas, including Knowledge Power (developing deep knowledge of natural, cultural, and historical assets among stakeholders, including youth), Lands and Waters (better management of natural assets), Village Works (communities serving as hubs for regional assets such as resource conservation, heritage-based businesses), and Mountain Made (promoting the region's "signature" products). In each program area, project leaders are seeking student involvement. The Land and Waters team, for example, is interested in linking with outdoor recreation groups in schools to help with asset mapping in high-value recreation areas. In Skowhegan, students have contributed images and text for a downtown walking tour (Village Works project).

MCHN has turned to the Rural School and Community Trust to help forge partnerships with local schools and youth to support local community development initiatives. Working with Hazard, the Rural Trust identified four western Maine schools eager to participate in heritage-based development efforts. The schools include Forest Hills K–12 School (Jackman), Madison Public Schools (Madison), Mount Abram High School (Salem Township—serves five towns covering a 600-square-mile region), and Skowhegan Middle School. Students are being tapped to provide creativity, research, analysis, and labor to the emerging market opportunities for heritage-based development in each of these western region communities. "The link with schools isn't always easy. Matching up the learning agenda with the community development agenda can be harder than it looks. That's why we sought help from the Rural School and Community Trust to help engage with schools as a community development resource," comments Hazard (personal communication, 2005).

Skowhegan's Model for Connecting Schools and Community Revitalization Efforts

Located in north-central Maine on the Kennebec River, Skowhegan has a long and colorful history, much of which is directly associated with its location on the Kennebec. Over several thousand years, the river was used as a travel way, first by Indians, then by Euro-American explorers and settlers. In the early 19th century, thousands of immigrants from both French Canada and Ireland traveled the Old Canada Road, settling in Skowhegan, the first major town settlers encountered in the "new world." The surging waterfall at the head of the gorge provided ample power (still producing electricity) to drive a variety of manufacturing concerns. During the 19th century, this vital and diverse economy produced a thriving commercial district and supported a range of community and cultural institutions. Today, Skowhegan's residents are trying to capitalize on the town's rich history and natural resources to develop new entrepreneurial ventures. Students are a major partner in these efforts.

Three years ago, Skowhegan's local historical society (called the History House) formalized a collaborative relationship with local schools by creating an online archive called Maine Memory Network to archive all the documents, photographs, artifacts, and letters collected by students, making them accessible to schools and historical societies throughout Maine. Local historical society members worked hand in hand with students to upload images and documents in a course called Skowhegan's Local History, team-taught by teacher Laura Richter and Lynn Perry of the History House. "In a very few years, people of their generation will become the keepers of our local history and perhaps this effort will start some of them down that road," comments Perry. The benefits of the school's collaboration with the History House extend far beyond either institution's door—thanks to the computer savvy of the middle school students. They are not only learning about their town's rich history, but also making it accessible to others, says Richter. Students launched a Skowhegan Community Website 3 years ago that archives students' research projects on important historical events and economic issues in the community.

Fostering relationships between town officials, residents, and students is a "calling" for 19-year veteran teacher Richter, who serves as the school's technology integration specialist as well as a teacher of history, social studies, and geography. She says:

> It's difficult to interest students in history when they learn from a textbook only. It doesn't allow them to have kinship or connection to the people and places they study, but when they handle primary resources—whether a canteen Benedict Arnold's men left on Skowhegan Island or the Civil War letters from a Skowhegan soldier to his girlfriend—they really come to see themselves as part of a tradition passed down.

She encourages her colleagues, working together across disciplines in heterogeneously grouped Grade 7 and 8 teams, to use the community as their classroom.

Students use sophisticated tools such as iMovie and PowerPoint to make compelling multimedia presentations, which have become very visible in the community and beyond. Their Web site documents students' numerous interviews with town officials and residents as well as current event information. Richter says:

> Students have become interested in town government and how decisions are made. They've located primary sources and photographs of many old buildings in town that have been torn down over the years and become concerned when they hear that buildings like the Grange Hall might become a parking lot. They go to town meetings with their laptops and create newsletters and web-based stories from the proceedings to influence town planners' thinking about the future of these buildings.

Pat Dickey, Skowhegan's recently retired Town Manager and town employee for over 40 years, refers to the Skowhegan Middle School students as "impressive and articulate ambassadors" for the town. Dickey observed:

> When town residents complain about their tax bills, I direct them to the impressive accomplishments and contributions of our middle school students—our future leaders that we want to stay in, or return to, Skowhegan when they finish their education. Residents tend to be more amenable to supporting the local schools' budgets when they see the students' contributions to the community.

In her tenure as Town Manager, Dickey would frequently direct prospective employers inquiring about possible relocation to Skowhegan to the students' Web site. She hosted students at Town Council meetings and did everything she could to make town records and information available to students conducting research. Student involvement in the town's community and economic development efforts has become routine. They create Web sites for local officials, participate in community development projects, research the local lake's water quality issues, and write newsletters for the town. Dickey notes, "I'm sure businesses will recognize that we have a future workforce that is able to handle more upscale jobs, including those related to lucrative high technology."

This year, students are focused on some of the heritage projects identified by Hazard's MCHN, including a "Run of the River" initiative to recognize the Kennebec Gorge surrounding Skowhegan as a regional, and perhaps national, whitewater training facility, bringing canoe and kayak enthusiasts from all over the northeastern United States to Skowhegan. Students, working closely with town planners, are busy creating a Web site, designing a logo, and other activities to support the project. Responding to a request from Maine's Department of Transportation, students are also designing interpretive signs and maps for a heritage trail along the Kennebec River (known as the Scenic Byway Project).

Skowhegan's community-centered approach to learning may well hold the key to keeping one of Maine's most precious resources—its young people—as vital contributors to the local and state economy.

Expand Students' Aspirations, Academic Performance, and Skills

Ten years ago, Maine began exploring school reform efforts to reverse the alarming trends it was seeing among its students, particularly those living in poverty. Although its fourth- and eighth-graders ranked near or at the top on national and international measures of achievement, only 37% of its seniors were enrolling in college. Although Maine's high school graduation rates led the nation, its most disadvantaged schools failed to graduate almost a third of their entering freshmen classes. And, for the 37% going on to higher education, half ended up taking remedial courses during the first 2 years of college. Despite being ranked as one of the best places in the United States to raise a family, Maine has seen the steady out-migration of its youth mentioned earlier.

In 1998, a diverse group of stakeholders from education and business released a template for secondary school redesign in Maine called *Promising Futures* (Maine Commission on Secondary Education, 1998). The document, a compilation of research and lessons learned about effective secondary education, describes a highly personalized and democratic school culture where equity of opportunity is the norm and there is an expectation that all students will achieve rigorous academic and global competencies for futures filled with promise and possibility. The guiding principles have been influenced by the work Maine schools have done with the Rural Trust since 1995. One of the five guiding principles, in fact, promotes curriculum and instruction that integrates place-based pedagogy across content areas. "Maine's connection with the Rural Trust has demonstrated the power of connecting students to their communities through authentic, problem-based curricula. We hope place-based pedagogy will also create jobs and expand young people's sense of pride in living and supporting their local community's rich history and heritage," says Pam Fisher, co-chair of the Promising Futures task force (personal communication, 2006).

Much of the work the Rural Trust is currently doing in Maine—technical assistance and evaluation to schools around place-based instruction, as well as support for policy initiatives and community-building efforts—is improving student engagement. A recent volume of the *Journal of School Health* (Blum & Libbey, 2004) documents that 40% to 60% of all students are chronically disengaged from schools. This "culture of detachment" argues Johns Hopkins University's Robert Blum, "decreases students' prospects for academic success and promotes a variety of high-risk behaviors." Engagement is a critical factor in improving academic achievement. A 2003 review of research conducted by the Coalition for Community Schools and contributed to the Rural Trust confirms that "students learn best when they are actively involved in understanding and helping solve meaningful problems. This is true across all ability levels and grades" (McLaughlin & Blank, 2004, p. 34).

In our work across the country, there is evidence that when students are involved in learning that focuses on community needs and interests, and community members serve as resources and partners in teaching and learning, their academic accomplishments exceed the most rigorous educational standards. Ultimately, this place-based approach can accomplish three expectations for schools: improved academic performance and preparation for college level academic work; acquisition of skills essential for the workforce; and knowledge and practical experience as active citizens and community builders.

The NOAA Local Fisheries Knowledge Project (LFK).
A project launched by the Rural Trust in 2002 in partnership with the National Oceanic and Atmospheric Administration (NOAA) and two Maine schools is proving to be a model for expanding student aspirations,

academic performance, and skills. This interdisciplinary place-based project encourages students to explore the connections between fisheries, marine environments, their communities, and their own lives by documenting and preserving the knowledge and experiences of local fishermen and others in marine-related industries. As part of their academic studies, students use a combination of interviewing techniques and the latest in digital recording technology to create a rich database of local knowledge about the environment, fisheries, and their community's heritage. The information collected in the interviews and supporting documents is entered into an online publicly accessible database created by NOAA. In the process of interviewing individuals in fishing-related industries, gathering and analyzing scientific data, and archiving information in the database, students gain understanding in how decisions are made about our coastal and ocean resources and may contribute information that is valuable in making those decisions. In the first 2 years, 275 high school students in the two schools interviewed over 100 residents, with a waiting list of 140 interested candidates.

Teachers are witnessing changes in students' career aspirations. In one school, Jonesport-Beals, a remote coastal community where the economy is still based on fishing, students' aspirations have centered on securing commercial fishing licenses so they can continue pursuing fishing careers as their families have for generations. Thirty-five of the 104 high school students at Jonesport-Beals have commercial fishing licenses and earn between $6,000 and $9,000 a summer lobstering. These students would rather be working to pay for their own boats than attending high school. In fact, some have dropped out of high school to do so. Through involvement in the LFK project, these students are beginning to recognize the importance an education can have in securing reliable careers in marine sciences and management, as well as the fishing industry. In addition to broadened career aspirations, teachers are witnessing increased reading, writing, listening, and analytical skills. Jonesport-Beals High School student scores on the state assessment test jumped from close to the bottom at 99th out of 127 schools to 12th in the state this past year. The teachers and superintendent believe one of the factors contributing to the improvement in test scores has been the LFK project.

From a community and economic development perspective, students' interest in protecting, restoring, and managing the use of coastal and ocean resources has increased. "Students have a broader understanding of how their community relies on the marine environment, economically, socially, and ecologically as a result of this project," comments

Pam Smith, instructor of the "We Mean Business" course at Jonesport-Beals and coordinator of the project there. For the past 2 years, students from the LFK project have been part of a focus group in Maine's Washington County discussing coastal access issues and the impact on the fishing industry and culture in the county.

In the process of interviewing community residents, students' work has revived the dormant Jonesport Historical Society. Beginning with five active members in 2002, the Society now has over 140 paid members (some of whom are students). Youth and adult members together conduct, record, transcribe, and archive oral histories documenting the community's local maritime heritage. Students have introduced Historical Society members to new technologies for recording and transcribing oral history interviews, while Historical Society members have helped students locate potential interviewees and reviewed their interviews. In 2005, the Historical Society received one of six U.S. Preserve America grants to develop a local Heritage Center in Jonesport.

The Project has also reduced the communities' negative perceptions of the regulatory agency. Historically, fishermen have felt that NOAA does not listen to what they know about fisheries and their local marine environment. Student historians are building bridges between the two entities.

Make Learning Relevant and Useful

Many students question the relevance of what they're learning. "When and where will I ever use this?" is a common refrain. Research shows that students learn best when engaged in solving problems that are meaningful to them and useful to larger audiences. McTighe, Seif, and Wiggins (2004) state that "Students are more likely to make meaning and gain understanding when they link new information to prior knowledge, relate facts to 'big ideas,' explore essential questions, and apply their learnings in new contexts" (p. 26).

In addition to not understanding the relevance of what they're learning, students often feel the products of their learning are pointless. There is a difference between passing high-stakes tests and possessing the knowledge needed to accomplish something. In this era of accountability, the public and its policymakers need to remember that education ought to be about learning how to do significant things with what students know and not just acquiring knowledge. For most young people, learning matters when it is personal and serves a public purpose.

Barbara Cervone, creator of What Kids Can Do (WKCD), a national nonprofit organization that promotes the value of young people working with teachers and other adults on projects that combine powerful learning with public purpose, agrees. She believes deeply in the contributions of young people as citizens and knowledge creators. WKCD seeks out and publicizes examples of student accomplishments across the country, featuring their stories, voices, and research.

Poland High School

Educators at Poland High School are joining with community organizations to give students a chance to apply what they are learning in authentic contexts. Six years ago, the communities around Poland, Maine, decided to leave a large consolidated district and build their own high school. Having not had a secondary school for over 50 years, this group had no model for how to work with the school. Also, mixed feelings about supporting a local school remained from the less than congenial break from the previous regional system. Thus, the new high school decided to make establishing community partnerships a school improvement goal. One of the first teachers to step forward with ideas of projects that could address the needs of the community was science teacher Michelle Garcia. Michelle's Grade 11/12 students approached the local planning board with a 6-year plan for correcting an erosion problem surrounding the school property. It seemed that when the school was built 5 years earlier, plantings had been installed near a major road to avoid a potential erosion problem. Unfortunately, none of those plantings survived. The town struggled with the ways and means to correct the problem. Part of the student's plan was to research and select plants that could reduce further erosion. The planning board voted unanimously to support the student's proposal.

Another biology class worked closely with the Tripp Lake Improvement Association and staff from the Androscoggin Soil and Water Conservation District to address erosion problems at the lake's Hemlock Campground, assess water quality, and conduct a purple loosestrife survey to monitor the location of this invasive species.

Linda Lasky, Tripp Lake Association President, believes the Association is fortunate to have the support of Garcia's class to address pressing issues outlined in their Management Action Plan. "Garcia's students are organized, dynamic, and determined to improve the quality of water on Tripp Lake. We are getting much for our money," says Lasky.

Grade 9 humanities students have developed and administered an extensive survey to gather information from residents of the three communities making up the region in an attempt to learn more about the communities' past, present, and future and build identity for the two feeder towns. Questions students hope will be answered by the survey include: Why did people settle here? How did people build a life for themselves? What has changed? What holds a community together? What is the future of these three communities? What role do we (students) play in the present and future? Students consulted both local and national experts such as Kretzman and McKnight from the Institute for Policy Research at Northwestern University on assets mapping and surveying strategies. In the spring of 2005, 150 freshmen surveyed over 500 youth and adults in the community. Students plan to provide information from survey responses (maps, Web site, resource guide) to raise community and student awareness about existing resources and needs in Mechanic Falls, Minot, and Poland. They hope the data will be used to inform local decision making by government agencies, businesses, and youth for the betterment of the community. Teachers overseeing the project observed that surveys like the one created by students are usually done by adults outside the school earning thousands of dollars for this kind of asset analysis.

In an effort to connect and build alliances between the three rural communities sending students to Poland High School, students have already begun turning the school into a living history exhibit with murals and artifacts depicting the past and present of the towns.

THE CHALLENGES

Stories like the one in Poland, Maine, create a powerful case for connecting schools, students, and community development organizations in important and meaningful revitalization efforts. Helping young people develop the habits, skills, and convictions to shape safe, sustainable, and just communities can be an important mandate of public education. Regarding youth as valuable resources for revitalizing communities, however, requires a shift in mind-set for both educators and community leaders. What obstacles stand in our way and what strategies can we draw from to address these obstacles?

Rigid Schedules and Instructional Mandates

Unfortunately, conventional curricula, school schedules, and accountability mandates focused on test scores have created an unreceptive environment for community-based learning. Recent federal and state regulations, such as state standards and No Child Left Behind (NCLB), have put significant restraints on the scope, content, and methodology of teaching and learning. Teachers, feeling pressured to "cover the content," have narrowed the scope of the curriculum. School schedules with 50-minute classes often prevent students from attending community meetings. And, liability issues can restrict students from leaving school grounds.

The Rural Trust contends that place-based learning connected to community revitalization efforts can raise student test scores, meet and exceed standards, cultivate students' civic competencies, and improve the quality of life in the community simultaneously. In fact, it is the school–community synergy that makes learning compelling.

The Trust has developed an assessment system that addresses a number of goals and processes not currently addressed in state and national standardized assessments but critical for improving teaching and learning. These include connecting schools and communities, pairing intellectual content knowledge with real world applications, measuring the full impact of learning inside and outside the classroom, strengthening youth voice and youth–adult partnerships, and using the evidence these strategies yield for curriculum improvement. These assessments are meant to complement standardized tests and other teacher-driven assessments of how individual students are progressing.

Maine also supports a comprehensive system of both local and state assessment measures to insure successful achievement of the learning results by all students. This mandate gives the local school and community more flexibility in designing assessment processes that support project and place-based curricular activities. Rural Trust experience suggests that when schools become committed to place-based learning, scheduling and liability issues tend to take care of themselves.

Teacher Training

Many teachers are unfamiliar with how to connect their instructional practices with real-world issues in the community. Moreover, they often reside outside the community they teach in and have few connections or contacts within the community where the school is located. Teachers need training in how to link standards-based curriculum concepts to community issues. Some colleges and universities like Antioch New England Graduate School, Lewis and Clark College, and Washington State University offer education courses in community and place-based education. In Maine, higher-education faculty are partnering with K–12 schools on a number of place-based projects. A recent grant from the National Science Foundation (NSF) to the Island Institute will network faculty from the University of Maine Machias, Bowdoin College, the College of the Atlantic, and 14 Maine island and coastal schools, forming a community of students, teachers, and professionals with heightened database development, GIS mapping, and ethnographic research skills to address community and marine-related issues. Higher-education faculty will work side-by-side with middle and high school teachers and students as they engage in ethnographic and technology-related projects connected to development issues such as coastal access, resource conservation, entrepreneurial economic efforts, and preservation of local history.

School systems like the Hudson Public Schools in Massachusetts offer a graduate credit-bearing course for new teachers that focuses on enhancing teacher understanding of the community and its organizations. Through the course, teachers develop a partnership with at least one community-based organization and create community-based projects for students.

Attitudinal Barriers

Engaging young people as partners in community building is not standard practice. In fact, youth are often marginalized by adults. Both youth and adults have issues about working together. Many adults do not believe students have the capacity or understanding to work on complex community issues, nor do they have the time to bring young people "up to speed" on issues. Adults are hesitant to make the investment, knowing students will graduate and probably leave the community. Control and authority are often entrenched behaviors for older people, even for those who strongly believe in the intergenerational model. Young people often feel their opinions are not respected or valued by adults. Training is needed to build strong relationships between the two age groups. The best way to build trust and respect between generations is through real work at ground level in the community.

There are a number of good resources for addressing the challenges of shifting attitudes around partnerships between and among youth and adults. The Vermont Children's Forum, working with a diverse group of youth and adults, has created a public education program—Our Voices, Our Community—that provides a series of tools and curriculum activities that address both youth leadership and meaningful partnerships with community members of all ages. The "curriculum" focuses on the resilience and strength of individual participants, embracing the idea that all people can be capable leaders if given the right tools.

Another resource is the Innovation Center's *Building Community: A Toolkit for Youth and Adults in Charting Assets and Creating Change* (2001). The toolkit contains a number of activities that help diverse age groups "build readiness" to start planning new community development projects that promote community change. *Building Community* describes a process by which youth and adults in communities can explore the strengths and gifts of people, place, past, present, and future.

The Rural Trust has a number of training tools drawn from their experiences working with schools and communities the past 10 years. A training module, *Connecting Schools and Communities*, addresses the challenges of bringing diverse stakeholder groups together and using effective communication and consensus-building strategies to sustain collaborations over time. Another module, *Designing and Implementing Projects for Multiple Outcomes*, guides youth–adult groups through the steps needed to create community development-oriented projects that simultaneously address academic and community priorities.

Different Languages

As mentioned in Rachel Tompkins' chapter in this volume, community activists, educators, and youth are not used to working together. All too often, community developers and schools operate independently. The work of community-based development efforts proceeds without involvement by young people or the schools. And the schools do not think very creatively about how they might support a new generation of place-conscious leaders in the local community. Often their approaches to problem solving are radically different. Therefore, it is important to bring someone who knows both the school and community well to the table to facilitate conversation among the parties.

In Wisconsin, the director of Wisconsin Rural Challenge, a rural schools network, is also the president of the state's Rural Economic Development Council. He has helped state and local development agencies understand that schools care about promoting healthy communities and young people need to be regarded as viable assets. Partnerships like the joint venture in western Maine between the Rural Trust, Mountain Counties Heritage Network, and the Northern Forest Center, provide a support network for developing relationships and finding mutual agendas between school and community groups.

Political Ramifications

Some schools are reluctant to involve students in controversial issues. They discourage students from critically analyzing the broader ideological and political issues generating problems and injustices. These attitudes can limit students' opportunities for involvement in the political process, thus limiting the prospects for a more participatory democracy. A community-based organization can support students' political activities when school-based educators are unable or unwilling to offer such support.

CONCLUSION

The time is right for a bold initiative that simultaneously addresses the interrelated challenges of school improvement and community revitalization. Many small towns are at risk of disintegration from the loss of jobs, the flight of their young people, and in some cases, the loss of their school through consolidation. Leveraging schools and youth as resources for their communities can break this downward spiral. As the examples in this chapter demonstrate, involving youth in important community work can simultaneously raise test scores, cultivate civic responsibilities of students, and improve the quality of life in the community simultaneously. Bringing young people into the company of adults working on matters of importance in their communities creates a synergy that not only values youth but also makes learning compelling. This larger mission of education holds particular relevance in rural states like Maine where the well-being of communities is inextricably linked to the health and vitality of their schools. Skowhegan's community-centered approach to learning may well hold the key to keeping one of Maine's most precious resources—its young people—as vital contributors to the local and state economy. Engaging young people as resources in revitalizing communities is a win-win strategy for maximizing the potential academic and civic benefits of schooling.

FOR MORE INFORMATION

Innovation Center for Community and Youth Development http://www.theinnovationcenter.org

Maine Memory Network Web site: http://www.mainememory.net

NOAA Local Fisheries Knowledge Project http://www.st.nmfs.gov/lfkproject/

Rural School and Community Trust http://www.ruraledu.org

Skowhegan, Maine Community Web site: http://www.msad54.k12.me.us/MSAD54Pages/SAMS/Heritage/Heritage.html

Vermont Children's Forum Web site http://www.childrensforum
.org

What Kids Can Do Web site http://www.whatkidscando.org

REFERENCES

Blum, R. W., & Libbey, H. (Eds.). (2004). School connectedness–strengthening health and education outcomes for teenagers. *Journal of School Health*, 74(7), 229–299.

Innovation Center for Community and Youth Development. (1999). *Youth development in the context of isolation: Challenges and opportunities*. Takoma Park, MD: Author.

Innovation Center for Community and Youth Development. (2001). *Building Community: A tool kit for youth and adults in charting assets and creating change*. Takoma Park, MD: Author.

Johnson, J., & Strange, M. (2005). *Why rural matters: 2005*. Washington, DC: Rural School and Community Trust.

Kretzman, J., & McKnight, J. (1993). *Building communities from the inside out: A path toward finding and mobilizing a community's assets*. Institute for Policy Research. Evanston, IL: Northwestern University.

Maine Commission on Secondary Education. (1998). *Promising futures: A call to improve learning for Maine's secondary student*. Augusta, ME: Author.

McLaughlin, M., & Blank, M. (2004, November 10). Creating a culture of attachment: A community-as-text approach to learning. *Education Week*, 24(11), 34–35.

McTighe, J., Seif, E., & Wiggins, G. (2004, September). You can teach meaning. *Educational Leadership*, 62(1), 26–30.

Putnam, R. (2000). *Bowling alone: The collapse and renewal of American community*. New York: Simon & Schuster.

Putnam R., & Feldstein, L. (2003). *Better together: Restoring the American community*. New York: Simon & Schuster.

CHAPTER 5

Environmental Justice in Egleston Square

Elaine Senechal

When I arrived to teach science at Greater Egleston Community High School, located in Roxbury, Massachusetts, in the Spring of 1996, I had no knowledge of urban ecology or the environmental justice movement. When I left 8 years later, my students were powerful activists and recognized leaders in their community, working for equality and justice in the environmental issues of their neighborhood. This is the story of our journey to gain power and understanding in order to improve the quality of life for my students, their families, and other residents of Roxbury. In looking back to the beginning, there is no way I could have imagined this story. I feel, however, in order to honestly and effectively meet the academic needs of my students, this path was my only choice.

The most important factor in our success was the unique character of Greater Egleston Community High School (GECHS) and the surrounding community. GECHS is a small, alternative high school within the Boston Public School system. It began, however, outside the public school domain. This school was founded by the residents of the low-income, minority community of Egleston Square. They started the school to meet the needs of their youth who were dropping out of the Boston Public Schools. At the time of its inception, youth gang activity and youth violence were at a high level in the neighborhood. The residents felt that a different program was required to serve their youth and bring them off the streets into an academic program that met their needs and offered them hope for the future.

The school was established with a 3-year grant from the Department of Labor. When the grant ran out, the school was invited to join the Boston Public Schools as a pilot program that would continue to serve youth at risk of dropping out of high school. From the beginning, one of the goals of the school was to create community leaders. As phrased in the school's mission statement, "Building leaders, building community, begins right in the classroom and then is transferred to the community outside the school walls" (Greater Egleston Community High School, 1998).

When I was hired in 1996, there was no science program at GECHS. My task was to build a program that met both educational goals and science standards, as well as the school's vision to create community leaders. I found community-based learning to be a successful strategy for teaching the required skills and competencies in science. I developed a curriculum that was connected to community and provided the students at the school with opportunities to take leadership roles in the community.

This chapter documents the development and implementation of a community-based science curriculum. It provides a rationale for community-based learning as a successful teaching strategy. Finally, it reflects on the process of community-based teaching and learning. My hope is that this chapter can serve as a tool to inform other teachers who are considering community-based projects or curricula.

HISTORY OF THE ENVIRONMENTAL SCIENCE/ ENVIRONMENTAL JUSTICE PROGRAM AT GREATER EGLESTON COMMUNITY HIGH SCHOOL
Community Mapping, Asthma, and Air Quality: 1997–2000

The Environmental Science program at Greater Egleston Community High School began as a collaboration between neighborhood and community groups concerned about issues of health and environment, and myself, representing the science program at the high school. Several factors facilitated the collaboration with these groups. In our school building were the offices of several community groups, including Ensuring Stability through Action in the Community (ESAC) and the Egleston Square Neighborhood Association (ESNA). ESNA had a committee that worked on environmental justice issues in Egleston Square. I joined this committee; among its members were representatives from Alternatives for Community and Environment (ACE). This organization worked on environmental justice issues in the Roxbury area and beyond. Through this connection I met the community organizers from the Roxbury Environmental Empowerment Project (REEP), who work specifically with youth and environmental justice concerns. The focus of the program was on the environmental issues that were of importance to the neighborhoods that surround the school. With the help of community organizations, the students became leaders and role models in the environmental justice movement in the community. They worked in partnership with community organizations to bring about positive change in the quality of their lives and the lives of citizens in their community.

The environmental justice movement is an international movement of poor, minority, and people of color who seek to address inequities in environmental policies and to advocate for fairness and justice in the environmental arena. Poor communities and communities of color have often been the dumping grounds for environmental problems that more affluent, and mostly White, communities "do not want in my backyard." Roxbury is one such effected community. It has eight times the state hospitalization rate for asthma as a result of environmental policies that do not protect the health and well-being of all its citizens.

The Environmental Science program at GECHS began in the winter of 1997. In collaboration with the Egleston Square Neighborhood Association (ESNA), students joined the efforts of the community in completing a Community Environmental Awareness Project. The goal of this project was to find and record areas of environmental concern in the neighborhood around the school. This information was joined with information gathered by residents to create a neighborhood map of environmental concerns that would bring awareness of these concerns and assist them in targeting their energy and resources. A multidisciplinary project was developed by teachers of math and humanities, as well as myself. Students observed and mapped the area, showing both areas of environmental concern and those areas where sensitive individuals were found. These included schools, day-care centers, and elderly housing. Students did investigations to find out what activities were occurring at various sites and evaluated these activities in relation to their effect on the environment. They learned a method for gathering soil samples for testing. They tested the soil in a vacant lot for contaminants and analyzed the data for presentation to the community. This project was a great success as both an environmental and an academic project.

There are several factors that contributed to this project's success. One was the involvement of youth in collaboration with the community to meet a real need in the neighborhood. Many of these young people had previously dropped out of school and had been involved in negative activities, such as gangs. Another factor was the thoughtful planning and implementation of this project using the resources of the school and community. It was developed through months of weekly meetings between the teachers of humanities, math, and me, as well as meetings with community organizers. In addition, the project had the full support of the Director of GECHS, Beatriz Zapater. She arranged teaching schedules to facilitate meeting times and student work in the community. She encouraged and supported the submission of the project to the Center for Leadership Development and the Coalition of Essential Schools.

In June of 1997, the students, teachers, and ESNA received the Greenleaf Community Environmental Activist Award from the Environmental Diversity Forum. The Environmental Diversity Forum was an organization that brought together groups from around the region that were working on environmental justice issues in low-income and minority neighborhoods. ESNA was a member of the Forum. The project also received recognition from educational organizations. In the summer of 1997, the project was chosen to be presented in the summer teacher workshops of the Center for Leadership Development in Boston. It received national recognition when it was chosen to be presented at the annual conference of the Coalition of Essential Schools in San Francisco in the Fall of 1997.

The development of the community-based science program continued in the 1997–1998 school year. As mentioned earlier, in the Fall of 1997 I began collaborating with a local environmental group called Alternatives for Community and Environment (ACE) and their companion organization, Roxbury Environmental Empowerment Project (REEP). This partnership, along with a continued collaboration with ESNA, led to the development of a course in environmental justice. Through a community mapping project and material presented in the class by REEP community organizers Klare Allen and Jodi Sugarman-Brozan, students learned of the high asthma rates in their community and the relationship of poor air quality to asthma. They also learned that the large number of truck and bus lots as well as trash transfer stations placed in their community (Roxbury has eight of the nine trash transfer stations in Boston) were sources of the problem. Students working with community members conducted a diesel vehicle count at the intersection outside the school. An astonishing 100+ diesel vehicles passed in front of the school per hour. Many were empty, out-of-service busses returning to their lots in the neighborhood. Klare and Jodi worked with the students in this class on the leadership skills needed to plan and carry out a march and rally to bring awareness of these air-quality issues to the community and public officials.

This was the start of a working relationship that was to continue for the next 7 years. Jodi and Klare brought the issues and needs of the community to the classroom, as well as opportunities for leadership. I took this information and developed projects and curriculum connected to state and local standards in science. For me as a teacher, the REEP organizers were an invaluable resource for connecting the community to the classroom. They came to my class every week to bring information and inspiration that helped move our projects forward. In our work together, we were copresenters of this course.

The march and rally that the students helped organize focused on the enforcement of a Massachusetts anti-idling law as a means to reduce emissions in the neighborhood, especially from diesel vehicles. The anti-idling law states that vehicles cannot idle their engines for more than 5 minutes. The students prepared flyers, banners, and informational "tickets" to hand out to idlers during the march. They spoke at the rally on the issues. Other speakers included the State Environmental Affairs Secretary, the regional Environmental Protection Agency chief, and representatives from state and local government. This event was a great success and received extensive coverage by the media. It resulted in two other events that students helped plan and participate in. Because of publicity regarding the march, a company that produced products to help asthma victims donated a large number of items to the community. Community organizers put together a community event called "Clean Air for the Holidays" to distribute the products and to inform residents of the environmental problems that were affecting their health. Students in the environmental justice class participated by preparing and presenting information about environment and health and conducting a survey of asthma sufferers to gain more information on the extent of the problem. Students also surveyed resident after resident, each with accounts of their own, or their family's, suffering from asthma. Residents brought their small children and babies who were victims of the disease. Some arrived carrying their vital oxygen supplies. This event led us to experience a lot of pride for what we had accomplished in the community and also opened our eyes to the extent to which our neighbors were suffering.

Another result from the publicity around the march and subsequent letters to newspapers that students had sent on air-quality issues was the willingness for the Massachusetts Bay Transit Authority (MBTA) to sit down with the students and hear their concerns. The MBTA was a big polluter in the neighborhood with large bus depots of diesel vehicles and long periods of idling for most busses. The MBTA ran empty busses through the neighborhood in sizeable numbers to its parking facilities. The meeting took place on February 9, 1998. I have no way of knowing what the MBTA was thinking would come out of this meeting because the person they sent was unprepared to face the students and the issues. The students, on the other hand, were very prepared. After participating in numerous community events, they knew the issues. Their questions and demands were prepared; they were ready to present their case. As my students pressed their issues, the representative became more and more flustered. At one point, in frustration I suppose, he told the students that next time they had issues they should send their parents instead! This was said to a group of students who were 16 to 22 years old and who had spent many hours working with the community to understand and present these concerns. My students kept their cool and won commitments from this representative, including prioritizing the use of less polluting alternative fuels in the neighborhood, working to reduce idling of busses in the community, and building garages outside the neighborhood to store busses. Eventually all these demands would be won, but it would take a long and dedicated commitment by the community and the students.

In the winter of 2004, the MBTA was fined for excessive idling and required to reduce the idling of its busses and to continue replacing diesel vehicles with alternative fuels, such as natural gas, that produce much less pollution. The demands of the students and the community that were initially presented at the 1997 anti-idling march led to this outcome.

The years 1998 through 1999 were very active ones for the environmental justice class. In addition to presenting a workshop at the Essential Schools Fall Forum in San Francisco, students prepared a presentation on air quality and asthma in Roxbury for the Spring 1998 "E.J. in the Hood" conference. During the same time, the Superintendent of the Boston Public Schools proposed charging students in Boston for their transportation to school. High school students in Boston do not travel to school on school busses. They are given bus passes to ride public transportation during school hours. The Superintendent's proposal was to charge the students for these passes to help balance the school budget. Many students in the Roxbury community come from low-income families who are struggling to provide the basic needs for their families. This additional expense would be especially difficult for these families. My students were outraged. They felt that it was an unfair proposal that would place the greatest burden on those least able to afford the cost, possibly preventing young people in the community from completing high school.

The community organizers heard the students' concerns and suggested that they use the skills gained from organizing around air quality and respiratory health issues to fight this proposal. The students prepared a letter to the Superintendent and school committee members and other government officials stating the reasons for their objections to the proposal. They also prepared a statement that was faxed to other schools for students and parents in those schools to sign, objecting to the proposal. They organized students and residents to attend the School Committee meeting where this proposal would be brought to a vote. A local School Committee member and the student representative with the backing of students and the community made a strong objection to the proposal. These are quotes from a letter dated April 7, 1998, from the Superintendent of the Boston Public Schools:

> This will acknowledge receipt of your recent letter forwarded on behalf of your Environmental Justice Class. Your class expressed concern regarding the proposal I submitted concerning high school transportation. Your students should know that the student representative on the School Committee made a strong presentation in opposition to this budget cut. In addition, members of the School Committee expressed reservations. As a result, I have prepared other options for their consideration.

The students had won; this proposal was abandoned by the Superintendent.

In the fall of 1998, students in the environmental justice class accepted two new projects to continue their work on air quality and related health issues. One was a public rally organized with the Egleston Square Neighborhood Association to bring awareness and publicity to these issues. This project was to continue the effort to put pressure on the MBTA to implement changes that would reduce diesel emissions in the community. The rally, called "Bad Air Takes a Toll," was held in the center of Egleston Square. It was well attended and received much publicity in local papers.

Indoor air quality was also an issue in the community, especially in the schools. Students began a project to measure the air quality in their own school. Working with the Roxbury Environmental Empowerment Project (REEP), students conducted a health survey among school building occupants to determine the frequency of health problems related to poor air quality. The students surveyed the rooms in the school and measured CO_2 levels and airflow of vents using equipment borrowed from the Environmental Protection Agency (EPA). They presented their results to scientists from the EPA, who validated their work. The data the students gathered were used to inform decisions made when the school underwent a renovation in order to improve air quality. The EPA scientists were as surprised by the high readings of CO_2 outside the school as inside the school. The air quality in the community was not regularly monitored, but this was to change.

One of the greatest victories in the community's struggle for improved air quality came to fruition in the Fall of 1999. The community, with its partners, had received a grant to build a state-of-the-art air quality monitoring station on the ground in the center of the community, Dudley Square, Roxbury. The activism of the students and residents in bringing awareness to air quality and health issues was a factor in the community's ability to secure this grant. This new air-quality monitoring station would take hourly readings of the levels of the most significant pollutants. These levels would be posted on a Web site to inform the community of the air quality and its health risks. My students were invited to participate in the opening ceremony for the station, called AirBeat, along with government officials, community leaders, and scientists. The students spoke about the importance of this station to the community and the need for the government and environmental and health organizations to go beyond monitoring air quality and to work together to bring about the changes needed to reduce asthma rates.

Also in the fall of 1999, my students and I learned that we had received a grant to collaborate with Roxbury Community College to develop joint projects on air quality and asthma issues. This grant included the opportunity for my students and me to take a course at RCC on environmental issues in the Spring of 2000. My students and I were, over time, partners and recipients of several grants. Most of these were acquired through the efforts of community organizations such as ACE/REEP and ESAC (Ensuring Stability through Action in the Community). Our first project was to develop a method to get information on air quality from AirBeat out to the community on a daily basis. My students, working with an intern from Roxbury Community College, developed a system using flags of different colors to announce the air quality of the day to residents. The colors were coordinated with the colors on the Air-Beat Web site: green for good air quality, yellow for moderate, and red for poor. The flags were constructed with money from the grant and hung by the students each day in Egleston Square and at the ACE/REEP headquarters in Dudley Square. In addition, students began to work with researchers from the Harvard School of Public Health to compare asthma data from the local health clinics to data from the air-quality monitoring station. They hoped to establish a correlation between poor air quality and poor respiratory health.

Students were able to meet with representatives from several local health clinics. The outcome was the same at each meeting. The health clinics did not have the personnel resources to gather the information from their records. Many staffs were already overextended. A substantial influx of funds and resources would be needed to enable them to provide the information.

Documenting a History of Community Action

As part of our collaboration with Roxbury Community College, my students and I were asked to present the history of our environmental work in the community to students and faculty at RCC. At this time I was in a graduate program in education and was keeping careful records of my own practice. The graduate program in which I was enrolled at Simmons College emphasized looking at our own teaching practice. The program gave me the opportunity to step back from a process in which I was involved in order to put some time into documenting our activities as an educational process. This effort to document our own history, therefore, is a window into daily experiences in the classroom. One of the problems I faced was how to guide my students to present our school's work. They would have to explain work done over years mostly by students who had graduated. The information was buried in files containing flyers, newspaper clippings, photographs, and former students' portfolios, journals, and posters. With the help of the computer teacher, we arrived at a solution. We planned to document a history of our school's environmental activism in the community in a PowerPoint presentation format.

I faced several challenges in guiding this process. I felt it was very important for my students to understand the history of what preceded them. They would be put in a unique situation because they were being asked to report on situations with which they were not personally involved. The creation of the PowerPoint would give us a tool for presentations; it would also be a learning experience for my students. They would become the chroniclers of this history. It would actually be a research project from which they could learn the environmental and health issues in the community and what actions the community had taken. The students would have the opportunity to see their place in the process and to predict what would need to happen in the future. Because of my minimal skills with PowerPoint, collaboration with our computer teacher was essential for the success of the project. One other person joined me: the coordinator of the collaboration that links Roxbury Community College with our high school. She was a graduate of both RCC and Tufts University with a degree in environmental science. I was also fortunate that several of my students were very skilled on the computer and had some knowledge of PowerPoint.

As one can see from the people involved, this project required extensive cooperation, something that is different from the way many public high school teachers operate. Part of the reason I could do this is because I teach in a progressive, alternative setting that supports my work. The other reason is that much of my working life had not been spent in a traditional public school setting. My way of working with my students reflected the way I operated in the "real world." I feel it reflected the way most people work. To get a project completed required collaboration and team work with other people who bring their own talents and expertise to the project. When I was the supervisor of the biological laboratory at a local university, I worked with many other people and depended on them to complete our tasks successfully. These people included employees, maintenance workers, and researchers. My classroom was untraditional in appearance and structure. Frequently, my classroom looked like a three-ring circus, or busy laboratory; like a three-ring circus, everyone was very involved in the success of the performance.

Once the PowerPoint was nearly finished, Jodi and Klare, the community organizers from ACE/REEP, joined us to complete the community research project. The students' presentation of their work to the community organizers was a very moving experience for all of us. I made the following notation in my journal of January 20, 2000:

> My students, who completed their PowerPoint work, did a wonderful presentation. Klare and Jodi were moved to tears. They explained to the students how much this presentation meant to them. It was a documentation of their work as organizers with youth in the community over the years. It is a tool they can use to present to other organizations who want to learn about community projects. Of course, it is also a record of my students' work with the community on environmental issues over time. Jodi will take the PowerPoint program to present in Los Angeles at a conference

of Jewish leaders in the environmental movement. The students will present their documentation at RCC and at the Spring "E.J. in the Hood" conference.

This project was successful in producing a useful tool for the school and the community. The students gained skills in technology and learned about environmental issues that affect their lives. They demonstrated the aptitude necessary to make successful presentations. Their work was recognized by a greater community beyond the school. It had value in the real world. These students were considered failures and dropouts in their previous school settings. To me, this type of teaching and learning is not only effective; it is also humane. It focuses on a collaborative effort, not competition where some are destined to fail. It begins with the skills that each student brings; it enhances and broadens these skills. It provides an opportunity for students to make a real contribution and receive recognition for that contribution. This approach works well for the students I teach.

A Bill, a "Silver Lie," Budget Cuts, and Bioweapons: 2000–2005

The students continued to work on the issues of air quality, respiratory health, and issues with public transportation through the Spring and Fall of 2000. An issue arose early in 2001 that led me and my students to become more closely involved with the political process. A bill was being considered by the Massachusetts State Legislature that could have an important positive environmental impact on the community. This bill recognized that some communities bore a disproportionate burden of environmental hazards. It affirmed equal protection of all citizens. To protect those who were unequally burdened, it would designate areas of critical environmental justice concern. In these areas, a standard of environmental review would be established. Essentially, it would give human communities similar protections that certain wildlife areas, such as wetlands, enjoy. An opportunity to advocate for the bill came up when students were asked to join other community organizations in testifying in support of the bill at a hearing of the State Legislature's Natural Resource Committee. Jodi and Klare worked with the students to prepare them to speak at the hearing. This is a reflection written by one of the students who testified:

On May 17th, 2001 we went to the State House in Boston to testify before the Natural Resources Committee on Senate Bill 1145, the environmental justice bill. When we first appeared at the State

House we had a rally outside. Then we headed inside the court-room; there were so many lawyers, doctors, and different residents from in and outside of Boston. It was so crowded that people were standing up and sitting on the floor. The difficult part was waiting two hours to speak and standing in that hot crowded courtroom listening to people talk about other bills. The successful part was finally testifying to Representative Robert Koczera and the Natural Resource Committee. I was so nervous at first; then I started talking and telling them about the problems in the community. The Representative was so proud of the class and me; he not only gave us feedback, but also applauded us.

This effort was successful; the bill moved out of committee for a vote by both houses of the legislature.

In the winter and spring of 2002, the students, in conjunction with other organizations, began a letter-writing campaign to their representatives in the legislature, urging them to vote for this bill. They were represented by Senator Dianne Wilkerson, a firm supporter of the legislation. When we were looking up students' representative in the House, we were surprised to learn that almost every student had a different representative. The students were not widely scattered; it was clear to me what had happened. The community had been chopped up and small pieces doled out to a variety of representatives, thus weakening the political voice of the people. This issue was to come forward in a Federal investigation the year after I left my teaching position at GECHS. Because of the student activism, we were contacted by Senator Wilkerson, who visited the class and talked to the students about the political process and what further efforts were needed to make this bill a reality. In the end, the bill passed unanimously in the Senate but failed to receive enough votes in the House.

The other issue the students began working on at this time was one involving transportation. In Boston, public transportation consists of subways, rail lines, and busses. The community historically was linked to downtown Boston by a subway and rail line called the Orange Line. The subway and rail lines are all named with a color and the word "line"; the busses have route numbers. The old Orange Line was dismantled before I came to Roxbury and replaced with temporary bus routes. A new Orange Line was built but not along the same route as the old line. A similar service was promised to the community to replace the old Orange Line. The community had asked for light-rail service but what they got instead was the Silver Line. The Silver Line was to be a bus, the only bus route with the name "line." The community was outraged. State Representative Gloria Fox reacted in this way: "This is discrimination against people of color. We pay more. We have services that are lacking. Busses that are overcrowded. Busses that are dirty."

My students began working with others in the community, such as the Washington Street Corridor Coalition, to fight for light rail. It was not a matter of money; the light rail would actually cost less. There were many political issues that led to the decision not to replace the subway with light rail. The community clearly felt the action was discriminatory. Students wrote to the newspaper and to the head of the MBTA, Michael Mulhern, expressing the community's feelings about this issue. In response, Mr. Mulhern agreed to meet with the students and answer their concerns. He was not convincing and was clearly uncomfortable facing questions from well-informed students. At this point I became ill and was out of school for a couple of weeks. I returned to find that two of my environmental justice students had been working with the computer teacher and the community organizers to produce a video that would be an exposé of the situation. They called the video "The Silver Lie." It was shown on the Boston Neighborhood Network, a local cable channel, and followed by an interview with both students about its creation. The Silver Line began operating in the neighborhood that summer; at least the busses were fueled by natural gas, a less polluting alternative to diesel. This project by the students again illustrates the collaborative nature of the work. They can continue without me because I am only one of many individuals working with the students on these issues. It was this constant collaboration with the community, plus the support of the administration, that led to our successes.

Two separate articles in major Boston newspapers reported on the inequities of the Silver Line. A *Boston Globe* article on February 23, 2004, reported the following in an article titled "Silver Line Not the Shiniest Commute":

> Getting downtown in the morning on the Silver Line takes approximately 25 percent longer than on the Red, Orange, and Green MBTA lines, according to a week long test conducted by the *Globe* this month. Still, the results echo the complaints of people of the Roxbury neighborhood—among the poorest, where many residents don't have cars and rely on public transportation—that they don't get the service other parts of the city enjoy. (Flint, 2004, p. A1)

A second article appeared in the *Boston Herald* on February 22, 2005. This article, like the *Globe*'s, was front-page news. The following statements are from the article titled "Silver Line's Tarnished."

> The MBTA's Silver Line, heralded as a traffic-free ride for underserved Roxbury commuters has become a dangerous obstacle course for mammoth busses constantly being forced into heavy traffic by illegally parked cars. The 60-foot busses that run along the Washington Street route are being blocked from a dedicated travel lane meant to speed them past traffic. "This is not bus rapid transit," said Roxbury activist Bob Terrell, referring to the term officials use to describe the Silver Line. "All they did was take a diesel bus, change the engine, paint it silver and run it down the street through traffic." (Ross, 2005)

In the spring of 2003, Klare and Jodi gave the students in the environmental justice class an opportunity to choose an issue that was most important to them. The students chose the state budget cuts to education. There were schools being closed and many programs cut, which affected the students and their families. This choice may seem unusual for an environmental justice class. However, both the community and the environmental justice movement broadly define "environment" and "environmental justice" to include all elements of the community, not only the natural components. Environmental justice includes issues of equality and self-determination. The students were aware that cuts to school budgets would mean the elimination of programs that supported their success. This had the potential of increasing the dropout rate, which could lead to an escalation of gang activity and youth violence.

The students decided they needed an event that brought awareness to the issues and put pressure on the elected officials to restore money to education. The event they chose was a rally at an elementary school that was slated to close, followed by a march to the home of the powerful Speaker of the House of Representatives, Thomas Finneran, who lived near the school. They were not protesting Representative Finneran, but asking him to take a more active role in opposing the cuts to education put forward in the governor's budget. It was quite an undertaking for the students to assume prime responsibility for organizing a large rally. They invited school committee members and government officials, including Representative Finneran and Governor Mitt Romney. They invited students and parents in schools from all over the city. They had to work out all the logistics and get the necessary permits. They were in charge of designing and distributing flyers. They developed rules for proper behavior during the rally and worked to set a positive tone. Finally, they ran the entire rally, giving speeches and introducing officials who spoke. This is one student's description from his class portfolio of his roles:

> I did research about the budget cuts and why it [is] happening in Massachusetts. I wrote letters to the school site council and also the teacher[s]. Another role I played was to lead the rally to [Representative] Thomas M. Finneran's house in Mattapan, to express the feelings we had about the budget cuts in Massachusetts and tell him students and teachers aren't standing for it. I also was one of the marshals [that] controlled the rally to [Representative] Thomas M. Finneran['s] house. The marshal's job was to keep everyone under control and on the sidewalk so they wouldn't get arrested by the police that escorted us.

As the students were planning the rally, they received unexpected attention. Two state representatives, on separate occasions, asked to come to the class and speak to the students. Both represented sections of the community and both had the same message. They asked the students to abandon their plans for the march and rally. The rationale for their request was not very clear to the students or me, although recent allegations against now former House Speaker Finneran may have been related to their actions. I suspect some pressure was being put on them in the legislature. The students and I talked about our rights under the Constitution. I gave the final vote to them whether to continue with their plans or not. They decided to go forward with their plans.

The event was a great success. The speakers included the Superintendent of the Boston Public Schools, other community leaders, and youth. The march was positive and peaceful. The students felt very empowered. They received the publicity they sought with a report and picture in a major Boston newspaper and a radio interview. This action did not immediately restore any funds; however, it did make representatives aware of the community's concerns.

The last issue that my students and I faced before I left my position at the school was not one we would have ever chosen. It is a nightmare foisted onto the community against its will. We learned in the fall of 2003 that a Level 4 BioLab was being planned for Boston and that it would be placed in the Roxbury neighborhood. The organizers came to the environmental justice class to ask for their help in opposing the lab. These labs work with the most dangerous diseases used for biological weapons. This was first time such a lab would be placed in a residential neighborhood. The students' first task was to research Level 4 BioLabs to find out what criteria gives a lab that designation. The next research project involved studying the diseases themselves, their identity, and their effects. It was hard work and very depressing to all of us. The students learned that the diseases researched in these labs are easily transmitted; they cause a high mortality rate, with no cure. They included ebola, anthrax, botulism, and the plague. Students presented their findings to residents at community meetings who were trying to grasp the situation in order to launch effective opposition. Students also wrote letters to city councilors, spoke before city council hearings, made informational pamphlets, and participated in rallies to oppose placing this lab in their community. This struggle continues on as the community fights another environmental injustice.

At the end of the school year of 2003, students met with members of the Boston City Council who wanted to hear of concerns from neighborhood residents as they prepared their budget for the city. One of the groups they requested to hear from was the students in the environmental justice class at Greater Egleston Community High School. The students, through their activism over the years, had established themselves as community leaders and credible spokepersons for the residents of their neighborhoods. They chose the issues they wanted to present to the council. Air-quality issues and education budget cuts were on the docket, of course; however, they also presented issues concerning better job opportunities, improved road and pothole repairs, affordable housing, increased trash receptacles for cleaner sidewalks and streets, more youth programs at community centers, and more effort to reduce youth violence. They spoke eloquently and sincerely about each issue. As a teacher, I look on our youth as a great resource to their community. They care deeply about the issues and have great energy and resourcefulness in working toward better neighborhoods. This is a reflection of a student on her experiences in the environmental justice class:

> I am proud of my accomplishments in environmental justice this trimester. Most importantly I have been able to gain confidence to speak in front of large groups of people. Before presenting to the City Council I was very nervous. But after watching them and my classmates somewhat debate I realized they are regular people just like my family, my teachers, and my friends, and I should not be nervous when it comes to speaking my mind.

Another student gave a moving and eloquent address to the councilors. She spoke about the need for funding for youth programs because they save lives. The funding for these programs was not restored and youth violence escalated in Boston.

SELF-REFLECTION ON COMMUNITY-BASED TEACHING

Teaching connected to community transforms the traditional role of the teacher. I have experienced it as a deep connection between what is happening in the community to what is happening in the classroom. I have been involved in community projects that span years as the Roxbury community struggles for environmental justice. The classroom is no longer an entity within itself, totally under the control or guidance of the teacher. In community-based teaching and learning, the teacher is part of a cast of different individuals working with students toward a common cause or goal. This presents both opportunities and challenges for the teacher. The opportunity is to connect learning to something authentic, to give students experiences in the real world outside the classroom. The challenge is to make these opportunities meet the skills and competencies required of the students. I have found that learning is enhanced when connected to community. My community-based activities are embedded in the school curriculum, not in extracurricular activities.

To be successful in community-based learning, I feel that the teacher must become involved in the community and its issues. I was active in the environmental movement in the neighborhood in which I taught. I was a member of the Egleston Square Neighborhood Association's Environmental Committee. I worked closely with Alternatives for Community and Environment (ACE) and the Roxbury Environmental Empowerment Project (REEP) and with the Environmental Studies Department at Roxbury Community College. Together, we decided on the direction for the class. Usually the community partners chose which projects were most important; I wrote lessons connected to these projects that were also tied to skills and competencies.

This type of teaching is far removed from "teaching from the text." I have to find resources and develop lessons using many sources. It requires flexibility and creativity. It also constantly changes. The issues and tasks of one year may not be the same the next year; it progresses over time as victories are won and new issues arise. Many of our projects are funded by grants; we were never certain which would be funded. These grants came from our community partners. The students change, too; they graduate and move on. In a way, I began over again with the students, while moving forward with the community tasks. I had to find ways to introduce the environmental problems and the history of community efforts and to prepare students to become participants in the action. I learned to take broader community projects and break them down into concise tasks for a class of students with lessons tied to skills and competencies. I used resources from my community partners in the planning and teaching process.

Work on community issues also changes the traditional roles of students and teacher. My students and I were partners when working on environmental issues. Our participation in the opening of *AirBeat,* the new "state-of-the-art" air-quality monitoring station in Roxbury, was an example of a partnership between a teacher and her students. The heads of environmental organizations and government officials were at the opening. My students did not have rehearsed speeches. We had gone over the issues concerning air quality, and they had their own personal experiences. I trusted my students to speak to the issues. This is exactly what they did; their presentation was extremely successful. One of my students and I were interviewed by the *Globe* and were mentioned in an article the following Wednesday. The students received a very positive response from all attendees. On Wednesday I received a call from Kasey Kaufman from Channel 4. She came to my class and interviewed the students and me.

One of the students went on to become a spokesperson on community issues. At the next rally, he was interviewed by two radio stations; I was not part of the interviews. This was not unusual; some of my students gave interviews or spoke at rallies, and I found out after the fact. The leadership skills they gained took them beyond the classroom; we became partners in our work on community issues. In this situation, the role of teacher and student becomes more fluid. Because we work as partners, my students and I needed to have respect and trust in each others' skills. My activism and commitment to community issues and the ways I work in collaboration with other community organizations served as a role model. Change can happen; however, it takes energy directed in effective ways and an understanding of both the issues and the forces that prevent change. This was the focus of our environmental justice effort. My experiences over the years in the environmental movement and my knowledge of the issues helped me work with our various partners and guide my students toward successful activism. Even with its challenges, I found connecting learning to the community to be an effective and exciting process. My students felt empowered and motivated when they were able to participate in positive community actions and when their work was valued by the community.

COMMUNITY-BASED LEARNING: A SUCCESSFUL STRATEGY FOR AT-RISK MINORITY STUDENTS

In my teaching experience, I have found that community-based learning is a successful strategy for teaching at-risk minority students. The elements that make this strategy an effective tool for educators working with this population of learners have been identified by my research and the research of others. These element are as follows:

- Reduction of alienation and isolation by providing a culturally familiar setting for learning.
- Increased engagement, motivation, and mastery of skills.
- Enhancement of self-concept.
- Acquisition of strategies to effect social change.

My reflective work on my teaching practice, as a graduate student, led to this research. There are numerous references in the educational literature regarding the success of connecting student learning to the community. A few of them are presented here. With this extensive research and multiple examples of the enhancement of student learning through this connection, I continue to wonder why it is not a more common practice in our educational institutions.

Reduction of Alienation and Isolation by Providing a Culturally Familiar Setting

One factor, which my students have often identified, that puts them at-risk for dropping out is the feeling of alienation they experience when attending public school. Schools are often not closely connected to communities or to community issues. Students become disconnected when they leave their own communities and cultures to enter a world where norms and expectations are those of the dominant culture. Although an understanding of the dominant culture is necessary, for some students it is so unwelcoming and unfamiliar that they may give up before completing their education. Frau-Famos and Nieto (1993), in their study of Puerto Rican youth and dropping out of school in Holyoke, Massachusetts, found a similar reaction in the students they investigated: "Holyoke students' own voices reinforce the importance of feeling comfortable in the school setting" (p. 163). Frau-Ramos and Nieto (1993) go on to elaborate:

...the three students did offer cogent messages about their school experiences. All three, whether they had completed high school, or not, described feeling alienated by their school experiences. "Fitting in" was an issue for all three students despite the fact that two had been in the school system for six years or more. The urge to belong and "fit in" cannot be over emphasized; it has come up as a primary concern of Latino students in national studies. (p. 163)

Delpit (1995) in *Other Peoples' Children: Cultural Conflict in the Classroom,* describes a parent's sentiment about sending her children to school: "When children go to school, they go to an alien place, they leave their parents, they leave their gardens, they leave their homes, they leave everything that is their way of life. They sit in a classroom and learn things that have nothing to do with their own place" (pp. 88–89). This feeling of alienation may be the result of overt hostility or negative perceptions of the minority student. Rodriquez (1996) speaks to this experience: "I'd walk into the counselor's office for whatever reason and looks of disdain greeted me—ones meant for a criminal, alien, to be feared. Already a thug" (p. 84).

In their study of Puerto Rican high school students who had dropped out of school in New York City, Savaria-Shore and Martinez (1992) report feelings of alienation in more subtle and indirect ways. One student commented: "Those guys (the teachers) didn't care about the student...nobody really cared whether you made it or not. If you couldn't take it that was just tough" (p. 237). Zanger's (1993) study of social marginalization of Latino students at a high school in Boston found that Latino students had "a feeling that the teachers wished that they were just not there" (p. 175). I found that students at Greater Egleston Community High School (GECHS) felt the same about their previous schools. As one student told me: "In my old school certain teachers didn't want to help the kids that wanted to learn, like me. Half the kids that wanted to learn dropped out of school. The teacher–student relations toward each other were unfair. I feel some students got better opportunities than others."

As a White teacher in an all-minority school, it has been necessary for me to face my own negative preconceptions of my students, as learners, in order to create a comfortable and supportive learning environment. In retrospect, I realize that this trusting classroom environment did not happen overnight. It developed slowly as I became more comfortable with the students and they with me. My biggest challenge was connecting with the Black and Hispanic male students. I realized what an impact all the negative publicity about this group has had. I had to work to overcome my mistrust, go beyond the images, and reach out to them as individual human beings.

Education that is connected to community places minority students in a more comfortable and familiar setting. It provides students with the opportunity to work with adults who share their cultural values and issues. Students are viewed as valued members of a larger society, the future leaders of that society. This statement is from the school evaluation portfolio of Greater Egleston Community High School, a high school that was started by the community: "Building leaders, building community, begins right in the classroom, and then is transferred to the community outside the school walls." In a 1999 speech about the rise in youth violence, Canada, author of *Fist Stick Knife Gun: A Personal History of Violence in America* (1995), addressed this connection to community, suggesting that its absence was one of the causes behind the escalation of youth violence. When youth feel abandoned by, or of no value to, the society around them, antisocial behavior escalates. This may include dropping out of school.

Increase in Engagement, Motivation, and Mastery of Skills

Curriculum that involves students with their community is also a powerful tool for engagement and motivation. It provides opportunities to connect students' experiences to learning. Delpit (1995) gives several examples of the importance of relevancy to learning: "One teacher explained that her Black students were much more likely to learn a new operation successfully when they understood to what use the operation might be put to in daily life" (p. 65). Community issues have meaning for the student; they are very interested in these activities. Wells, in *Literacies Lost: When Students Move From a Progressive Middle School to a Traditional High School* (1996), found a lack of relevancy to be a factor in students' lack of progress in the high school: "The students' analysis of their work in the two schools is telling. They made clear distinctions between work that was meaningful to them and work that wasn't" (p. 157). Skelton (1998), in a lecture to educators at Simmons College, raised the question: "What are the opportunities to apply knowledge in the broader community?" Learning experiences can be structured to connect to students' community and, also, to teach the skills needed in the dominant culture. In *Literacies Lost*, Wells (1996) states:

...depending on elements such as supporting community, perceived mission, and leadership, schools might function to transmit knowledge and understanding that are particular to their local communities, as well as those that are widely represented in the larger culture. (p. 4)

In his essay, "Home Culture—An Essential Curriculum," Wigginton (1995) advocates for educational experiences that are focused on students' cultures. Based on his 25-year experience as an English teacher with the *Foxfire* Project, where students were involved in studying their Appalachian community, he makes a strong case for the worth and effectiveness of learning based on community and culture. He states: "...also fact is the nearly universal conviction among former students and their families that the work they did on the *Foxfire* Project was abundantly worth doing" (p. 245). In addressing the need for students to meet skill requirements and prepare for standard testing programs, he observes: "...I can target, directly and effectively, every one of those requirements—be it reading, research, writing, grammar, mechanics, even origin of the English language—through our study of the Appalachian region" (p. 246).

In my classroom I have also found that community-based learning enhances students' ability to gain these necessary skills. Students are much more motivated to read, write, or express themselves in other ways when there is a purpose in which they are invested. My students have made great strides in their literary development through these community-based projects. Some have progressed from fear of expressing themselves, even in the classroom, to become presenters of workshops at community forums. When there is real purpose for their expression and respect for their views, which are available through community activities, the gaining of literacy (or any other kind of skill) becomes a much easier process.

Enhancement of Self-Concept

As educators of minority students, we must be aware of the effect that negative messages from the dominant society can have on our students. Abdi (1998), during a Simmons College lecture about the experiences of Somalian students attending Boston Public Schools, stated: "Negative messages about themselves and their future are constantly being heard." Although our public schools claim equal education for all students, minority students have less success despite various attempts at school reform. Latino students continue to have the highest dropout rates of any group and, even if they stay in school, often receive less than a high-quality education (Frau-Ramos & Nieto, 1993; Turner, Laria, Shapiro, & Del Carmen Perez, 1993; Wheelock, 1993). Savaria-Shore and Martinez (1992), in their study of Puerto Rican students in New York who dropped out, note:

> We would add that continuing attention must be paid to the racism, sexism, and class biases in our society which are reflected in schooling, in research design as well as in policy implementation. It is equally important to attend to the double and sometimes triple burden of prejudice which must be borne by ethnic and language minority youngsters in a society which often seems to harbor negative attitudes towards its youth. (p. 248)

Obiakor (1992), in his article about African-American students, makes recommendations for enhancing the self-concept of these learners. One of his suggestions involves "modifying external factors that influence students' self-concepts, such as environmental, teaching strategies, assessment tools and interpretations" (p. 164). Community-based learning provides the opportunity for this modification by placing students in a setting where their contributions are valued and they are looked on in a positive light. Again and again, I have seen the positive effects that community-based projects have had on my students.

My students in environmental justice discussed the presentation they made to Jodi and Klare (community organizers with REEP). They knew they did a good job; a grade from me was secondary. Their work and effort were validated by members of their own community. They made a substantial contribution and that contribution was, and will continue to be, recognized.

In speaking to the students, Klare requested that they include pictures of themselves in the presentation. She explained the importance of presenting themselves in a positive way to counteract all the negative publicity about urban minority youth. She felt they should leave a legacy so their work would continue to be recognized after they have left high school. The exposure students receive while working on beneficial community projects helps build a new public perception of urban, minority teens. This is the power of community-based learning. It provides opportunities that enhance self-concept of minority youth and support their success as learners.

Acquisition of Strategies to Effect Social Change

The issues of equality in our society that were previously discussed cannot be ignored by educators of minority students. We should view teaching and learning in its social and cultural context. Within the isolated world of the classroom, we may strive for equality of all students, but we need to recognize that our minority students are burdened by the inequalities of the society around them. In most school settings, minority students enter the unfamiliar world of the dominant culture that controls the education system. The elements in control do not always look favorably upon minority students. Freire (1998) addressed this in his "Letters to Those Who Dare Teach":

> We have a strong tendency to affirm that what is different from us is inferior. We start from the belief that our way of being is not only good but better than that of others who are different from us. This is intolerance. It is the irresistible preference to reject differences. The dominant class, then, because it has the power to distinguish itself from the dominated class, first rejects the differences between them but, second, does not pretend to be equal to those who are different; third, it does not intend that those who are different shall be equal. What it wants is to maintain the differences and keep its distance and to recognize and emphasize in practice the inferiority of those who are dominated. (p. 71)

Freire's words hold true of the reality in which I teach. I came to the same conclusion as Freire in my effort to explain why these strategies are not more widely implemented. We are teaching students in a school system established and controlled by the dominant culture. In spite of their own and their families' desire for education, and their own intelligence, skills, and potential, they are often viewed negatively as learners. The education system often does not meet their needs or enhance their capabilities. Effective strategies exist. We as educators need to continue to implement these strategies and to push for support for this implementation.

If we truly care about our students' success, I feel that we as teachers must become active in areas of social change. I have found that community-based learning is a tool for empowering students; it gives them the tools to organize and advocate for their rights. By taking on community projects that involve justice and equality, I am able to give students skills that will help them in their struggle for equitable opportunities in the society in which they live. In reacting to Freire's conviction that education is political, I have to make this part of my role as teacher. In order to give my minority students the best education, I must be an advocate in the political arena. I must teach my students to be advocates for themselves and their community. The public school system is a government institution and exists within the political domain. For the most part, it is controlled by the dominant culture that often views my students negatively. Many of these political leaders either do not believe in my students' ability to succeed or do not wish their success. Minority students are very aware of how they are regarded by the dominant culture; this knowledge can be demoralizing. I feel it is necessary to educate students about the political process to show them how they can organize with others in their community. These activities will help them to gain the power and resources that they have been denied. If I am not in the struggle for equality in education for my students, I am passively supporting the status quo.

CONCLUSION

My final year as a teacher at GECHS was 2003–2004. The decision to leave was difficult, but circumstances in my life and in the school had changed. I was now living farther away from Roxbury, making the commute difficult. A change in administration at the school resulted in a more challenging environment for the types of collaboration necessary for this community-based teaching and learning. The Roxbury community continues its struggle for environmental justice. In July 2005, a complaint regarding the violation of the Civil Rights Act was filed by minority residents of Roxbury and the South End. This complaint states that placing the BSL4 Laboratory in predominantly African-American and Latino neighborhoods is discriminatory and violates the regulations of the U.S. Department of Health and Human Services. Also, the community continues to work with its youth on environment and justice issues through REEP and ACE.

In the Spring of 2004, a federal investigation began regarding Thomas Finneran, the State Speaker of the House. This probe looked into his statements about his role in redistricting that left the minority neighborhoods of Boston with representation divided among many individuals, weakening their political power in the House. My students and I had noted this impact of the redistricting process when we sought support for the environmental justice designation bill. This situation may have been related to the pressure put on students not to conduct a rally at the Speaker's home in the Spring of 2003, although our issue was the governor's cuts to the education budget. Speaker Finneran resigned from the legislature in the Fall of 2004 and was charged in 2005 in federal court with committing perjury and obstructing justice in a case alleging that he and others intentionally discriminated against the minority voters of Boston. The investigation is continuing.

I now teach in a school in a small suburban town north of Boston. The structure of this school reminds me of the high school I attended, also in a small suburban town. When I arrived at the school, there was a ban on using the town's drinking water because of a pollutant found in the water. My ecology students entered the town's essay contest on recycling. One of my students won the contest. I have joined the recycling committee. For me it begins again: learning the issues, connecting to the community, and involving my students in the process. Each morning at the beginning of the school day we hear the Pledge of Allegiance, "…with liberty and justice for all." Because of my experiences in Egleston Square, I am aware that for many citizens this is a goal, not a reality. Day-to-day they struggle against discrimination for the equality and justice they deserve.

REFERENCES

Abdi, S. (1998). *Literacy, schools, and community.* Lecture at summer course, Simmons College M.S./C.A.G.S. Program in Teaching and Leadership. Boston, MA.

Canada, G. (1995). *Fist, stick, knife, gun: A personal history of violence in America.* Boston: Beacon Press.

Canada, G. (1999). *Issues of youth, violence, community, and education.* Speech at the Coalition of Essential Schools, Fall Forum, Atlanta.

Delpit, L. (1995) *Other people's children: Culture conflict in the classroom.* New York: The New Press.

Franklin, M. E. (1992). Culturally sensitive practices for African-American learners with disabilities. *Exceptional Children, 59*(2), 115–122.

Frau-Ramos, M. & Nieto, S. (1993). I was an outsider: An exploratory study of dropping out among Puerto Rican youths in Holyoke, Massachusetts. In R. Rivera & S. Nieto (Eds.), *The education of Latino students in Massachusetts: Issues, research, and policy implications* (pp. 147–169). Amherst: University of Massachusetts Press.

Freire, P. (1998). *Teachers as cultural workers: Letters to those who dare teach.* Boulder, CO: Westview Press.

Greater Egleston Community High School. (1998). *School portfolio.* Boston: Author.

Obiakor, F. E. (1992). Self-concept of African-American students: An operational model for special education. *Exceptional Children, 59*(2), 160–167.

Rodriguez, L. (1996). Always running. In W. Ayers & P. Ford (Eds.), *City kids, city teachers: Reports from the front row* (pp. 11–24). New York: New Press.

Ross, C. (2005,February 22). Silver Line's tarnished. *Boston Herald*, A1.

Savaria-Shore, M., & Martinez, H. (1992). An ethnographic study of home/ school conflicts of second generation Puerto-Rican adolescents. In M. Savaria-Shore & S. Arvizu (Eds.), *Cross cultural literacy: Ethnographies of communication in multiethnic classrooms* (pp. 227–251). New York: Garland.

Skelton, J. (1998). *Literacy, schools, and community.* Lecture at summer course, Simmons College M.S./C.A.G.S. Program in Teaching and Leadership.

Turner, C., Laria, A., Shapiro, E., & Del Carmen Perez, M. (1993). Poverty, resilience, and academic achievement among Latino college students and high school dropouts. In R. Rivera & S. Nieto (Eds.), *The education of Latino students in Massachusetts: Issues, research and policy implications* (pp. 191–216). Amherst: University of Massachusetts Press.

Wells, M. (1996). *Literacies lost: When students move from a progressive middle school to a traditional high school.* New York: Teachers College Press.

Wheelock, A. (1993). The status of Latino students in Massachusetts public schools. In R. Rivera & S. Nieto (Eds.), *The education of Latino students in Massachusetts: Issues, research and policy implications* (pp. 11–34). Amherst: University of Massachusetts Press.

Wigginton, E. (1995). Home culture, an essential curriculum. In A. Ornstein & L. Behar (Eds.), *Contemporary issues in curriculum* (pp. 245–250). Boston: Allyn & Bacon.

Zanger, V. V. (1993). Academic costs of social marginalization: An analysis of the perceptions of Latino students at a Boston high school. In R. Rivera & S. Nieto (Eds.), *The education of Latino students in Massachusetts: Issues, research and policy implications* (pp. 170–190). Amherst: University of Massachusetts Press.

CHAPTER 6

Creating a Place for Indigenous Knowledge in Education
The Alaska Native Knowledge Network

Ray Barnhardt

This chapter describes a 10-year educational restoration effort aimed at bringing the Indigenous knowledge systems and ways of knowing that have sustained the Native people of Alaska for millennia to the forefront in the educational systems serving all Alaska students and communities today. The focus is on describing how Native people have begun to reintegrate their own knowledge systems into the school curriculum as a basis for connecting what students learn in school with life out of school. This process has sought to restore a traditional sense of place while at the same time broadening and deepening the educational experience for all students. Included is a discussion of the role of local Elders, cultural atlases, traditional values, cultural camps, experiential learning, and cultural standards. All serve as the basis for a pedagogy of place that shifts the emphasis from teaching about local culture to teaching through the culture as students learn about the immediate places they inhabit and their connection to the larger world within which they will make a life for themselves.

A refrain commonly heard in conversations among Native people in Alaska is in reference to the challenges associated with "living in two worlds," one being the locally derived Native world with which they are intimately associated, and the other being the externally defined world that has enveloped their existence. The tensions between these two worlds have been at the root of many of the problems that Indigenous peoples have endured throughout the world for several centuries as the explorers, armies, traders, missionaries, and teachers have imposed their worldview and ways of living onto the peoples they encountered in their quest for colonial domination. These tensions between the ecologically (and thus locally) derived ways of Indigenous peoples and the macrosystems associated with colonial economic and geopolitical interests are a direct reflection of the tensions between local diversity and globalization embedded in the theme of this book. As Indigenous people reassert their worldviews and ways of knowing in search of a proper balance between these "two worlds," they offer insights into ways by which we can extend the scope of our educational systems to prepare all students to not only make a living, but to make a fulfilling and sustainable life for themselves. What follows is a detailed example of how the Indigenous peoples of Alaska have sought to reconcile these tensions and accommodate the differences between their ways of life and those of the outside world while at the same time strengthening critical features of their own diverse cultural histories and traditions. In so doing, they offer strategies for overcoming the tendencies toward "replication of uniformity" that are so deeply ingrained in the bureaucratic structures associated with globalization (Barnhardt, 1992), and instituting a more locally grounded, place-based approach that has the potential to integrate "the best of both worlds" (Gruenewald, 2003).

OLD MINTO CULTURAL CAMP

OUR MISSION IS TO HONOR OUR ANCESTORS by preserving and protecting Athabascan values, knowledge, language, and traditions. We aim to facilitate the passing on of these things from elders to youth, and to share our culture with others in the land of our grandmothers. We carry out these goals in the spirit of healthy lifestyles and education, and with respect for ourselves, the Earth and all life.

—*Cultural Heritage and Education Institute*

For nearly two decades, the University of Alaska Fairbanks, in cooperation with the Cultural Heritage and Education Institute of the village of Minto, has been offering an opportunity for university students in selected summer courses to spend a week at the Old Minto Cultural Camp on the Tanana River under the tutelage of local Athabascan Elders and their families. The program is designed as a cultural immersion experience for teachers and others new to Alaska, as well as for students entering the UAF graduate programs in cross-cultural studies.

Participants in the Old Minto Cultural Camp are taken 30 miles down the Tanana River from Nenana by river boat to the site of the former village of Minto, which was vacated in 1970 when the new village of Minto was constructed 25 miles away near the Tolovana River on the north end of the Minto Flats. In 1984, the Elders from Minto set up the Cultural Heritage and Education Institute as a nonprofit entity with Robert Charlie as director, to help them regain control over the old village site and put it to use for cultural and educational purposes. In addition to the UAF Cultural Camp, the site has been used in the ensuing years by the Minto Elders to provide summer and winter cultural heritage programs for the young people of Minto, as well as for others from as far away as Anchorage, Yukon Territory, New York, England, and Australia. In addition, the Tanana Chiefs Conference (a tribal organization serving Interior Alaska) has been using Old Minto as the site for a successful alcohol and drug recovery camp. Despite State restrictions on the use of the site (until title was regained by the Minto Tribal Council in 2004), participants in the various Old Minto programs, including the UAF faculty and students, have helped to restore several of the old buildings, clean up the cemeteries, clear two campsites, and construct a fish-wheel, a smokehouse, drying racks, outhouses, kitchen facilities, a dining hall, and 10 cabins for year-round use.

Participants in the summer cultural immersion program spend eight days at Old Minto, arriving in time for lunch on Saturday and then spending the remainder of the first day "making camp," including collecting spruce boughs for the tents and eating area, bringing in water and firewood, and helping with the many chores that go with living in a fish camp. Except for a few basic safety rules that are made explicit upon arrival, everything at the camp for the remainder of the week is learned through participation in the ongoing life of the people serving as our hosts/teachers. Volunteer work crews are assembled for the various projects and activities that are always under way, with the Elders providing guidance and teaching by example. Many small clusters of people—young and old, Native and non-Native, experts and novices—can be seen throughout the camp busily working, visiting, showing, doing, listening, and learning from each other. Teachers become students and students become teachers. At the end of the day, people gather to sing, dance, joke, tell stories, play games, and watch the midnight sun hover over the Tanana River. On the last evening, a potlatch is held, with special foods prepared by the camp participants and served to over 100 guests in a traditional format on the ground adjacent to the riverbank, followed with speeches relating the events of the week to the life and history of the area and the people of Minto.

By the time the boats head back upriver to Nenana on Saturday, everyone has become a part of Old Minto—connected to the place and the people whose ancestors are buried there. It is an experience for which there are no textbook equivalents. What is learned cannot be acquired vicariously because it is embedded in the environment and the learning experience itself, although not everyone comes away having learned the same thing. In fact, one of the strengths of the program is that participants comes away having learned something different and unique to (and about) themselves.

The Old Minto Camp experience (which occurs during the middle week of a 3-week course) contributes enormously to the overall level of cross-cultural understanding that students achieve in a relatively short period of time—a level of understanding that could not be achieved in a year's worth of reading and discussion in a campus-based seminar. Part of the reason for this is that students come back to class during the third week with a common experience of immersion in a culture deeply rooted in a particular place, against which they can bounce their ideas and build new levels of understanding. More significantly, however, students have been able to immerse themselves in a new cultural milieu in a nonthreatening and guided fashion that allows them to set aside their own predispositions long enough to begin to see the world through other peoples' eyes. For this, most of the credit needs to go to the Elders of Minto, who have mastered the art of making themselves accessible to others, and to the Director, Robert Charlie, who makes it all happen. For the Minto people, it provides an opportunity to reconnect with their own heritage and ancestral place, and to enlist the teachers' help in experimenting with new ways to pass on that heritage to their children and grandchildren (as indicated in the Cultural Heritage and Education Institute mission statement).

The greatest challenge for those of us teaching the courses associated with the camp experience is to help the students/teachers find ways to transfer what they have learned at Old Minto to their future practice as educators, while at the same time helping them to recognize the limitations and dangers of overextending their sense of expertise on the basis of the small bits of cultural insights they may have acquired on the banks of the Tanana River. By taking the teachers to a traditional camp environment for a cultural immersion experience of their own, our intent has been to encourage them to consider ways to use cultural camps and Elders' expertise in their own teaching. At least one graduate of the program has taken the experience to heart and has developed a graduate course in "Place-Based Education" into which he has incorporated a week's stay at Old Minto for his summer class.

Teachers, schools, and communities throughout Alaska have sponsored similar camps for a wide variety of purposes, but in many instances the camps are treated as a supplementary experience, rather than as an integral part of the school curriculum. We hope that graduates of Old Minto will lead the way in making cultural camps and Elders the classrooms and teachers of the future in rural Alaska, which is why "Elders and Cultural Camps" has become one of the key initiatives implemented over the past 10 years through the Alaska Rural Systemic Initiative/ Alaska Native Knowledge Network in each of the five major cultural regions in Alaska.

ALASKA RURAL SYSTEMIC INITIATIVE

In an effort to address the issues associated with converging knowledge systems in a comprehensive, in-depth way and to apply new insights to address long-standing and seemingly intractable problems with schooling for Native students, in 1995 the Alaska Federation of Natives, in collaboration with the University of Alaska Fairbanks and with funding from the National Science Foundation, entered into a long-term educational restoration endeavor—the Alaska Rural Systemic Initiative (AKRSI). The underlying purpose of the AKRSI has been to implement a set of initiatives to document systematically the Indigenous knowledge systems of Alaska Native people and develop school curricula and pedagogical practices that appropriately incorporate local knowledge and ways of knowing into the formal education system. The central focus of the AKRSI strategy has been the fostering of connectivity and complementarity between two functionally interdependent but historically disconnected and alienated complex systems—the Indigenous knowledge systems rooted in the Native cultures that inhabit rural Alaska, and the formal education systems that have been imported ostensibly to serve the educational needs of Native communities. Within each of these evolving systems is a rich body of complementary knowledge and skills that, if properly explicated and leveraged, can serve to strengthen the quality of educational experiences and improve the academic performance of students throughout Alaska (Boyer, 2005).

Figure 6.1 Cultural regions and participating school districts.

The most critical salient feature of the context in which this work has been situated is the vast cultural and geographical diversity represented by the 16 distinct Indigenous linguistic/cultural groups distributed across five major geographic regions, as the map in Figure 6.1 illustrates.

The diverse Indigenous cultural and language systems that continue to survive in villages throughout Alaska have a rich cultural history that still governs much of everyday life in those communities. For over six generations, however, Alaska Native people have been experiencing recurring negative feedback in their relationships with the external systems that have been brought to bear on them, the consequences of which have been extensive marginalization of their knowledge systems and continuing erosion of their cultural integrity. Though diminished and often in the background, much of the Indigenous knowledge systems, ways of knowing, and worldviews remains intact and in practice, and there is a growing appreciation of the contributions that Indigenous knowledge can make to our contemporary understanding in areas such as medicine, resource management, meteorology, biology, and in basic human endeavors, including educational practices (James, 2001).

In response to these conditions, the following initiatives were developed and have constituted the major thrusts of the AKRSI applied research and educational restoration strategy:

Alaska Native Knowledge Network
Indigenous Science Knowledge Base
Multimedia Cultural Atlas Development
Native Ways of Knowing/Pedagogical Practices
Elders, Cultural Camps, and Traditional Values
Village Science Applications, Camps, and Fairs
Alaska Standards for Culturally Responsive Schools
Native Educator Associations

Over a period of 10 years, these initiatives have served to strengthen the quality of educational experiences and have been shown to improve consistently the academic performance of students in participating schools throughout Alaska (AKRSI Final Report, 2005). In the course of implementing the AKRSI initiatives, we have come to recognize that there is much more to be gained from further mining the fertile ground that exists within Indigenous knowledge systems, as well as at the intersection of converging knowledge systems and worldviews. The depth of knowledge derived from the long-term inhabitation of a particular place that Indigenous people have accumulated over millennia provides a rich storehouse on which schools can draw to enrich the educational experiences of all students. However, this requires more than simply substituting one body of knowledge for another in a conventional subject-based curriculum—it requires substantial rethinking of not only what is taught, but how it is taught, when it is taught, where it is taught, and who does the teaching. With these considerations in mind, we established the Alaska Native Knowledge Network as a key component of the AKRSI effort to serve as a framework for documentation, analysis, dissemination, and application of information about Indigenous knowledge systems and their relevance in the contemporary world.

NATIVE WAYS OF KNOWING AND TRADITIONAL VALUES
Indigenous peoples throughout the world have sustained their unique worldviews and associated knowledge systems for millennia, even while undergoing major social upheavals as a result of transformative forces beyond their control. Many of the core values, beliefs, and practices associated with those worldviews have survived and are beginning to be recognized as being just as valid for today's generations as they were for generations past. The depth of Indigenous knowledge rooted in the long inhabitation of a particular place offers lessons that can benefit everyone, from educator to scientist, as we search for a more satisfying and sustainable way to live on this planet (Barnhardt & Kawagley, 2005).

Actions currently being taken by Indigenous people in communities throughout the world clearly demonstrate that a significant "paradigm shift" is under way in which Indigenous knowledge and ways of knowing are recognized as constituting complex knowledge systems with an adaptive integrity of their own (Barnhardt & Kawagley, 2004). As this shift evolves, Indigenous people are not the only beneficiaries—the issues are of equal significance in non-Indigenous contexts. Many problems manifested within conditions of marginalization have gravitated from the periphery to the center of industrial societies, so that new (but old) insights emerging from Indigenous societies are of equal benefit to the broader educational community.

Over many generations, Indigenous people have constructed their own ways of looking at and relating to the world, the universe, and to each other (Barnhardt & Kawagley, 1999; Eglash, 2002). Their traditional education processes were carefully crafted around observing natural processes, adapting modes of survival, obtaining sustenance from the plant and animal world, and using natural materials to make their tools and implements. All of this was made understandable through demonstration and observation accompanied by thoughtful stories in which the lessons were imbedded (Cajete, 2000; Kawagley, 1995). However, Indigenous views of the world and approaches to education have been brought into jeopardy with the spread of Western values, social structures, and institutionalized forms of cultural transmission.

Over the past 10 years, Native Elders and educators from every cultural region in Alaska have sought to reconnect with their cultural traditions through a variety of initiatives aimed at making explicit their expectations for drawing on their own ways in the upbringing of their children and grandchildren. For example, the following cultural values were drawn from several lists of values adopted by Alaska Native Elders from each cultural region in the state to serve as the core values by which the community members, students, and school staff are expected to engage with one another and by which educational practices are to be implemented:

Respect for Elders
Respect for Nature
Respect for Others
Love for Children
Providing for Family
Knowledge of Language Wisdom
Spirituality

Responsibility
Unity
Compassion
Love
Dignity
Honoring the Ancestors
Honesty
Humility
Humor
Sharing
Caring
Cooperation
Endurance
Hard Work
Self-Sufficiency
Peace

Such universal values, once identified and adopted by Native communities, provide an invaluable basis on which to construct an educational system that is not only applicable to Native students but has relevance for all students. The metaphor we've used to describe the processes we are engaged in with the Native communities and schools is that of converging streams of knowledge, as illustrated in Figure 6.2.

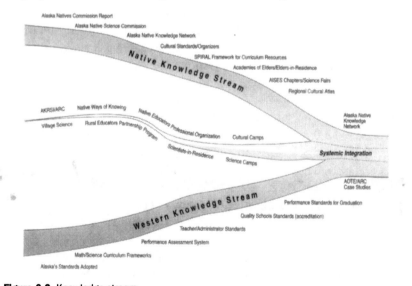

Figure 6.2 Knowledge stream.

A variety of initiatives have been implemented aimed at documenting the makeup of the Native knowledge stream to make it more accessible to schools, along with parallel initiatives aimed at loosening up the structure of the Western knowledge stream to make room for the local contributions. In addition, initiatives such as the Old Minto Camp have illustrated how both knowledge streams can come together in mutually productive ways. The goal of these efforts has been to demonstrate the complementarity that can be achieved by understanding the interaction of these knowledge systems in ways that increase both the depth and breadth of learning opportunities for all students.

Recently, many Indigenous as well as non-Indigenous people have begun to recognize the limitations of a monocultural, single-stream education system, and new approaches have begun to emerge that are contributing to our understanding of the relationship between Indigenous ways of knowing and those associated with Western society and formal education. Our challenge now is to devise a system of education for all people that respects the epistemological and pedagogical foundations provided by both Indigenous and Western cultural traditions. Although the examples used here to illustrate that point are drawn primarily from the Alaska Native context, they are intended to be illustrative of the issues that emerge in any context where efforts are under way to reconnect education to a sense of place and its attendant cultural practices and manifestations.

ALASKA NATIVE KNOWLEDGE NETWORK: CONNECTING EDUCATION TO PLACE

As the AKRSI effort began to accumulate a widening range of examples of the successful merging of Indigenous and Western ways of making sense of the world, we sought to develop curricular and pedagogical strategies that incorporated the experiential features that served to bring the two systems of thought together. Sharing the insights gained from this process and promoting the exchange of materials and ideas among educators throughout Alaska and beyond became the central task of the Alaska Native Knowledge Network. To achieve this end, we developed a curriculum database, an extensive Web site and listserv, and a publication production and distribution facility. The following section illustrates some of the kinds of resources that have been developed under the auspices of the ANKN.

The primary vehicle for promoting experiential, inquiry-based pedagogy has been the development of curriculum materials that guide teachers into the use of the local environment and cultural resources as a foundation for all learning. A key incentive for such practices has been the sponsorship of Alaska Native Science Camps and Fairs in which students work with local Elders to identify topics of local interest and develop projects illustrating the use of "science" in everyday life in their community and environment. The science project opportunities have been unlimited as Elders have shared their accumulated knowledge derived from living on the land over many generations. For example, the Minto Elders identified 72 uses of birch trees, many of which provided intriguing opportunities for students to test the scientific principles imbedded in the Elders' knowledge (e.g., Why is bark for baskets harvested at a certain time of the year?).

Elders as well as scientists judge student projects, using two sets of criteria to ensure that the students have incorporated both culturally accurate and scientifically valid principles and practices. This is a learning process in which the teachers, Elders, and students have all been eager and willing participants, and we now have numerous examples of integrated science/culture camps and fairs that clearly illustrate the ways in which an extended period of experiential inquiry in a traditional camp environment can serve as the stepping stone toward in-depth curriculum and instruction back in the classroom (http://www.ankn.uaf.edu/anses/).

One of the major ANKN initiatives in the area of curricula has been the creation of a clearinghouse and database to identify, review, and catalog appropriate national and Alaska-based curriculum resources suitable for Indigenous settings, and make them available throughout the state via the ANKN Web site (http://www.ankn.uaf.edu). Access to these resources has been expanded to include a CD-ROM collection of the best materials in various thematic areas relevant to schools in Alaska. In selecting culturally relevant materials for the database and CD-ROM collections, we have sought to reach beyond the surface features of Indigenous cultural practices and illustrate the potential for comparative study of deep knowledge drawn from both Native and Western streams. Examples of topical areas for instruction that provide opportunities for linking local knowledge with the textbook curriculum are illustrated in the lower portion of the following iceberg analogy (Figure 6.3).

The knowledge and skills derived from thousands of years of careful observation, scrutiny, and survival in a complex ecosystem readily lend themselves to the in-depth study of basic principles of biology, chemistry, physics, and mathematics, particularly as they relate to areas such as botany, geology, hydrology, meteorology, astronomy, physiology, anatomy, pharmacology, technology, engineering, ecology, topography,

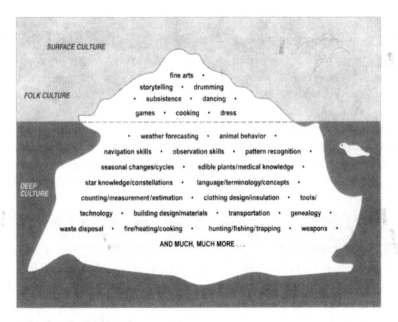

Figure 6.3 Iceberg analogy.

ornithology, fisheries, and other applied fields (cf. Carlson, 2003; Denali Foundation, 2004). Requests for the ANKN curricular materials listed in the ANKN database have grown steadily, with over 800,000 "hits" from nearly 40,000 different individuals recorded on the Web site each month. The CD-ROM containing *Village Science* (http://www.ankn.uaf.edu/VS/index.html), the *Handbook for Culturally Responsive Science Curriculum* (http://www.ankn.uaf.edu/handbook/), and *Alaska Science Camps, Fairs and Experiments* (http://www.ankn.uaf.edu/Alaska_Science/) has been an instant hit and is being used extensively in schools and professional development programs throughout the state. It is the ready availability of these resources that has given teachers the impetus to revamp their curricula to integrate the place-based approach to education that has been championed through the AKRSI.

The integration of the curricular and pedagogical strategies just outlined into everyday practice in schools has been fostered in several ways. The first has been through the promotion of Indigenous "organizers" as the basis for bringing all the elements of the educational experience together in a framework that is grounded in the cultural and physical environment in which the school is situated. Guidelines and models to assist teachers and districts in such development are now included in the Alaska curriculum frameworks documents distributed by the Alaska

Department of Education, as well as through ANKN (cf. Scollon, 1988). A recent addition to the arsenal of professional development activities that expose teachers to available curriculum resources has been the regional implementation of cross-cultural orientation programs for new teachers, modeled on the Old Minto camp.

One of the vehicles for bringing coherence to the ideas imbedded in the initiatives promoted by the AKRSI has been the development of a culturally oriented curriculum framework for purposes of organizing all the curricular and cultural resources that are emerging from the schools as a result of the various initiatives. The "Spiral Pathway for Integrating Rural Alaska Learning" (SPIRAL; see Figure 6.4) is structured around 12 themes and grade levels, so that the compilation of curriculum resources can be accessed by clicking on the appropriate theme and grade level, which will then produce a codified list of available materials, many of which can be downloaded directly from the ANKN Web site.

To take the place-based curriculum structure imbedded in the SPIRAL thematic chart a step further, a group of Native educators from the Athabascan region of Interior Alaska developed a 7–12 charter school in which the entire curriculum is based on the SPIRAL framework and is implemented in a 3-week modular format where students enroll in one course at a time and rotate through each of the 12 themes on an annual year-round schedule. The specific components that make up the curriculum are summarized in Figure 6.5, all of which have been aligned with the State content standards.

Another area in which the AKRSI is promoting initiatives impacting student–teacher, school–curriculum interactions is in the use of technology to extend and deepen learning opportunities for Native students. For those schools that have full technology access, we have been providing training in implementing "cultural atlases"—a CD-ROM/Web site development project in which students research any aspect of their culture/community/region and assemble the information in a multimedia format through the use of technology. Cultural atlases engage students in information gathering and compiling processes that simultaneously enhance learning of subject matter, technology applications, and cultural knowledge, with the results often of direct interest and service to their communities. Areas in which cultural atlases have been developed by students in various schools around the state include life histories, genealogies, place-names, language documentation, uses of local flora and fauna, subsistence practices, community histories, traditional arts and crafts, mapping projects, and weather knowledge. The AKRSI staff

SPIRAL PATHWAY
for
INTEGRATING RURAL ALASKA LEARNING

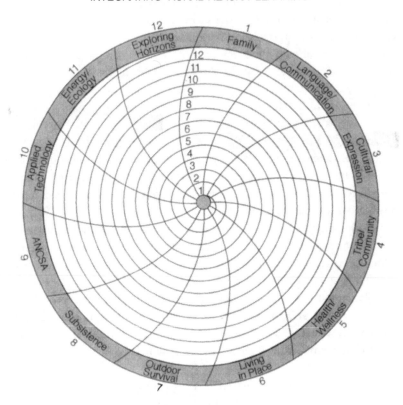

S.P.I.R.A.L. Curriculum Chart
Outer Ring = Themes (Values)
Spiral = Annual Cycle of Learning

Figure 6.4 S.P.I.R.A.L. Curriculum Chart. Outer ring = themes (values); spiral = annual cycle of learning.

member responsible for the cultural atlas initiative was invited to attend a UNESCO-sponsored conference on "Multimedia and Invisible Culture," to illustrate how technology can be used to help students connect and contribute to their place (King & Schiermann, 2004).

ALASKA STANDARDS FOR CULTURALLY RESPONSIVE SCHOOLS

One of the major constraints in achieving long-term improvement of any kind in rural schools in Alaska is the persistent high turnover rate

Theme	Level 7	Level 8	Level 9	Level 10	Level 11	Level 12
FAM	Fall language/culture immersion camp	Native values in practice	Cultural camp	Genealogy preparation	Family/Elder history	Child-rearing/parenting
L/C	Language immersion follow-up	Translation project	Cultural journalism	Place names project	Life history of an Elder	Mentor/apprentice for local language
CE	Visual art project	Traditional songs and dancing	Traditional crafts	Storytelling	Traditional ceremonies	Host a traditional potlatch
T/C	Community services map project	Land use planning	Tribal/clan history	AFN Youth/Elder Conference	Tribal/state/federal relationships	Service Learning Project
H/W	AK Native games I	Nutrition and food preparation/preservation	AK Native games II	Ethno-botany	Alaska Native games III	Traditional healing/wellness I-search project
LP	Elements of the Universe	Boreal forest	Life in the sub-arctic	Cultural atlas	Rural/urban interface	Sense of place
OS	Life in winter camp	Traditional shelter and clothing	Weather	Geospatial surveying and cult situated design	Migration and Navigation	Winter excursion
SUB	Soos Curriculum	Subsistence way of life	Trapping	Fisheries	Waterfowl	Hunting
ANC	Business plan preparation	School-based enterprise	History and impact of ANCSA	Regional Corporations	Alaska Native law	Native corporation internship
AT	Native science fair	Digital tools	Village science/math	Traditional modes of transportation	Boat/snow machine maintenance	Senior project
E/E	Math story problems	Snow science	Alaska geography	Contaminants	Arctic biology	Arctic geophysics
EH	Alaska history	U.S. history/geography	World history/geography	Close-up	Upward Bound/RAHI	Travel program/senior trip

Figure 6.5 S.P.I.R.A.L. curriculum thematic summary.

among educational personnel (an average of one third annually in rural schools), coupled with a statewide Alaska Native teaching staff of under 5% although the Native student population constitutes 24% of the school enrollment. Therefore, the emphasis of the AKRSI has been on implementing changes that can bring about a degree of stability and continuity in the professional personnel in the schools, particularly through the preparation of qualified Alaska Native teachers and administrators, and engaging Elders and local experts in the educational process. This has led to a focus on capacity building through the formation of a series of regional Native educator associations to foster leadership development on the part of those teachers for whom the community/region/state is their home.

A turning point in the AKRSI efforts took place in 1998 when the Native educators from each of the regional associations collectively produced and adopted the Alaska Standards for Culturally Responsive Schools, which have since been endorsed by the State Board of Education and are now in use in schools throughout the state. The "Cultural Standards" embody the cultural and educational restoration strategy of the AKRSI and have had ripple effects throughout Alaska, in urban as well as rural schools. These standards have provided guidelines against which schools and communities can examine the extent to which they are attending to the educational and cultural well-being of their students. They include standards in five areas: for students, educators, curriculum, schools, and communities. The emphasis is on fostering a strong connection between what students experience in school and their lives out of school by promoting opportunities for students to engage in in-depth experiential learning in real-world contexts.

Culturally responsive education is directed toward culturally knowledgeable students who are well grounded in the cultural heritage and traditions of their community and are able to understand and demonstrate how their local situation and knowledge relates to other knowledge systems and cultural beliefs. This includes:

- providing multiple avenues for the incorporation of locally recognized expertise in all actions related to the use and interpretation of local cultural knowledge and practices as the basis for learning about the larger world;
- reinforcing the positive parenting and child-rearing practices from the community in all aspects of teaching and engaging in extended experiences that involve the development of

observation and listening skills associated with the traditional learning ways of Native people;

- incorporating cultural and language immersion programs and the organization and implementation of extended camps and other seasonal everyday-life experiences to ground student learning naturally in the surrounding environment.

As articulated by the Native educators, the Alaska Standards for Culturally Responsive Schools point to the need for educators who:

- incorporate local ways of knowing and teaching in their work;
- use the local environment and community resources on a regular basis to link what they are teaching to the everyday lives of the students;
- participate in community events and activities in an appropriate and supportive way;
- work closely with parents to achieve a high level of complementary educational expectations between home and school;
- recognize the full educational potential of each student and provide challenges necessary for them to achieve that potential. (ANKN, 1998, pp. 9–12)

Subsequently, the Native educator associations have elaborated on the Cultural Standards through the preparation of Guidelines for the Preparation of Culturally Responsive Teachers (which are now being put to use in preservice and in-service programs around the state), as well as a set of Guidelines for Respecting Cultural Knowledge, Guidelines for Nurturing Culturally Healthy Youth, Guidelines for Strengthening Indigenous Languages, Guidelines for Cross-Cultural Orientation Programs, and Guidelines for Culturally Responsive School Boards (the latter have been adopted by the Alaska Association of School Boards). These cultural standards and guidelines are all designed to assist schools and communities in the appropriate integration of Indigenous knowledge in all aspects of their operations, and are all rooted in the belief that a form of education grounded in the heritage language and culture indigenous to a particular place is a fundamental prerequisite for the development of culturally healthy students and communities.

With regard to participation, the standards and guidelines themselves emphasize the importance of extensive community and parental interaction and involvement in their children's education, both in and out of school. Elders, parents, and local leaders are encouraged to be involved in all aspects of instructional planning and the design and implementation of programs and curricula. Culturally responsive schools foster extensive ongoing participation, communication, and interaction between school and community personnel. Elders are accorded a central role as a primary source of knowledge throughout the standards and guidelines. An important element for building on the traditional learning styles of Indigenous peoples is the creation and maintenance of multiple avenues for Elders to interact formally and informally with students at all times. This includes opportunities for students to engage in the documenting of Elders' cultural knowledge on a regular basis, thereby contributing to the maintenance and transmission of that knowledge. The cultural and professional expertise of Elders is essential and is to be used in appropriate and respectful ways, as illustrated by the Old Minto example cited earlier.

As they were being developed, all of the cultural standards and guidelines were deliberately phrased in positive and proactive terms, rather than dwelling on and delineating the negative aspects of past educational practices. Some of the multiple uses to which Native educators envisioned the cultural standards being put are as follows:

- They may be used as a basis for reviewing school or district-level goals, policies, and practices with regard to the curriculum and pedagogy being implemented in each community or cultural area.
- They may be used by a local community to examine the kind of home/family environment and parenting support systems that are provided for the upbringing of its children.
- They may be used to devise locally appropriate ways to review student and teacher performance as it relates to nurturing and practicing culturally healthy behavior, including serving as potential graduation requirements for students.
- They may be used to strengthen the commitment to revitalizing the local language and culture and fostering the involvement of Elders as an educational resource.
- They may be used to help teachers identify teaching practices that are adaptable to the cultural context in which they are teaching.
- They may be used to guide the preparation and orientation of teachers in ways that help them attend to the cultural well-being of their students.
- They may serve as criteria against which to evaluate educational programs intended to address the cultural needs of students.

- They may be used to guide the formation of state-level policies and regulations and the allocation of resources in support of equal educational opportunities for all children in Alaska.

Since their adoption in 1998, the Cultural Standards have been used for all these purposes and many more, including serving as model criteria for an accreditation system for Indigenous-serving higher education programs and institutions.

For educators new to the use of the Cultural Standards, a helpful resource has been the *Handbook for Culturally Responsive Science Curriculum,* which provides further insight, practical information, and examples of how to incorporate traditional knowledge in science curricula and integrate it with Western science, how to relate curriculum topics to the cultural standards, and examples of culturally appropriate strategies for instruction and assessment. The *Handbook for Culturally Responsive Science Curriculum* provides useful information on how to approach and involve Elders as teachers, and highlights how traditional teaching and learning can be combined with strategies for teaching inquiry-based science. Some of the compatible strategies identified include:

- community involvement and cooperative groups;
- multiple teachers as facilitators of learning;
- investigate fundamental science questions related to life, seasons, and environment;
- investigate questions from multiple perspectives and disciplines;
- learn by active and extended inquiry;
- use of multiple sources of expert knowledge including cultural experts;
- diverse representations and communication of student ideas and work to classmates and community. (Stephens, 2000, p. 28)

In this respect, the incorporation of the *Alaska Standards for Culturally Responsive Schools* in all aspects of the school curriculum and the demonstration of their applicability in providing multiple alternative avenues to meet the State content standards is central. As indicated in the cultural standards, culturally responsive curricula:

- reinforce the integrity of the cultural knowledge that students bring with them;
- recognize cultural knowledge as part of a living and constantly adapting system that is grounded in the past, but continues to grow through the present and into the future;

- use the local language and cultural knowledge as a foundation for the rest of the curriculum and provide opportunities for students to study all subjects starting from a base in the local knowledge systems;
- foster a complementary relationship across knowledge derived from diverse knowledge systems;
- situate local knowledge and actions in a global context: "Think globally, act locally";
- unfold in a physical environment that is inviting and readily accessible for local people to enter and utilize. (ANKN, 1998, pp. 13–19)

SUMMARY

The following statement taken from the introduction to the *Alaska Standards for Culturally Responsive Schools* summarizes the primary thrust of the Alaska Native Knowledge Network in its effort to create a place for Indigenous knowledge in education:

> By shifting the focus in the curriculum from teaching/learning about cultural heritage as another subject to teaching/learning through the local culture as a foundation for all education, it is intended that all forms of knowledge, ways of knowing and worldviews be recognized as equally valid, adaptable and complementary to one another in mutually beneficial ways. (ANKN, 1998, p. 3)

Although much remains yet to be done to fully achieve the intent of Alaska Native people in seeking a place for their knowledge and ways in the education of their children, they have succeeded in demonstrating the efficacy of an educational system that is grounded in the deep knowledge associated with a particular place, on which a broader knowledge of the rest of the world can be built. This is a lesson about "living in two worlds" from which we can all learn.

REFERENCES

[Most of the references cited in this article can be found on the Alaska Native Knowledge Network Web site at http://www.ankn.uaf.edu]

Alaska Rural Systemic Initiative. (2005). *2005 Final report*. Fairbanks, AK: Alaska Native Knowledge Network (http://www.ankn.uaf.edu/arsi.html), University of Alaska Fairbanks.

Alaska Native Knowledge Network. (1998). *Alaska standards for culturally responsive schools*. Fairbanks, AK: Alaska Native Knowledge Network (http://www.ankn.uaf.edu/standards/), University of Alaska Fairbanks.

Barnhardt, R. (1992). Administration across cultures. In D'Oyley, V., Blunt, A., & Barnhardt, R. (Eds.), *Education and development: Lessons from the Third World*. Calgary: Temeron Press.

Barnhardt, R., & Kawagley, A. O. (1999). Education Indigenous to place: Western science meets indigenous reality. In G. Smith & D. Williams (Eds.), *Ecological education in action* (pp. 117–140). New York: State University of New York Press.

Barnhardt, R., & Kawagley. A. O. (2004). Culture, chaos, and complexity: Catalysts for change in Indigenous education. *Cultural Survival Quarterly, 27*(4), 59–64.

Barnhardt, R., & Kawagley, A. O. (2005). Indigenous knowledge systems and Alaska Native ways of knowing. *Anthropology and Education Quarterly, 36*(1), 8–23.

Boyer, P. (2005). Alaska: Rebuilding Native knowledge. In P. Boyer (Ed.), *Building community: Reforming math and science education in rural schools*. Washington, DC: National Science Foundation.

Cajete, G. (2000). *Native science: Natural laws of interdependence*. Santa Fe, NM: Clear Light Publishers.

Carlson, B. (2003). Unangam hitnisangin/unangam hitnisangis: *Aleut plants*. Fairbanks, AK: Alaska Native Knowledge Network (http://www.ankn .uaf.edu/Unangam/), University of Alaska Fairbanks.

Denali Foundation. (2004). *Observing snow*. Fairbanks, AK: Alaska Native Knowledge Network (http://www.ankn.uaf.edu/ObservingSnow/), University of Alaska Fairbanks.

Eglash, R. (2002). Computation, complexity, and coding in Native American knowledge systems. In J. Hankes & G. Fast (Eds.), *Changing the faces of mathematics: Perspectives on Indigenous people of North America* (pp. 251–262). Reston, VA: National Council of Teachers of Mathematics.

Gruenewald, D. (2003). The best of both worlds: A critical pedagogy of place. *Educational Researcher, 32*(4), 3–12.

James, K. (Ed.). (2001). *Science and Native American communities*. Lincoln: University of Nebraska Press.

Kawagley, A. O. (1995). *A Yupiaq world view: A pathway to ecology and spirit*. Prospect Heights, IL: Waveland Press.

King, L., & Schiermann, S. (2004). *The challenges of Indigenous education: Practice and perspectives*. Paris: UNESCO.

Scollon, R. (1988). The Axe Handle Academy: A proposal for a bioregional, thematic humanities curriculum. In R. Barnhardt & K. Tonsmeire (Eds.), *Lessons taught, lessons learned*. Fairbanks, AK: Center for Cross-Cultural Studies (http:// www.ankn.uaf.edu/axehandle/index.html), University of Alaska Fairbanks.

Stephens, S. (2000). *Handbook for culturally responsive science curriculum*. Fairbanks, AK: Alaska Native Knowledge Network(http://www.ankn.uaf.edu/ handbook/), University of Alaska Fairbanks.

II

Reclaiming Broader
Meanings of Education

The chapters in this section explore some of the reasons for adopting an approach to teaching and learning that is more grounded in students' experiences of particular places. Each of the authors deepens the conversation about the role of place in education and culture; each brings a unique perspective to the question of what place-based education could contribute to the development of young people better able to deal with the variety of social, economic, and environmental challenges that currently face humanity.

In the first chapter, co-editor David Gruenewald discusses the potent relationship between a commitment to "diversity" in education and a commitment to "place." He argues that professional educators have reified the discourse about diversity to such an extent that it has become increasingly hard to see the ways in which standardized schooling is fundamentally homogenizing and monocultural. He suggests that by attending to the relationship between culture and place, educators will become better able to sustain rather than undercut cultural diversity. Attention to the tasks of decolonization and reinhabitation—an approach that marries the social critique of Paulo Freire with the environmental awareness of Rachel Carson—will also better prepare young people to diminish the domination of mainstream institutions and open the possibility of creating communities characterized by equity and ecological sustainability.

Next, Robert Michael Pyle brings a specific focus to this broader theme by considering the way that nature study can become a political act. Pyle, a prolific author and widely known natural historian, warns that place-based education, no matter how holistic or culturally grounded, must foster the experience of nature as an everyday act. Without such experiences, people are at risk of the profound illiteracy of not knowing how to name, and not knowing how to care for, the life around them. If place-based education focuses only on human communities, it will do little to rectify the disharmony that currently threatens the integrity of natural systems and our own well-being.

Focusing next on human systems, Rachel Tompkin's chapter describes the vision of the Rural School and Community Trust, which she directs, and its long record of success in promoting youth as assets in their own communities. Tompkins argues, as did Dewey, that rather than considering young people to be potential *future* citizens in a particular community, they can and should be initiated as citizens *now*, even in such complex and typically adult tasks as developing a healthy, and thriving, local economy. She offers numerous examples of places around the United States where such partnerships are stimulating entrepreneurial and cultural activities that are proving to be a source of revitalization and hope for communities increasingly marginalized by the forces of globalization.

In the final chapter of this section, Paul Theobald, author of *Teaching the Commons* (1997), and his co-author John Siskar, deepen the conversation about the role of place in defining community. One of the potential criticisms of a place-based approach to education is that it focuses on the rural and neglects urban contexts, or that it takes for granted a nostalgic homogeneity that does not sufficiently appreciate the complexity and diversity of contemporary life. In this chapter, Theobald and Siskar provide a theoretical framework for "community in diversity," drawn from the writings of Montesquieu, that demonstrates the appropriateness of a place-based approach to all communities.

Taken as a whole, these chapters illustrate a diverse set of meanings about the power of place in education. Urban, suburban, and rural education, social justice, economics, ecology, and environment—all of these potent, and often neglected, educational themes are brought up close and made meaningful in the context of place-based approaches to education.

CHAPTER 7

Place-Based Education
Grounding Culturally Responsive Teaching in Geographical Diversity

David A. Gruenewald

INTRODUCTION

Writing about the significance of place to culture, anthropologist Clifford Geertz (1996) observed, "No one lives in the world in general" (p. 259). That is, our cultural experience is "placed" in the "geography" of our everyday lives, and in the "ecology" of the diverse relationships that take place within and between places.

In the past two decades, the terms *multiculturalism, diversity,* and, more recently, *culturally responsive teaching* have been used frequently by educators concerned with equity, social justice, and democracy, and who are working to undo the damage perpetrated in schools by all forms of oppression. These culturally loaded terms, I argue in this chapter, need to be contextualized in order to avoid the abstraction that often accompanies their institutionalization and decontextualized overuse. Indeed, "No one lives in the world in general," and the concept of place can help to make concrete the cultural thinking promoted by many progressive and critical educators. By focusing on place and place-based cultural thinking, I hope to invite educators committed to social justice, antioppression, and the non-neutrality of teaching into an expanded conversation about *why* educators must be responsive to culture and diversity and *how* we can be responsive through local inquiry and action.

Since I began teaching in the 1980s, "diversity issues" and "multicultural education" have been two of the most visible themes promoted in the schools and universities in which I have worked, eclipsed only by the themes of "standards, testing, and accountability." In my current role as a faculty member in a college of education, I hear and see these words constantly. I am even evaluated each year, in part, for how I include "diversity" in my teaching, scholarship, and service. No other word holds such power in the evaluation process or in the culture of my department and college. Like many colleges and universities, mine also offers various courses on diversity, convenes several diversity committees, and staffs both a multicultural center and a center for equity and diversity. Quick searches for any of these terms on our Web site's homepage will net tens of thousands of hits. Clearly, multiculturalism and diversity are important to educators, and for good reason. Once institutionalized, however, these terms are used with such frequency that their meaning and purpose have become unclear.

My treatment of diversity, identity, and difference in this chapter is far from complete. I focus on these and related concepts to call their meanings and educational usefulness into question, and to suggest the appropriateness of place-based pedagogy as one pathway toward clarifying and expanding some of the common aims of critical, multicultural educators in diverse places.

DIVERSITY AND THE INSTITUTION OF SCHOOL

The language of educational theory, practice, and policy includes many clichés—"leave no child behind," for example. Often these terms, such as *democracy, social justice, equity*, and *diversity* are used as if they are unproblematic and universally understood and accepted. Who would want to leave a child behind? Who wouldn't want to "increase achievement for all kids" or "close the achievement gap"? Yet, through sheer repetition, such slogans and words such as *diversity* have been reified— that is, their everyday use now suggests a taken-for-granted concreteness and righteousness, when, in fact, such words and slogans are rhetorical abstractions that can only be understood by analyzing the contexts in which they are used and the purposes to which they are put.

Responsiveness to diversity, cultural competence, or culturally responsive teaching have become nearly ubiquitous phrases in the education literature, popular especially among progressive and critical teacher educators. To be responsive to diversity in education generally means that one understands how the power dynamics of difference in race, class, gender, sexual orientation, ability, and other forms of "otherness" play out in schools and classrooms, and that one has the skills or the cultural competence to teach for equity, social justice, and democracy. These are important ethical goals that exist in education because people from oppressed groups have taken the political action necessary to influence the policies and discourses around the historically colonizing practices of schooling. A key reason for attempting to train teachers for cultural competence in the United States is that while the teaching force remains overwhelmingly White, students are increasingly diverse in terms of race, culture, ethnicity, nationality, and language. Without teachers who are sensitive to and knowledgeable about differences among individuals and groups, "other people's children" can be marginalized, neglected, undervalued, poorly served, and even greatly damaged by their experience of school (see, e.g., Delpit, 1995; Gay, 2000; Ladson-Billings, 1995, 2001).

Teaching "diversity" to predominantly White teachers and teacher education students is a delicate challenge that is often met with resistance, especially by some White students who frequently believe that racism and prejudice are ancient history. Diversity lessons and field experiences designed by teacher education faculty can have a transformative impact on some students and help them understand the political dynamics surrounding other people's experiences. These same lessons, however, can raise the defenses of other students and cause them to become even more dismissive of differences in educational or social opportunity based on race, class, gender, or sexual orientation. But underneath the unresolved pedagogical challenge of how to teach White teachers about diversity, a more serious problem looms: that is, once diversity discourse is institutionalized in schools and universities, its meanings become standardized, shaped, and absorbed by the institutional culture.

In my own institution, diversity has become a code word that, paradoxically, is not at core about diverse cultural perspectives and diverse cultural ways of being. Instead, the word represents the progressive project of addressing inequality by providing greater support and institutional access to individuals from cultural groups that have suffered institutional violence. For the most part, the code word diversity is simply the safer substitute for the word race, although it also sometimes means class, gender, or sexual orientation. In teacher education, the standard or common definition of a culturally competent and responsive teacher is one who can help an individual from one of these "othered" groups succeed in schools or universities. This is an important goal that I fully support, especially when connected to the goal of raising teachers and students' "sociopolitical consciousness" (Ladson-Billings, 1995, 2001) of the cultural and institutional practices that help to maintain oppressive relationships. However, the complex and contested issues surrounding "sociopolitical consciousness," or what Freire (1993) called *conscientization*, is often reduced in schooling and other institutions to the issue of individual and group access to opportunities that have been denied. Greater institutional access does not equate to greater cultural diversity; indeed, institutions like schools, universities, and governments, through their assimilating regimes of standardization and power-laden rituals of credential granting, have proven remarkably good at epistemological homogenization and the creation of a global monoculture.[1]

Moreover, the emphasis on diversity in the paradoxically prescriptive path toward teacher certification has focused teacher education faculty and students' attention mainly on classroom interactions between teachers and students. This focus tends to deflect attention away from a larger analysis of political economy, diverse cultural ways of being and knowing, and the relationship between education and specific geographical/cultural communities—places. When diversity issues are framed as classroom problems instead of cultural problems, the purpose of cultural competence can be reduced to "leaving no child behind" or "closing the achievement gap." In the institution of school as a whole, such noble rhetorical aims currently manifest in tightening regimes of standardization, test preparation, and remediation—each of which works against the elusive value of "diversity."[2]

PUBLIC EDUCATION OR HOMOGENOUS SCHOOLING?

As a White, male, educated-class heterosexual, I am wary that problematizing diversity may be misunderstood as intolerant, uninformed, or racist by some educators working to improve the experience of students from diverse cultural backgrounds within the existing educational system. My purpose is not to discredit diversity as an important educational term, but to describe the relevance of place to critical, multicultural educators committed to diversity issues. Three key assumptions about public schools underlie my argument. First, I want to acknowledge the fact that most conversations about public education, critical or not, are actually conversations about schooling. As schooling is only one aspect of the much broader field of education, terms such as "educational research," for example, are remarkably misleading. In everyday use, the proper term should be "schooling research," a narrower, specific, and institutionalized form of education limited by countless taken-for-granted rules and conventions. The fact that education and schooling are confused, even by those who identify as critical educational researchers, reflects the power of institutions to shape our language practices and confine our thinking to the usual acceptable categories. My first assumption, therefore, is that the broader field of education should inform the narrower subfield of schooling. Currently, the narrower subfield of schooling dominates and distorts the broader fields of educational research, theory, and practice.

My second assumption, which follows from the first, is that most critical educational research, when primarily focused on schooling, reinforces the power of school discourse to limit educational discourse. There are good reasons for the focus on schooling. Schooling as a whole is an exceedingly expensive and inequitable enterprise that, according to most critical educators, privileges some and disempowers others. Within the framework of schooling, this is obviously the case. Even the No Child Left Behind Act is premised, at least on the surface, on equalizing educational opportunity and outcome. Critical educators do try to go much further in addressing inequities than what is required by current legislation. In response to the multiple ways that schools enact violence on identities and communities, critical educators seek to acknowledge and redress the multiple imbalances of power endemic to schooling. Although I fully support and embrace this goal, my second assumption is that conversations about diversity and schooling, once institutionalized, fall short of questioning the educational value of schooling itself and its relationship to specific communities—human and nonhuman. In efforts to close the achievement gap, the underlying structure and purpose of school, which can be described as meritocratic competition for scarce social and economic rewards in a capitalistic society, remains largely unchallenged. For the most part, critical educators have been successful at establishing diversity as a construct important to the discourse of schooling, at least at the level of rhetoric. However, in their effort to promote changes in schooling practices, educators committed to diversity often get trapped in what Tyack and Cuban (1995) call "the grammar" of schooling. This grammar or logic, focused as it always has been on efficiency and short-term thinking, and more recently on efficiency, short-term thinking, and standards and testing, has tamed the conversation about diversity into one about equity and access within the grammar of schooling. What's often missing is an open challenge to the grammar of schooling and critical questions about the meaning of school success and achievement in the wider context of the communities and cultures in which education, and schooling, take place.

My third assumption is that there is a sad and difficult irony surrounding the continuing push to acknowledge and teach for diversity in schools: that is, schools as public institutions are some of the least diverse places imaginable. What is the meaning of diversity when the basic grammar of schooling segregates children by age and regulates them by the hour and minute for 12 to 16 years or more? What is the meaning of diversity when the only adults students typically see in schools are official representatives of the institution, the very custodians of its grammar? What can diversity possibly mean when school curriculum is unabashedly standardized and managed as official knowledge? What becomes of diversity when schools isolate—by law and often by lock, key, and sometimes barbed wire—teachers and learners from the wider community of which schools are only a small and homogenous part? Although the ethical project to respond to diversity and teach for equity and social justice is a noble project that I support and embrace, the piece I want to add to the puzzle is that from a structural, organizational, temporal, spatial, architectural, cultural, intellectual, and ecological perspective, schools lack diversity big time. This *fundamental lack of diversity*, the isolated, regulated, and narrow nature of schooling, its disconnection from and disregard for community life—these are issues that critical educators need to take seriously.

PLACE, EXPERIENCE, AND POLITICS

Public education in the United States has always been synonymous with state-controlled schools and regimes of standardization that work against cultural diversity. It is therefore necessary to look outside of schools and classrooms in order to find the actual diversity that has become so important to educational discourse. Places are a good place to begin.

"Place" has, in recent decades, become a powerful theoretical construct in many disciplines, including philosophy, literature, environmental science, health, geography, history, human ecology, and many others (Casey, 1997). Philosopher Bruce Janz's Web site, Research on Place and Space, is a growing catalog of thousands of articles and books on the topic (Janz, 2005). Snyder (1990) sums up well why so many academics, writers, and cultural groups embrace place: "The world is places" (p. 25). That is, places are where people and other beings live their lives. The concept of place, especially when informed by this multidisciplinary scholarship on place, can potentially concretize the notion of culture and cultural difference in the lived experience of people in their diverse and unique environments (see e.g., Harvey, 1996; Massey, 1994, 1995).

The movement for place-based education has only begun to borrow from this rich reservoir of place-consciousness in politics, aesthetics, geography, philosophy, cultural studies, anthropology, sociology, architecture, and so forth. For the most part, place-based educators use the term "place" synonymously with "community." Indeed, both place-based and community-based educators advocate using diverse communities as "texts" for curriculum development and engaging teachers and learners in direct experience and inquiry projects that lead to democratic participation and social action within the local environment. However, unlike community-based education, and unlike much of the literature around place and space, the literature around place-based education is self-consciously nonanthropocentric.[3] For many place-based educators, place also signifies what social and cultural theory, as well as diversity advocates, most often overlook: "the land," "the natural environment," and "the nonhuman world." Place is essential to education, then, because it provides researchers and practitioners with a concrete focus for cultural study, and because it expands a cultural landscape to include related ecosystems, bioregions, and all the place-specific interactions between the human and the more-than-human world.

Place-based educators are especially interested in the power of place as a context for diverse experiences that do not and probably cannot happen in the institution of school. It is diverse places that make possible diverse experiences and diverse cultural and ecological formations. The attention to experience in place-based education locates its pedagogy in the broader traditions of experiential and contextual education and in the philosophical tradition of phenomenology. Places, and our relationships to them, are worthy of our attention because places are powerfully pedagogical. Casey (1996) writes, "To live is to live locally, and to know is first of all to know the places one is in" (p. 18). Such an idea may seem obvious. But when considered against the background of standardized educational practices or the homogenizing culture of global capitalism, claiming the primacy of place is revolutionary: It suggests that fundamentally significant knowledge is knowledge of the unique places that our lives inhabit; failure to know those places is to remain in a disturbing sort of ignorance (see Gruenewald, 2003b).

As long as there have been cultures, cultures and their related politics have been entwined with places. Thus, places are far from strictly geographical locations; they are not precultural or presocial; places are at least partly social constructions or cultural products. Williams (2001) formulates this equation: "Place + People = Politics." People, in other words, are not only shaped by places, but we are place-makers, and what we make of our places, and the character of the places we leave behind over generations, reflects much of our political and cultural lives, as well as our theories of knowing and being. But to call people place-makers is to invoke an incredible responsibility on every human community, every member of the species *Homo sapiens*. It is also probably a dangerous kind of hubris to assume the godlike role of place-maker. This is so because, although humans are only one species among many, we have the power to make any place, or the planet itself, unsuitable for particular forms of life, and also unsuitable for particular (culturally diverse) ways of belonging to human communities.

Recognizing that people and cultures are place-makers suggests a much more active role for schools in the study, care, and creation of places. Educationally, this means developing connections with diverse places that allow us learn from them. From the perspective of democratic education in diverse societies, schools must provide more opportunities for students to participate meaningfully in the processes of coming to know places and shaping what our places will become. Educational disregard for places works against diversity and democracy, and makes unlikely the cultural competence sought by many multicultural educators.

RECONNECTING CULTURE AND ENVIRONMENT IN PLACES

Conversations about diversity, culture, and schooling, focused as they often are on race, class, gender, and so forth, make it very difficult to talk about "the land" or "the environment"—*all the diverse ecological places that make possible any cultural formation, any identity, and any idea.* Somehow the natural environment or even the physical environment, in which the culture environment is *always* embedded, continues to be neglected in most cultural and educational theory. Within schools and universities as a whole, environmental studies remain a subfield of various sciences, and are rarely the concern of those focused on diversity and the conflicts of cultural politics. In schooling, environmental education itself is rare, and rarely intersects with culturally responsive teaching. Place helps to bridge this culturally constructed epistemological divide.

When I was a graduate student trying to bring a passion for the land into a cultural studies program, I initially met resistance from faculty and students focused instead on issues of race, class, gender, identity, difference, and other forms of anthropocentric "othering." I remember being challenged by one of my professors over wine at Thanksgiving dinner.

With his usual passion, he asked me point blank: "How can you talk about 'the environment' when people in South America are killing stray cats for dinner?" His question baffled me. I did not yet have the intellectual experience needed to articulate the many ways that killing cats for food exemplifies the intersection of culture and environment. I remain grateful to my pre-ecological professors for introducing me to several critical traditions through which I am beginning to make sense of people's different cultural experiences of their different environments, or places.

Recently in my seminar on Environment, Culture, and Education, a doctoral student studying communications reminded me again of why so many people are reluctant to allow "environmental" discourse into the cultural conversation. The student, who describes himself as an African-American/queer community activist, put it pretty plainly: "It's hard to be concerned about 'the environment,'" he said, "when someone's foot is on your neck."

Without question, the word "environment" has taken on many connotations from White, middle-class environmentalism; for some people, such connotations diminish the word's power to describe contested cultural situations. For many educators advocating cultural responsiveness, environment is not a high-priority concept and is, in fact, often ignored or resisted. A broader view of the environment, however, one that is informed by the traditions of environmental justice (e.g., Bullard, 1993), social ecology (e.g., Luke, 1999), ecofeminism (e.g., Warren, 2000), indigenous knowledge (e.g., Cajete, 1994), and ecojustice (e.g., Bowers, 2001), recognizes that the poverty and violence described by my former professor and student are environmental problems. Poverty and the violence of exploitation and racism have for hundreds of years been connected to patterns of colonization that impact people and their geographical–cultural environments. Talking about the cultural constructs of racism and poverty without talking about geography and environment is to abstract these concepts from where they have been constructed and experienced. Still, arguing that the environment is a critical cultural construct is difficult work in social and institutional contexts such as schools and universities, probably no less difficult than arguing the enduring significance of race. As a critical cultural and educational construct, place can be described as the nexus of culture and environment; places are where we constantly experience their interconnection. We only need to learn to pay attention to see that the distinction between things cultural and things environmental is artificial. No one lives in the world in general.

RECOVERING RELATIONSHIP AND INTERDEPENDENCE WITH LAND

Each one of us is a product of a lifetime of environmental and cultural education that includes our embodied experience of places. When Orr (1992) said, "All education is environmental education," he may as well have said "All education is cultural education." Whether we are conscious of it or not, environmental and cultural education is happening to all of us, all the time. There are, however, important differences in the core foci of cultural and environmental studies. Central to environmental education are the concepts of *relationship* and *interdependence*. The science of ecology is about studying the relationship and interactions between different parts of a system, and the interactions between systems. Although there are undoubtedly great differences between people and cultures, from an ecological perspective, people, cultures, and places are inescapably interconnected in relational systems. In cultural studies, these systems are sometimes described as a "political ecology"[4] of power relationships that privilege some groups or individuals over and at the expense of others; the result is the many "faces of oppression" (Young, 1990) experienced today and throughout human history. However, the exercise of power, colonization, imperialism, and exploitation have always involved people *and* land, culture *and* the places that make culture possible. To borrow postmodern geographer Soja's (1989) phrase, we need to "reinsert" the land into our critical educational theories.

I acknowledge that for some people, because of our differences in experience, because of our differences in race, class, gender, and other categories of otherness, there is a hierarchy of appropriate entry points into conversations about people, place, culture, and education. It really *is* hard to talk about the environment when someone's foot is on your neck. Critical race theorists, Marxists, and gender studies people all have their own literatures and their own agendas. These agendas are crucial to understanding identity, difference, culture, and education, and they help to explain the neglect, the marginalization, and the atrophy of ecological attention. As important as cultural studies is, in its various incarnations, to theorizing education, the silence in this field toward ecological reality can only be described as a kind of intellectual hegemony, a disciplinary practice, and an egregious act of institutional, biological, and cultural violence.

Cultural studies as a field is concerned with the production of discourses, and the power of these discourses to shape and limit our thinking and experience. If there is a dominant, or hegemonic, theme in the cultural studies literature that informs schooling, that theme is *difference*.

Broadly speaking, cultural studies, cultural politics, and cultural thinking (the kind that is currently in vogue among educational theorists) is about deconstructing and reconstructing identities and communities through the construct of difference. This is an incredibly important, powerful, and complex project: How can we better understand ourselves, one another, and our differences? How can we act on these understandings? If cultural studies are concerned with deconstructing and reconstructing identities and communities through the construct of difference, I argue that ecological studies are concerned with deconstructing and reconstructing identities through the construct of *relationship*.

Perhaps for good reason, the idea of relationship in cultural studies is looked on with great suspicion. How can you know me when your experience is not mine? The related literature of postmodernism and postcolonialism are full of words to warn off the concept of "sameness" (which is not the same as relationship): the last thing you want in a cultural studies environment is to be accused of utterances that are totalizing, homogenizing, universalizing, or essentializing. Phrases like "common humanity" and even the word "we" have become taboo; the idea of *difference* is privileged over the idea of *relationship*. The result is that there is very little ecological or relational (not to mention species-level) thinking in cultural studies, or in educational discourses informed by cultural studies perspectives. Difference, rather than relationship, has become what Foucault (1980) called "a regime of truth" or what is often referred to among critical theorists as "official or high status knowledge." Thus it is possible to speak of the "hegemony" of cultural studies, and its own "totalizing" discourse that has "marginalized" ecological thinking and has in many cases "disqualified" the very idea of relationship or of the human family.

As "ground-zero"—where culture and environment come together—place can help to reclaim the idea of relationship and interdependence between different parts of the cultural/ecological system. Place-based pedagogy, then, offers two key challenges to the discourse of culturally responsive or relevant pedagogy. The first is to inform the concept of cultural relevance with place-specific cultural and ecological study. This means expanding the focus of cultural competence well beyond classroom interactions between White teachers and non-White students. Without a focus on a diversity of places and the relationship between them, the sociopolitical consciousness-raising important to diversity advocates will lack specific and diverse cultural grounding. The second challenge, if we are to live together peaceably on a finite planet, is to seek more balance between the concept of *relationship* and the concept of *difference*.[5] The privileging of the discourse of difference in cultural study reinforces an anthropocentric stance that obscures the relationship between all people and the land, between all cultures and the diverse environments out of which all cultures emerged. The great irony here is that the discourse of diversity in cultural studies and schooling neglects biological diversity, the vast "diversity of life" (see Wilson, 1992) that makes all life possible and worth living. The ecological reality and cultural necessity of biodiversity can remind educators and cultural theorists to pay more attention to relationship. Educators concerned about culture and the possibilities for democracy need to continue to work to understand our differences, our relationships, and our interdependence. This does not mean advocating "one world" thinking. It means acknowledging that we live on one world. Despite our differences, the process of learning cannot be limited to individualistic political claims between me and you. It needs to be about us—and we are only one species among many.

A CRITICAL PEDAGOGY OF PLACE: CULTURALLY AND PLACE-RESPONSIVE EDUCATION

The phrase "culturally responsive teaching" begs an important question that needs to remain open: that is, to what in culture should educators be responsive? Diversity educators have successfully foregrounded one answer to this question: culturally responsive educators must be responsive to differences among students so that no child is left behind. I have argued that this response, as important as it is, tends to trap classroom teachers in the grammar of schooling and limit the role of teaching to a relatively narrow set of increasingly prescribed classroom interactions. Place-conscious educators propose a different but related focus for educational attention and cultural responsiveness: the cultural/ecological places common to the lived experience of learners (see e.g., Bowers & Apffel-Marglin, 2005; Cajete, 1994; Gruenewald, 2003a, 2003b; Hart, 1997; Lai & Ball, 2002; Prakash & Esteva, 1998; Reisberg, Brander & Gruenewald, 2006; Smith, 2002; Sobel, 2004; Theobald, 1997). A focus on the lived experience of place puts culture in context, demonstrates the interconnection of culture and environment, and provides a locally relevant pathway for multidisciplinary inquiry and democratic participation.

This is not to say that all examples of place-based education successfully integrate all of these possibilities. Much place-based education continues to foreground local environmental study while neglecting the more politically charged cultural environment. However, place-conscious or place-responsive education proposes fertile ground for educators dedicated to diversity or cultural competence.

I have previously proposed the phrase "a critical pedagogy of place" to signify the potential confluence of cultural and ecological thinking in the emerging discourse of place-based education (see Gruenewald, 2003a). Although critical pedagogy has been challenged by Bowers (1991, 2003, 2005), Bowers and Apffel-Marglin (2005), and others as nonresponsive to diverse cultural ways of being, the intent of the phrase, "a critical pedagogy of place," is to combine the critical tradition that has historically been concerned with human oppression, difference, and radical multiculturalism with geographically and ecologically grounded (i.e., place-based) cultural experience. A critical pedagogy of place posits two fundamental goals for education: decolonization and reinhabitation. Decolonization roughly equates with the deeper agenda of culturally responsive teaching: to undo the damage done by multiple forms of oppression. Reinhabitation roughly equates with the deeper agenda of many environmental educators: to learn how to live well together in a place without doing damage to others, human and nonhuman. Pedagogically, these two interrelated goals translate into a set of questions that can be put to any group of learners on any place on earth: What is happening here? What happened here? What should happen here? What needs to be transformed, conserved, restored, or created in this place? As Jackson (1994) asked, How might people everywhere learn to become "native" to their places?[6] Such questions provide a local focus for socioecological inquiry and action that, because of interrelated cultural and ecological systems, is potentially global in reach. In other words, place-consciousness suggests consciousness not only of my place, but of others, and the relationship between places.

Obviously, these inquiry questions point to a very different kind of school experience than what is typically assumed by multicultural education or culturally responsive teaching. These questions turn one's gaze outward from schools to the culturally and ecologically rich contexts of community life. This does not mean abandoning the classroom, but rethinking its relationship to the wider community. The institution of school and the space of the classroom cannot be expected to solve cultural or ecological problems. This is especially so when schools remain disconnected from actual communities outside their own institutional boundaries. The juxtaposition of culturally responsive and critical, place-based pedagogy suggests several additional focusing questions important to the development of place-based education:

- To what in places should teachers and learners be responsive?
- What forms of cultural, economic, and political colonization impact multiple places?
- To what forms of grassroots resistance and reinhabitation might educators pay attention?
- What is the role of indigenous knowledge in reinhabitation and decolonization?
- How can a focus on the local also provide opportunities for intergenerational, interregional, and international communication and collaboration?
- What kinds of experiences are needed for people to learn how to perceive, critically analyze, and act on their human and nonhuman environments and relationships?

One of the main goals of place-based education is to expand the landscape of learning opportunities among and between students, educators, and community members. It may be that culturally responsive teaching in diverse communities is only possible when students and teachers encounter the cultural and ecological diversity that is threatened or extinct in schools, but still endemic to places.

ENDNOTES

[1] The current Bush administration, for example, can boast the most diverse Cabinet in the history of the American Presidency. Yet the members of this Cabinet speak in the White voice of the political right wing.

[2] This does not mean the discourse of diversity or cultural responsiveness always gets reduced to classroom interactions between teachers and students for the purposes of closing the standardized achievement gap. The work of the Alaska Native Knowledge Network (1998), the Coalition for Community Schools (2005), and the Rural School and Community Trust (2005) are notable exceptions. Their publications on culturally responsive teaching, schools, curriculum, and communities are fundamentally concerned with the relationship between culture, education, and place. Other exceptions include Haymes (1995), hooks (2003), and Gutstein (2003).

[3] See Bowers (1993, 1995, 1997) for a discussion of anthropocentrism as one of the "root metaphors of modernism."

[4] The appropriation of the word "ecology" can only be seen as ironic whenever it neglects nonhuman systems and interactions.

[5] The converse of these challenges also holds true: culturally responsive pedagogy challenges place-based pedagogy to pay more attention to classroom interactions and to difference.

⁶ Increasingly I am convinced that, despite problems of appropriation, Native, Indigenous, First Nations, and Aboriginal educational processes and epistemologies need to be at the center of place-based, culturally responsive teaching. Only through studying Native experiences will educators understand the enduring legacy of colonization and the possibility for diverse cultural ways of being.

REFERENCES

Alaska Native Knowledge Network. (1998). Alaska standards for culturally responsive schools. Anchorage, AK: Alaska Native Knowledge Network. Retrieved October 12, 2005, from http://www.ankn.uaf.edu/.

Bowers, C. A. (1991). Critical pedagogy and the "arch of social dreaming": A response to the criticisms of Peter McLaren Curriculum Inquiry, 21, 479–487.

Bowers, C. A. (1993). Education, cultural myths, and the ecological crisis. Albany: State University of New York Press.

Bowers, C. A. (1995). Educating for an ecologically sustainable culture: Rethinking moral education, creativity, intelligence, and other modern orthodoxies. Albany: State University of New York Press.

Bowers, C. A. (1997). The culture of denial. Albany: State University of New York Press.

Bowers, C. A. (2001). Educating for eco-justice and community. Athens and London: University of Georgia Press.

Bowers, C. A. (2003). Can critical pedagogy be greened? Educational Studies, 34, 11–21.

Bowers, C. A. (2005). How Peter McLaren and Donna Houston, and other "Green" Marxists contribute to the globalization of the West's industrial culture. Educational Studies, 37, 185–195.

Bowers, C. A., & Apffel-Marglin, F. (Eds.). (2005). Rethinking Freire: Globalization and the environmental crisis. Mahwah, NJ: Lawrence Erlbaum Associates.

Bullard, R. (Ed.). (1993). Confronting environmental racism: Voices from the grassroots. Boston: South End Press.

Cajete, G. (1994). Look to the mountain: An ecology of indigenous education. Durango, CO: Kivaki Press.

Casey, E. (1996). How to get from space to place in a fairly short stretch of time. In K. Basso & S. Feld (Eds.), Senses of place (pp. 13–52). Santa Fe, NM: School of American Research Press.

Casey, E. (1997). The fate of place: A philosophical history. Berkeley: University of California Press.

Coalition for Community Schools. (2005). Retrieved October 12, 2005, from http://www.communityschools.org/.

Delpit, L. 1995. Other people's children. New York: New Press.

Foucault, M. (1980). Power/knowledge: Selected interviews and other writings. (C. Gordon, Ed.). New York: Pantheon Books.

Freire, P. (1993). Pedagogy of the oppressed. New York: Continuum. (Original work published 1970.)

Gay, G. 2000. Culturally responsive teaching. New York: Teachers College Press.

Geertz, C. (1996). Afterword. In S. Feld & K. Basso (Eds.), Senses of place (pp. 259–262). Santa Fe, NM: School of American Research Press.

Gruenewald, D. (2003a). The best of both worlds: A critical pedagogy of place. *Educational Researcher, 32*(4), 3–12.

Gruenewald, D. (2003b). Foundations of place: A multidisciplinary framework for place-conscious education. *American Educational Research Journal, 40*(3), 619–654.

Gutstein, E. (2003). Teaching and learning mathematics for social justice in an urban, Latino school. *Journal for Research in Mathematics Education, 34*(1), 37–73.

Hart, R. (1997). *Children's participation: The theory and practice of involving young citizens in community development and environmental care.* London: Earthscan, Unicef.

Harvey, D. (1996). *Justice, nature, and the geography of difference.* Malden, MA: Blackwell.

Haymes, S. (1995). *Race, culture, and the city: A pedagogy for black urban struggle.* Albany: State University of New York Press.

hooks, b. (2003). *Teaching community: A pedagogy of hope.* New York: Routledge.

Jackson, W. (1994). *Becoming native to this place.* Lexington: University of Kentucky Press.

Janz, B. (2005). *Research on place and space.* Retrieved October 12, 2005, from http://pegasus.cc.ucf.edu/~janzb/place/geography.htm.

Ladson-Billings, G. (1995) Toward a theory of culturally relevant pedagogy. *American Educational Research Journal, 32*(3), 465–491.

Ladson-Billings, G. (2001). *Crossing over to Canaan: The journey of new teachers in diverse classrooms.* San Francisco: Jossey-Bass.

Lai, A., & Ball, E. (2002). Home is where the art is: Exploring the places people live through art education. *Studies in Art Education: A Journal of Issues and Research, 44*(1), 47–66.

Luke, T. 1999. *Capitalism, democracy, and ecology: Departing from Marx.* Urbana: University of Illinois Press.

Massey, D. (1994). *Space, place, and gender.* Minneapolis: University of Minnesota Press.

Massey, D. (1995). *Spatial divisions of labor: Social structures and the geography of production.* New York: Routledge.

Orr, D. (1992). *Ecological literacy.* Albany: State University of New York Press.

Prakash, M., & Esteva, G. (1998). *Escaping education: Living as learning within grassroots cultures.* New York: Peter Lang.

Reisberg, M., Brander, B., & Gruenewald, D. (2006). Your place or mine? Reading art, place, and culture in multicultural children's picture books. *Teacher Education Quarterly, 33*(1), 117–133.

Rural School and Community Trust. (2005). Retrieved October 12, 2005, from http://www.ruraledu.org/.

Smith, G. (2002). Place-based education: Learning to be where we are. *Phi Delta Kappan, 83,* 584–594.

Snyder, G. (1990). *The practice of the wild.* New York: North Point Press.

Sobel, D. (2004). *Place-based education: Connecting classrooms and communities.* Great Barrington, MA: Orion Society and Myrin Institute.

Soja, E. (1989). *Postmodern geographies: The reassertion of space in critical social theory.* London: Verso.

Theobald, P. (1997). *Teaching the commons: Place, pride, and the renewal of community.* Boulder, CO: Westview Press.

Tyack, D., & Cuban, L. (1995). *Tinkering toward Utopia: A century of public school reform.* Cambridge, MA: Harvard University Press.

Warren, K. 2000. *Ecofeminist philosophy: A Western perspective on what it is and why it matters.* Lanham, MD: Rowman & Littlefield.

Williams, T. T. (2001). *Red: Passion and patience in the desert.* New York: Pantheon Books.

Wilson, E. O. (1992). *The diversity of life.* Cambridge, MA: Harvard University Press.

Young, I. (1990). *Justice and the politics of difference.* Princeton, NJ: Princeton University Press.

CHAPTER 8

No Child Left Inside
Nature Study as a Radical Act

Robert Michael Pyle

Human denizens of modern industrial cultures are profoundly ignorant of the living and physical world around them. This state of ecological illiteracy makes itself abundantly clear in the United States, and I think it is not much less dire in other first-world countries. Personal acquaintance with local flora and fauna—once an essential knowledge and later at least commonplace in most cultures—has become scanty to absent. Although millions of people call themselves birdwatchers in the United States, modern naturalists of depth and breadth are so rare as to be considered a priesthood of shamans, a motley host of weirdos, or an insignificant population of marginal obsessives.

The American Nature Study movement, during a window of some 50 years, considered and promulgated local knowledge of nonhuman lives and processes as a fundamental part of ordinary education (Comstock, 1911). Nature Study comprised a normal part of everyday primary education in schools across the United States. Basic acquaintance with local fauna and flora on the part of schoolchildren was considered desirable and realistic. Now, for another half-century, nature literacy as a fundamental educational objective has been sidelined if not forgotten (Pyle, 2002). From a purge of naturalists in the universities to the marginalization of nature study in the public schools, the current Dark Age of place-centered knowledge is deeply, dangerously maladaptive (Pyle, 2003). How can a culture confront imperiled ecosystems when a large majority of the members have no functional knowledge of the system's working parts?

Place-based education, no matter how topographically or culturally informed, cannot fully or even substantially succeed without reinstating the pursuit of natural history as an everyday act. Prior to its subversion and distraction by "No Child Left Behind," American education was making a spirited attempt at human inclusiveness in K–12 studies. The idea of neighborliness still has currency in the classroom, and this is good. But what we desperately need, if the society is to persist in the face of climate change and every other challenge to survival, is a strong sense of our more-than-human neighborhood. This cannot come, by definition, without knowing something of the neighbors. Yet to a great degree, environmental education has abandoned species-level objectives. Many educators seem to think it's enough to teach a modicum of process and function, while confronting organisms at a coarse and shallow level, and then briefly. New approaches in place-based education too often make the same mistake. Place, of course, is fundamental; but place is nothing but geology without its plants and animals, and they all have names and faces. Making an effort to know some of them is simply good manners among neighbors. Consigning them to some abstract category called "nature," in contrast, is not only impolite, but ultimately suicidal. In a stunning irony, developers and some self-described "deep ecologists," deep in belief yet unmindful of ecological details, unintentionally conspire to perpetuate a fallacy of false security based in blissful ignorance of the nuanced physical world around us.

Ecological illiteracy aids and abets environmentally regressive governments. In this chapter, I have no intention of pussyfooting around the fact that we are presently subject to an actual pogrom leveled against environmental protections, legislation, and regulations, and against habitats themselves. The George W. Bush administration unveils new enormities against the past century of conservation progress almost weekly, retreating in turn on clean air and water, roadless areas, Arctic protection, old-growth forests, national parks, endangered species, and on and on. While free-trade globalism and unsustainable population growth threaten the very functioning of the planet's climate and currents, American policies seem designed to hasten the process of environmental decline and the era of social and biological reckoning. If Americans were better informed about natural conditions—if they were not plumb ignorant—I doubt they would be so compliant.

Ecological sophistication always threatens an establishment rooted in capital expansion at all costs, unrooted in the land, and dependent on global dissociation. After all, no one citizen who understands what such a course means for the earth and all its life-forms could conceivably countenance an administration—or vote for it—that beggars the public estate and depletes all supportive resources in service of military adventurism and mercantile plutocracy. All forms of public education that undergird such a government agenda, through teachings of blind patriotism and faith in the status quo, are essentially corrupt regardless of any other merit they might possess. Yet since the state funds and regulates the schools in large part, it can manipulate trends that might prove counterproductive to its purposes. "No child left behind," for example, eclipses critical thinking with linear testing, and helps suppress the time-consuming place-based education that all sensible nations should enshrine under the motto "No child left inside."

But children *are* left inside. I have argued (Pyle, 1993) and others have concurred (Finch, 2003; Kahn & Kellert, 2002; Nabhan & Trimble, 1994) that the *extinction of experience* resulting from a loss of local diversity necessarily results in a descending spiral of alienation, apathy, inaction, and further extinction: a destructive cycle of alienation and loss. The antidote, many agree, is immersion in the so-called natural world, particularly in those special places (Sobel, 1993; Stafford, 1986; Thomashow, 1995) where initiation and imprinting on nature take place. To some degree, the autodidacticism inherent in the ritual of outdoor play has made up for the absence of actual nature study in the schools. Children may become sensitized to the out-of-doors and its sensations by scrambling about their forts and crawdad holes, even if they know few of the animal and plant occupants' names. But I am deeply concerned that this traditional avenue toward natural intimacy is closing down.

Often while lecturing to groups of naturalists, students, writers, environmental professionals, and other congregations, I ask them to imagine their special place of childhood—"the spot you blame or bless for being here." Then I ask them to immerse their minds in the memory and to evoke the sensations and stories of that place. The gathered faces become deeply peaceful as they do this, only to grimace or even tear up later when I ask how many could find their special place substantially unchanged today. The litany of places varies only a little from group to group, usually including fields, creeks, ditches, rocks, trees, thickets, backyards, vacant lots, grandparents' farms and gardens, and every other sort of open space locus of discovery and initiation. Common currency of this realm of youth includes the building of forts, catching bugs, tadpoles, and crawdads, rites involving the opposite sex or its absence, and all manner of imaginative role-playing games. The concrete social values of outdoor play are well summarized and documented by Winters (2004) and White (2004), and Mergen (2003) provides an extraordinarily thorough review of the literature of children in intimate contact with nature.

Virtually every naturalist and person of kindly disposition toward the natural world can recite the particulars of such a grounding in a particular place. So can many others, giving at least an opening to their better nature as regards the environment. I feel I have gotten through to people who did not consider themselves environmentalists through connection with a place they hold in their hearts. In fact, the number of adults in my audiences incapable of naming a "first place" is vanishingly small. But in recent years, I have been distressed to discover that many younger people have no such sites or experiences to relate. Graduate students and older undergraduates of my acquaintance may still respond positively, but many younger college and high school students have no idea what I am talking about.

A recent book, *Last Child in the Woods*, (Louv, 2005) took this problem on directly. Richard Louv maintains (p. 7) that if we experienced the out of doors when we were young, "then we were bound to the natural world and remain so today." Yet interviewing some 3,000 children and many of their parents, Louv found widespread abandonment of the out-of-doors in favor of the sedentary virtual world. One child responded that he didn't like the outdoors because there were no electrical outlets.

Louv concluded that we are facing a dangerous syndrome he calls *nature deficit disorder*. Indeed, the seduction of computer-mediated recreation—video games, iPods, cell phones, messaging, and e-mail, not to mention the old standby television, are collectively one of the main drivers of the extinction of experience. This overlies the "original" cause, the actual loss of habitats within the radius of reach of children and others: when a town in-fills, it may help prevent sprawl on the edges, but it also abolishes vacant lots and the neighborhood wilderness they represent. What, after all, is less vacant to a curious child than a vacant lot (Pyle, 2002)? As outdoor educator Megan McGinty put it:

> As a kid, I was absolutely captivated by the idea that the mundane things in my backyard could be connected to bigger, more exotic things that lay far beyond. Suddenly, pretending to be exploring the Amazon while catching and identifying spiders in the vacant lot next to my friend's house did not seem so farfetched. In fact, it made the spider-hunting seem less like playing and more like training for someday exploring the great unknowns that still remain in the wild-lands. (McGinty, 2004)

The third force driving kids from the woods is fear: parents' fear of abduction, molestation, or other dangers to their children. Many people speak of their special places in terms of unmediated liberty. More boys than girls enjoyed the freedom of the day that many in my generation knew, but even among females over 30 or so, "'Bye, Mom, see you at dinner" was not an uncommon afternoon's salutation. Nowadays, out-of-school hours are either scheduled to the minute between soccer and what-not, or sequestered within safe bounds, and probably plugged in. The kind of personal sovereignty over children's playtime that my peers and I enjoyed is almost extinct, even if a kid actually wants to abandon his Game-Boy or her iPod for field and wood. Now there are few fields and woods, organized activity has supplanted free agency, the computer rules, and invisible fences of fear have arisen between kids and the nearby wild. Finch (2003) explored all of these factors separating young Americans from the land, especially what he calls the bogey-man phenomenon.

The forces aligned against free exploration are not new. The 1941 American Youth Commission Report, entitled "Time on Their Hands," criticized parents for allowing their children solitary recreation (Cranz, 1982). This followed a 1910 dictum from Lester Gulick, Chief Secretary of the Playground Association of America, who said, "It is not enough to give everyone the chance to play. We must also direct that play to specific as well as attractive ends" (Cavallo, 1981). Yet it is the unbounded liberty to prowl and poke about, whether alone or with comrades, that fertilizes the generous and curious instinct in the immature human mind. As a recent writing student of mine perfectly put it, "We were the neighborhood pack of children that beat back the pavement as we endlessly circled the neighborhood streets, creating a mission where there wasn't one before, finding pockets of wild, behaving badly, eating dirt, sinking fingers into creek muck, smelling of sweat and decomposing creek silt" (Marsh, 2005).

Three vignettes from recent experience highlight varieties of the problem:

1. A college professor whose class I visit praises the concept of children's special places, then informs me that her own 7-year-old is not allowed out of his home cul-de-sac—a protective regime under which I would have withered, possibly perished.
2. On a visit to the Vancouver, Washington Mall, just before closing, I observe boys skipping stones in the central water feature—only they aren't stones, they are quarters the lads have fished out of the fountain. When I ask whether they got so good by practicing on a local pond or creek, they reply that they have no such place nearby; only the mall. I am both heartbroken by

their loss, and heartened that their basic instincts have survived their abandonment in the 'burbs.

3. Passing through a Target store in Missoula, Montana, I pause to look over the shoulder of a boy soldered to a video screen. He is playing a mountain-biking game, replete with realistic habitats. Then I notice that the object of the game is to whack hikers, strollers, birders, anyone who comes along the trail on foot: Mad Max on two wheels, offing pedestrians instead of aliens. Is it any wonder that wandering in the out-of-doors can no longer be counted on as an antidote to the extinction of experience, in the absence of nature study in school?

Still another factor has arisen in opposition to spontaneous place-based inquiry. Lucky children who still have access to natural fragments of land commonly find them managed, fenced, interpreted, way-marked, and tangled more with rules than underbrush. Nature Conservancy preserves, Audubon Centers, community nature centers, parks (if they retain any wildness), and most other accessible open-space reserves bristle with regulations. Visitors must remain on trails (an automatic turn-off to the exploring impulse), nothing may be picked, plucked, dug, or collected, no tree-forts or brush-structures may be built (fatal flaw, right there), and much of what's worth learning is pointed out on plaques, numbered stakes, and booklets, or (even worse) by adult guides. As a former Nature Conservancy regional land steward and parks interpreter, I well understand the need to protect ecologically sensitive sites from these kinds of disturbances and to provide intelligent interpretation for visitors in some sites. The problem lies, just as with the national parks, in the imperative for the same acres to serve wildly different purposes: public recreation, scientific discovery, free play, *and* protection.

So it is that we see the irony of children's special places being protected and ruined in a single stroke. In Aurora, Colorado, the fortunate kids in one neighborhood enjoyed a remnant cattail marsh, cottonwood grove, and prairie, where countless, nameless adventures continued to take place at a time when much of the town was immured in a seeming infinitude of tract housing. The wild patch inevitably came under threat from developers. A coalition of parents, open-space advocates, the City of Aurora, the Trust for Public Lands, and others brokered a heroic and unlikely agreement to save Jewell Wetlands. But the bargain included water management structures, as well as formal developments such as a lawn and a butterfly garden in place of partially native grassland, an ADA-accessible paved trail, and sidewalks. Some of the habitat has indeed remained intact, and the conservationists doubtless did the best they could. The outcome beats the alternative of more houses, and the place may have more appeal for the general public as a park than it did as a thicket. But now, when you penetrate to the most intimate, intriguing depths of the swamp, you do so on asphalt, and you find an interpretive sign awaiting you. The kids it was all supposed to be for will have to work much harder to feel as if they have discovered anything for themselves (Pyle, 1998).

A subset of the regulatory obstacle may be found in the discouragement of collecting. True enough, children need to understand the need to leave living things alone as a default, if no need exists to interfere with them, especially in sensitive places under lots of people pressure. On a recent visit to a busy Puget Sound beach with my grandchildren, I was appalled to see child after child (and their overseers) coming out of the water with handfuls of bright sea stars, only to let them dry and die in the bright sun, then be left to rot or feed the lucky gulls. This might or might not hurt the population, but it seemed wanton: wonderful that the kids spotted the sea stars and picked them up and admired them, but then they should have returned them to the cold water.

The definition of "need" here should be interpreted broadly. If kids feel the need to catch crayfish or insects to satisfy their curiosity, hunter instinct, and nervous energy, fine—most invertebrate organisms, unlike easily depleted tide pools, can take much incidental predation—especially if children eventually release most of their take. But the occasional child who entertains the inclination to make a study collection should be treasured, nourished, and encouraged to do so—not disciplined by adults' vague notions of a nonconsumptive imperative developed for vertebrate populations under pressure. Just think if E. O. Wilson's parents had forebade him from collecting insects (Wilson, 1994)!

However, insect nets are commonly looked on with aspersion these days, banned from many parks and reserves, and not widely available. The North American Butterfly Association pointedly discourages the use of nets for children. Yet this is an elitist and unrealistic attitude (Robinson, 2005). Most children cannot afford close-focusing binoculars (NABA's prescribed tool of choice), nor are they remotely patient enough to use them. Keane (2005), trying to demonstrate for an audience of ecocritics how the practice of butterfly pursuit has changed and in so doing taking my own writing badly out of context, argues for abandonment of the net in favor of the camera. "The ecstasy of connection may now be abstracted," he writes, "but the throbbing of the wild is preserved." But children on adventure are not normally equipped with close-up cameras, nor the exquisite patience it takes to photograph butterflies. Nor do they give a hoot for abstraction. They do, however, love to swing a butterfly net, with almost atavistic fervor and adeptness. Insect nets are cheap, easy to use, and just plain fun, as I rediscover time after time while teaching field classes with both children and adults. And it is exactly the sort of abstraction that Keane condones that kills the impulse of the throbbing wild for children (Pyle, in press).

Bug and fish nets have always been the number one medium for curious kids to discover a real interest in biology, and long may they wave. Environmental and outdoor educators should make nets available, but not required, for the children they take outside, along with words about care, sensible use, and gentle release of anything the catcher does not mean to collect and properly curate. If killing the insect is not necessary for a collection, catch-and-release is easy to accomplish with a net and is what I mostly do in teaching. Too, fine collections may be made from road-killed insects, abundant along any roadway, another reason why abandoning nets is silly as well as counterproductive: Every driver kills vastly more butterflies in summer than any army of collectors. Indeed, more butterflies are killed in a week in Illinois than exist in the cumulative holdings of major U. S. museums (McKenna, McKenna, Malcolm, & Berenbaum, 2001). Children are keenly attuned to such hypocrisies: A culture that has entire television channels devoted to bass fishing, eats meat, and "fogs" for mosquitoes should not try to tell a child not to catch common insects. Nor should the techniques of making a simple collection be swept away before the nonconsumptive wave. Assembling and taking responsibility for curating a study collection can be a powerful accomplishment for a youngster, and it furnishes a much faster learning curve than mere watching.

In the post–Nature Study era, it is possible for an individual, gifted, and risky teacher to re-create either the pedagogical basis for knowing something of nature or the rich possibility of outdoor discovery or, rarely, both. One of the finest natural history teachers I have ever known was James Fielder, who taught courses in ornithology, wilderness ecology, and animal behavior in a public high school in Bellevue, Washington, in the early 1970s. Fielder gave the basics of field biology in class, then took his lucky students on extensive birding field trips throughout the Pacific Northwest. Several of his graduates found real direction through these experiences, joining the earliest classes at The Evergreen State College where they studied with legendary Evergreen teachers Steve Herman, Al Weideman, Robert Sluss, and others, and became lifelong naturalists and conservationists.

By way of contrast, my own high school biology tutelage was a singularly undistinguished business conducted by the football coach. Even so, I had the immense good fortune that two other biology teachers named Ed Butterfield and Keith Anderson ran a lifesaving, after-school ecology club. I also benefited from amateur butterfly collectors of my acquaintance, and parents and grandparents who knew something of the natural world, as well as the freedom of the day and easy access to adequate habitat along a country ditch where I learned about butterflies. Among all these, I gained the rudiments of what would have been routine in an earlier time (Pyle, 1993, 2000). Comstock (1911) claimed that her voluminous *Handbook of Nature Study* "does not contain more than any intelligent country child of twelve should know of his environment; things that he should know naturally and without effort, although it might take him half his life-time to learn so much if he should not begin before the age of twenty" (p. xi). But most people today lack such boons as I enjoyed, and don't live in the country. Here is where place-based educators can make all the difference.

To emphasize this important point, I will cite two more graduate students from a class I taught at the University of Montana in the 2005 spring semester entitled "Writing as If the World Matters." Brian Williams had come to Missoula from the Northeast, felt alien, and decided to enter on an intensive homing through self-taught natural history exploration. He wrote, "In Missoula, I'm clearly out past the fringe of my home territory, on unfamiliar soil. Yet each discovery I make, the date the larch drop their needles in fall, the first buttercup of the year, the last Bohemian waxwing of winter, drops a counterweight to that alienness, helps root me here" (Williams, 2005). So bracing and invigorating did he find this practice that, as a part of his Master of Science portfolio in the Department of Environmental Studies, he undertook to teach a course in field natural history through EVST and the Montana Natural History Center. Each week concentrated on a different aspect of life studies, including a field trip. Taking part in the entomology exercise, I was able to observe the enthusiasm and zeal of the diverse class of graduates, undergraduates, and townspeople. There was no pretense of complete coverage, and the instructor was still learning alongside the students. Yet I have no doubt that each member went forth with much wider eyes and enhanced knowledge of natural systems and players, never to take the more-than-human world for granted again. Whether this course continues will depend on the appearance of another such teacher.

Joe Sullivan was a doctoral student in education when he took my writing course. He'd come back to graduate school after teaching high school in his native Washington state in the early years of this century. Dissatisfied with the state of affairs in the classroom and corridors of the schoolhouse, Joe developed the idea to take students outdoors in an unstructured, spontaneous-as-possible series of rambles, "devoting," as he said, "one day a week to nature." He wrote:

> Our unspoken pact was that we could each do as we wished, experience the world on our own, and collectively go where the day took us. Together, we forged new trails and named them as we went. I demanded no learning from anyone, and did my best to stay out of the way as they inevitably absorbed the natural world. We better understood the physical struggle of life when we counted hundreds of pacific gumboot chitons washed up on a short stretch of storm-ravaged beach, their pink flesh faded and shredded by the sand. We knew the impact of our culture when our spontaneous necropsy of a ling cod revealed a stomach bloated by foam flotation. And we saw a different side of ourselves when we watched scientists chainsaw a cross section through a beached orca. Often, we learned about the joy we could bring to each other, carving bulbs of bull kelp into the heads of sinister baby dolls, finding hidden fields for Frisbee, or running backwards on our snowshoes.

> Constrained by the hours of after-school daylight, we limited our reach to places within an hour of our town, Sequim, in northwest Washington. This became one of the great joys of the club: revisiting the same places with new people, at different times of the year, in the context of different seasons and phases of life. We found half a dozen favorite spots where we could feel small without going far, and visited each a couple times per year.

> Once, only ten minutes from the classrooms where we felt the forfeit of our days, we walked a hundred-foot-high ocean bluff, closed our eyes, and took the sandblasting of a sixty mile-per-hour wind. In spring, we trekked up a favorite foothill to look down on the fingers of Puget Sound and the Strait of Juan de Fuca, nearby islands, far off volcanoes, and the overwhelming greens and blues of all the earth we intimately knew. In fall, we marched muddy trails in the rain, gazed across valleys at foggy slopes, and warmed at the thought of more valleys and slopes beyond that fog. These

scenes drew out the best in us. We sat in silence, grew smiles, and challenged each other in reckless downhill sprints: animals in our element. (Sullivan, 2005)

Sullivan's phrase "the forfeit of our days" captures as well as anything I have ever heard the tragedy of childhood lost indoors. Inasmuch as we deem school to be necessary, an outdoor complement such as Joe developed in his school can go a long way toward reconciling that forfeiture. I will never forget (and I was a relatively happy student) the excruciating pang of required indwelling once spring took hold. Today's calendar of last day in June and first day in August would have been intolerable, and the concept of year-round school, a popular topic of discussion in those baby-boom-crowded days, simply inconceivable. The reason Comstock's program of Nature Study was tolerable to many children was that the classroom time held out the promise of an outdoor corollary. And this is what Ed Butterfield, Keith Anderson, Jim Fielder, Brian Williams, and Joe Sullivan made possible, along with many other field-oriented teachers around the country—many, but vastly too few.

The problem with all of these models is their exceptionality, and the ephemerality of any given regime. Ed Butterfield retired, and most of his usual teaching habitats became developed. Jim Fielder, with his iconoclastic ways, ran afoul of administrators and left teaching for river rafting, then writing. Brian Williams graduated and moved on to become the chief naturalist for the King Ranch in Texas. Joe Sullivan discovered certain internal limitations to his outdoor club: How can you take everyone who wants to go? Failing that, how do you avoid sponsoring a clique, or advantaging some students over others? Such pioneering teachers also face the challenges of principals afraid of liability in these litigious times, conflicts with other extracurricular activities and after-school jobs, overprotective parents, and a battery of electronic blandishments. But the sheer rarity of such teachers, who know natural history or are eager to learn it as they teach, is the greatest obstacle to natural literacy through individual initiative. Comstock wrote, "The reason why nature-study has not yet accomplished its mission, as thought core for much of the required work in our public schools, is that the teachers are as a whole untrained in the subject" (Comstock, 1911, p. xi).

If maverick teachers can never be enough, how about formal environmental education? I'd like to think that EE has functionally taken the place of Nature Study, but except in rare and charmed circumstances, usually dependent on individual teachers, it has not. My own experience with one environmental ed center over several years gave me reason to doubt what it was accomplishing. The teachers were committed, and the students on the whole enjoyed coming into the country. But it seemed to me that little was learned of a lasting nature, in both senses; nor was an exploratory goal satisfied. The experience smacked more of summer camp than nature study: flag ceremonies, ropes courses, rambunctious group hikes, token awards at regimented mealtimes, and raucous camp-fires characterized the days—and this, just one week in sixth grade out of their whole school career. The high side included older outdoor school veteran kids coming back as counselors, and at least some exposure to habitats and species and to conservation ethics. If it should steer a few kids toward life studies, or toward the back door, such EE is definitely worthwhile. It's better than basketball camp, but I cannot imagine that a one-time exposure to such thin gruel will change many lives to the same degree that a daily or even weekly period of nature study in class might do. Speaking at the 20th annual meeting of the Maryland Association of Environmental and Outdoor Educators in 2005, I was encouraged by the energy and innovation of many members, and by the high quality of many Chesapeake Bay–area programs. Yet with no slight intended toward EE professionals, whom I consider front-running candidates for group beatification, I doubt that the majority of strapped American school districts are dispensing outdoor education of much depth.

Still another resource for place-based, experiential studies may be found in the catalogs and facilities of private nature organizations. I've already mentioned the problem with nature centers being too often and too much out of bounds to substitute for the local bush. At least their presence validates a child's impulse in this direction, and might substantially stimulate its growth. The National Audubon Society has committed itself to 1,000 nature centers around the country (Flicker, 2002). In truth, some of the "new" facilities under the NAS banner have simply replaced existing neighborhood centers, and officers of several local chapters have accused National Audubon of predatory practices vis-à-vis their established programs, buildings, and members' volunteer energies. Nevertheless, NAS at least in principle has affirmed the organization's fundamental dedication to natural history learning.

The National Wildlife Federation, however, has wavered in this respect. For some 20 years, I taught at the Federation's Conservation Summits, summer nature camps for families, teachers, and anyone else who wished to spend a week in a conducive location taking classes on flora and fauna and many other outdoor topics. Several summits took place each summer, in various locations around the country, such as the YMCA of the Rockies in Estes Park, Colorado, or the campus of the University of Vermont, or Western Washington University. I found these programs extraordinarily effective, exposing thousands of people to an array of excellent instructors, experiences, habitats, organisms, outdoor skills, and lore. But the Federation whittled down its education department, then the summits, holding fewer of them and those largely at expensive resorts, and devaluing instructors. Managers demanded "metrics" to demonstrate that the summits actually affected conservation outcomes—thus signaling a loss of faith in the essential mission of promoting nature study. Eventually, the program dwindled to a single summit per summer, then flickered out. A group of former instructors has lately resusitated the effort under the name "Family Summits." Yet, in my opinion, the Conservation Summits were one of the most valuable initiatives in NWF's history. Undertaken on a much wider scale, such a model would be of immense national value. NWF Backyard Wildlife Coordinator Craig Tufts (personal communication) recently wrote to me that the organization is reaffirming its commitment to nature study.

However, a recent draft overview for a program entitled "NWF Connecting People to Nature" (NWF, 2005) contained among its 33 bulleted points no fewer than six major components that are to be online, television-, or video-based.

I have great admiration for another branch of the independent arm of contemporary place-teaching, namely, the several institutes based around national parks and other large ecosystems. Great Smokies, Yosemite (and its subsidiaries, Headlands and Olympic Parks Institutes), and North Cascades Institutes are three of the strongest entities in this arena. NCI, independent and still under its founding director Saul Weisberg's vision, is one of the oldest and perennially most successful of these nonprofits. By offering a wide array of in-depth field seminars in ecology and the arts for 20 years, NCI has initiated thousands of participants in the ways of wildlife and wild places as mediated by the Greater North Cascades Ecosystem. In the summer of 2005, NCI's long-awaited North Cascades Environmental Learning Center opened on Seattle City Light's Diablo Lake in the Ross Lake National Recreation Area. This purpose-built facility will allow even greater depth, variety, and intensity of instruction and experience for adults, while housing graduate students who assist in teaching Mountain School for kids. Likewise, Olympic Park Institute maintains the Rosemary campus on Lake Crescent on the Olympic Peninsula for similar purposes. OPI, however, has eliminated its adult courses in favor of an aggressive program of learning experiences for schools. A reasoned argument can be made for each approach, and an ideal institute would be strong in both. A present danger to school programs of this sort is the set of constraints laid down by No Child Left Behind and its state-required corollaries, under which a nonprofit can become merely a surrogate for overstretched schools, an agent of delivery of rote facts to satisfy standardized testing: the antithesis of discovery.

Not that there is no place for rote learning in place-based education: quite the opposite. Comstock and her many emulators (Pyle, 2001) stressed the learning of names and lifeways in the classroom, augmented by discovery afield. This can be a powerful combination, more potent than either element without the other. One reason people shrink from learning flora and fauna is that they feel they can never catch up, so why learn any? Another is that they never get much of a chance to see the application of the admittedly tedious memory-work in the real—actually real—world. All of the private, nonprofit initiatives help redress the deficit in ecological literacy, but they are limited by their ambit and funding, the small part of the population they can reach, and their distance from population centers. And, although each of them has scholarship programs, they remain foreign to most people of little means, and overwhelmingly White.

Clearly, nature study must extend well beyond the wildlands into the cities themselves. Some well established nature centers recognize this, and act on it. The Nature Center at Shaker Lakes is situated in one of Cleveland, Ohio's most affluent districts, but not far from sections of radically lesser means. The center offers nature study services to children and parents from both clienteles, and the shrinking one in between, hoping to lessen the distinctions in at least this one area.

Happily, so-called waste ground and vacant lots are well suited to nature discovery, if safety issues can be overcome (Pyle, 1993). But as mentioned before, in-filling and gentrification are making an endangered species of vacant lots. This is not the case everywhere: Yale forest sociologist William Burch told an audience of nature reserve professionals recently that Detroit's brownfields represent a huge gift of potential urban forests, though the stands may consist largely of ailanthus. Think, he was suggesting, what this undervalued resource could represent to the children of Detroit, who are unlikely to venture outside the inner city to the nature centers of suburbia. "Detroit experienced a decline in population of 600,000 people between 1965 and 1990 alone," wrote Grove and colleagues (Grove, Vachta, McDonough, & Burch, 1993, p. 25), "as over 45,000 families moved out of Detroit. This led to a large number of vacant homes in the city; the problem became so severe that in 1989 the city instituted a widespread demolition project to remove 'dangerous and abandoned' buildings. Consequently, Detroit lost 60,385 housing units resulting in 65,000 vacant lots." Such hand-me-down habitats are what British naturalist Mabey (1973) calls "unofficial countryside," and they may support a surprising degree of natural diversity, accepting that some proportion of the biota will be alien, adventitious species, like the pandemic primates currently considering these topics.

So what may be done? Or rather, what *must* be done? If one accepts, as I do, that global ecocatastrophe is all but certain under the current model of population growth and capitalist expansion (Monbiot, 2005; Speth, 2002), and that the American public in its ecological illiteracy is subject to lulling by ideological or Pollyannish bromides to the contrary (Crichton, 2005), then it follows that greater collective knowledge of the way the world works in all its constituent parts may lead to resistance at the polls or in the streets. It is far from certain at this point that citizen activism could forestall, let alone prevent, systemic collapse or disruption. But it is clear that without a popular revolt against ecological forfeit on the alter of war, domination, and global economic growth, no such reversal will be possible. Environmental scholar Thomas Fleischner (2005) shows why those moved by natural history experience a deep commitment toward conservation. "Natural history holds promise of a wiser, more grounded form of resource management," he insists, "not only because of more informed science, but also because of gratitude for the uplifting beauty of the world, and the humility this engenders" (p. 13).

It follows that no measure could be more salutary when it comes to remedial education for the people and the land than reinstatement of Nature Study as a regular part of every school day. If people knew even a little about the plants, animals, soils, waters, and atmospherics of their places, and how they fit together in a fragile and functioning whole that utterly supports us, I don't believe they would permit our present course. This is why Nature Study writ large is a radical, subversive, even deeply seditious act against the status quo.

In response to the enthusiastic reception for his book *Last Child in the Woods*, Richard Louv has founded the Children and Nature Network. Already this initiative has seen anti-nature deficit legislation introduced in several states. "No one among us," wrote Louv (2007), "wants to be a member of the last generation to pass on to its children the joy of playing outside in nature." Changing the curricula of all school systems to replace No Child Left Behind with No Child Left Inside may be a quixotic goal given the current Congress and legislatures. Meanwhile, I can imagine a scenario to advance many of the same goals. It has three parts. Some of these are parallel with a program for general social change in this direction that I put forward in an essay entitled "Nature Matrix: Reconnecting People and Nature" (Pyle, 2003), but they are more specific:

1. Give all possible support and encouragement to existing place-based education programs as mentioned earlier, and elsewhere in this book. They aren't enough, but they help hold the dike against utter anthropecentrist extremes from bursting ("anthropecentrism" here being ironic because what is defined that way is by logical extension misanthropic).

2. Press school districts and school boards in every way possible to increase resources and mandates for place-based programs, classes, clubs, and field trips, drawing on local amateur naturalists whenever possible, and reinstating a sense that local flora and fauna are as well worth knowing as numbers, letters, and computer screens. Press to substitute direct experience for virtual encounter whenever possible. Be relentless and tedious in this, both with educators and children themselves. Encourage parents to banish television and restrict computer time to nighttime hours between homework and bedtime.

3. Establish a loose system of alternative open space reservations where the primary function is seen not as native plant and animal protection as much as child exploration and autodidactic play. Make these as large as possible. Provide no trails, interpretation, or rules, other than kindness, no bullying, and no drugs or weapons. Furnish insect nets. Forts and treehouses allowed. Recruit parents for remote supervision: maintaining safe boundaries, without evident restriction, presence, or interference. Build small structures at the edge for purposes of shelter in case of violent weather, emergency bathrooms, picnics, and housing a modest library of field guides and references for questions that arise; perhaps also synoptic collections, and a simple lab. Such places could as easily be established in farmed-out fields and woods at the edge of Milwaukee as they could in the Tree of Heaven forests in downtown Detroit and the blackberry ravines of Seattle. Tax exemption and benefits

would need to be crafted to benefit both owners and donors of sites. Parents may need to sign releases from liability as a condition for turning their kids loose within.

Whether such a system of unofficial countryside reserves could duplicate the special place experience for children otherwise deprived, and thereby hold back the extinction of experience and the dangerous rise of nature deficit disorder, I cannot say. But it's worth a try. Whatever works to rub young noses in nature must be done, before the out-of-doors becomes as quaint to the average child as the slide rule or the slide projector, the film or the typewriter. Even if it takes something as radical as that gentle pursuit of yore, Nature Study.

REFERENCES

Cavallo, D. (1981). *Muscles and morals: Organized playgrounds and urban reform*, 1880–1920. Philadelphia: University of Pennsylvania Press.

Cranz, G. (1982). *The politics of park design: A history of urban parks in America*. Cambridge, MA: MIT Press.

Crichton, M. (2005, December 5). Let's stop scaring ourselves. *Parade*, 6–7.

Comstock, A. B. (1911). *Handbook for nature study*. Ithaca, NY: Comstock.

Finch, K. (2003, October–December). Extinction of experience: A challenge to nature centers? (or, how do you make a conservationist?) including several related sidebars by G. T. Maupin. *Directions*, 2–10.

Fleischner, T. L. (2005). Natural history and the deep roots of resource management. *Natural Resources Journal, 45*, 1–13.

Flicker, J. (2002). *Audubon, the second century: Connecting people with nature*. New York: National Audubon Society.

Grove, M., Vachta, K. E., McDonough, M. H., & Burch, W. R. (1993). The urban resources initiative: Benefits from forestry. In P. Gobster (Ed.), *Managing urban and high-use recreation settings*. General Technical Report NC-163. St. Paul, MN: U.S. Dept. of Agriculture, Forest Service, North Central Forest Experiment Station.

Kahn, P. H., Jr., & Kellert, S. R. (2002). *Children and nature: Psychological, sociocultural, and eolutionary investigations*. Cambridge, MA: MIT Press.

Keane, D. (2005). Butterflies, beer cans, and the peril inherent. *ISLE, 12*(1), 185–192.

Louv, R. (2005). *Last child in the woods: Saving our children from nature deficit disorder*. Chapel Hill, NC: Algonquin Books.

Louv, R. (2007). Leave no child inside. *Orion, 26*(2), 54–61.

Mabey, R. (1973). *The unofficial countryside*. London: Collins.

Marsh, G. J. (2005, Spring). *Under the road and whispering*. Unpublished manuscript, University of Montana, Missoula, MT.

McKenna, D. D., McKenna, K. M., Malcolm, S. B., & Berenbaum, M. R. (2001). Mortality of Lepidoptera along roadways in central Illinois. *Journal of the Lepidopterists' Society, 55*(2), 63–68.

McGinty, M. (2004, Fall). Wolverines, wonder, and wilderness, or, Why the wolverine matters to a kid who has never seen a racoon. *Clearing, 117,* 26–28.

Mergen, B. (2003). Review essay: Children and nature in history. *Environmental History, 6*(4), 643–669.

Monbiot, G. (2005, February 15). Mocking our dreams. *The Guardian,* 21.

Nabhan, G. P., & Trimble, S. (1994). *The geography of childhood: Why children need wild places.* Boston: Beacon Press.

Pyle, R. M. (1993). *The thunder tree: Lessons from an urban wildland.* Boston: Houghton Mifflin.

Pyle, R. M. (1998). Foreword to the 1998 edition, *The thunder tree* (paperback edition). New York: Lyons Press.

Pyle, R. M. (2000). *Walking the high ridge: Life as field trip.* Minneapolis, MN: Milkweed Editions.

Pyle, R. M. (2001). The rise and fall of natural history. *Orion, 20*(4), 8.

Pyle, R. M. (2002). Eden in a vacant lot: Special places, species, and kids in the neighborhood of life. In P. H. Kahn, Jr., & S. R. Kellert (Eds.), *Children and nature: Psychological, sociocultural, and evolutionary investigations* (pp. 305–327). Cambridge: MIT Press.

Pyle, R. M. (2003). Nature matrix: Reconnecting people and nature. *Oryx, 37*(2), 206–214.

Pyle, R. M. (in press). In praise of butterfly nets: A reply to David Keane. *ISLE.*

Robinson, M. W. (2005). Reply to "The birth of butterflying." *American Birding, 37*(4), 356, 358.

Sobel, D. (1993). *Children's special places; Exploring the role of forts, dens, and bush houses in middle childhood.* Tucson, AZ: Zephyr Press.

Speth, G. (2002). A new green regime: Attacking the root causes of global environmental deterioration. *Environment Yale, 1*(2), 20.

Stafford, K. (1986). *Having everything right.* Lewiston, ID: Confluence Press.

Sullivan, J. (2005, Spring). Tuesday Life Club. Unpublished manuscript, University of Montana, Missoula, MT.

Thomashow, M. (1995). *Ecological identity.* Cambridge, MA: MIT Press.

White, R. (2004). *Benefits for children of play in nature.* Retrieved on September 3, 2005, from http://whitehutchinson.com/children/articles/benefits.shtml.

Williams, B. (2005, Spring). An etiquette of place. Unpublished manuscript, University of Montana, Missoula, MT.

Wilson, E.O. (1994). *Naturalist.* Washington, DC: Island Press.

Winters, M. (2004, August 11). Get out and play! *Chinook Observer,* A4.

CHAPTER 9

Overlooked Opportunity
Students, Educators, and Education Advocates Contributing to Community and Economic Development

Rachel Tompkins

For the past 10 years, the Rural School and Community Trust has worked with rural schools and communities to engage young people as resources in community building and to support adults and youth to learn about what makes a good school and then act on that knowledge. We have also provided research and networking to groups working to improve state school policies (particularly finance systems) and helped to build understanding of the connections between good schools and healthy, thriving communities.

Today the Rural Trust has success stories to tell about accomplishments and lessons learned from this decade of work. Beginning inside schools in very diverse places in the United States, educators and students have connected with business leaders, government officials, and community activists to fashion academically challenging curricula that connect students with their culture, with solving community problems, and with understanding their economies. In Howard, South Dakota, inspired teachers have made their schools and their students active partners in community and economic development. In Edcouch-Elsa, Texas, young people have returned home to create a school-based organization, the Llano Grande Center, that is committed to engaging young people and their families in building on the strengths of their community.

In other places in the country, rural citizens concerned with the quality of their schools and the future of their communities have fought for well-financed and well-managed schools, with excellent teachers close to home. In low-income rural communities in West Virginia, South Carolina, Arkansas, and Mississippi, parents and other community members have studied issues, devised solutions, and built public support for education improvements or have fought off bad policy ideas. They are building new organizations, connecting former isolated rural individuals across communities in associations that cross boundaries of age, race, geography, and class. In so doing, they have increased the number, quality, and diversity of community leaders, added capacity for community problem solving, and expanded democracy.

These stories from diverse parts of the country give life to the idea that schools as institutions are an important, although often overlooked, component of community and economic development. These stories are about active rural citizens of all ages—students included—and their homegrown organizations fighting efforts to close local schools, demanding more of their schools, and creating new politically effective organizations. In their work, they contribute to school improvement and help build more sustainable communities. Similarly, students and teachers combining school learning with community improvement add to a community's ability to solve problems and enact programs of improvement. Some of these success stories begin with activists in the community, pushing on and working with educators to build stronger schools and better communities. Others begin in the school, with educators understanding that students can learn and contribute to their communities at the same time. Indeed, no matter where the source, the stories are about schools and communities getting better together, sometimes with and because of each other, sometimes in spite of each other, and in creative conflict.

The opportunity to harness and build on the lessons learned from this work will be lost unless rural community and economic development professionals, practitioners, and local government officials understand and act to use the potential. Although rural development strategies have shifted in the past 25 years from looking only to external sources for solutions to focusing on building local strengths, policymakers and practitioners concerned with development still do not often include schools, educators, education activists, and students as resources and allies in their strategies. Educators, struggling to meet requirements of standards and accountability systems with high-stakes tests as the only outcome measure, are concerned that civic education and place-based learning will not immediately raise test scores. And they worry that they lack competence to engage students in real work in the community that is also challenging academically. Interestingly, it is the education activists in low-income communities who most often understand the connections between their work to improve schools and their work to improve their communities generally.

This chapter lays out the changes in rural America that have altered strategies of rural development, outlines the role of schools in community and economic development, and tells six stories from the work of the Rural Trust that are examples of the potential connections. It concludes with some lessons learned and some ideas for seizing the opportunities suggested by the stories.

CHANGES IN RURAL AMERICA

The market forces of the global economy, the telecommunications revolution, and government policies that continue to encourage concentration, centralization, and standardization have profoundly altered rural America at the beginning of the 21st century. As one writer puts it:

> The increasing competitive global economy has forced major restructuring in rural regions and communities in many painful ways—whether we are talking about prices for farm commodities or the collapse of textile and carpet manufacturing or the structure of the retail sector. (Dabson, 2005, p. 1)

As rural America has changed, so, too, have ideas and appropriate strategies for rural development. Until the early 1980s, conventional wisdom had it that rural development depended on recruiting industry from elsewhere to employ local people. For many years, rural regions were able to recruit manufacturing enterprises interested in cheap labor, easy access to natural resources, and limited regulation. States competed to see who could give the most land, infrastructure, and tax breaks to attract industry. Every small town either had or was working hard to get an industrial park into which it could lure a factory.

While this strategy always had a handful of winners and many losers, it was not until the global economy became a reality that rural places understood that not enough of them could win for this to be a very effective strategy. When the competition was Mexico or Brazil or Indonesia, with wages that were pennies on the dollar to the minimum wage, there was no way that towns in the United States could compete for or retain those firms driven to pay the lowest wages.

In the same period, natural resource extraction-based economies in rural regions faced international competition and relentless pressure to consolidate into larger units, in part driven by government policy, but also because of competition. Communities that were dependent on timber or coal or fish or cattle all suffered losses in a number of enterprises due to consolidation or markets lost to foreign competition. Regulation to protect endangered species and to curb damaging air and water pollution contributed to the existing economic difficulties of marginal farms and became a lightning rod for criticism. Twenty farms turned into one large farm; mines and sawmills closed; employment plummeted. Many of these communities joined the search for low-wage manufacturing.

While the global movement of capital was one impetus for changes in thinking on rural development, another was the technological revolution that built a communication highway connecting even the most remote places to the mainstream grid. Rural towns could now be locations for enterprises that used communications technology as a main part of their business, such as call centers for online retailers, insurance, and utility payments. This also contributed to a surge in enthusiasm for entrepreneurship—small niche information-related businesses could be created in small towns at lower cost to supply and serve larger firms. And for professionals, a "Lone Eagle" operation could be located anywhere using a satellite dish, Internet access, and UPS or FedEx to move information back and forth.

Thus over the past two decades, strategies pursued for rural economic development have shifted from recruiting industry externally to cultivating entrepreneurship locally and building on community assets. There is more attention now to bringing rural people together in communities and regions in order to understand economic and demographic changes that are affecting their lives and to develop a new shared vision for their economy and communities. The new language of building or strengthening social capital has become a common parlance in many rural places. Even the policies and practices aimed at poverty reduction have begun to focus on asset-building strategies.

In the same period, equally profound changes have come in expectations, policies, and practices in public schools. School systems are now expected to teach all children to high levels and are held accountable through state standards and systems of testing. This centralization and standardization of school curriculum conflicts with traditions of local control of schools and with the efforts of local citizens to have schools serve as important partners in community development. In fact, state and federally mandated school policies and their even more restrictive implementation often run counter to promising practices in asset-based community and economic development.

ASSET-BASED RURAL COMMUNITY DEVELOPMENT

Three separate and interrelated strands of research and practice have contributed to current thinking about asset-based development: (a) Kretzman and McKnight's inner-city work in Chicago (1993); (b) social capital studies made popular by Putnam (1993, 2000); and (c) the multiple capitals analysis of Cornelia and Jan Flora (Flora & Flora, 1993; Flora, Flora, & Key, 2004).

The same economic forces that affected rural America sent thousands of industrial jobs out of central cities, leaving only low-paying service jobs for neighborhood residents and high-paying professional jobs for people who live in the suburbs or in gentrifying neighborhoods. Older city neighborhoods needed new strategies to create opportunity. These changes in urban America led a group of policy researchers at Northwestern University, headed by John McKnight and John Kretzman, to rethink strategies for community development in poor inner-city neighborhoods in Chicago.

McKnight and Kretzman rejected the traditional path of describing the needs or deficiencies of these urban neighborhoods in order to acquire services. They viewed this thinking as locking urban community members into being consumers and never producers, into being clients of services rather than self-reliant problem solvers. They were also persuaded by historic evidence that community development occurs when local people are committed and invest their time and energy in the effort. And they were convinced that most urban communities would never receive the kind of external help from either private investment or public largesse that would lead to significant development.

In related research, Putnam's (1993) work on regional development in Italy concluded that relationships of trust and reciprocity developed over centuries of associational life in northern Italy explained why development occurred there and not in the south, where patron–client relationships dominated in both public and private life. He used the term *social capital* to describe these relationships, drawing on the earlier work of Bourdieu (1986) and Coleman (1988, 1990). He expanded on this concept in a very popular book on the United States called *Bowling Alone* (2000), which suggested that the United States was losing its stock of social capital. Today there is a cottage industry of study on social capital and many projects designed to develop it (see the Web site for Saguaro Seminar in references). But there is general agreement that building social capital alone will not lead to economic improvements and that more complex ideas are needed.

In the early 1980s, the Floras and others (Flora, Gale, Schmidt, Green, & Flora, 1993; Green, Flora, Flora, & Schmidt, 1993) analyzed rural communities that thrived and those that did not and found that the thriving communities had a combination of local leadership, entrepreneurship, and relationships built within the community and with outside expertise. Over the next several years, Cornelia Flora expanded Putnam's analysis to incorporate the multiple capitals needed for development—human, financial, social, cultural, physical, environmental, and political (Flora et al., 2004).

Within the economic development community, there is increasing interest in entrepreneurship as the most appropriate strategy for rural regions, in part because recruitment and retention no longer work and in part because it fits best with an asset strategy. The rural economy is composed largely of small enterprises that are often the most dynamic and innovative parts of any economy. And small enterprise fits the scale of the rural environment. A recent competition by the Kellogg Foundation for proposals to build stronger community systems of support for entrepreneurship netted 182 proposals from 47 states involving over 2,000 organizations.

The asset-based development path espoused by McKnight and Kretzman, reinforced by Putnam's research on social capital, and highlighted by the Floras' continuing work, is to build development strategies on the capacities, skills, and capital of people and communities. All of these community-connected researchers have developed tools for mapping community assets—assets of individuals, associations, and institutions. Kretzman and McKnight, working in some very low-income places where citizens have been convinced they have little to offer, begin by encouraging a listing of the gifts, skills, and capacities of individuals. Their approach acknowledges that everyone is gifted, everyone has something to contribute.

For Putnam and the social capitalists, mapping the network of formal and informal community associations is a critical part of understanding where development begins. For the Floras and other community developers, mapping the formal institutions is critical—businesses, churches, schools and colleges, libraries, health care institutions, and the like—anything that could be construed as an asset. All are convinced by evidence from both U.S. and international research and practice that planning for the future based on a careful assessment of community assets leads to economic choices that distribute benefits more broadly in the community. Communities develop in a much more sustainable way when they use external resources wisely, but are not totally dependent on them.

THE DISCONNECT BETWEEN COMMUNITY DEVELOPMENT AND SCHOOLS

The connection between asset-based rural development thinking and schools is, on the surface, obvious. Schools are a clearly evident asset in a rural community—filling economic, social, cultural, recreational, and political roles as well as their traditional educational role. The school building itself, along with its gymnasium, auditorium, cafeteria, and playing fields, serves as a community center in many places. It is the location of cultural and sporting events, where local cooks prepare dinners for visiting dignitaries, the meeting place for community discussion of major issues, and the location of voting booths for elections. In several communities that we know about, it is also the location for weddings and funerals too large for small country churches. Perhaps most importantly, school students and teachers are resources and can become incredible assets for community problem solving and planning.

While community leaders and local government officials in rural places now routinely think about rural development as asset building—taking advantage of the "capital" that exists in their communities and strengthening that as a way to maintain or grow their economy—not very many of them engage schools or educators in community planning and action. They tend to focus on housing, health care, social services, and job creation strategies. Even those who work on early childhood education and adult education tend to do so apart from the school system. Likewise, educators who believe that the best education connects students to real-world problem solving and to the culture, history, economy, and natural resources of their place have not made many connections to the community and economic developers.

The reasons for this are numerous but they cluster around two factors: community development activists find school officials unapproachable, bound by too many bureaucratic rules and practices; educators often do not believe they have the time or skill to engage students in place-based work and are worried that such work will distract from the push for higher test scores. Neither side has had much experience or training in developing collaborative relationships. And so each waits for the other to initiate the conversations and to provide the energy and leadership to connect and plan together (Coalition for Community Schools, 2002). In some communities with a history of racial or class divisions, a legacy of distrust must be overcome. In other places, schools are perceived by community activists as engines of talent removal or of cultural destruction (e.g., in Native places), and "community" is viewed by school officials as something to liberate kids from. Both groups have a lot of practitioners who reject the premises of the other group.

THE ROLE OF SCHOOLS IN COMMUNITY AND ECONOMIC DEVELOPMENT

Schools produce social capital—educated students—that is very often not reinvested in the local community, as many students leave upon graduation or are not being used to their fullest potential as community members while in school. Therefore, much of the local investment in rural schooling is ultimately lost (Beaulieu & Mulkey, 1995; Gibbs, Swaim, & Teixeira, 1998). Rural citizens bemoan the loss of young people, and researchers write about the "brain drain," but few remedies have even been tried. Most economic developers talk about the importance of an educated workforce and espouse increased percentages of students going on to college and developing professional skills, but they do not link that to strategies and policies that might encourage these well-educated young people to stay in a rural place. The most ubiquitous rural school policy of the last 50 years—school consolidation—has, in fact, further exacerbated population decline and sent even more young people away from rural places. Keeping a small school in a rural community is literally a life or death matter for the community.

Economically, schools are the largest employer, especially in many poor rural communities. The purchasing power of the school and its employees makes up a large percentage of local retail sales. They are therefore an anchor, a catalyst, and an economic engine in many rural communities. Even though school consolidation has been the most prevalent rural school policy of the last century, little attention has been focused on what is lost when schools close. A small number of studies have chronicled the loss in retail sales, bank loans, and the number of businesses overall when a school closes. Others have noted the accelerated population decline in towns that close their school (Lawrence et al., 2002).

A recent study by Cornell University sociologist Thomas A. Lyson (2002) focused on 352 incorporated villages and towns with populations of under 2,500 in New York State. He divided these communities into two groups—the 71 with 500 or fewer people, and the 281 with more than 500 people. Almost three fourths of the larger group had a school (73.7%), whereas only about half (52.1%) of the smaller group did. Historical data indicate that nearly all of the towns and villages had a school at one time. Those with and without schools in each of the size categories have similar age-level profiles, percentage of households with children, and percentage of children enrolled in school. But the socio-economic differences between them are powerful. The study also found that among the smallest towns and villages:

- Sixty percent of the communities with schools saw population growth from 1990 to 2000; only 46% of those without schools grew.
- Average housing values in the communities with schools are 25% higher than in those without schools. Their houses are newer, and more likely to be served by municipal water and sewer systems.
- Communities with schools enjoy higher per capita incomes, a more equal distribution of income, less per capita income from public assistance, less poverty, and less child poverty.
- Communities with schools have more professional, managerial, and executive workers; more households with self-employment income; 57% higher per capita income from self-employment; a higher percentage of residents who work in the village; and fewer workers who commute more than 15 minutes to their jobs (Lyson, 2002).

The differences between larger rural communities with schools and those without were similar, but not as extreme as the differences in the smaller communities. It is clear from Lyson's report that the smaller the community, the more having a school matters. In short, if a community has a school, it is likely to be more stable and more prosperous, with more people working close to home in jobs in which they are decision makers.

In addition to this powerful institutional role of schools in the local economy, the people in schools can become significant assets for planning and implementing community building ideas. Students and teachers can be researchers, planners, conveners, project managers, and leaders in community development efforts as part of the regular school curriculum. Students can learn the skills of business planning while actually starting a business through entrepreneurship classes (Hobbs, 1995).

The chapters in this book outline many examples of this work. In addition to student learning and leadership, place-based education can also support adult learning broadly conceived. Adults in the community, parents and others, who come together to work for improved schooling are building their civic competence, their ability to analyze complex issues, participate in dialogue and debate, make decisions, move an agenda to action, and lead. In low-income communities where adults have often been marginalized, these are significant personal and organizational assets essential to strengthening democracy in each community and altogether in the nation. Indeed, the skills of active citizenship in this democracy are strengthened for everyone in a process that engages students, educators, and community members in carrying out and improving instruction.

BEGINNING IN THE SCHOOL

Educators and students have made important contributions to community and economic development in several communities in which the Rural Trust has worked. Two examples are Howard High School in Miner County, South Dakota, and the Llano Grande Center at Edcouch-Elsa High School in South Texas. In both places, more than a decade of school and community collaboration has supported both student learning and community sustainability.

Howard, South Dakota

In 1995, the Howard School District, through the Program for Rural School and Community Renewal at South Dakota State University, began receiving funding totaling $150,000 over 4 years from the Annenberg Rural Challenge (the predecessor of the Rural Trust) for projects to connect rural schools with their communities (Miner County Rural Revitalization Web site, www.mccr.net). The project was based on the ideas that change was needed for the community to sustain itself and that youth were more open to making that change. They also believed that adults might really listen to the ideas of young people. The Howard Rural Challenge involved teachers, students, and community residents focused on developing a sustainable community that:

- Met the basic needs of the people (food, water, shelter, clothing, jobs); that is, the community is only as well off as its most destitute citizen.

- Grew and developed within its ecological limits; that is, the people of the community must inhabit it in ways that sustain it for future generations.

The first step was to create a Rural Resource Center in the school and encourage community members to come visit and interact with the students. Students, staff, and community members worked together on special themes throughout the years, learning more about the place where they live. For one project, students interviewed all the veterans in their community and collected memorabilia from several wars for display in the Resource Center. A community celebration recognized all of the veterans and their stories, bringing dozens of people with no children in school into the school building to see student work.

The Future Business Leaders of America students conducted a community cash flow study investigating where residents spent their money and their views of local businesses. Students put together a presentation describing changes residents would like to see in Main Street businesses, for example, evening hours and an ATM machine at the bank. They also analyzed the sales necessary to generate tax revenue to support the town budget and shared that with the community. By both making residents more aware of the need to spend locally and also making businesses more aware of community needs, gross sales in Howard increased 41.1% in the following year and stabilized over the next 3 years. Other student-led projects included widely attended adult computer training classes, obtaining a U.S. Department of Agriculture grant for a state-of-the-art greenhouse and community garden, a schoolwide study of cancer clusters in the county, and several community celebrations.

The Howard Rural Challenge sponsored community vision meetings in Fall 1997, bringing together people from Miner County to discuss concerns and issues. Students and adults worked together setting up the agenda and presentations. Three large meetings of about 150 people were held, interspersed by two small meetings consisting of 15 to 17 people meeting at 12 to 14 homes. The small groups included a mix of youth, elderly, farmers, businesspeople, clergy, teachers, and low- and high-income residents. Participants discussed Miner County's weaknesses and strengths and got to know each other. A Miner County Task Force, made up of 22 members from different parts of the county, including youth and elderly, evolved from the community visioning meetings to work on economic development and county beautification, the top priorities identified in the meetings.

As a result of this work, Miner County was selected by the Northwest Area Foundation as one of the places in the northern Great Plains that showed promise for reducing poverty and developing a thriving economy. The Foundation resources have enabled the county to create Miner County Community Revitalization (MCCR), a community nonprofit that guides the implementation of a 10-year community plan. Committees that include young people and adults work on six issues considered critical: economic development; agriculture and conservation; housing; education and youth; elderly; and health care. An outreach committee was added to encourage additional involvement in revitalization, especially among those most disadvantaged and least heard.

MCCR has struggled with the challenges of planning, building community understanding and involvement, and initiating successful projects. Tangible projects are important for building community support and motivation. New businesses in wind energy production and maintenance and organic beef production and sales, together with housing developments and community service projects, are all solid evidence of progress (Eig, 2005).

Edcouch-Elsa, Texas

The Llano Grande Center for Research and Development, located at Edcouch-Elsa High School, has evolved from an oral history project into a regional intellectual and economic nerve center for Mexican-American communities in South Texas (adapted from Null, 2001). Students working through the Llano Grande Center have documented the historical contributions of the people of Mexican descent who pioneered, settled, and worked in the area and have implemented many other projects that have revitalized the region's educational, cultural, civic, and economic life. The work was started by Francisco Guajardo, a graduate of the school who went to the University of Texas at Austin and returned home to teach and encourage others to follow his path. In the 15 years since Francisco returned, hundreds of students have gone to college (many attending the most selective colleges in the United States), graduated, and continued their connection to the center whether they return to South Texas or work elsewhere. "The Ivy League college effort is not important in and of itself," says Guajardo. "What matters is that the Ivy League symbolizes what we can accomplish, what can be possible. Students in our schools are lifting their sights and aiming for a future based on knowledge, skills, and information" (in Null, 2001). A supportive and often informal network of teachers, students, alumni, and community members continues to collaborate and expand on the objectives they defined when they began the center.

The children involved in the Llano Grande Center programs come from two of Texas's poorest school districts, where about 60% of children are from families living below the federal poverty line. Agriculture, the mainstay of the economy for decades, has declined, unemployment is high, and the largest employer is the school district. Most parents of Edcouch-Elsa students never finished high school and have a limited grasp of English. Most have worked as agricultural laborers in the area and traveled the migrant routes. Today, about 40% of Edcouch-Elsa High School students still follow the crops with their families. Within a few weeks, the school population can expand or shrink by hundreds of students. Many students attend two school systems.

Llano Grande student researchers have interviewed older residents and reconstructed the history of the region from the perspective of the workers. These have been recorded, transcribed, and archived by students— usually in Spanish. Then they are translated and the transcriptions are edited into narratives for publication in both English and Spanish, thereby honing the dual language skills of these students and making them very successful on SAT tests in English composition and Spanish. The narratives now supplement regular history books in elementary schools and are studied and used by children at all grade levels. Students have reworked the stories into documentaries, plays, and other narratives that have been used by the Smithsonian and PBS in major productions.

All of this attention to learning connected to the families, traditions, and struggles of the region has resulted in increased community involvement in the school, higher motivation for learning, and much improved academic outcomes. Indeed, since 1998, this school with many very poor children has been successful on the Texas achievement tests and ranks as a "recognized school."

Equally important has been the work of the Llano Grande Center in developing job opportunities for students, alumni, and others who have developed skills in information research, collection, and management. At one point, employees and interns, most of them students, were transcribing oral history records on a contract basis for the King Ranch; the Institute of Texan Cultures at the University of Texas, San Antonio; and Texas A&M University–Kingsville. A Houston executive of a survey research firm, whose mother was interviewed by Llano Grande oral history researchers, helped students learn survey research skills, which, coupled with their excellent ability to speak two languages, makes them qualified for bilingual interviewing by the firm. The Center continues to create good jobs for young professionals, including organizing community forums, running a Spanish immersion institute, operating digital storytelling workshops, and conducting teacher training workshops and youth leadership trainings. The Edcouch Chamber of Commerce is located in the Center's office in the school. A returning graduate developed several plans for job-creating enterprises. These include a publishing house to print items for the school and the local government that would be processed in a nearby city without a local enterprise and a Spanish Language Immersion Program that uses Spanish-speaking elders in the community as tutors and mentors for professionals who must be bilingual to work successfully in South Texas business, health care, or government positions. Students also learn to write grant proposals in the Social Science Research Methods high school class and have been successful in generating funds for community and school projects.

Many outstanding college graduates have returned to teach in the school and to work in the communities. Other school alumni who do not return remain part of the e-mail network of the Center and assist the community in learning about grant and business opportunities.

These two examples illustrate the diverse ways students can be engaged in community and economic development. But there are others. For example, REAL Enterprises (e.g., Rural Entrepreneurship through Action Learning; online at www.realenterprises.org) has pioneered strong school curricula teaching young people business-planning skills and helping them prepare and seek investment for real businesses in their communities. Operating in several states, REAL is the beginning of what could be a much more systematic K–12 entrepreneurship training effort.

BEGINNING IN THE COMMUNITY

In many regions of the country, educators are not the leaders in developing place-based curriculum and have, in fact, distanced themselves from the surrounding community. Educators and other community elites sometimes view low-income and working-class parents as incapable of contributing to student learning or making good decisions about school policy. In places such as these, curriculum connected to place does not flourish unless citizens organize themselves and advocate for a curriculum that honors their culture and contributions.

Connecting school and community begins with parents and community members who insist on being involved in the school in more than peripheral ways. In places where educators do not have high expectations for children and where large achievement gaps exist for minority and poor children, parents and citizens often begin by demanding changes in the way the school operates. School officials may resist the pressure. Working through these initial exchanges to build a common school and community partnership takes time and patience. School officials have to change expectations and practice; community members need to learn about educational practices and understand those that are effective for their children. They must also develop the kind of civic competence that enables them to work effectively with school boards and school systems. The Rural Trust has worked with several of these groups from West Virginia and South Carolina to Mississippi. Their members have become knowledgeable, skillful, persistent advocates for children, for small community-based schools, and for collaborative school and community relationships.[1] Once this community-school relationship develops, place-based learning can flourish.

Challenge West Virginia

In West Virginia, poor parents won a lawsuit declaring the state school finance system to be unconstitutional in 1974. Over the next 25 years, the state closed hundreds of schools, arguing that large consolidated schools that were centrally located in each county were the only way to meet the State Supreme Court's requirements for funding. By the mid-1990s, only a few community high schools remained, and elementary schools began to be consolidated. Long bus rides over winding mountain roads—some as long as 2 hours each way—started becoming the rule for 6-year-olds as it had been for 16-year-olds.

Starting in 1997 with funds from the Annenberg Rural Challenge, Challenge West Virginia, a small nonprofit organization, began to create chapters of parents and interested citizens in rural counties across the state committed to maintaining and improving small community schools. The county chapters sent one person, called a community fellow, to monthly meetings where they shared information about activities and issues in their counties and were briefed on a variety of education issues. The fellows studied state policy and recommended that bus rides for elementary children be capped at 30 minutes each way and that no child of any age ride a bus more than one hour each way. Dismissed for many years as backward rabble-rousers, the fellows continued to build their capacity and expand their numbers. And armed with a growing pile of research, they continued to educate policymakers about the benefits of small schools close to home.

In 2002, a couple of enterprising education reporters for the state newspaper, the *Charleston Gazette*, began to study the impact of school consolidation. They found that the claims made by proponents were unfounded—there were actually more administrators not fewer, the promised rich curricula had not materialized in the consolidated high schools, no money had been saved, and the state spent more dollars on transportation per pupil than any other state. The paper had long been a supporter of consolidation, but changed its editorial stance in part because one of the reporters actually lived a "day in the life" of a student, going to school in one of the state's mountainous counties, riding the bus, and attending school. His view was that no one should be required to do that every day. The series won national journalism awards including Education Writer of the Year from the Education Writers Association (Eyre & Finn, 2003).

Today, Challenge West Virginia has chapters in more than half of West Virginia's counties and can rally hundreds to support positions on improving community-based schools. Legislation limiting bus rides was introduced in 2005 as one of the Governor's primary pieces of legislation. Although it did not pass, Governor Manchin made it clear that he is committed to halting the rush to consolidation and will be able, through his appointments to the State Board of Education and to the State School Building Authority, to influence policies for years to come.

Fellows who have been part of Challenge West Virginia have been elected to school boards in their counties and have learned the skills of governance, developing policy alternatives, and transparent decision making. They have begun to focus more attention on improving the quality of instruction in the schools and on implementing place-based curricula. Using their newfound knowledge and skills, they are poised to connect their schools to asset-based community development.

South Carolina Rural Education Grassroots Committee

The South Carolina Rural Education Grassroots Committee began 4 years ago with assistance from the South Carolina Appleseed Legal Justice Center and the Rural Trust as a group of rural people concerned about their schools and willing to spend a year of study, thinking, and talking about good education policy for their children and communities (South Carolina Rural Education Grassroots Committee, 2003). They made six broad recommendations in a report at the end of the year:

1. Strengthening rural communities is an important first step in improving rural schools.
2. Districts should create a positive learning environment, evaluate school discipline policies to reduce the disproportionately high number of minority exclusions, and report progress to the community.
3. The achievement gap should be eliminated and local communities should be actively involved in setting goals for closing the gap.
4. School leaders should provide both inexperienced and veteran teachers with the tools they need to be successful with diverse groups of students.
5. All school boards should be elected in nonpartisan elections.
6. Resources should be provided by the state to cover the actual cost of providing children with the opportunities they need to meet state and federal standards.

While this group of concerned rural citizens from around the state called upon policymakers and educators to make changes, they also outlined their responsibilities as parents, businesspeople, government officials, and community leaders to do their part to help make the necessary changes. And they have kept their part of the bargain.

They have added members to their group in the past 3 years, and they continue to meet monthly to study school improvement ideas and proposed policies. They regularly attend their local school board meetings, attended sessions of the trial on the constitutionality of the school finance system, and participated with urban parents and community leaders in advocating for increased funding for schools. Several members are active as tutors and supporters to help children achieve high levels of reading. Some members are active in local community improvement groups on South Carolina's island communities and have engaged young people as active members of their groups. They have worked to maintain historic school buildings and use them as community centers. The Rural Trust is also working with two school board members and teachers and students in two schools on a civic engagement curriculum.

In 2005, the Grassroots Committee worked with African-American church groups to educate the public about tuition tax credit bills. These bills promised to "put parents in charge," but would have siphoned public money to existing students in the state's large network of private schools, most of which were created as segregation academies following the *Brown* decision. Despite strong support from the Governor and private school supporters, the bill was defeated.

South Carolina has a growing and effective network of local community development corporations (CDCs) and a strong state CDC association. To date, they have not connected much with the Grassroots Committee, but they share common aims of building local capacity in low-income communities and should become allies and supporters of each other's work. As students engage more in community work, it may be possible to build these alliances. Even without this connection, the South Carolina rural community activists are a force for maintaining and improving local schools.

Mississippi Education Working Group/Southern Echo

The Mississippi Education Working Group (MEWG) is a collaboration of grassroots community groups working through an intergenerational model to create a quality, first-rate public education system for their respective communities. They pool their strength and resources, enabling parents and students to influence the formation of education policies at the local level, and also to join forces across community lines to impact the formation of education policies at the state level.

MEWG operates as part of a long-standing civil rights group called Southern Echo and concentrates its local organizing work in 13 school districts and 11 counties, within the Mississippi Delta and in the southwest part of the state. At the state level, the impact of the organizing work on education policy affects all 152 Mississippi school districts, but focuses on equality of educational opportunity delivered in the 35 counties that serve an African-American majority.

MEWG provides a systematic program of training, technical, and legal assistance for grassroots community organizations to build the capacity of parents and students to interact knowledgeably and effectively with school officials and elected representatives. Each local group creates a clear vision, effective strategies, and meaningful programs to form a foundation that will broaden the base of support needed to transform the public education system. In part, the training is aimed at providing community people with an understanding of where they have been, where they are, and where they need to go so that they can work honestly and fearlessly toward their goals.

MEWG has many local and state successes. Southern Echo and MEWG helped get Mississippi's school aid formula fully funded for the first time in history in 2003, and in 2005, helped prevent adoption of a budget filled with education cuts. They also won passage of a comprehensive Juvenile Justice Reform Act that replaces incarceration with teaching, learning, and social services for nonviolent juvenile offenders, earning formal praise from the Legislature for its efforts. Less visible but as important, MEWG members are running for and getting elected to their local school boards.

At the local level, community members in one county successfully challenged the practice of allowing citizens who do not reside in their school district to vote for the district's superintendent. In yet another success, a local community group protested the lack of special education services and, as a result, were able to air their concerns during a visit scheduled for this purpose by an associate state superintendent. This associate superintendent also set up hearings in eight other sites in Mississippi, including three in the Delta, to hear additional parental concerns. He used the information to prepare the job description and work plan for a new state director of special education.

In these four states, citizens in low-income communities have developed knowledge and skills to be effective advocates for their children. They are committed to education for their children that develops their citizenship knowledge, skills, and dispositions as well as the knowledge and skills for college and work. Many members of these groups are now running for school board and other local offices and are assuming leadership roles in community development. In fact, many of these education activists discovered their interest in government and public issues while part of community improvement associations and started working on education issues because they understood that schools and education are essential to thriving communities.

These groups of education activists are excellent examples of expanding social capital through strong associations, building human capital by increasing the knowledge of citizens, and increasing political capital by effectively organizing to influence public decisions. The research from both Putnam and the Floras would argue that these are significant community assets essential for community and economic development. If they were joined with the community and economic development groups whose work is focused on building physical (houses, businesses, infrastructure) and financial (venture capital, loan funds) capital, a broad strategy of tackling persistent areas of poverty could be pursued.

One excellent method of encouraging these types of connections is engaging educators and students either with the community development organizations doing research and analysis projects for community planning (as in Howard, South Dakota) or with education activists in school improvement and community pride projects (as in Edcouch and Elsa, Texas). As in all reciprocal relationships, the in-school activities of places like Howard and Edcouch-Elsa cannot be sustained absent active community support for retaining and improving small schools and for generating the resources necessary to recruit and retain competent teachers. When schools and communities build collaborative relationships place-based learning thrives.

LESSONS LEARNED

Schools as institutions are significant assets for community and economic development. Maintaining small schools in rural communities is an important key to sustaining the community. Losing a school in a rural community already suffering population decline is a sure way for decline to continue and increase. Therefore, community and economic development organizations should join in efforts to maintain and improve existing small schools. They should also offer innovative solutions that join a community's need for housing, health, job creation, and other investments to the school.

Students, teachers and education activists are important collaborators for asset-based community economic development. Students have talent, energy, and ideas that can contribute to community efforts to reinvent the economy or reinvigorate a community. They can learn to do good research and hone their writing skills by writing good grant proposals, applying for historic or scenic designations for town attractions, or developing brochures for tourists, all for towns that have no staff to do those tasks. They can learn science by studying animal and fish habitat for forest and stream protection designation, for information for hunters and fishermen, for beautiful brochures of the region's wildlife. They can expand their artistic horizons by doing murals, designing logos, or doing computer graphics for the town or business Web site. They can start actual businesses through entrepreneurial training. All of these curricula can be designed to meet state standards, increase knowledge and skill, and engage students in real work with purpose. It may be that through this they will see promise and possibility in living and working in their home town. That is the lesson of Llano Grande.

Community development NGOs need to be educated about the benefits both of small community-based schools and also of collaboration with educators and schools. Community development professionals are skeptical about engaging with the schools. They usually avoid involvement in school consolidation battles. It will take a campaign of information about successes and additional models to share to show them the ways to do this. And it will take educators willing to open the doors, take some risks, and work at developing ideas and programs.

One possibility involves creating summer placement opportunities for teachers inside community development organizations, giving them a chance to understand the work of the organizations, and to develop curricula that connect students with community issues.

Models of rural school and community development need to be implemented along with robust research and evaluation to determine the effectiveness of various strategies. Longitudinal research on places like Howard and Edcouch-Elsa and on other models of school–community connections is badly needed. What are student learning outcomes over time? Do specific students decide to come back home or stay? Which ones? How are the leadership and civic competency skills developed in education advocacy work applied over a lifetime? Does this impact other community and economic development efforts? What community indicators change when school and community connections are strong—is there hope for the future or are multiple projects for improvement undertaken, new businesses launched, regional planning undertaken? There are several good systems of monitoring changes within a community that use indicators that are precursors to changes in economic statistics.

Building the skills of rural citizens to be knowledgeable, effective, and persistent advocates for good schools helps to build the assets of a community for further development. Almost all research on rural development concludes that leadership matters, but few studies give much attention to how one develops and continues to replenish the leadership base of a place. The patient building of education activists in the fellows programs of West Virginia and South Carolina is one strategy. The creation of small local groups connected to a central training and support system like MEWG and Southern Echo is another variation.

Connecting students to community development teaches them to be good citizens of any place and builds their leadership capacity. When students are connected to a place like Llano Grande, they continue to be tapped for help even after they go to college and take jobs elsewhere. Again, tracking what happens in these communities over the next generation will tell us more about the effectiveness of both strategies.

Educators, students, and community activists are important assets for rural community development. But the potential they represent will go unrealized unless they and rural development practitioners take advantage of the resource they bring. Understanding the stories of successful connections between schools and communities is a first step. Encouraging more examples and developing a policy climate that supports school and community collaboration are essential if this work is to grow to be more than a few good stories.

ENDNOTE

[1] Material for these examples is contained in reports from these groups to the Rural School and Community Trust. See www.ruraledu.org for more information.

REFERENCES

Beaulieu, L. J., & Mulkey, D. (1995). *Investing in people: The human capital needs of rural America*. Rural Studies Series. Boulder, CO: Westview.

Bourdieu, P. (1986). The forms of capital. In John G. Richardson (Ed.), *Handbook of theory and research for the sociology of education* (pp. 241–258). New York: Greenwood Press.

Coalition for Community Schools. (2002). *Education and community building*. Washington, DC: Institute for Educational Leadership.

Coleman, J. (1988). Social capital in the creation of human capital. *American Journal of Sociology, 94*(Suppl.), S95–S120.

Coleman, J. (1990). *Foundations of social theory*. Cambridge, MA: The Belknap Press of Harvard University Press.

Dabson, B. (2005, June 2). *Entrepreneurship as a core economic development strategy for rural America*. Presentation to the Advisory Committee for Strengthening America's Communities Initiative, Clearwater, FL.

Eig, J. (2005, March 25). In the bid to hang on, Miner County, SD, downsizes, dreams. *Wall Street Journal*, A1.

Eyre, E., & Finn, S. (2003). *Closing costs*. http://www.wvgazette.com/section/senses/ closing+costs

Flora, C., & Flora, J. (1993, September). Entrepreneurial social infrastructure: A necessary ingredient. *Annals: American Academy of Political and Social Science, 529*, 49–58.

Flora, C., Flora, J., & Key, S. (2004). *Rural communities: Legacy and change* (2nd ed.). Boulder, CO: Westview.

Flora, J., Gale, E., Schmidt, F., Green, G., & Flora, C. (1993, August). *From the grass roots: Case studies of eight rural self-development efforts*. Washington, DC: United States Department of Agriculture, Economic Research Service.

Gibbs, R., Swaim, P., & Teixeira, R. (1998). *Rural education and training in the new economy*. Ames: Iowa State University Press.

Green, G., Flora, J., Flora, C., & Schmidt, F. (1993, November). *From the grass roots: Results of a national study of rural self-development projects*. Washington, DC: United States Department of Agriculture, Economic Research Service.

Hobbs, D. (1995). Capacity building: Reexamining the role of the rural school. In J. L. Beaulieu & D. Mulkey (Eds.), *Investing in people: The human capital needs of rural America* (pp. 259–284). Rural Studies Series. Boulder, CO: Westview.

Kretzman, J., & McKnight, J. (1993). *Building communities from the inside out: A path toward finding and mobilizing a community's assets.* Institute for Policy Research. Evanston, IL: Northwestern University.

Lawrence, B., Diamond, B., Hill, B., Hoffman, J., Howley, C., Mitchell, S., Rudolph, D., & Washor, E. (2002). *Dollars and sense: The cost effectiveness of small schools.* Cincinnati, OH: Knowledge Works Foundation.

Lyson, T. A. (2002). What does a school mean to a community? Assessing the social and economic benefits of schools to rural villages in New York. *Journal of Research in Rural Education, 17,* 131–137.

Miner County Rural Revitalization Web site. http://www.mccr.net

Null, E. (2001). Llano Grande Center's oral history project sparks cultural and economic renewal in Texas's Rio Grande Valley. http://www.ruraledu.org/projects/project0400.html

Putnam, R. (1993) *Making democracy work: Civic traditions in modern Italy.* Princeton, NJ: Princeton University Press.

Putnam, R. (2000). *Bowling alone: The collapse and renewal of American community.* New York: Simon & Schuster.

Rural School and Community Trust Web site. http://www.ruraledu.org

Saguaro Seminar: *Civic Engagement in America at Harvard University.* http://www.bettertogether.org

South Carolina Rural Education Grassroots Committee. (2003). *Building strong rural schools in South Carolina: The foundations we need.* Washington, DC: Rural School and Community Trust.

CHAPTER 10

Place

Where Diversity and Community Can Converge

Paul Theobald
John Siskar

Diversity and community are two concepts commonly thought to be at odds with one another. Diversity popularly implies heterogeneity, whereas community typically suggests the opposite. Each can be seen as a great societal strength—or weakness—for quite different reasons. Diversity is sometimes viewed as a source of cultural richness and sometimes as a source of divisiveness or conflict. Community is frequently assumed to be a source of social solidarity, but it is just as frequently viewed as a catalyst for segregation and discrimination. In this chapter we argue that, far from being at odds, these concepts are in reality intimately connected. Diversity without community signals a lack of any kind of collective action. Community without diversity is a harbinger for intellectual and cultural stagnation. Neither scenario is conducive to a well-functioning society committed to democratic principles.

Place, it turns out, is a central component to both diversity and community. As a concept, it is attracting more and more scholarly attention these days. Prior to the past few decades, few people were inclined to systematically examine place as a force in the lives of individuals, or as an important component of diversity or community. But things change. Geographers, in particular, have spearheaded the study of place, as well as environmental scholars, and, increasingly, educational theorists (Bowers, 1993; Dolce & Morales-Vasquez, 2003; Gruenewald, 2003; Noddings, 1996; Smith, 2002; Theobald and Curtiss, 2000). In fact, we are at a point now—and this volume stands as evidence of this—where it is possible to discern something like an educational movement, albeit a fledgling one, and one dwarfed by the larger and officially sanctioned "standards and testing" movement. When reference is made to the growing popularity of pedagogy informed by place, it generally goes by the phrase "place-based" or "place-conscious education."

The label sometimes creates confusion, however, for the movement is tightly connected to what others often refer to as "community-based" or "community-oriented studies." Place-based education nevertheless remains the preferred term, for there isn't a great deal of clarity regarding what is meant by the term community—for reasons we broach later. And it is generally accepted that it is possible to go to school where no community exists. By contrast, barring online schools, it is simply not possible to go to a school that is no place. But the larger rationale for using the phrase "place-based" has to do with the fact that the full range of an individual's humanity will unfold someplace, whether or not we would choose to call that place a community. That place then becomes a kind of stage on which political, social, economic, educational, and religious lives become manifest, however well- or ill-developed these might be. And the interaction between these lives in that place contributes to a certain kind of enacted story told time and time again whenever the place is described.

Most often, that description creates a picture of a particular community, but here's the catch: Community is not an either/or concept. Rather, it is one that exists on a continuum. And to further complicate the matter, the criteria for its existence reside largely in the subjective realm of feeling, which accounts for the popular reference to a "sense" of community. The degree to which a particular place in fact constitutes a community depends not on the number of people living in close proximity to one another, but on the amount of life circumstances that are shared. A small number of ranch families spread out across vast spaces within a particular watershed may be more of a community than a densely populated suburb.

Emerson once joked about the farmer who wanted all the land bordering on his own. Until the day that this farmer gets his wish, there is one dynamic that belongs to all places: at some fundamental level they are shared; and thus all places have at least one ingredient on which to build a sense of community. The word itself, coming from the two words "common unity," speaks to the constitutive criterion of "sharedness" in its definition. The more that political, social, economic, educational, and religious lives are shared in a particular place, the greater the sense or feel of community that will exist there.

But at some level the centrality of "sharedness" to community is worrisome. Is it not possible, for example, for a group of people to share their hatred for ethnic minorities, or for members of a particular religious group, or for those with a different sexual orientation? This is another reason why some place-based education advocates prefer that term to "community-based," and it is also why many advocates of multicultural education are sometimes wary of community-oriented studies (Noddings, 1996). There is a very legitimate concern here, and it is one that highlights a pivotal tension in all societies, but particularly in modern democracies that are fundamentally committed to the value of human freedom. If I am free to pursue my own life and lifestyle, am I not free to exclude from it those who are different from me? Don't I possess the right to reject diversity in my life?

The term *diversity* has gradually come to describe all manner of efforts designed to end America's history of discrimination and oppression toward various minority groups. Even conservative scholars (D'Souza, 1998; Schlesinger, 1998) acknowledge that this history was brutal and violent. More mainstream scholars also point out that the impact of this history continues to negatively affect the lives of minority group members today (Banks, 1996; Grant, 2002; Sleeter, 1996). Promoting "diversity," therefore, has increasingly become synonymous with promoting racial, ethnic, religious, linguistic, and cultural tolerance—through various types of political, economic, and educational policies and practices—in the hopes that such efforts will eliminate the injustices that continue to define the nation.

Because diversity seems to celebrate differences and community seems to promote commonality, the two concepts are often thought to be at odds with one another. Many spokespersons for diversity worry that advocates of community will harbor narrow-minded views or fundamentalist moralisms, whereas many spokespersons for community worry that advocates of diversity will render society devoid of solidarity or a clearly defined sense of the common good. These worries constitute a large part of the public discontent with the status quo: discontent about whether average citizens have lost control of the forces that shape their lives and livelihoods, and discontent about whether the moral fabric of the nation is disintegrating before their very eyes. For some, the answer to these problems lies in the restoration of community; for others, in a societal embrace of diversity. What is not yet well understood, or so we argue, is that diversity and community are intimately connected and, furthermore, that the great public project facing the United States in the 21st century is a concerted effort at the mutual development of each. We further argue that schools have a huge role to play in this endeavor, a role that we believe would be best realized through the use of place-based pedagogy.

SOME HELPFUL HISTORY

Despite the fact that diversity and community may seem to be at odds, the reality is that both are tightly connected to notions of human freedom. But rather than clarifying the matter, this fact further complicates things, for there are many differing conceptions of what constitutes human freedom. For example, diversity advocates are drawn to conceptions of freedom that focus on individual rights, whereas those promoting community are more focused on processes that extend to all members of the community a voice in how life will unfold in their neighborhoods and in larger societal arenas. It turns out that we can trace the historical developments that have led to differing definitions of freedom—an effort that will explain how we arrived at this crossroads, this point at which community and diversity are routinely construed to be in opposition to one another.

We get our best glimpse of this by going back to the days of the American Revolution. Feeling oppressed by heavy taxes and other burdens imposed by the government of George III, the 13 colonies declared themselves free of the feudal arrangements the "mother country" represented. In many ways, America's revolution against England represented the death knell of feudalism and a starting point for the rise of democracy. Colonial attempts at imagining a more democratic future were significantly aided by what came to be known as "Enlightenment" philosophy, a set of new ideas about how man ought to be governed, how an economy ought to be orchestrated, even how an education ought to prepare individuals for citizenship. Behind all the various ideas were philosophical arguments about man and his ontological makeup—what man is essentially. In this regard, the main sources for the various arguments were two philosophers, John Locke of England and Charles de Montesquieu of France.

Both of these gentlemen, and many others among those who are thought to be a part of the Enlightenment, spent a great deal of time theorizing about how human conditions would unfold in a "state of nature," far from the interference of kings, priests, and lords. There was a crucial distinction to be made about man in the state of nature, and it turns out that these two philosophers, Locke and Montesquieu, differed profoundly in this regard.

For Locke, man roaming the forests would first turn his attention to looking for food—gathering acorns and apples to eat. The implication is that man is fundamentally an economic being. This being the case, Locke determined that the role of government was to orchestrate the economy, make a level playing field, adjudicate any clashes between individuals, and, when necessary, create an army to defend the people from foreign invaders. The people would in effect enter into a contract with those who would form the government and perform these vital functions. Citizens could then go about their private affairs and pursue their economic self-interest. In this Lockean worldview, community played no particular role. In fact, just as multiculturalists sometimes suspiciously inspect the notion of community-based education, Locke and his followers looked at community as a possible obstacle to the exercise of human freedom.

By contrast, Montesquieu saw the state of nature much differently. In his view, man's first act in the forest would have been to search for a friend, someone with whom he could move through life, someone who would make economic activity worth the effort. Thus, for Montesquieu, man is fundamentally social, and consequently a political being. This suggests a rather different role for government than that envisioned by Locke. For Montesquieu, government ought to be the collective voice of the people, ascertained in numerous ways. And although modern states were too large to replicate the Athenian assembly, citizens could exercise their political voice through all manner of local associations that animate community life. A major function of government, then, was to serve as a catalyst to community health and well-being. In contrast to Locke, Montesquieu looked at community not as a possible detriment to the realization of human freedom, but as the vehicle through which that realization could take place.

It doesn't take much insight to recognize that Locke's perspective won the day among many of our founders, especially those who gathered in Philadelphia during the summer of 1787. The constitution writers effectively minimized any political role America's citizens might play, for all intents and purposes confining that to the mere exercise of the vote once every 2 years—and even this limited democratic space was reserved for those who held sufficient property. Furthermore, the economic essence of human nature as perceived by Locke and his American followers made man out to be an acquisitive being, someone who required assistance to keep his appetites in check. Witness the remarks of two prominent constitutional architects. Said James Madison, "If men were angels, no government would be necessary." And Hamilton, "Why government? Because the passions of men will not conform to the dictates of reason without constraint" (Wright, 1996, pp. 160, 356).

In hindsight, it looks as if Montesquieu's views were hardly noticed at the point of our founding, but nothing could be further from the truth. Our sacred governmental trinity—executive, legislative, and judicial—is straight from Montesquieu, as is giving each governmental branch a kind of power check over the others (although there is increasing scholarly speculation concerning the extent to which the rules governing the Iroquois Confederation were a significant influence on early American statesmen).[1] We do know, though, that the delegates in Philadelphia took from Montesquieu what they thought was useful, and discarded the rest.[2] High on the list of ideas headed for the trash heap was Montesquieu's conception of the role local associations should play in the maintenance of a healthy republic. But that doesn't mean that this idea, or any others emanating from Montesquieu, for that matter, went unheeded in the early republic. In fact, an examination of some of America's lesser statesmen—some of the antifederalists who opposed the Constitution, even some of the early clergy—reveals that the idea that government ought to cultivate the well-being of communities was widespread.

As the American story progressed, there was ample evidence to suggest that Montesquieu's views were surprisingly alive and well despite our Lockean-inspired Constitution. By the 1830s, for example, frontier settlement had advanced into the interior at such a rapid clip that the centralized government was not able to manage the process. Matters had to be dealt with locally, and as a result, the nation witnessed dramatic growth in local associations. This in turn ushered in a great democratic era (albeit one marred by discriminatory practices aimed at Blacks, Native Americans, and women; more on this shortly) demonstrated by such things as the ascendancy of "log cabin presidents," the abolition of property qualifications for the vote, the establishment of free common schools systems, prison reforms, park construction, and many other democratic developments.

Alexis de Tocqueville (1956) described much of this in his classic study entitled *Democracy in America*, originally published in 1836. Said Tocqueville, "In every case, at the head of any new undertaking, where in France you would find the government, or in England some territorial magnate, in the United States you are sure to find an Association"

(p. 198). He elaborated further, "If an American should be reduced to occupying himself with his own affairs, half his existence would be snatched from him, he would feel it as a vast void in his life" (p. 167). Tocqueville's analysis suggests that Montesquieu was right. Local associations could provide the stage on which ordinary citizens insert a political dimension in their lives, thus invigorating democracy and greatly enhancing a sense of personal fulfillment.

Montesquieu, more than Locke, was enamored by the success of the Greek and Roman republics. Citing Aristotle, Cicero, and others who believed that the quality of government rested on the quality of its citizens, Montesquieu was an advocate of what is sometimes called the republican or civic republican tradition of political theory. Locke and his followers became spokespersons for what is generally called liberal political theory (not "liberal" in current parlance, meaning largely the political "left," but liberal in the sense that it hinged decisively on human freedom).

Liberal political theory rested on the idea that freedom meant a level economic playing field, not a seat in Congress or a voice in political decisions. In contrast to Montesquieu, there was no burden to improve citizens within the political theory of Locke and his followers. In Immanuel Kant's famous words, "...the problem of setting up a state can be solved even by a nation of devils...for such a task does not involve the moral improvement of man."[3] This was a rather stark contrast to the republican tradition, which maintained that citizen formation was an absolute necessity, a political project that could not be overlooked. Another way to view the discrepancy is to contrast the educational views of America's most steadfast political liberal, Alexander Hamilton, with those of America's most steadfast political republican, Thomas Jefferson. In the huge corpus of Hamilton's writings, there is virtually no reference to improving the intellectual qualities of American citizens. In fact, Hamilton's exceedingly rare references to youth had to do mostly with the use that could be made of them, "at a tender age," in the nation's factories. Jefferson, on the other hand, tried three times to get his native Virginia to pass free school bills—although always unsuccessfully.

At one level, at least, this lack of a citizen formation project in liberal political theory is conceptually consistent. As noted earlier, the primary motivation behind this theoretical trajectory was maximizing human freedom, more specifically, what Berlin (1958) defined as "freedom from," freedom as defined by the removal of restraints. Underlying this concept is the notion of equality that Kelly (2002) identifies as equality of opportunity, where all are treated the same regardless of situation or need. The best society, in the view of Locke, Hamilton, and other liberals, was one that guaranteed citizens the right to pursue their own ends—their own religion, their own career, and their own education. In fact, they worked to create a governmental system that would safeguard these choices by maintaining complete neutrality in the policy arena with respect to such ends.

It should be fairly obvious, then, that advocates of diversity would find the ostensible policy neutrality within this theoretical trajectory appealing. At first glance, at any rate, it seems to allow individuals from diverse backgrounds a fair shake at maintaining their diversity while still advancing within mainstream society. And the appeal of this vision for society was heightened additionally by one troublesome drawback to republican political theory: the fact that its history had always been tainted by a degree of exclusivity. The logic behind exclusionary efforts within the civic republican tradition generally went something like this: If citizens are going to come together to deliberate matters affecting the public good, they are going to need certain qualities—intelligence, reasonableness, sound judgment, and so on. Starting with Aristotle's Greece, Cicero's Rome, and continuing through the highpoint of republican theory in the United States during the 19th century, all kinds of groups have been deemed to be lacking these qualities: slaves, freedmen, women, Catholics, indigenous peoples, and immigrants from a rather large assortment of nations considered, on some level or another, inferior.

However, the idea that gender, race, religion, or cultural background permanently renders one unfit for a political role as a citizen is not a part of republican theory itself. Many republican theorists have rejected such stereotyping. Interestingly, Montesquieu ultimately rejected a republican form of government in favor of a limited monarchy. He argued that a republic would require a system of schools capable of delivering "the full power of education," something he was quite certain France did not possess in the middle of the 18th century.

But at the high point of Montesquieu's influence in the United States—the 1830s and 1840s, we set about the task of creating just such a system. We established common schools in virtually all the northern states before the Civil War, and in all the southern states just after it. The schools were designed to provide an education common to all citizens of the republic regardless of race, gender, religion, or class. To be sure, historians continue to debate the question of whether or not the ideal of the common school was ever reached or even approximated. Perhaps it never was. But this doesn't reduce the significance of the vision behind the establishment of free schools, a vision that was profoundly democratic and an integral piece of modern republican political theory.[4]

This brief glimpse at some early American history helps us to see that as our nation was founded and later as it moved through its formative years, it had two theoretical options to choose from when setting up a government and creating a new society. The liberal theory option generally looked at community as a potential obstacle to human freedom; therefore, the well-being of communities was not considered a criterion for policymaking. On the other hand, the liberal option did hold some promise as an avenue toward a free diverse society, for making one nation out of many cultures, for *e pluribus unum*. By contrast, the republican political theory option prized community life as the best expression of freedom, but it came with a history of intolerance toward difference. The perception that diversity and community are at odds was born as a result of these differing theoretical perspectives.

In the end, as noted earlier, we opted for a system predicated on liberal theory. In some measure, this is why a group of scholars who have been critical of the status quo, especially how it has been hard on community life in America, have come to be called *communitarians*, although we should point out that they hardly ever use that term to describe themselves. One reason they haven't warmed to this label is that the demise of community under the current system is not their only lament. They are equally concerned about the fate of diversity in contemporary society. For despite its theoretical promise to create a level playing field irrespective of race, gender, religion, or cultural background, America's track record in this regard has been poor at best.

It turns out that there was a huge ideological development near the end of the 19th century that had a number of significant effects. First and foremost, it banished lingering elements of republican political theory to the very margins of American society, further endangering the fate of community in America. But on top of this, it struck a severe blow at diversity, or the potential for diversity that lay within the commitment to policy neutrality at the heart of liberal theory. We turn now to examine this development and then to what generally has been called the communitarian critique of modern liberal theory.

SPINNING DARWIN SOCIOLOGICALLY

The individualism of Locke's worldview received even greater legitimation from ideas related to Charles Darwin's great work of modern biology, *The*

Origin of Species. Darwin never saw his efforts in anything other than biological terms, although that wasn't the case for many of his subsequent followers. Herbert Spencer and William Graham Sumner (Dickens, 2000; Peel, 1972) are two of the most prominent examples of men who translated evolutionary concepts into contemporary sociology. The end result was what we casually refer to as Social Darwinism (it would have had more explanatory power if we had simply called it racism), a severe blow to the potential for diversity within the liberal worldview.

But beyond the condemnation of diversity inherent in Social Darwinism were other societal conceptions that gave additional strength to the already quite strong Lockean-inspired individualism in American culture. For instance, most social Darwinists came to see society as a kind of organism, with the individuals in society analogous to cells. As all cells play an identifiable role in the health of the organism, all individuals have an identifiable role to play in the interest of a healthy society. This insight became the wellspring for all manner of attempts to "socially engineer" the school, the workplace, even the church.

Recall that it was at the height of Montesquieu's influence in America—the 1830s, described and documented by Tocqueville—that we finally began to adopt a system of free common schools for all (with some lamentable exceptions). By the first decades of the 20th century, we were so convinced by Darwinian logic, so sure that each individual had an "evident and probable destiny," to quote longtime Harvard president Charles Eliot (Preskill, 1989), that we believed education had to be differentiated, not common, where individual strengths were accurately matched to societal needs.

In keeping with our earlier embrace of Locke's views, schools were increasingly designed to prepare students for economic roles. The idea that there might be a curriculum common to all citizens of a democracy was scarcely acknowledged in the heavily Darwinian milieu of the early 20th century. And of course some individuals were more fit than others—those would receive a college-bound curriculum en route to the important jobs in society and government. Later in the century, another Harvard president, James Conant, added more resolve to the development of meritocratic principles through his tireless promotion of gifted education.

The point here is that we have moved in a certain direction in this society, a direction first set by our founders in their selection of Lockean views to create a social praxis. The cultural development set in motion by those decisions has in effect promoted the idea that we are a nation of individuals living among strangers. The heavy emphasis on individualism sewn into our cultural makeup from the outset—which is one and the same as saying the heavy doses of suspicion reserved for community as a possible deterrent to freedom—received an ideological boost from the ascendancy of Social Darwinism. In fact, some scholars are convinced that American society has come to be dominated by a kind of hyperindividualism—referred to by the late Lasch (1979) as a "culture of narcissism"—and that the drawbacks from this have begun to seriously outnumber the benefits. Communitarian scholar Michael Walzer describes our current circumstances this way:

> We are perhaps the most individualist society that ever existed in human history. Compared certainly to earlier, and Old World societies, we are radically liberated, all of us. Free to plot our own course. To plan our own lives. To choose a career. To choose a partner or a succession of partners. To choose a religion or no religion. To choose a politics or an anti-politics. To choose a lifestyle—any style. Free to do our own thing, and this freedom, energizing and exciting as it is, is also profoundly disintegrative, making it difficult for individuals to find any stable communal support, very difficult for any community to count on the responsible participation of its individual members. It opens solitary men and women to the impact of a lowest common denominator, commercial culture. It works against those committed to the larger democratic union and also against the solidarity of all cultural groups that constitute our multiculturalism.[5] (Walzer, 1992, pp. 11–12)

At the heart of Walzer's and other communitarians' critique is an argument that goes something like this: America's preoccupation with acquisitive, or possessive, individualism is directly implicated in the demise of community in America. It has led to a fracturing of communal solidarity, which in turn has resulted in the diminishment of a sense of political efficacy among citizens. Worse still, it has elevated the most privileged in American society while condemning historically oppressed groups to ever more rigid socioeconomic circumstances. Because communitarian arguments call for a reconsideration of the value of community across the full spectrum of the human condition, because it calls for a repudiation of the racism that has infected the post-Darwinian development of American institutions, it has become a part of the intellectual rationale undergirding place-based education. That rationale generally takes two forms—one dealing with the utility of place-based approaches for the generation of deep-level understanding in traditional school subjects, which we turn to shortly, the other having to do with the potential of place-based education for developing citizens capable of wielding democratic processes. By using school subjects to examine circumstances germane to a particular place and following this up with genuine and substantial contributions to the quality of shared life in that place, the school can make a contribution to community vitality. In the process, both teachers and students can learn, firsthand, what Montesquieu argued over 200 years ago: (a) that life is more than an economic endeavor and (b) that a fulfilled life requires a political dimension—one that enables individuals to experience the sense of satisfaction that comes with positively affecting the lives of friends and neighbors. In this way, place-based education holds potential for advancing the welfare of community in this country, as well as enhancing the strength of our commitment to diversity.

COMMUNITARIANISM

The lines of argument taken up by communitarian scholars are quite diverse. MacIntyre (1984) has been most concerned with the development of moral theory in a society dominated by individualist views. Taylor (1989) has been most concerned with the development of modern identity; Walzer, with the distribution of social and economic justice. And there are many others (Kymlicka, 1989; Sandel, 1996; Selznick, 2002). Some of the arguments are highly sophisticated and only readily comprehended by trained philosophers. Others, like Etzioni (1993), have taken great pains to lay out communitarian arguments that can be easily grasped by average citizens.

But the main point of departure for communitarians as they critique the status quo goes back to the state of nature. That is, they deny, as did Montesquieu, the Lockean claim that we are distinct "presocial" or "prepolitical" individuals first, and only later enter into relationships that require commitments, obligations, and so forth. They argue, rather, that it is only through relationships and commitments that an individual can come to acquire any identity, unique or otherwise. This crucial distinction eventually leads to quite different pathways as it relates to policy development, as we shall soon see.

Perceiving individuals to be solitary beings, advocates of Lockean perspectives extend to them an array of delineated and inalienable "rights" that some believe were bestowed by the "Creator" and others believe were merely identified as "self-evident" with the application of enough rational power. Regardless, for communitarians, when the defense of rights becomes the first order of business for a governmental structure, it tends to mitigate against the development of other life-sustaining concerns. Glendon (1991) succinctly captured the essence of the critique of our rights-oriented society that emanates from the individualistic perspectives of the Lockean tradition:

> ...current American rights talk...is set apart from rights discourse in other liberal democracies by its starkness and simplicity, its prodigality in bestowing the rights label, its legalistic character, its exaggerated absoluteness, its hyperindividualism, its insularity, and its silence with respect to personal, civic, and collective responsibilities. (p. x)

She goes on to contend that our embrace of rights talk "...works against the conditions required for the pursuit of dignified living by free men and women" (p. xi).

Communitarians are not opposed to the concept of rights, but they do not see them as a universal feature of the human condition—something that existed in Locke's presocial state of nature. They see them, rather, as collectively created rules that are generated in response to contextually and historically dependent circumstances. In Locke's world, every human being is endowed with a right of personal autonomy—the right to choose how he or she will live, what he or she will do, and so on. Part of government's role is to protect the individual's right to choose—and then to stay out of the business of assessing the quality of those choices. According to communitarians, this is a serious flaw, for individual choices can impinge on the ability of others to pursue what they take to be the good life. This became an especially serious flaw when in 1886 the U.S. Supreme Court extended the rights of "personhood" to business corporations, enabling them to buy one another up, to exercise the right of free speech through campaign donations, the distribution of antiunion pamphlets, and so on.

When a corporation pulls up stakes and moves its operations abroad, it does so by exercising its individual right to choose. It is under no obligation—nor is anyone else—to determine the quality of that choice by, say, measuring the hardship it might create in the community it has decided to leave. And the same can be said related to all kinds of policy enacted in this country—the way it affects a community is not a concern. One could point to the way the nation's auto manufacturers bought out intracity public transit systems and lobbied for the creation of megahighways to promote automobile consumption as one illuminating example

(Jacobs, 2004). The end result was the disintegration of America's inner cities and prolonging the separation of races in this country due to the White flight these policies enabled. Or one might point to a common 20th-century school consolidation policy that literally robbed thousands of small rural communities of their schools, claiming they lacked sufficient economic and educational efficiency. Those responsible for such policies were either blind or indifferent to the effect of these policies on community life.

If communitarians are correct, if there is indeed no such thing as a presocial individual identity, then contributions to individual well-being cannot be so easily separated from the well-being of the communities of which individuals (or the corporate "person") are a part. Communitarians are asking for the elevation of community well-being in the policy arena because (a) human beings need more than the ability to invoke rights to lead fulfilled lives and (b) healthy communities provide the platform (through Montesquieu's local associations) for individuals to play a political role with their lives—thus contributing to the overall health of the United States as a democratic society.

Although the philosophical arguments behind the communitarian agenda can get quite convoluted, the agenda itself is simple: We have gone too far with our individual orientation in this society, and we need to find a better balance between the protection of individual rights and the promotion of community well-being. Or, put another way, we need to find a way to insert community well-being into the list of criteria used to determine the formation of all manner of social policy, be it political, economic, or educational.

One essential piece of this project is to bring an end to what communitarians call "difference-blindness" as it relates to policy. Perhaps the central precept of liberal theory is that individuals are free to choose their own paths in life. The logic of liberal theory, therefore, suggests that policy decisions must be "difference blind," lest they advantage some individuals more than others. Communitarians see many shortcomings in this. First, they doubt whether this kind of neutrality is possible. Furthermore, even if it were, they don't believe it is desirable. Communitarians like Fraser (1997), Young (1990), and Kymlicka (1995) point to the experience of minorities in this country, their persistent overrepresentation among the poor, lingering inner-city blight, and so on, as examples that prove that attempts at difference-blind policy, perhaps even very well-meaning attempts, inevitably privilege the status quo. In its place, communitarians ask for "particularity" in policymaking—meaning well-considered attention to differing circumstances, differing cultures, differing histories. Such a policy strategy, they argue, would much more effectively advance the cause of diversity in American society.

Martin Luther King, Jr., clearly saw the need for healthy communities in the quest for a society that would ultimately heal the cultural wounds created by the implications of Social Darwinism and the earlier legacy of slavery itself. Commenting on the decades-long strategy of waiting for the NAACP to win major judicial victories, King remarked, "When legal contests were the sole form of activity, the ordinary Negro was involved as a passive spectator. His interest was stirred, but his energies were unemployed. Mass marches transformed the common man into a star performer" (King, 1967, p. 566). In his essay "Where Do We Go From Here: Chaos or Community?" King betrayed a keen awareness of the deep link between community and diversity. Far from viewing them to be at odds, King saw them as indispensable to one another. Judges might hand down prodiversity decisions, lawmakers might pass civil rights legislation, but without healthy communities that offered citizens a platform to play a political role with their lives, the nation's commitment to diversity would remain chimerical. Said King, "How shall we turn the ghettos into a vast school? How shall we make every street corner a forum … every houseworker and every laborer a demonstrator, a voter, a canvasser and a student? The dignity their jobs may deny them is waiting for them in political and social action" (King, 1967, p. 611).

In King's quest to turn the ghetto into a vast school and the street corner into a political forum one can identify the best attributes of republican theory, as well as the essential points of the communitarian critique of liberalism. Free people require a political dimension in their lives in order to live with dignity. Making the most of one's political contribution can only come with the improvement of the nation's citizens. In other words, what King saw in 1967 is just as true today: America stands in need of the simultaneous and mutually reinforcing development of diversity and community.

DIVERSITY, COMMUNITY, AND EDUCATION

It is interesting that educational proponents of diversity and community are so suspicious of one another when they share overlapping goals. They both are attempting to address issues of alienation that students and the public at large experience every day. They both wish to see students develop into individuals who are empathetic to others and act in socially responsible ways. They both embrace the critical pedagogical notion that education should be socially transformative. And frequently, communitarians seem to blur the communitarian–multicultural distinction by identifying recognition of reasonable cultural diversity as a norm that needs to be treated the same as freedom and equality (Taylor, 1994). Additionally, communitarians and multiculturalists each argue that they hope to produce students who are empowered, emboldened, and who shoulder responsibility well.

However, the resolution of these positions is neither simple nor straightforward. The differences are real, and they start with how one goes about achieving desired goals. Nevertheless, consider how well the emphasis of multicultural educators on who you are and where you come from contrasts with the focus of place-based educators on where you are and your responsibility to your community. Both educational traditions can draw from a huge curricular reservoir germane to a given place. But multicultural and place-based educators typically have not taken advantage of the ability to strengthen each of their designs by adopting elements of the other's practice. The dynamic between the development and welfare of the individual and the community creates an opportunity for a checks-and-balance system that would well serve learners whom Dewey, in the tradition of Montesquieu, rightly defined as *social individuals*. Dewey's individual, like Vygotsky's child, can only grow in and through social interaction.

This is not to say that others have not identified the relationship between multicultural and place-based education. It is apparent in both rural and urban contexts. In both settings there is recognition that "community life is being undermined by capitalistic development patterns" (Gruenewald, 2003, p. 5). Others (Castells, 1983; Giroux, 1993; Haymes, 1995; hooks, 1990; Keith & Pile, 1993; Williams, 1988), whom Gruenewald (2003) refers to as *radical multiculturalists,* argue that any discussion of cultural education must include recognition of the hegemonic power exerted by the dominant class through the use of place. This is consistent with the analysis of those who look at place from a rural perspective (Hass & Nachtigal, 1998; Theobald, 1997; Theobald & Curtiss, 2000).

It is clear that multicultural and place-based educators could complement each other in a reform effort. For example, a place-based curriculum would be well served by the watchful eye of multiculturalists on the lookout for sexist, racist, and misogynistic tendencies that are possible when one is trying to cultivate a connection and identify with all the individuals within a place or community. Multicultural concepts infused within a place-based curriculum would help balance the tension between respecting each member of the group and creating a common identity for all. But it is not simply a matter of developing curriculum that can fully embrace the conceptual underpinnings of both positions. Instead, it is the positive nature of the tensions inherent between the two positions that will maximize the success of any potential educational reform. Schools, especially those in high-need urban and rural areas, would be well served by having faculty and administrators who understand and are passionate about the ideas that drive multicultural and place-based education.

We have often seen in the past, when one group or another proposed a more radical change in how schools should operate, that the emphasis was on changing content at the expense of identifying processes that schools and teachers might adopt. Whether the call came from the left or the right, it included what appears to be an unintended attempt to indoctrinate students with a new set of beliefs—moral, ethical, understanding and acceptance of others, critical awareness of society, and so on. We believe as well that place-based and multicultural content needs to be identified and integrated into the curriculum, but adding content alone is not sufficient. We suggest that for schools to simultaneously cultivate the development of a sense of community and an appreciation of diversity in children, more emphasis on process is critical. It is not enough to ask what students should know; it is also necessary to decide on how they will come to know it.

If the goals of diversity and community are to be met, students need to experience and become comfortable using processes that are democratic and that require critical analysis. We find it hopeful that educators across the country have been embracing a constructivist stance toward education because inherent within a constructivist pedagogy are processes that are social, democratic, and inclusive of critical inquiry.

Improving the nation's citizens, developing healthy communities, promoting an embrace of diverse ways of life and living, these are societal efforts to which schools can make a legitimate, though partial, contribution. It should be obvious that we believe place-conscious curriculum and instruction of the sort described in this volume is the best way to move in that direction. But it is worth noting that even if one believes that larger societal goals should not be a part of the public school project—that schools exist solely to fulfill the intellectual needs of individual students—place-conscious education, from a learning theory standpoint, nevertheless remains well warranted.

As noted earlier, new views about human learning are a typical part of the rationale for place-based studies. Older views, like most post-Darwinian intellectual trajectories, were cast in individual terms. Behaviorism dominated the field for decades, and that was followed by a brief period dominated by information-processing models. These were largely usurped by the advent of constructivism, however, and we are only now beginning to understand that learning, like other distinctly human traits, is largely a social undertaking, thus the popularity of the phrase "social constructivism." And one step further, the social nature of the learning process meshes well with Montesquieu's conception of humans as primarily social beings.

At the root of constructivism is an understanding that culture informs the way we process information, think, and come to understand anything. Bruner (1986) is sympathetic to Vygotsky's view that "...man was subject to the dialectical play between nature and history, between his qualities as a creature of biology and as a product of human nature" (p. 71). Bruner goes on to say, "Society provides a tool kit of concepts and ideas and theories that permit one to get to higher ground mentally" (p. 73). Bruner is by no means alone in recognizing that the way one constructs the world is socially dependent (Cahan & Kocur, 1996; Dewey, 1916; Efland, Freedman, & Stuhr; 1996; Gadamer, 1976; McLaren, 1989; Neperud, 1995; Orr, 1992). This concept is at the root of constructivist thinking and has been influenced by many throughout the history of the development of American education. Perhaps no one is more eloquent in expressing this idea than Dewey (1916), who noted:

Society not only continues to exist by transmission, by communication, but it may be fairly said to exist in transmission, in communication. There is more than a verbal tie between the words common, community, and communication. Men live in a community by virtue of the things which they have in common; and communication is the way in which they come to possess things in common. What they must have in common in order to form a community or society are aims, beliefs, aspirations, knowledge—a common understanding—like-mindedness as the sociologists say. Such things cannot be passed physically from one to another, like bricks; they cannot be shared as persons would share a pie by dividing it into physical pieces. The communication which insures participation in a common understanding is one which secures similar emotional and intellectual dispositions—like ways of responding to expectations and requirements. (p. 4)

We can see this as the emphasis on developmental theory has moved from a Piagetian perspective to one that embraces the notions of Vygotsky. Piaget focused on identifying the individual stages a child goes through as he or she matures. Piaget's emphasis on a laissez-faire model, where educators are supposed to wait until the individual child is ready for the content, contrasts sharply with Vygotsky's notion that child development is an inherently social process. One key component of Vygotsky's theory was his Zone of Proximal Development, "the distance between the child's current level of independent problem solving and what he or she is able to do under adult guidance" (Prawat, 1993, p. 10). The role of the teacher is to identify both benchmarks (the child's current status and his or her potential) through social interaction with the child. Once the benchmarks are established, scaffolding activities, activities that are appropriate for the child to reach that potential, are designed to help the child reach that goal. The teacher may model behavior, set up activities in which the teacher works with the child, or structure the class so that the student is working with a peer. Where Piaget would have us wait, Vygotsky encourages us to design experiences where the student must interact with others.

Dewey's (1916) observations reinforce this perspective:

A society which makes provision for participation of all its members on equal terms and which secures flexible readjustments of its institutions through interaction of different forms of associated life is in so far democratic. Such a society must have a type of education which gives individuals a personal interest in social relationships and control, and the habits of mind which secure social changes without introducing disorder. (p. 112)

Gutmann (1987) is even more succinct: "Children must learn not just to *behave* in accordance with authority but to *think* critically about authority if they are to live up to the democratic ideal of sharing political sovereignty as citizens" (p. 51).

Put simply, understanding traditional school subjects is augmented by social interchange and by grounding subjects in the immediate lives of students. What this suggests is that even if our goal was as narrow as raising test scores, place-based education is probably the best route to getting there. But its appeal is greatly aided by the promise it holds for the development of individuals willing to allow relationships and commitments to enter into self-definition.

A particular place on earth can be a kind of curricular lens through which all traditional school subjects may be closely examined. The immediacy and relevance of place in the lives of students can be a huge catalyst to deep learning—learning at the level of understanding. The discovery that develops in attempts to find out why the place looks and feels as it does yields a kind of intellectual satisfaction that cannot be matched even by the complete mastery of a disconnected textbook curriculum.

Because every place faces different circumstances, of course, it is impossible to be prescriptive about place-conscious units and lessons. An inner-city school with high levels of diversity may need to spend more time on lessons that help students critically examine the forces that have brought them together in a particular neighborhood. What decisions contributed to the creation of ghettos and to what degree were those decisions anchored in social Darwinist logic? Most important, what kind of work can be undertaken to improve the sense of community both in and around the school?

On the other hand, students in a relatively homogeneous rural community may need to critically examine the lack of diversity in their lives. Where are the original inhabitants of that place? How were they treated? Why were they removed? Why are there so few African-Americans in the community? Was it because when European settlers first claimed ownership of the farms and community businesses, Blacks were still being held in bondage?

Regrettably, the current standards and testing regime doesn't allow a great deal of space for the curricular imagination of the nation's teachers—a very lamentable circumstance. But the pendulum will soon return, for if Americans decide they must make a cultural corrective by simultaneously elevating the value of community and diversity, one essential part of the process will be more widespread use of place-conscious education. The examples shared in this volume demonstrate that students can learn well by using place-based approaches to curriculum and instruction. The greater contribution, though, may well be the enculturating effects of asking students to shoulder some obligation for the well-being of their communities and for nurturing an embrace of diversity for the benefit of us all.

ENDNOTES

[1] A growing number of scholars are now beginning to acknowledge the influence of the native American Iroquois government—represented by the Great Binding Law of the Iroquois Confederacy—as perhaps the single most important,

and probably only, model for the 1754 Albany Plan of Union, a precursor to the American Articles of Confederation and, some claim at least, the Constitution itself. (See Mander, 1991, pp. 230–231.)

[2] An examination of the *Federalist Papers* (Benjamin F. Wright, Ed., 1996) reveals that Montesquieu was a source of guidance and direction as the former colonials went about the business of creating an independent state. When it suited their purposes, as was the case for "checks and balances," they cited him as an authority and referred to him as the "celebrated" Montesquieu, "the oracle who is constantly cited on the subject" (p. 337). When it did not, such as Montesquieu's marked preference for a collection of small republics, they rejected him as misinformed. Said Hamilton in "Number Nine," taking Montesquieu's advice would have us "splitting ourselves into an infinity of little, jealous, clashing, tumultuous commonwealths, the wretched nurseries of unceasing discord, and the miserable objects of universal pity" (p. 126).

[3] The remarks are from Kant's essay, "Perpetual Peace," written in 1795, which is reprinted in *Kant's Political Writings,* (1970) edited by Hans Reiss, Cambridge: Cambridge University Press, 112–113.

[4] We should point out that the acceptance of statewide education systems was coincident with ever increasing rates of urbanization, industrialization, and immigration and all of the many social ills that accompanied these developments. Many claim that the adoption of school systems was more a response to these problems than a delayed response to the vision of a democratic republic buttressed by schools designed for "the diffusion of knowledge." Some believe that the failure to reach this ideal vision was in part due to a misplaced emphasis on equality of opportunity. They argue that equality of outcomes, or what an educator might refer to as equity, would be the better goal. Instead of an educational system where everyone is treated the same, the system should make sure that each learner receives the resources that he or she needs, recognizing that needs vary.

[5] Robert Dahl (2002) provides further evidence of this in his little book *How Democratic is the U.S. Constitution?* He documents the fact that the United States has slipped to the bottom of the top 25 "first world" nations in virtually every measure that defines a democracy.

REFERENCES

Banks, J. A. (1996). *Multicultural education, transformative knowledge, and action: Historical and contemporary perspectives.* New York: Teachers College Press.

Berlin, I. (1958). *Two concepts of liberty.* Oxford: Clarendon Press.

Bowers, C. A. (1993). *Education, cultural myths, and the ecological crisis: Toward deep changes.* Albany: State University of New York Press.

Bruner, J. S. (1986). *Actual minds, possible worlds.* Cambridge, MA: Harvard University Press.

Cahan, S., & Kocur, Z. (Eds.). (1996). *Contemporary art and multicultural education.* New York: Routledge and The New Museum of Contemporary Art.

Castells, M. (1983). *The city and the grassroots.* Berkeley: University of California Press.

Dahl, R. A. (2002). *How democratic is the American constitution?* New Haven, CT: Yale University Press.

Dewey, J. (1916). *Democracy and education.* New York: Macmillan.

Dickens, P. (2000). *Social Darwinism: Linking evolutionary thought to social theory.* Philadelphia: Open University Press.

Dolce, P. C., & Morales-Vasquez, R. (2003). Teaching the importance of place in the world of virtual reality. *Thought and Action, 19,* 39–48.

D'Souza, D. (1998). *Illiberal education: The politics of race and sex on campus.* New York: Free Press.

Efland, A. D., Freedman, K., & Stuhr, P. (1996). *Postmodern art education: An approach to curriculum.* Reston, VA: The National Art Education Association.

Etzioni, A. (1993). *The spirit of community: The reinvention of American society.* New York: Touchstone Books.

Fraser, N. (1997). *Justice interuptus.* New York: Routledge.

Gadamer, H. G. (1976). *The relevance of the beautiful and other essays.* (N. Walker, Trans.). Cambridge, UK: Cambridge University Press.

Giroux, H. A. (1993). *Living dangerously: Multiculturalism and the politics of difference.* New York: Peter Lang Press.

Glendon, M. A. (1991). *Rights talk: The impoverishment of political discourse.* New York: The Free Press.

Grant, C. (2002). *Educator's guide to diversity in the classroom.* New York: Houghton Mifflin.

Gruenewald, D. A. (2003). The best of both worlds: A critical pedagogy of place. *Educational Researcher, 22*(4), 3–12.

Guttmann, A. (1987). *Democratic education.* Princeton, NJ: Princeton University Press.

Haas, T., & Nachtigal, P. (1998). *Place value.* Charleston, WV: ERIC Press.

Haymes, S. N. (1995). *Race, culture, and the city: A pedagogy for black urban struggle.* Albany: State University of New York Press.

hooks, b. (1990). *Yearning: Race, gender, and cultural politics.* Boston: South End Press.

Jacobs, J. (2004). *Dark age ahead.* New York: Random House.

Kant, I. (1970). Perpetual peace. In H. Reiss (Ed.), *Kant's political writings* (pp. 112–113). Cambridge, UK: Cambridge University Press. (Original work published 1795.)

Keith, M., & Pile, S. (1993). *Place and the politics of identity.* New York: Routledge.

Kelly, P. (2002). Introduction: Between culture and equality. In P. Kelly (Ed.), *Multiculturalism reconsidered* (pp. 1–17). Cambridge, UK: Polity Press.

King. M. L. (1986). Where do we go from here? Chaos or community? Reprinted in J. M. Washington (Ed.), *A testimony of hope: The essential writings and speeches of Martin Luther King Jr.* (pp. 566–567). New York: HarperCollins. (Original work published 1967.)

Kymlicka, W. (1989). *Liberalism, community, and culture.* Oxford: Oxford University Press.

Kymlicka, W. (1995). *Multicultural citizenship.* Oxford: Clarion Press.

Lasch, C. (1979). *The culture of narcissism: American life in an age of diminishing expectations.* New York: W. W. Norton.

MacIntyre, A. (1984). *After virtue: A study in moral theory.* South Bend, IN: University of Notre Dame Press.

Mander, J. (1991). *In the absence of the sacred.* San Francisco: Sierra Club Books.

McLaren, P. (1989). The emergence of a critical pedagogy. In P. McLaren (Ed.), *Life in Schools* (pp. 159–207). New York: Longman.

Neperud, R. W. (Ed.). (1995). *Context, content, and community in art education: Beyond postmodernism.* New York: Teachers College Press.

Noddings, N. (1996). On community. *Educational Theory, 46*(3), 245–267.

Orr, D. W. (1992). *Ecological literacy: Education and transition to a postmodern world.* Albany: State University of New York Press.

Peel, J. D. Y. (1972). *Herbert Spencer: On social evolution.* Chicago: University of Chicago Press.

Prawat, R. S. (1993). The value of ideas: Problems versus possibilities in learning. *Educational Researcher, 22*(6), 5–16.

Preskill, S. (1989). Educating for democracy: Charles W. Eliot and the differentiated curriculum. *Educational Theory, 39,* 351–369.

Sandel, M. J. (1996). *Democracy's discontent: America in search of a public philosophy.* Cambridge, MA: Harvard University Press.

Schlesinger, A. M. (1998). *The disuniting of America: Reflections on a multicultural society.* New York: W. W. Norton.

Selznick, P. (2002). *The communitarian persuasion: A public philosophy for our time.* Baltimore: Johns Hopkins University Press.

Sleeter, C. M. (1996). *Multicultural education as social activism.* Albany: State University of New York Press.

Smith, G. (2002). Place-based education: Learning to be where we are. *Phi Delta Kappan, 83,* 584–594.

Taylor, C. (1989) *Sources of the self: The making of modern identity.* Cambridge, MA: Harvard University Press.

Taylor, C. (1994). The politics of recognition. In A. Gutmann (Ed.), *Multiculturalism and the politics of recognition* (pp. 25–73). Princeton, NJ: Princeton University Press.

Theobald, P. (1997). *Teaching to the commons: Place, pride, and the renewal of community.* Boulder, CO: Westview Press.

Theobald, P., & Curtiss, J. (2000). Community as curricula. *Forum for Applied Research and Public Policy, 15,* 106–111.

de Toqueville, A. (1956). *Democracy in America.* New York: Mentor Books. (Original work published 1836.)

Walzer, M. (1992). *What it means to be an American.* New York: Marsilio.

Williams, B. (1988). *Upscaling downtown: Stalled gentrification in Washington, D.C.* Ithaca, NY: Cornell University Press.

Wright, B. F., (1996). *The federalist.* New York: Barnes & Noble Books.

Young, I. M. (1990). *Justice and the politics of difference.* Princeton, NJ: Princeton University Press.

III

Global Visions of the Local in Higher Education

Too often in formal schooling, one stage of education is discussed with little thought about what comes before and after. In this volume we have tried to show the relevance and power of place-based education to every stage of formal schooling. This final section explores ways that educators at the university level are attempting to reconfigure their courses or programs to introduce students to the potentialities of place as the site of democratic practice, personal and political awareness, and education.

Three of the four chapters demonstrate the significance of place-based thinking to understanding the global context of contemporary life. Because of its focus on specific localities, place-based education has been critiqued as narrowly provincial or disconnected from the larger and more complex problems of the global age. However, as many of the chapters in this volume suggest, it may be only through a close examination of the local that the impact of global relationships can be properly understood.

Where "extension" and "outreach" services have long been part of the college and university mission, today's rhetoric has shifted to the concept of active engagement with particular communities. Although the word *engagement* can frequently be found in mission statements and strategic plans, the discipline-specific nature of university departments, as well as their frequent isolation from one another, can make a larger, coordinated effort at engagement difficult to achieve. Michael Mahaly Morris describes his long commitment to the development of leadership within the context of specific places. Morris is that rare academic who has constructed a career for himself that blends scholarship and activism. One of his most recent projects involved the creation of an institute in Albuquerque, New Mexico, that brought together community activists and educators with the aim of cultivating grassroots leaders willing and able to address a variety of difficult local issues.

The following chapter by Freema Elbaz-Luwisch describes an even greater challenge for people concerned about place—the discovery of commonality in a region divided by prolonged violent conflict. She reminds us that war is, shockingly, an everyday event on our planet. Although citizens of the world's only military superpower, people in the United States have not typically thought about the impact of war on actual places. Elbaz-Luwish describes this impact from the perspective of the Jewish and Palestinian students with whom she shares a learning space at the University of Haifa in Israel. Her reflections, and those of her students, remind us that even in contested territory, the discovery of place is essential to our coming to feel at home in the world, and that this experience of at-homeness can potentially serve as a basis for transcending ethnic and national differences.

It is a long way from Israel to the Blue Mountains of John Cameron's Australia. There, Cameron has been "practicing place" and place-responsive education in ways that blend depth experience in natural and wild places with the development of critical social and ecological consciousness. Cameron shows that the political possibilities of social transformation need to be nurtured by the imagination, and that imagination can be recovered through contact with places apart from the daily round. The rhythm Cameron describes between the familiar and the strange prompts deep reflection about the value of direct experience with diverse places.

Community-based and place-based education currently under way at universities from New Mexico to Israel and Australia can challenge educators at all levels to consider the role of place in their own teaching. The final contributors to the book, Matt Dubel and David Sobel, describe how place-based educational thinking can be accomplished in teacher education here in the United States. Sobel is one of the preeminent voices in the current movement for place-based education. His record of "institutionalizing" an approach to education that turns a face outward toward communities and places can instruct and inspire similar efforts elsewhere.

If the residents of the industrialized world are to embrace ways of thinking and acting characterized by social equity and environmental stewardship, people of all ages must encounter formal and informal educational experiences that direct their attention to the local—its assets and its challenges. Our hope is that people who assume the role of teachers in whatever capacity will see the value of incorporating place into their work with children and adults. Only in this way will the alienating messages of the global media and conventional schooling be offset by the experiences of at-homeness, care, and commitment.

CHAPTER 11

Place in Leadership Formation
The Institute for Educational and
Community Leadership (IECL)

Michael Malahy Morris

Place contextualizes us—it provides a grounding for where we are from, where we have had profound experiences, and what communities we identify ourselves to be from. Place influences our personal sense of nature, hometown, socioecological values, and the visions we hold for the world. Place affects our sense of problems and priority issues that we believe our primary communities ought to deal with and why. Moreover, place contextualizes what we believe leadership to be and our assumptions about how best to exercise those qualities.

Over the last quarter century, more and more cities, geographical regions, and civic-minded organizations have begun to sponsor public leadership programs oriented toward the needs, opportunities, and/or problems associated with American communities. Community leadership programs emerged as civic orientation mechanisms for preparing a new generation of leaders for nonprofits, community associations, corporate and governmental institutions, and the diverse networks required to maintain a higher quality of community life and deal with complex local problems. Most public leadership projects guide their participants toward recognizing the assets of particular locations and seek to build long-term relationships among project participants in order to carry forward shared visions for community improvement.

The Institute for Educational and Community Leadership (IECL) was unusual in this regard. IECL was created as a special outreach project of the College of Education at the University of New Mexico and the Division of Educational Leadership and Organizational Learning. Coordinated by the Policy Center of the College of Education, IECL required a 1-year commitment on the part of participants; at IECL's conclusion, each participant was to receive a special certificate in community leadership, and 18 academic credit hours. IECL was organized around weekend workshops and retreats, including two intensive summer sessions and a concentrated practicum. Over a 3-year period (1997–2000), more than 60 students ranging from high school aged to retirees participated in three separate cohorts.

IECL's design was a response to a specific moment in time, an experiential and academic answer to the issues confronting particular people and places in the southwestern part of the United States. IECL was intertwined in the lives, work, and home places of educators and community workers who actively sought to better understand who they were, where they were from, what challenged families and children, and, most importantly, how to change community and educational conditions.

What made IECL unusual, beyond its staying power with select participants, was its underpinning in place-based learning—rural, urban, and tribal communities—and how it established a space for participants to contextualize problems and examine issues grounded in personal experience and real places. In the process, IECL's community learning orientation informed participants' sense of shared problems and possibilities across urban, small-town, and Indigenous communities.

Although IECL would deal with complex social problems and major institutions, such as schools and health care entities, its entire orientation was toward place and relationships. This included not only New Mexico as a bioregion or Albuquerque as a unique cultural area, but the actual places people lived, worked, and went home to every evening. IECL's focus was on the places people found themselves in every day.

As IECL emerged and evolved into a distinct community leadership program, the relationships among people, the stories they shared, and how they came to energize and inspire one another, made this a memorable group experience that has simply become known as "IECL."

PLACE, LEARNING, AND LEADERSHIP

Community learning originates within our individual life experiences and the various settings we become immersed in. In terms of leadership formation, place becomes a teacher that is always present, no matter how many times we move or relocate. As we become more attentive to what community has to teach, the lessons of place seem never ending, perpetual, and often paradoxical.

My own development from young boy to adolescent, into adulthood and now aging father and community member have all been influenced by the places I have lived, explored, and worked in over the course of life's journey. These experiences, accumulated learning garnered from each influential place, continue to steer my curiosity and direct my intellectual interests.

My boyhood adventures with community learning began by jumping trains and riding into the countryside, past "the colored section" of town into the rural rolling hills, where I saw the name Tecumseh on a roadside sign for the first time and acquired a permanent interest about all things Native. Boundaries, neighborhoods, the "wrong side of the tracks," and borders between the city and farmlands became my escape routes. These pathways allowed me to enter into rural and urban environments, into nature and learning outside institutional buildings.

Immediately after high school, I spent 2 years reading gas and electric meters in Dayton, Ohio, where I would find myself one day in poor neighborhoods, the next in middle-class suburbs, then downtown in the urban basements of skyscrapers and small shops. This let me see a variety of residences, commercial enterprises, and family living conditions. My day job became a sociological walkabout in an American city divided by racial and class lines, embodied in diverse neighborhoods and stark economic disparities.

Next came the American civil rights era, where my interest in social justice struggles and regional differences drew me to Mississippi. I remained on the sidelines in Hattiesburg until Dr. Martin Luther King, Jr.'s murder in 1968. "What side are you on?" became more than a movement song. Working on voter education and "get out the vote" campaigns in the Black neighborhoods in South Dallas, Texas, solidified a personal pull toward studying community power, race relations, and local organizing.

Graduate studies in social psychology in Dallas, Texas, convinced me that traditional higher-education institutions required radical change and reform. The nature of academic structures, conventional academic course work, teaching methods, semester credit-hour systems, and assumptions about core knowledge seemed an impractical way to organize learning in an era of war, civil rights conflicts, and emerging social movements. As a result, my attention turned toward American traditions in innovation and experimentation within colleges and universities, in both historical and contemporary terms. I sought to discover places dedicated to alternative visions and ways of approaching learning.

My doctoral research on academic change pointed me toward the experimental institutions—Antioch College (which I had passed as a young boy countless times on my trips through the countryside), Goddard College in Vermont, and the New Colleges in Alabama, California, and places like Hofstra that sprang up during the '60s. In response to a national call to redesign learning options for diverse populations and adults—such entities as the University Without Walls movement, the Union for Experimenting Colleges and Universities, Evergreen State College, Alverno College, Empire State College in New York—all became significant contributors to my sense of what is possible in post-secondary education and the critical importance of creating access for those blocked from attending college (at the time, women, minorities, special populations, and older adults).

These experimenting institutions were places where learning was centered on individual development through interdisciplinary study; problem-based or project learning, guided by learning agreements and personalized contracts, with extensive use of structured field experiences that emphasized community participation and civic involvement. The ideas associated with how learning could be more de-institutionalized and made more community oriented would hold my attention for more than three decades.

While completing my dissertation (1976–78), I did a two-year stint coordinating a national network for a Danforth Foundation funded Center for Individualized Education (CIE), promoting adult learning and new adult degree programs. Based at New York's Empire State College's administrative offices in Saratoga Springs, my work revolved around strengthening the eight-institution network of CIE and organizing the first international conference ever held on adult learning in the United States. However, faculty development workshops and conference organizing soon became too detached; they seemed very disconnected from place, community, and the lives of everyday people.

CHEROKEE TEACHINGS

Therefore, in the July summer sweltering heat of 1978, my wife, 18-month-old daughter, and I moved to eastern Oklahoma to live and work among the Cherokees, America's second largest Indigenous tribe. We hoped to do something that would be much more community oriented. My role, in both teaching and administration, would be as a full-time social science faculty member with one of the nation's first innovative tribal colleges, Flaming Rainbow University (FRU).

Created with Ford Foundation support, FRU was the only Native American college founded to replicate the University Without Walls approach—assessment of prior learning, learning contracts, small topical classes, combined with many field projects. My primary assignment was to teach the introductory courses in Political Science, Sociology, and Social Problems and try to make learning as applied as possible. In addition, serving as Social Science Division Director, I was to develop programs dealing with cooperatives, community studies, and assist with the preparation of accreditation study documents.

A year later, Wilma Mankiller, a former FRU student who had been working in the planning department of the Cherokee Nation of Oklahoma, and Scott Gregory, the chief financial officer for the tribe, urged me to apply for the Tribal Development Officer vacancy. A new senior planning position reporting directly to the Principal Chief of the Cherokee Nation, the Tribal Development Officer (TDO) led the planning department (which included Health, Education, Social Services, and various Community Projects). The TDO also was to prepare new federal and state grant submissions, assist communities with planning and program development, and establish new partnerships with national and state foundations.

A month into this new position, in early November 1979, our family's little world was forever changed when my wife, Sherrye Ethridge Morris, was killed in a head-on car crash near our home. My barely three-year old daughter Meghan and I were left to heal in a small cabin at the edge of Lake Tenkiller. In a sympathetic and caring reaction, the Cherokee people held us close to them in familial ways. Tribal elders invited us into the spiritual life of the communities. We were permitted to live more intimately among the people and take part in their daily trials and joys.

The hopes and dreams Sherrye held for the entire Cherokee experience were transported into my new position. In the process, my educational background and training were deeply tested. New learning occurred around river bottom mineral rights, historic building restoration, negotiations with the Bureau of Indian Affairs, implementation of the new federal Tribal Self-Determination laws, and the tug-of-war challenges associated with contract negotiations between various federal agencies. My cultural and historical ignorance about the Cherokees further challenged me. Extensive learning opportunities propelled me into subjects and social problems that no degree in education or public policy could possibly have prepared me for.

Seven years later, my knowledge about communities and Indigenous approaches to development were permanently transformed. My sense of how people and place were intertwined was lived out in both everyday terms and through the conscious development of a new government with roots and representation tied directly to place and communities.

The Cherokee experiences produced innumerable lessons—enough to fill a book in its own right. Two incidents, in particular, stand out in terms of place-based learning and leadership formation.

LISTEN TO THE PEOPLE

One morning, Fan Robinson, a student of my wife's who was an environmental community health planner for the tribe, invited me to her office. Immediately upon entering the portal of her door, sitting to the side in a small chair, still wearing his cowboy hat with an eagle feather in the headband, was a Cherokee elder. Fan introduced him as Crosslin Smith.

As soon as I heard the name, I knew this was one of the traditional medicine chiefs, a hereditary descendent of the Keetowah's (the religious society) spiritual leaders. In an instant, Fan announced she needed to run an errand, picked up some papers, and left me standing before Mister Smith.

As she was departing, Crosslin began the long version of the Cherokee creation myth. He then went into the full explanation of the meaning and importance of each of the seven tribal clans. Becoming exceedingly nervous and unsure about what was happening, nearly 40 minutes standing witness to this endless stream of stories, I waited for him to pause and simply jumped in: "Uncle, why do you tell me all these things?"

His instructions still echo in my ears. "Son, you have been given a great responsibility. You have been asked to lead the Cherokee planning department, to represent us in the halls of government, to create programs and projects for our people. You know nothing, really, about us. You are a stranger, a newcomer to our world and our ways. You do not know our origins, our medicine, our traditions, our values and beliefs. Before you make any major decision or choose a particular path for our people, you must listen to what we think should be done. Do not assume you know what to do. We know what we want to happen for our communities, our way of life, the next generation. Listen to the people; speak with the elders—we will tell you which way to go."

This simple but potent message has greatly influenced me in terms of place-based learning—listen to the people, they will point the way. People in every community and place know what they need, what is important to them, what they want to learn and do. Sometimes it may not be clear at first; there will be competing ideas and conflicting interests. But, the way will eventually be pointed out, if one listens to the people.

REMEMBER THE REMOVAL

By the early 1980s, there was a general recognition that the Cherokee children—elementary, middle, and senior high school aged students—were not receiving an adequate or historically accurate education about their people, the Cherokee contributions to society, their language, their removal from Georgia, North Carolina, and Tennessee, and the tribe's struggles with the federal government over centuries, within the public schools and state controlled education.

The Cherokee Nation Youth Leadership program was established to address this oversight and encourage a new generation of potential tribal leaders. Young people did not know each other as blood relatives; they tended to only meet through school-based academic or athletic competition. Too few knew their own tribal history, the clan structure, anything about the old ways and key words and concepts in the Cherokee language. The tribe started the youth leadership program outside the schools as a way to deal with tribal history and core cultural values.

In an effort to revive interest in tribal history, the Cherokee Nation Youth Leadership Program sponsored separate trips to retrace the Trail of Tears, the infamous routes over which Cherokees were transported from their homelands in the east (Carolina, Tennessee, and Georgia) to Indian Territory (modern day Oklahoma). Commonly known as the Trail of Tears by the Cherokees and several other Oklahoma tribes, these forced removals resulted in more than one-third of the tribal membership dying at the time (early 1830s) due to the arduous journey, various diseases, starvation, and freezing to death.

Historians have estimated more than 17,000 Cherokees perished in these forced removal trips from their eastern homeland to Indian Territory. The Trail of Tears marked the tribe's principal historical memory and was intensely implanted in every tribal members' consciousness. However, despite its cultural importance, only a few paragraphs appeared on this subject in the official State of Oklahoma history textbook.

In order to bring more prominence to this subject and rekindle a deeper interest in tribal history, the Cherokee Nation Youth Leadership Program embarked upon three separate trips back to the ancient Cherokee homelands to retrace removal routes. These trips began in the summer of 1983—first through actually hiking the remaining trails in Arkansas and southern Missouri, then retracing historical points in North Carolina, Georgia, and Tennessee.

The last trip in 1984—called Remember the Removal—sought to bring larger public attention to naming various parts of the 1400 mile long land route of the Trail of Tears as a federal designated trail system. Ultimately, this trip did contribute to the federal designation being granted, and the entire experience remains an important youth development achievement for many tribal leaders. Later in 1984, the national Association for Experiential Education (AEE), with urging from the National Youth Leadership Council's chief executive officer, James Kielsmeier, named The Remember the Removal Project one of the outstanding youth leadership programs in the nation.

Teaching cultural and political history on the road, in actual encampment sites reported in official removal documents, visiting gravesites and places with direct historical and cultural importance, changed these young people's perspectives and lives. It also taught me that government, political, and cultural history could be made more alive through meaningful site immersions and deep field-oriented learning. Using community and local people as teachers made the past come alive through stories, official records, and documents. All these were powerful pedagogical tools.

My experiences also taught me that history in place matters; cultural and community history shape and influence what we experience. Untapped, and often unrecognized and devalued, knowledge exists at the local level if we but seek to uncover it. Listening to the people, sharing stories, identifying what common visions people hold for their home places and the future, one can learn what folks believe are the right actions to take when faced with difficult problems. All these lessons would influence what became known as the IECL approach.

HIGHLANDER AND GRASSROOTS CHANGE

In modern American culture, few places have achieved the revered status as a site for sharing problems and democratizing leadership as has the Highlander Center in Tennessee. Founded during the Great Depression, Highlander became an Appalachian people's retreat and regional think tank for community activists and common folks wanting to make a difference in the life of their communities.

My awareness of Highlander began in the late 1960s. Civil rights friends and colleagues had been there, and many admired Highlander's role in training Dr. Martin Luther King, Jr. and others working to pursue nonviolence and civil disobedience. Social activists knew how Rosa Parks had been trained there before the famous incident on the Montgomery bus that helped ignite the contemporary era in the American Civil Rights movement. The Student Non-Violent Coordinating Committee (SNCC) also met at Highlander under the watchful eye and inspiring wisdom of Ella Baker. Highlander played an important role as a "safe house" for social justice and for organizing around social and political problems.

My life became more directly tied to Highlander during graduate school. One of my mentors, the late Royce "Tim" Pitkin, founding president of Goddard College, was a longtime family friend and ally of Myles Horton, also a founder of Highlander. Tim and Myles had traveled to the Danish folk schools as graduate students in New York. When Pitkin first heard my dreams for creating a rural learning center tied to community development, he strongly suggested that I meet with Myles and one of his former Goddard students, Frank Adams. These introductions later paved the way for my own relationship with both Myles and Frank (who wrote the initial history of both Highlander and Goddard).

Myles' first wife, Zilphia Mae Horton, was part Cherokee. So Horton's interest in eastern Oklahoma and the challenges of the Cherokee people were lifelong and genuine. He had several times visited that region pondering whether or not a Highlander replication project might make any sense. He told me that he concluded a Highlander adaptation could only work if native Cherokees led it from that region. Three of my Flaming Rainbow students had that potential—Wilma Mankiller, Julie Moss, and the late Georgianna Springwater. But none took on this critical task.

Over the years, my primary community learning interests would center on the facilitation process used at Highlander and its role in developing the Citizenship School model—a grassroots effort to train common people to pass the literacy tests in Southern states and secure their rights to full citizenship. Citizenship Schools were an informal learning system that allowed and encouraged people to understand democratic concepts and then practice through direct actions how average citizens could influence voter participation, issue articulation, and public policy.

Through the committed leadership of Septima Clark, Bernice Johnson, Eutaw Jenkins, and later Andrew Young and Dorothy Cotton, Citizenship Schools became a widely used tool for achieving voting rights and inspiring people to become involved in community leadership. Dorothy Cotton, the longtime director of the Citizenship Schools, recently told me, "There has never been a leadership program like the Citizenship Schools; it encouraged unlettered and often uneducated people to define what democracy meant to them and assume greater control over their public lives and the direction of their home communities."

Myles, Highlander, Frank Adams, and Dorothy Cotton taught me the power inherent in informal learning, the importance of people sitting as equals in a circle together sharing stories and concerns across communities, the fellowship and bonds that form when people express their innermost heartfelt and passionate concerns for life, their families and loved ones, and the hope they hold for their communities. Highlander also taught me what Friere suggested in his writings: People could make their own political and historical meaning from defining difficult words and ideas in their own terms—such as Bill of Rights, Freedom, Democracy, and Community Change.

Highlander also permitted me the opportunity to better understand shared leadership among colearners who gain power and perspective from the lives and encouragement of others, in extended dialogue and discussion with each other, while defining problems and issues on their own terms. This process—what we might call an informal, nonhierarchical, non-teacher-dependent, discussion and organizing practice—would become fundamental to how IECL sought to teach and create a community of learners in Albuquerque, New Mexico.

TIME AND PLACE: RISE OF GANG VIOLENCE, PLANT CLOSINGS, AND RACISM

The 1990s were unkind to New Mexico. The state and its people were in the throes of another boom and bust economic pendulum, an economy tied to tourism and military and war-related research, compounded by a bottoming out of oil- and gas-drilling revenues. Small towns across the state, especially rural villages and tribal pueblos, saw their stores and livelihoods either diminished or further transformed into commuter economies—driving greater distances for employment and household goods and services. Only urban magnets such as Albuquerque, Santa Fe, and Las Cruces continued to grow in population, despite these shifts in economic fortunes.

Albuquerque, the geographical center of New Mexico, sits at the actual crossroads of Interstates 40 and 25. Development in this city over the last half century would best be described as continuous sprawl.

Housing has spread up and down the Rio Grande River and into the mountain edges and western desert mesas, while the central city has struggled to maintain its infrastructure and vitality.

The core of the city, the downtown areas surrounding old Albuquerque, were designated "Pocket of Poverty" neighborhoods during the federal War on Poverty era in the 1960s. The 17 diverse neighborhoods that compose this "Pocket of Poverty" area had not only lost physical and commercial vitality, but a growing number of long-term residents as well. Neighborhoods such as East San Jose, Kirtland Corner, South Broadway, and Wells Park are composed of a large portion of low-cost housing and rent options that serve a more transient population, making these neighborhoods less rooted, less stable. Families with children, in particular, come and go in an almost constant fashion. Several schools in these neighborhoods lose 100% of their student body over the course of a school year.

At the city's boundaries, literally but a few miles away, lay the ancient tribal villages that surround modern Albuquerque—the pueblos of Isleta, Sandia, Santa Anna, San Felipe, and, only a few miles farther out, Laguna, Acoma, Santa Domingo, and Cochiti. These are traditional communities dating back hundreds of years, now seeking to shape more contemporary visions for how a Native American community lives.

By the 1990s, West Coast–style gang culture—stereotyped for the public by rampant drug usage, unbridled graffiti art, endless drive-by shootings, youth-led executions, and constant territorial battles—added an ever-heightened tension and more anxiety to New Mexico's sense of place: unsafe communities, neighborhoods, and tribal reservations. This produced a citywide, regional, and even statewide climate of fear and impending violence. Nightly newscasts further reinforced the crisis by running the normal 14 minutes of fear stories. Violence, burglaries, and youth mayhem captured headline after headline. Celebrated murders and shootings lingered in the news for months, not days.

In a conventional reaction, Albuquerque's mayor (recently re-elected, again), Martin Chavez, dispatched more and more patrol cars and declared a citywide youth curfew. Youth-service providers, however, sought a more deliberative solution by forming a Gang Strategy Coalition, external to city government but still funded by the city, to act as a public–private partnership to share ideas and develop new approaches. Led by Fred Griego III, a longtime community activist and youth-service advocate, this coalition sought to establish an interagency convening space where diverse people, ideas, and concerns could be freely expressed. Meeting monthly, the Gang Strategy Coalition provided a temporary space for sharing stories, hopes, and even visions about what the city might be able to do for its young. Although the coalition discussed many youth concerns, this temporary alliance helped frame the first focus question for IECL: What can we do to support our young people and create healthier communities and neighborhoods?

At exactly the same time, Levi-Strauss's corporate office in San Francisco was preparing for its final round of major plant closings in the United States. Still relying on sewing production in jeans and clothing, the company could no longer compete with foreign labor costs. The Levi-Strauss Foundation staff visited four cities where plants and sewing factories existed as major employers (Valdosta, Georgia; Knoxville, Tennessee; El Paso, Texas; and Albuquerque) to assess local needs and identify critical issues. A common theme, repeated by plant workers and local opinion leaders in surveys and interviews in each site, surfaced as a central barrier to individual worker, family, and community advancement and prosperity—racism. This label—*racism*—was defined as the institutional structures and cultural values and behaviors that intentionally and systematically discriminate against people on the basis of race, culture, and ethnic background.

In Albuquerque, racial history and interracial hierarchy remain much more challenging to decipher or explain. Not only does the state still have a significant population of Indigenous inhabitants (28 distinct tribal reservations), it also has a nearly majority Chicano and Hispanic population. Besides its small African-American citizenry, there are also growing numbers of Asian-Americans (Vietnamese, Cambodian, Chinese, Japanese, and others). Couple these groupings with a sizable mixed racial background populace, and any explanation of hyphenated interrelations gets very entangled and debatable.

Racism, within these intercultural and interracial dynamics, would prove to be extremely difficult to confront. In order to draw strategic consideration to the deep problems associated with interracial relations, racial discrimination, and correspondent disparities, three crucial institutions drew immediate attention: the banking industry, with its history of redlining and unfair lending practices; city government in its limited appointment of racially diverse commissioners and public board members; and public education through historical inequities and the problems of fairness for non-White youngsters within the public school and university systems.

Each of these institutions provided a unique organizing target for Project Change, a national antiracism initiative supported by the Levi-Strauss Corporation. Each required that a complex and detailed change strategy be applied, with the ultimate goal being to shift racial awareness and results for people of color, in loan practices, representation on boards and commissions, and how largely public schools truly support the success of all students, regardless of their racial and/or ethnic background.

Education proved to be an especially thorny problem in this regard. I served as Project Change's education chair during much of this time (1994–1998) and was repeatedly told by senior school administrators that educational equity and racism were problems of the city and general society and thus could not be adequately solved and/or addressed within the school system. These positions were articulated as if public schools were not a central socialization instrument for the society's racial prejudices as a whole.

After two full years of seeking even a brief preliminary public hearing and limited discussion on the issues and educational impacts associated with racism, the school board voted not to endorse Project Change's distribution of its Educational Equity booklets within the schools and pointedly discouraged Project Change's representatives from holding dialogues on these topics on school grounds.

Racism was just too divisive, Project Change board members were told.

These seemingly disparate social forces—youth violence, racism, and educational equity—marginalized, denied, and contested topics that they were, became the initial impetus for creating a new space to explore controversial ideas and community challenges.

IECL—MORE THAN A NAME

The term "educational" has ceased to be utilized on its own as a symbolic term that implies learning in any context; "educational" now equates largely to schooling or institutionalized learning. For many community members, however, schools and universities are now viewed as foreign institutions, organizations increasingly more loyal to their bureaucratic forms, representative of public corporations or "educational" enterprises external to the lives of ordinary people and their communities.

The Institute for Educational and Community Leadership (IECL) sought to directly link the challenges facing school reform and improvement to the life of the community. In this spirit, IECL would strive to balance the importance of leadership within each setting and strengthen the ties between the calls for institutional reform with the real tests facing communities—to erase the false barriers that have been constructed between institutional realities and community needs.

Within the field of leadership preparation, Community Leadership has come to be categorized as a subfield of leader practice. Those who exercise community leadership are often identified as public leaders—leaders who work for the greater good in largely public arenas. School, in a period of increased federal and state mandates, is often no longer seen as a public institution. Rather, in urban settings in particular, school has become a state institution managed by professional administrators and highly educated teachers. IECL sought to reconnect communities and schools to the natural interdependence that exists between education as learning, schools as organizations, and the context of learning that exists in the places both within and between community and these formal organizations.

Leadership for the average person is also increasingly viewed in elite and elevated terms. Average citizens do not see themselves as public leaders; this is something others do: elected officials, appointed public servants, administrators, people holding titles and positions. IECL sought to change this internalized perspective.

IECL declared that every person should have the opportunity to lead. In a highly professional and expert driven society, noncredentialed people have a harder time penetrating the power and prejudgments of formal leaders, educational and otherwise. IECL tried to level the playing field, to democratize how leadership could be shared and made more authentic and collaborative between professionals and people who may have limited formal education but considerable life experiences.

A profound example of this internalized chasm was stated in the very first IECL vision-building workshop. In these sessions, each participant articulated what they hoped would happen in their community, neighborhood, and/or institutional base, in terms of change and improvement. Irene Ballejos, a new neighborhood association president and dedicated youth violence prevention activist, framed her concerns for the future with this opening disclaimer: "I do not know as much about some of these things as many of you—I am only a mother."

Aghast at this comment, other IECL members promptly informed her that being a mother was the most important role of all! This catchphrase—I Am Only A Mother—became an oft-repeated remark when any IECL participant felt overwhelmed by the power of institutions or those who were in positions of power.

YOUTH, SCHOOLS, AND COMMUNITY

In a context of youth violence, plant closings, failing schools, and struggles with racism, IECL emerged from critical dialogues among Educational Leadership faculty at the University of New Mexico, those who prepare future superintendents and principals, and community leaders concerned with the future of children, youth, and families throughout New Mexico. The perspectives presented by these voices were especially important in defining how new leadership approaches and IECL's launching might address these challenges.

Education, in particular, has presented a constant challenge. New Mexico has rated at or near the bottom of every conceivable negative school and child indicator for nearly a decade: literacy rates, school completion, dropouts, teacher salaries, expenditure per child, teen pregnancy, access to health care—the list goes on.

Education has been further complicated by child and family poverty in the state. When you compare school performance with family income and diverse student populations, it is the poorest communities that comprise the highest number of schools and neighborhoods on the school-in-need-of-improvement list. This is where children often come to learn English as their second language, where economic realities undermine school success and school performance.

One other point warrants noting. In the early conceptual stage of IECL, community members stated that they did not see education solely as occurring in schools. Communities, neighborhoods, villages are places for learning, teaching, and enhancing human potential. Seasoned community leaders also did not interpret education as being separated from community; they saw formal and informal education as essential to the well-being and health of any strong community. In their words—you could not have authentic education without community; you could not have revitalization in schools until learning was more valued throughout communities.

IECL ANNOUNCEMENT AND CORE DESIGN

The language in the first promotional flyers clarified the principal ideas. IECL was promoted as a yearlong project committed to:

- Supporting a new generation of community-school leaders;
- Building more direct connections between parents, community workers, teachers, and administrators;

- Providing opportunities for extensive dialogue and discussion on critical community-school issues;
- Through strengthening community partnerships and collaborations.

The actual introductory brochure stated: "IECL is a field-oriented learning program focused entirely on strengthening the relationship between schools and communities and to enhancing the potential for collaborative community leadership." IECL would become more than a name; IECL would seek to actively engage its participants with new ways of improving community life and focusing energies and talents on change.

In order to apply to IECL, potential applicants were to be residents of the state of New Mexico. Persons need not be in graduate school or enrolled currently as a college student. A keen interest in community–school matters and the motivation to learn more about community involvement were essential to articulate in the application process. Youth and adults were eligible to participate and teams from neighborhoods, schools, existing community partnerships, and networks were encouraged to apply.

Potential participants were seen as people who possess a deep interest in learning more about:

- Participatory community problem-solving;
- Creating community learning options for young people;
- Building more engaged parent participation programs;
- Wanting to see communities respond more collaboratively to such matters as youth violence, substance abuse, accessibility to health care, and youth employment.

Twenty to twenty-five IECL participants were to be selected through a competitive application process. Efforts were made to ensure applicants came from urban, rural, and tribal community backgrounds. The first cohort had seven tribal members in it; all were youth workers in one form or fashion. Age, gender, and interracial balance were sought as well. Each IECL cohort was composed of teachers, school administrators, active parents, community workers, representatives of local and tribal government, and human-service providers interested in school and community issues.

IECL was organized into a four-semester cohort program tied to academic course work and direct field experiences. Each seminar was co-taught with university and community faculty. Three university professors with interests in education and democracy, healthy communities, and school reform were involved, along with the author. Steve Preskill, Tom Keyes, and Magdalena Avila each contributed major ideas to course content, the co-teaching flow of particular topics, and important community resources to the overall design and delivery of IECL. Community faculty members were experienced and seasoned leaders from health, education, social programs, and community organizing backgrounds, at all levels of community life—urban, rural, and tribal.

Each cohort functioned as a collaborative learning community; competition was downplayed in favor of collaboration and cooperative learning. Participants were encouraged to see one another as co-learners and co-creators of the IECL experience with faculty and sponsors. IECL participants:

- investigated critical local concerns,
- visited exemplary community partnerships,
- met with experienced community leaders,
- worked with collaborative initiatives in the Albuquerque area,
- spent concentrated time developing and refining action plans based on existing or proposed community projects,
- generated interpretations of appropriate leadership strategies from academic and community perspectives.

IECL was to be "an incubator for community learning and a safe place for the exploration of what it means to work collaboratively with others to improve schools and build healthier communities."

IECL's educational philosophy was not neutral.

Each participant was required to prepare a personal vision statement on what he or she sought to change or improve in education and the community and why. Participants accepted major challenges for their community leadership projects, rethinking what they were doing and where they might be going with their work and community commitments. This took the form of action plans presented before other IECL participants, community faculty, and advisory board members for review, feedback, and critique.

IECL stated it existed "largely to increase parent and community participation in education at all levels. IECL holds the belief that educators ought to work closely with parents, local community leaders, youth workers, health and human service agency personnel, and the business and corporate community, to enhance the total quality of community life."

The IECL approach held that schools, whether rural, tribal, urban, or suburban, are primary community resources and therefore have a special responsibility (really obligation) to become more actively engaged with the critical social and economic issues facing children, youth, families, and communities. IECL cohort members were to use their talents and energies to strengthen community assets and participate in local problem solving. IECL's intent was to be applied and experiential, grassroots focused, participatory, fully inclusive, practical in nature, school and community-based, and project driven.

IECL sought, through its operation and learning approach, to model the best practices of community partnerships, collaborative leadership, local advocacy, and current adult learning principles. It would stretch educational notions about the use of time, space, teachers, university learning, field experiences, practical problem solving, personal and community visions, projects, and collaboration. Learning would be based in community practice and take place in full recognition of prior learning (what students bring with them) and see classroom learning as only a part of learning. IECL also sought to extend learning out over semesters, places, and issues—this would not be a stand-alone course or single experience, but accumulated learning recognizing the uniqueness of individuals and settings and adding content over time.

The outcomes of IECL were intended to form new leadership skills, knowledge, and understandings. These were to include new community learning in such specific areas as:

- The nature of personal and community leadership;
- Development of broader community networks;
- The complexity and interdependence of community problems;
- Cultural diversity in Albuquerque and the Southwest;
- Communication and collaborative decision-making abilities;
- New strategies to build partnerships and collaboratives;
- Assessing and mapping community and local issues;
- How to identify, collect, report on community-generated data;
- The utilization of the media for raising community awareness;
- New approaches to conflict resolution.

Four core courses were developed as linked seminars to merge and interconnect this content: Introduction to Community Leadership, Creating Communities of Learners, Education's Role in Strengthening Communities Through Partnerships for Social and Economic Development, and Education for Democracy. Participants were exposed to new interpretations about leadership, recognizing community assets, learning how to sustain broad strategies for Healthy Communities—based on the World Health Organization projects approach and recent "healthier communities" activity throughout New Mexico.

Workshops emphasized storytelling, heartfelt exploration of who was in the room, where they came from, what challenges life had given them, and the communities each represented. Participants listened to each other give voice to the most difficult challenges in life: death, illness, failures, setbacks, and overcoming these setbacks through family support, relationships, courage, and faith.

Racial and ethnic experiences were placed at the center of these discussions. People studied the Project Change Equity Discussion books, triggering their own challenges with the educational system—public, private, tribal, and university levels. Intercultural dynamics became a central discussion topic, even when it brought tension and divisions. Some of the most difficult exchanges came from the stories and readings associated with racism. A few participants left the circle after these exchanges, due to what it stirred up in them, only later to return for other rounds of talk and exploration. Authentic dialogue became a premium throughout IECL.

IECL participants studied different leadership models, leadership traits and characteristics, and looked at various intercultural and community views on leadership. Sessions were held at community locations throughout Albuquerque and on the reservations, Laguna and San Ildefonso in particular, where members were able to meet tribal leaders and see public ceremonies and dances. Efforts were made to take cohort members into the communities they might not be familiar with. Experienced intercultural leaders spoke to the cohorts and described their projects and personal life stories with community leadership.

Considerable attention was also given to collaborative projects with a mix of partners and participants. Participants were asked to conduct summer and semester-long joint and collaborative research projects with fellow cohort members and people from their home communities. They were asked to cross boundaries and collaborate with people they might not normally work with. Journals and media were used to document key activities and for important activities. Occasional weekend retreats were held to go deeper into a particular topic. Special trainings were held with outside and community experts around: Vision Building, Asset Mapping, Collaborative Problem Solving, and Principles of Partnerships. Site visits were made to exemplary projects, to pilot partnership programs, and to experiments with intercultural cooperation in various settings.

An annual weeklong seminar was held with each cohort with an emerging Islamic scholar, Anouar Majid, a Moroccan whose cross-cultural writings and discussions on American society and globalization predated the 9/11 bombings and now serve as an essential reference point for IECL participants to understand how the Muslim world sees America and our people. The Majid sessions were always held during the final summer workshops on Education and Democracy, where participants were able to integrate what they had learned about New Mexico places with a global perspective on the challenges of democracy and education. Majid has gone on to become an international expert on interpreting the American experience to Muslims and Islam to Americans. His sessions served to connect each cohort to larger global dialogues on community and leadership.

The intent behind the content, exposure to different perspectives, and the process was to nurture within each IECL participant the desire to become more purposeful about community change and improvement efforts. This took many forms and has served to make IECL an important networking and collaborative benchmark for many participants.

INCUBATING CHANGE PROJECTS

The process of articulating a personal vision for change, listening to others do the same, and subsequently responding to reading, study, and reflection about what you as an individual were really seeking to accomplish with your life and why, had a profound impact on most participants.

It is rare in our society that we have the time and space to state what we hope for in our worlds and how we want to work on those dreams with others. Moreover, the process of giving voice to innermost hopes for a better world, a better community, a better school system, and being witness to others doing the same has an untold rippling effect on people; each vision inspires the next, and others still contemplating desired futures determine where to apply their full energies.

IECL sought to be an open space for community visions for change. Participants were given the time and safety to fully state their innermost thoughts, fears, hopes, and challenges. People vented their frustrations with one another around community life, isolation, government, major institutions like schools and universities, the challenges of parenthood, lost jobs and relationships, death, and the problems they saw as critical in life.

Such disclosure—often raw and emotional, frequently filled with anger and frustration—builds intimacy. It also leads to trust and deeper dialogue. This was true for all three IECL cohorts.

The process of stating where you want your work or project to go, listening to others do the same, learning about and studying collaborative projects for change, seeing efforts attempt to impact systems and institutions, hearing stories about community organizing and long struggles, either inspires people or drives them to surrender to the forces of the status quo. IECL participants did not surrender.

IECL became an incubator for change projects, and each cohort produced its own projects in that regard. An incubator is a place where people help make personal and community dreams real. An incubator for change is where people work on their projects in a supportive and encouraging environment, where coparticipants assume a contributive role with project design, strategy development, resource acquisition, and implementation.

The crisis with youth violence jumped right into the first IECL workshops, when Irene Ballejos described in vivid detail the murder of her oldest son in a drive-by shooting in the South Broadway neighborhood. Three teachers from Eugene Fields Elementary School, located in the South Broadway neighborhood, listened to Irene's story. The freshness and pain in this story tore at every member's heart. Irene's son had been shot to death in a case of mistaken identity related to a drug deal gone bad.

As a reference point, this story became one that did not go away over the entire 12-month IECL Cohort One experience. Renee Paisano, then a senior program manager with Save the Children/USA, kept thinking about how her work could connect to the needs she heard expressed in IECL. Six months into IECL Cohort One, the first group of participants in IECL, she informed the group of a pilot project–funding opportunity being launched by Save the Children/USA that sought to fund and create urban collaboratives for elementary-aged children designed to provide after-school programming. This funding opportunity—really a seed grant with limited operational monies—provided the impetus to look at how youth programming was occurring at the community and neighborhood level and how a bridge might be built between Irene Ballejos's community (Kirtland Corner) and the South Broadway neighborhood.

IECL participants, community faculty, advisors, and neighborhood allies, all discussed what the vision for such a community collaborative might be. Save the Children/USA staff believed one neighborhood collaborative ought to be formed. IECL participants and Policy Center affiliated faculty argued that this funding ought to seek to build two sites in partnership with one another—Kirtland Corner and South Broadway working together on after-school programming. Each place would develop its own unique community learning plan but work together on resource sharing, training, staff development, and learning opportunities and share what each site was actually learning about program design and youth development.

The after-school portion of this pilot would be called the Albuquerque Community Schools Project (ACSP) and seek to transfer Lloyd Tireman's Depression-era ideas about schools as centers of community life to the modern after-school arena. However, in the early stages, ACSP would emphasize that the community develop its own schools and operate primarily from storefronts and public spaces. The staff for these after-school programs would be part-time community adults from the neighborhoods combined with 10 UNM undergraduate and graduate students.

This student group would be called the University of New Mexico Service Corps and become a campus-based adaptation of the recently launched federal AmeriCorps program. The name UNM Service Corps was put forth in an attempt to establish a brand designation that could survive any potential demise of the federal program. AmeriCorps, in 1997, was still moving forward with tenuous support from Republican members in the United States Congress. It did not seem at all clear whether AmeriCorps would survive.

The first summer was a complete start-up operation for twin projects: the Albuquerque Community Schools Project and the UNM Service Corps. Four months into the projects, Save the Children/USA was encouraging the local partners to submit a grant to AmeriCorps for a National Direct Education award to support the UNM Service Corps and provide AmeriCorps stipends for the college students. The grant submission was successful, and by August 1998, UNM found itself with 80 part-time National Direct Education awards, a tremendous number of slots for any new program.

Under a new mayor, and with Jerry Ortiz y Pino's appointment as director of Albuquerque's Division of Family and Community Services, the partners were being encouraged to expand this after-school model into 10 additional communities. Ortiz y Pino wanted to change the way youth activities were carried out in city-sponsored community centers and saw these projects as a strategic instrument for doing that. After less than a year, the Albuquerque Community Schools Project and UNM Service Corps moved from two sites and 10 corps members to 12 community learning centers and 80 corps members.

All this expansion and subsequent program design was a direct result of the synergy and collaborative spirit inherent in IECL One, a spirit that would find its home with Cohort Two of IECL, composed entirely of after-school program workers—volunteers, city staff, national program personnel, interested teachers, parents, and school administrators. Youth violence and Irene Ballejos's story had stimulated the development of an entirely new impetus in after-school program design, recreating the local community schools movement, and infusing community service commitments from college students into community life.

Eight years later, these twin programs persist and are now prospering in 12 community sites, impacting nearly 5,000 youngsters each day. Other projects, perhaps not on the same scale as these two, emerged as well. IECL participants developed high school leadership projects, middle school programs targeted at African-American males, training programs on racism and antiracism curricula, parent involvement projects, new approaches to full inclusion for students with disabilities, even legislative agendas to influence how the federal-mandated tobacco settlement monies were to be deployed.

IECL emerged as a serious incubator for change.

CHALLENGES: PERSONAL AND ORGANIZATIONAL

The goals of IECL changed very little in its initial 3 years (1997–2000). What did change was the funding for IECL. Cohort One was supported with very little external funding. Jaime Tamez, then director of the Albuquerque Public School district Title I office, did support a small number of scholarships for parents and teachers from Title I funded schools to participate in IECL.

The rest of the participants paid their own way. This "pay as you go" pressure would place strains on certain participants. One-third of the first cohort were college students working on degrees or their graduate education. They simply built the IECL course work into their degree programs. Another third were school-related personnel who had difficulties balancing the demands of IECL (four semesters, 18 credit hours, evening and summer courses) and their family and school-related commitments. A number of school district participants would step out for one semester over the length of the entire IECL program.

The group most challenged by the academic demands included the neighborhood association leaders, community activists, or parents going to a university program for the first time. The weekly meetings, class assignments, readings, journals, and homework pressures were simply too much for many of them. There was a readiness factor, in terms of educational demands, that also inhibited this group. A third of the grassroots leaders (4 participants) would not make it to the final summer.

Years later, when you meet these grassroots folks at a community meeting or celebration, they will invariably say: "You know, I need to finish IECL." Even though the program has not been offered since the summer of 2000, these members still intend to finish.

IECL Cohort Two operated entirely on student funding. Several community participants asked if they could audit the courses and seminars—in other words, do the work but not pay the public tuition cost. This is a critical point because as a learning opportunity modeled after the Highlander Center, whether you link community learning to credit and course work determines how institutionalized you really become.

Highlander never concerned itself with credit and traditional academic course work. The model Highlander works from does not emulate higher education but seeks to stimulate dialogue for social change and action through workshop-based relationship building, sharing common concerns and collective action. The costs associated with this approach are tied to transportation, food and lodging, and minimal workshop fees, not those associated with institutionalized learning that modern colleges and universities now practice.

The key question for university faculty in this regard is: Can you develop an alternative learning approach inside the requirements and bureaucratic guidelines of established colleges, departments, credit-hour generation demands, faculty workloads, and grading systems? Cost and credit demands limit the flexibility higher-education institutions have with offering learning options to poor people and/or acting as sites for long-term community building. Most modern universities are increasingly driven by cost-conscious management and an organizational culture oriented toward income production. Courses and workshops, outside continuing education offerings, are tied up in ever-increasing complications related to cost effectiveness, faculty workloads, and revenue generation.

The IECL model remains antithetical to those concerns. This difference would be tested when the Levi-Strauss Foundation stepped back into the picture and fully funded Cohort Three.

In 1999, the local Project Change finally realized the dialogue and discussion approach to rational change would not move the Albuquerque Public School District board and senior administrators into looking deeply at racist practices in education. Project Change was forced to look for a viable alternative to prepare a cadre of change agents around racism and equity issues. Through their solicitation, the National Project Change board agreed to fully fund IECL to the level of 24 participants, covering full tuition cost, books, retreats, and special events. This would be the only year money was no object.

More candidates applied for the 1999–2000 cohort than any other. Selection was more difficult and teams submitted applications representing certain projects and/or neighborhoods. The balance between university-affiliated participants and community representatives was nearly equal. The group would be composed of high school students, school board members, international graduate students, neighborhood association presidents, community organizers, and every combination of youth, school, and community interest one could imagine.

The interests and the dynamics were the most challenging of any cohort. It is hard to understand, even after all these years, what really happened. But it is fair to say the tensions between institutional learning, conventional teaching and academic requirements (especially grading requirements), and the desire for a significant number of the group to be largely self-directed, literally pulled the group apart. Conflict grew to the point where the group could not hold itself together and the strain pulled it into two camps—university-affiliated versus community interests. The very essence of IECL, its purpose really, was not achievable in the center of this split. As Chinua Achebe titled his powerful novel, *Things Fall Apart.*

In one pointed and exacerbating exchange, Maria Hines, a leader from the Downtown Neighborhood Association, blurted out: "The problem with too many of you university faculty is you have become *institutionalized;* you no longer remember where you come from or why the community matters." This indictment went to the heart of the matter: How could faculty teach about community if they were disengaged from it?

Five years later (2000 to 2005) many who felt forced to choose sides see what transpired differently, myself included. Now IECL Three is seen as a great teacher in how institutional and community learning differs. One is driven by the requirements of the academy, the other by the realities and needs of community. The university requires course syllabi, reading lists, papers, and exams. The community wants to set these aside and act more immediately within the places where people live and struggle.

As stated earlier, it is not at all clear that this type of community leadership model can survive within the culture of academia. Such efforts may stand a better chance as informal, noncompetitive, and nongraded learning opportunities outside the university. Tuition cost, time, assignments, and the artificial measurements of credit hours and semesters, all contribute to impeding informal community learning and leadership formation. IECL existed in its own "wrinkle in time," in a small moment of opportunity, but the permanency that these change-oriented learning projects require may find more nourishing ground in natural community settings. The spirit of an IECL is in its people, their stories and struggles, not in "traditional classes" or conventional professor-led teaching.

In the end, more than 60 community members went through some portion of the IECL experience. Each cohort had the same titled course work and basic experiential sequence. Cohort Three was fully funded and externally supported. That made a qualitative difference in what participants were able to do and the support they received. Cohorts One and Two struggled to make it from semester to semester. Each IECL cohort was entirely different.

Evaluations and member reports continue to indicate that each cohort came away with a powerful sense of IECL as a space to discuss difficult and controversial issues. Each year focused on youth, schools, and community matters, and participants believed they were better prepared to deal with change across these domains. Many IECL graduates and even those who participated for two or more semesters have gone on to more significant leadership at the community and state level. More than a third of the IECL alumni have started their own projects or gone on to direct major community and youth programs.

The participants continue to see IECL as a significant experience in their educational and professional development. Recent research by the city of Albuquerque, where more than 100 city leaders and youth workers were interviewed about after-school programming, identified IECL as a force for change and suggested it be reintroduced as a city- and county-wide leadership development program. About a third of the actual participants say IECL influenced how they teach, work with community, look at community issues, became more engaged with antiracism work, clarified their life goals, and/or decided to return to college. This is no small contribution toward the initial goals and purpose represented by IECL.

EPILOG ON PLACE AND LEADERSHIP

Leadership formation is a relatively new concept for describing how cultures and communities become more deliberate about identifying and preparing future leaders. This subject is drawing global attention as societies find themselves responding to Western economic influences and the downsides of global capitalism. Those who see market forces as inevitable still seek to protect cherished aspects of community, older patterns of community life, traditional lifestyles, and core cultural values.

In a networked world, where people are increasingly isolated on a human relations level but connected to one another in a technological fashion—where headsets separate generations and mass media connects the same folks—how people come together to listen, witness, talk, define, and act in unison on issues that matter to them is increasingly becoming a filtered, if not compromised, process.

Local people continue to not realize how their particular issues with teen pregnancies or drug usage are now universal. Challenges to modern life, whether they be educational, health, or economic in origin, do not always permit for mediated dialogues.

When IECL One participants listened to the stories of family violence and the degradation of young women in a tribal setting, these became universal stories translated to every neighborhood, every place represented in the circle. The struggle of tribal women united to do something about these things knew no boundaries. The struggle was everyone's concern, held every man's and woman's outrage and hope. This level of human exchange cannot come solely from mediated sources. We must sit and talk with one another, listen to each other's stories, look into one another's eyes, hear our unique voices, and plan for change in collective as well as individual ways.

At its core, IECL was about leadership as relationship building. One leads from relationships as much, if not more, than from positions, role, or place. Place and geography are central to pedagogy, but relationships inspire people to see the seemingly invisible interconnections that bind us to one another and to the land. Community building comes from the exchange between people who are being real and present to one another as they struggle to make a difference.

Our isolation, the separateness explicit in contemporary life, distracts us from the shared struggles we all have and our "lived lives" as human beings. We share countless invisible and unstated agendas with one another that can only come to the surface when we hear each other's stories and challenges. The major gift of places like Highlander, besides merely surviving and being such an important gathering point, is that it has been a civic storytelling place for sharing people's struggles, a place to meet and talk, and more importantly, organize about the most difficult problems facing our communities and our poorest people.

We need hundreds of Highlander Centers across the country—formal and informal—that provide citizens of all ages with the gathering places to talk long and hard about what is happening to our nation and its communities, how we can work together to protect and improve community life, and how we organize to fight power in ways that preserve our most cherished places and diminish conditions of poverty. This can happen when we meet across communities, class, and contexts and articulate not only the challenges but also the visions for change we each hold, fully examining these plans for the hopes and themes they represent for each of us.

We also need community leadership programs that understand that modern crises are complex and interdependent. Issues impacting community life are not isolated from one another; they are interconnected and interwoven. What happens with the closing of a Levi-Strauss sewing plant does much more than translate into lost economic impact and jobs. It ripples through the lives of families, young people, schools, access to health care, and so on.

The challenges of the 21st century require critical thinking about not only the quality of life we want to see for our communities, but how we respond to globalization, complex technology, health care access, education, and the demands for community sustainability. This requires organizational and community learning that is much more interdisciplinary and applied than what normally is planned and implemented. It also requires us to address how leadership formation becomes more intergenerational, mixing young with the old in a process of mutual problem solving through deep and prolonged life experiences.

Place is what makes such visions real. In the United States, where simplistic analysis speaks of Red and Blue states, we have reduced our distinctive regions and incredibly diverse communities to colors that categorize and further divide us, not into citizens and problem-solvers who act. In order for me to understand the rural villages of upstate New York, the small towns along the Mississippi Delta, the villages of New Mexico's border counties, the distinct neighborhoods of Oakland, California, a Red or Blue analysis will never do.

Place requires us to go deeper with our understanding through observation, study, dialogue, and action; place requires us to lead from a sense of community history, human and ecological dynamics, and the practice of democratic action through common problem solving. Place provides the localized opportunity for us to better comprehend the complexities of what leadership means, as well as to become more active citizens and learners within our communities. This learning for action holds the promise that we can, indeed, transform our democracy.

SELECTED BIBLIOGRAPHY

Adams, F. (1975). *Unearthing seeds of fire: The idea of Highlander.* Winston-Salem, NC: John F. Blair.

Belenky, M., Bond, F., & Weinstock, L. (1997). *A tradition that has no name.* New York: Basic Books.

Bender, T. (1978). *Community and social change in America.* Baltimore, Maryland: Johns Hopkins University Press.

Benson, A. G., & Adams, F. (1987). *To know for real: Royce S. Pitkin and Goddard College.* Adamant, VT: Adamant Press.

Cajete, G. (1994). *Look to the mountain: An ecology of Indigenous education.* Denver, CO: Kivaki Press.

Dixon, E. M. (Ed.). (1991). *Antioch: The Dixon era, 1959–1975.* Saco, ME: Bastille Books.

Flowers, J. (1996). *Healthy cities—healthy communities.* Retrieved November 25, 2005, from http://www.well.com/user/bbear/healthy_communities.html

Gamson, Z., and associates. (1984). *Liberating education.* San Francisco: Jossey-Bass.

Grant, G., & Riesman, D. (1978). *The perpetual dream: Reform and experiment in the American college.* Chicago: University of Chicago Press.

Jacobs, D. (Ed.). (2003). *The Myles Horton reader: Education for social change.* Knoxville: The University of Tennessee Press.

Mankiller, W. (1994). *Mankiller: A chief and her people.* New York: St. Martin's Press.

Milton, O. (1975). *Alternatives to the traditional.* San Francisco: Jossey-Bass.

Morgan, A. E. (1984). *The small community: Foundation of democratic life.* Yellow Springs, OH: Community Service, Incorporated.

Price, V. B. (1992). *A city at the end of the world.* Albuquerque: University of New Mexico Press.

Sando, J. S. (1992). *Pueblo nations: Eight centuries of Pueblo Indian history.* Santa Fe, NM: Clear Light Publishers.

Tireman, L., & Watson, M. (1948). *A community school in a Spanish-speaking village.* Albuquerque: University of New Mexico Press.

CHAPTER 12

Multiculturalism, Conflict, and Struggle
Place as Meeting Ground in Israeli Education

Freema Elbaz-Luwisch

What sense of place can be elaborated in a setting marked by conflicting historical narratives, competing claims to "native" status, wide-ranging cultural diversity, and varying degrees of privilege in society? How does this impact on the lives and work of teachers in particular? These questions could be asked in many sites around the world; they arise for me with particular force in Israel, a country that sees itself as both Jewish and democratic, and in an educational system that celebrates some aspects of the country's multicultural diversity while it ignores or silences other aspects. In this chapter I examine these issues through a close reading of stories told by Jewish and Palestinian teachers and student teachers, and vignettes of education experience in which I have participated. I consider the diverse ways of narrating a sense of place that seem to be possible in the Israeli setting, and explore some of the implications of this narrative diversity for understanding the complex educational situation that it represents and the opportunities for intervening in it.

In personal narratives written or told at various times in their careers, teachers speak about different kinds of place: One story features the open spaces of a lost childhood, whereas another refers to the "here" and "there" of the immigrant teacher. One educator speaks with difficulty about the home that, she discovered, once belonged to another family that had been displaced; some students appreciate the heady freedom of an intellectual space provided by the university (Hertz-Lazarowitz, 2003). A wide variety of constructions can be and have been elaborated to provide a sense of meaningful place for these educators. Interestingly, most of these understandings of place manage to construe the violence of the volatile political situation as something that happens elsewhere, alongside but not within the various places where normal life is lived.

In exploring these diverse construals, I write as a former immigrant, having come to Israel from Canada twice: first in 1966 as a volunteer and student spending 7 years in the country, and again in 1983 when I settled with my family. I write as a woman and a mother, and as a person with a particular political orientation. In writing, I try to be aware of my own position and acknowledge it through my text, while at the same time making room for other positions to be present. My purpose is to make visible the complex and contested web of meanings surrounding place in Israel, and to raise questions rather than provide empirical ground for general claims.

As a faculty member at a university in the north of the country that has a more diverse student body and faculty than any other in the country, I've been involved in the education of practicing and prospective teachers who come from the different communities that make up the fabric of Israeli society. Over the years, I have searched for ways of engaging the students with their own life stories and those of their colleagues, believing that personal stories provide a fertile ground for meeting—with oneself and with others (see Berlak, 1996; Conle, 1996). It is not easy in the university classroom to create the conditions of safety and mutual respect that enable people from groups with conflicting positions to tell personal stories, particularly during times of political strife and violence in our immediate surroundings. The effort is not always successful but is often very rewarding, for participants as well as for myself as their teacher. Engaging with the personal and professional stories of teachers, one is struck by the difficulties of making a place for oneself in teaching, and by the many creative ways that individuals go about this task. Reading and listening to such stories across cultural and other differences, one finds that these stories ground a deeper understanding of lives in education; furthermore, one discovers that personal stories can serve as places of meeting. With a deeper understanding of how this comes about, education might help to elaborate the possibility of place as the ground or setting for personal and cultural experience to be shared, rather than property to be fought over or, at best, divided.

In what follows, I first provide some background into the particular setting of Israel and the Israeli educational system as the backdrop for many of the stories told by the teachers whose words I quote later on. I go on to examine some of the ways that place appears in the stories of Israeli teachers: Some tell stories of being reconciled with one's place, at home in teaching or in the country, whereas others tell stories of ongoing struggle and conflict. I then look at stories that seem to throw into relief the potential of stories as meeting-ground for people from different communities and backgrounds, providing a way to engage with and learn about one another. Finally, I consider what the implications of this series of stories might be both for the specific context of Israel and more widely.

THE MANY PARADOXES OF PLACE IN ISRAEL AND IN ISRAELI EDUCATION

Israel is a contradictory place in regard to the way that it enables various groups to belong; the country aims to be, simultaneously, a democratic country offering equality under law to all its citizens, and a Jewish state that honors both Jewish religious tradition and Zionist ideals. The country's ethos and institutions have been shaped by the experience of centuries of persecution and exile. The Holocaust has marked virtually every aspect of Israeli life: Many people feel that Israel exists so that the situation of European Jews who were arrested, deported, sent to concentration camps, and murdered, will never be repeated. Thus Israeli law includes a "Law of Return" that grants automatic citizenship to Jewish immigrants; this is the primary official act of positive discrimination on which there is almost universal consensus among Jewish Israelis, despite the obvious disadvantage to which it subjects non-Jewish citizens. The Hebrew term for immigration to Israel is "aliya"—*going up* to the holy land; for new arrivals, immigration to Israel often carries a sense of homecoming. The Jewish experience of disenfranchisement over centuries of diasporic living and the Biblical commandment to "honor the stranger who lives in one's midst" provide moral force to the provisions, enshrined in the country's declaration of independence, granting equality under law and freedom of worship to all citizens regardless of their background and religious or ethnic affiliation. Nonetheless, for the one sixth of the population that is not Jewish (primarily Moslem and Christian Arabs), their sense of belonging to the state is made problematic by the political situation and by pervasive, de facto inequalities in public services. The Arab citizens of Israel often regard their identity as Israeli citizens as a "historical accident" and tend to identify themselves as belonging to the land and to the Palestinian people, although they participate in the political process, are represented in the Knesset, and pursue their rights within the framework of the legal system.

Another paradoxical aspect of the Israeli ethos is its relation to modernity. Founded in 1948 by a United Nations resolution (which called for two states, Israel and Palestine, and was rejected by the neighboring Arab countries, which declared war on the new Jewish state), Israel is a very young country by world standards; the history of the Jewish people, however, goes back nearly 6,000 years, and the history of settlement of Jews in the region is documented going back more than 3,000 years. Thus a very long view of time and a connection to a particular place throughout that time are one of the distinguishing features of the culture. Giddens (1991) argued that one main aspect of modernity is the separation of time and space, with the result that the premodern sense of place is lost: We are no longer attached to particular places as meaningful within the cycle of our individual and collective lives. Locations become interchangeable, judged only by the "quality of life" available in them, no longer carrying unique historical and cultural meanings for those who belong to them. In Israel, the situation seems quite different: As a place that has been fought over, with many losses on all sides over the years, the sense of place and of belonging to place is no doubt altered but certainly not diminished by modern concerns. Almost 60 years after the founding of the state, the country is dotted by memorials placed on the sites of important battles in the 1948 war, as well as on the sites of more recent terror attacks; ceremonies are held at these sites on the Day of Remembrance for fallen soldiers, and other commemorative practices are common (naming public buildings after fallen soldiers, publishing books remembering their lives, and so on). Other, less official forms of remembrance have also grown up. For example, occasionally the families of people killed in automobile accidents place memorial plaques or objects beside the road, thus mimicking the practice for military losses.

In the Palestinian community within Israel, there are similar informal practices of remembrance, such as going to visit the sites of Arab villages that existed before 1948; in some places little concrete evidence of the village remains, but cemeteries, mosques, and churches have been preserved and serve to mark these sites. A joint Jewish–Palestinian organization, "Zochrot" (meaning remembrance) conducts tours that take people from both communities to visit various sites, provides information about what existed there before 1948, and sometimes places signs or plaques to inform people of the former Arabic names of streets or towns. Jewish settlers in the occupied Palestinian territories justify their presence there by appeal to the Bible and to a conception of the Biblical "land of Israel" as a place divinely promised to the Jewish people, which they see as their religious duty to settle and preserve. Holy sites in Jerusalem and Nazareth have sparked conflict and contention because more than one group stakes a claim of ownership to a particular site or holy place. Even Tel Aviv, a thoroughly modern and dynamic city where sentimentality about the past seems to have little place, has been declared a World Heritage Site by UNESCO because of the large number of buildings in the Bauhaus style built there in the first half of the last century by Jewish architects who emigrated from Germany. In short, modernism does not seem to have lessened the grip of the past on the local sense of place for either Jews or Arabs.

THE ISRAELI SCHOOL SYSTEM

The paradoxes of life in Israel extend to the school system, which is segregated according to language—two parallel systems teaching in Hebrew and in Arabic— and according to religion—the Jewish sector divided into religious and secular schools, whereas the Arabic-speaking schools take in Moslem, Christian, and Druse pupils (see Kalekin-Fishman, 2004, for a comprehensive treatment of the education of the diverse groups in Israel). In recent years, a small number of bilingual schools have opened; these schools have roughly equal numbers of Jewish and Arab pupils, and two teachers in each class (see Feuerverger, 2001, for an account of one such school and its community). The Jewish population is highly diverse in terms of ethnic background; a system-wide reform in the 1970s established a structure consisting of a 6-year elementary school followed by 3 years of junior high school and 3 years of high school. One of the purposes of this reform was to increase integration among different social and cultural groups. The reform was only moderately successful in this respect (see Yogev, 1989).

Military service brings young people at age 18 into increased contact with the diversity of Israeli society, but attendance at university may be the first time that many Jewish and Arab/Palestinian young people encounter one another. At the University of Haifa, Arab students make up 20% of the student body, paralleling their proportion in the population; about a third of the Jewish students are of Sephardic origin (coming from families who immigrated to Israel from North Africa and Asia), and about 20% of those of Ashkenazi (European) origin are themselves immigrants from the former Soviet Union. Thus, the university represents the diversity of Israeli society and provides a place of meeting, and sometimes confrontation, between the different groups (see

Hertz-Lazarowitz, 2003; Elbaz-Luwisch, 2001). In many instances, however, students study alongside one another without much interaction.

ATTENTION TO PLACE IN ISRAELI EDUCATION

There has been a widespread attitude favoring protection of the natural environment in Israel, long before environmental issues came to the forefront in Western countries, for reasons directly related to Zionist ideology: Touring the country and appreciating its natural beauty is seen as a way of expressing one's belonging and ownership. In Israeli schools, this attitude was given clear expression through regular trips to various parts of the country, which were seen as an essential part of the curriculum and have served as an important educational instrument in inculcating the discourse of Zionism. The study of the "homeland" (known as "moledet" in Hebrew) is a compulsory part of the elementary school curriculum, usually organized in a conventional way beginning with the child's immediate surroundings—home, family, and neighborhood—in the early grades, continuing with a study of the wider community, the town, and its institutions. In junior high school, the curriculum expands to include a study of the different regions of the country using the tools of geography, but now organized as a subject called "Shelach" in Hebrew—an acronym for the different components of the subject, field studies, national studies, and social studies. The subject incorporates regular field trips to learn about the country.

These field trips, hikes, and class overnight trips have been a particularly effective feature of Israeli schooling. Class trips have been seen as a medium for learning actively about one's environment and country, and for making connections among the different subjects in the curriculum as one relates the history and geography learned in class to the place being visited. The impact of school trips is reinforced by the work of informal educational organizations such as youth movements, which also draw heavily on hikes and overnight trips as part of their programs. The trip functions as a way of establishing one's belonging: as Casey comments about journeys, they "not only take us to places but embroil us in them" (1993, p. 276). Hiking tours have been the preferred way of coming to know the country because:

> When you hike in the desert you actively possess its wadis and rocky promontories. The circuitous mountain roads skirting dense pine forests become Jewish when you drive along them. Sighting gazelles, identifying wild plants, excavating archaeological sites

are all symbolic acts of possession. Caring about the homeland proves ownership. (Benvenisti, 1986, p. 23)

The author of these lines, Benvenisti, is a theorist and critic of labor Zionist ideology and a former youth leader himself; his comments are intended to convey a strong sense of irony regarding the way that "ownership" of the land has been socially constructed, and reinforced through the medium of the nature hike. This is illustrated by the story of a teacher named Lena who was a new immigrant from Eastern Europe: taking part in the end-of-year trip with her students was the final event in her account of her first year as a teacher in Israel. She told how her students were helpful and concerned, encouraged her on a difficult hike in the mountains, and gave her their last supplies of water. The story of the school trip (told without irony in this case) marked the culmination of her adjustment to life in Israel, and indicated her belonging not only to the school but to the country as well (see Elbaz-Luwisch, 2004). For adults who have grown up in Israel, their sense of identity, their choice of leisure activities, their understanding of the Bible, Jewish and Zionist history, and their attitudes to nature have all been markedly shaped by this aspect of formal and informal education.

In recent years the school trip has undergone significant changes. Whereas trips used to be organized entirely by the class teachers, schools have begun employing the services of outside organizations (like the Society for the Preservation of Nature) that provide more specialized guides to various sites, offering up-to-date scientific information as well as organizing activities thought to be more engaging or entertaining for the children, such as treasure hunts, dramatic simulations, or art activities. School trips are sometimes planned as "fun" outings to a water park or other site of entertainment. Parents are expected to cover the cost of school trips, including all the services provided. This commodification of the school trip coincides with a steady decrease in the popularity of youth movements (membership in which was once *de rigueur* for almost all children and youth) as the appeal of their altruistic ideological messages has faded. During the violence of recent years, some school trips were cancelled or rerouted, and, as part of industrial action, the teachers' unions for a time prohibited teachers from working outside of regular school hours, which made it impossible to conduct most trips. Despite such difficulties, however, the school trip is still seen as one of the taken-for-granted regularities of Israeli schooling that, persists, perhaps especially in times of trouble, as a way of showing that life continues as normal.

Most recently, in the light of apparent erosion of knowledge of Jewish and Zionist history, the Ministry of Education (led by a minister affiliated with the right wing of the political spectrum) developed a list of 100 essential concepts that teachers are expected to teach. This practice has been strongly and vocally criticized (if not ridiculed) by virtually every academic concerned with education: It seems destined to promote rote learning of a rather arbitrary set of notions in decontextualized fashion, rather than meaningful learning of one's own history closely anchored to its local context. However, the practice is in line with worldwide trends of going back to the "basics," to the teaching of easily evaluated content and the upholding of "standards"; it also speaks (if indirectly) to widespread concern with the falling standards of Israeli performance on international evaluations, particularly in mathematics and other highly valued subjects. As a result, this newly imposed task, which teachers are expected to implement on their own (no formal materials have been developed, and for the most part the concepts are already covered in existing curricula), has proved resistant to criticism. In fact, the Ministry has expanded the practice to cover concepts in science and social studies, each with their own list.

THE ENVIRONMENT AS A SITE OF COOPERATION/CONFLICT

Geographically, the eastern end of the Mediterranean basin is a region that served, in the course of its long history, as a corridor for travel and transport of goods throughout the Middle East (Keinan, 1998). As the term *corridor* suggests, it is a very small and narrow area, rich in natural diversity (beaches, mountains, swamp, desert, and forest as well as urban sprawl) but poor in resources, and environmentally at risk. Cooperation is desperately needed to safeguard the environment. Following the signing by Israeli and Palestinian leaders of the Oslo accords of 1993 (a groundbreaking document that provided a framework for a multistaged process through which an eventual peace agreement was to be worked out; these accords broke down at the end of 2000 with the beginning of the violence of the second Intifada), a number of nongovernmental organizations began to work in the area. Chaitin, Obeidi, Adwan, and Bar-On (2002) began a study in 2000 of organizations whose work was aimed "at enhancing not only the regional environment but also the development of peaceful relationships between the neighbours" (p. 65). However, the outbreak of violence in October 2000 not only made it difficult to collect data as planned but also made it almost impossible for the research team (composed of Israeli and Palestinian researchers) to continue their regular meetings. Nonetheless, they were able to portray an interesting picture of the work of environmental organizations in the region as related to the wider political situation. They found that both sides agreed that too much environmental damage had been incurred, that the issues (such as water, pollution, sustainable development, and public awareness) were common to both sides, and that there was urgency and a shared interest in addressing these issues. However, they also found important differences in perspective tied to the asymmetry between sides in the conflict:

> Palestinian environmentalists see the Israeli occupation of Palestinian lands, and their general disregard for the Palestinian people, as being *the* reasons that so much damage has been caused to the environment, whereas Israeli environmentalists see deterioration of the environment as being a result of general ignorance, disregard and low priorities on the part of state institutions. (p. 83)

Interestingly, the Palestinian organizations saw themselves engaged in cooperative work mainly because the issues demanded it, yet felt that discussion of the conflict was relevant to the environmental issues on which they were working. The Israeli organizations, on the other hand, often saw the joint work as an important purpose in its own right, with the potential to create bridges between the two peoples, yet they were less willing to actually engage with the political issues and feelings around the conflict, claiming that this kind of discussion was an avoidance of the environmental concerns. The study provides an interesting window into the ways that the complex political situation interacts with the diverse understandings of the environment and of issues around place in the local setting.

Yet another example of the politicization of place and the accompanying complexity of the issues surrounding the topic is provided by a recent event in the Faculty of Education at the University of Haifa. The teacher of a popular course in "Environmental Education" (an elective in the Masters program in Development of Educational Systems, of which I am the coordinator) planned with her students to hold a "Green Day" to raise awareness of environmental issues among students and teachers in the faculty. I was enthusiastic about this plan and passed it on to the Department Head and to the Administrative Head of the Faculty. Both were positive about the idea but raised concerns: The plan, submitted about a month before the scheduled date of the event, called for tables to be set up in the lobby of the Education Building, where representatives of different environmental organizations, invited by the students, would be able to display information and speak with people using the building. We were told that because the lobby of the building was considered "public space," several different offices within the university administration would have to give their approval, beginning with the university vice president and moving on down to the building maintenance supervisor. Approval might be granted, but it would take considerable time for the paperwork to be processed. In addition to the bureaucratic aspect, one main concern was that of security: Approval for the event would likely be contingent on the provision of additional security personnel in the building during the event. A second concern was economic: The spaces that the students had planned to use for the displays—an area of the lobby where tables and chairs were set up for students who gathered to drink coffee and eat while doing assignments together—had, we learned, been rented out to the cafeteria as extra seating space. The cafeteria managers would no doubt object to the space being designated for another purpose without financial compensation. Thus, the lobby of the building, which we thought of as a convivial place meant for educational activity, was overlaid by administrative, security, and commercial interests that all but displaced the educational purposes formulated by the students and their teacher. This episode illustrates the particular Israeli version of how "the discourses of economism and governmentality narrow the purposes of education" (Gruenewald, 2004), while simultaneously limiting the ways that place can be imagined and used.

IN AND OUT OF PLACE

Casey (1993) tells us that "we are rarely securely in place and ever seemingly out of place" (p. xvii). As I have been suggesting, Israel is a country where belonging and maintaining one's hold on one's place have been important and contested matters, historically and politically, personally and socially, for many years. Thus it is not surprising that being "out of place" is a frequent theme that recurs in the stories of Israeli teachers. In the Arab sector of the Israeli school system, teachers are in a particularly complex position, as they have to contend with the dilemmas of teaching in the Israeli school system in a Jewish state where the Arab citizens constitute a significant minority. As individuals, most of these teachers—except for those who have chosen to teach the Hebrew or English languages—are working in their first language, within their own culture and very often in their hometown or nearby. However, since 1948, it is their native place itself that has changed, becoming part of the Jewish state; this event is referred to in Arabic by the term "Nakba" meaning disaster, a term that only in recent years has become familiar to Jewish Israelis.

The practices of exclusion that mark the situation of Palestinian Arab citizens of Israel are multiple and pervasive. In a discussion of Israeli culture that examines changing understandings of Zionism, Silberstein (1999) points out that "Zionist discourse takes it as a given that the land of Israel, also known as Palestine, is the legitimate home of the group represented as the Jewish people.... Insofar as Zionist discourse takes for granted the legitimacy of the Jewish nation's claim to the land, it denies the Palestinian Arab claim" (pp. 22–23).

Silberstein discusses the ongoing debates within Israeli society concerning the founding myths of Zionism and the questioning of these myths by recent scholarship. He points out that post-Zionist scholars have incorporated into their narratives the previously silenced voices of the Palestinian "Other," but, with a small number of exceptions, those writing about the Palestinians' experience have been members of the hegemonic Jewish group. Gur-Zeev (2001) similarly argues that both Jewish Israelis and Palestinians refuse to acknowledge the "otherness of the other" by ignoring the other side's collective memory and experience of catastrophe. It is a common feature of situations where groups are in conflict that members of each side view their own situation in all its fullness, while decontextualizing and even dehumanizing the other side.

Paying attention to context thus becomes particularly important for developing an understanding of the relationship to place where groups are in conflict. Research on teaching, particularly research conducted from a narrative perspective, has developed ways of attending to context, looking at teaching in terms of the concrete details of biography, school settings, relationships, educational systems, and political and historical frames while still attending closely to the voices and stories of individual teachers (Clandinin & Connelly, 1996, 2000; Elbaz-Luwisch, 2005; Goodson, 1997; Gudmundsdottir, 1991; Phillion, He, & Connelly, 2005). However, even studies that pay close attention to context do not always provide a sense of the teacher teaching in a "place": a location that is not only specific and distinct from other locations but that holds meaning for the persons who inhabit it. Erkkila (2001) has begun to examine the experience of teachers in Lapland, paying attention to the understandings of place held by Saami teachers (who are native to the sparsely populated far northern region, belong to the indigenous Saami culture, and speak the Saami language as well as Finnish) and by other Finnish teachers who moved there from the southern part of Finland. Issues of identity and belonging arise in different ways for both groups of teachers. The Saami teachers deal with the problems of maintaining their language and culture and have the task of developing materials to teach the Saami language and heritage, whereas teachers from the south entertain ongoing questions about their place in the northern culture. Phelan (2001) explores the difficulties of "unearthing place" in teacher education in Northern Ireland, where political issues arising from the conflict between the Protestant and Catholic communities regularly intersect educational practice but are generally silenced by prevailing educational discourses. Yet the rarity of studies such as these only emphasizes the absence of a sense of place in the study of teaching. These examples also underline the fact that, perhaps not surprisingly, the presence of cultural difference and competing claims around place is an important motivation for attending to the theme of place in teaching. In the Israeli context, the situation of Arab/Palestinian teachers is illuminating: Many Arab/Palestinian teachers' stories give expression to an experience of struggle around finding or making one's place, whereas other teachers seem to be able to create a sense of belonging within teaching. It may be useful to look at these two kinds of stories in turn, as the contrast between them serves to highlight many of the issues that arise around "place."

The Classroom as Home
In an early study, Clandinin (1985) highlighted the story of Stephanie, an elementary-school teacher for whom the theme of "home" was central to the way she understood her work and organized life in her classroom; the theme of classroom as a homelike place recurs in the stories of many teachers and in the literature (e.g., Butt & Raymond, 1989). This theme appears to be a basic one both to the understanding of teaching and for the understanding of how teachers construe "place" itself: the idea of "classroom as home" not only gives expression to an educational philosophy (as broad, multifaceted, and vague as it is common), but also expresses the existential grounding of teachers in their schools and classrooms as workplaces and as sites where they can put their ideals into practice and make meaning in their professional lives. Thus, it seems to provide a useful point of entry for the present discussion.

The theme of classroom as home appears in the stories of Palestinian women teachers in Israel with a particular flavor. A teacher named Saidah, an experienced elementary-school teacher, described the classroom as her home, indeed as her world, expressing her commitment to her work in the way she made her classroom into a place that felt like home: *I did repairs in the classroom, I painted it and hung up a bulletin board, and painted the furniture...I felt that the classroom was my home. I still feel that way, I try to fix up and decorate the classroom as if it were my home.* In the past, Saidah had aspired to an administrative position and was disappointed to find that others with local connections were promoted in her stead; she had refused to use her own "family connections" to help her obtain the desired position and was both critical of this practice and angry. Yet rather than turning her against teaching, this experience led to Saidah's grounding herself even more firmly in her classroom: She would still like to work as an advisor, but from her classroom as a home base, she is confident that she can contribute and help other teachers regardless of her formal responsibilities. Thus her vision of the classroom as a home motivated her to attend in-service programs, learn about alternative pedagogies, and make regular changes in her classroom work.

Saidah's story is not unlike that of many other Palestinian women teachers within the Israeli school system. The traditional worldview of Arab society views teaching as one of few accepted professions for women, and despite some erosion of the status of teachers in recent years even in the Arab sector, being a teacher still offers women a respected role as a professional within their community. In addition, teaching provides an opportunity to make a meaningful contribution to society and grants a measure of financial independence. In contrast to Saidah's story, consider the narrative of Paula, an elementary-school science teacher in the Jewish sector, for whom the sense of her place in teaching has been made problematic. In the past, Paula particularly enjoyed the possibility of awakening children's interest in their environment: "If a child opens his eyes and looks around he learns to see things he didn't notice before, suddenly he opens his eyes...and comes during recess to ask a question, for me that's something that makes me happy in my work." But after 9 years, Paula finds that teaching tires her; she is irritated by the rude behavior of many children, and tired of "...teaching the same material year after year, dealing with the same problems year after year, sitting in the same teachers' room with the same teachers." Seeking change and stimulation in her work, Paula had trained to become a computer coordinator but a promised new position did not materialize; frustrated, she was no longer able to sit in the teachers' room, but spent her breaks at different places in the school. School was no longer a place where Paula felt at home.

Although Saidah and Paula are individuals and their stories can't be generalized, they do seem to reflect a pervasive trend within Israeli education. School can still be a meaningful place within society for Palestinian women teachers, for whom entry to other workplaces is more difficult, and who often seem to be relegated to the sidelines of public life; for Jewish Israeli teachers, in a more individualistic culture oriented toward financial success, teaching school sometimes seems like a default position rather than a place invested with significance and opportunity.

These stories are also gendered, which becomes more obvious as one reads additional stories of men and women teachers from the Arab sector. The gender difference begins in the stories that teachers tell about their childhood. Hasan, describing a village childhood in the 1940s and 1950s, says:

> We climbed trees, to the top of the fig tree...we made swings on the olive trees and flew through the air to great distances, we went into deep caves, not afraid of animals or snakes. We hiked in the fields and woods and mountains, and drank water from the rocks.... During the olive season we gathered olives, and in the fig and carob season we gathered the fruit...and in the construction work I helped the family, I took nails out of boards and watered the concrete.

Hasan, who became a teacher and later an inspector, is now retired; he was an important influence on his daughter, who chose to become a math teacher like her father. Maha, another experienced teacher who told her story to her daughter, described her childhood in the 1950s as an equally positive experience, but its ingredients are entirely different:

> Mother worried a lot about my studies and helped me a lot...I was spoiled at home and at school, and I remember it as the most beautiful period of my life. We played with "thinking" games, like dominos or the "snake game," and I played chess with my friends or the neighbors. We played only at home...to this day I still have the games at home, I gave them to my children to play with, and now I give some of them to my grandchildren.

Maha's and Hasan's descriptions portray the stereotypically adventurous outdoor childhood of a boy and the well-behaved indoor childhood of a girl. Few Arab or Jewish children would be able to tell such stories today, as there are fewer possibilities for outdoor wandering; in Israel, as in other countries, computers and television fill much of the time of both boys and girls. Both stories are also told in a historical fashion: Maha and Hasan were children during the 1948 war, when many Palestinians were forced to flee their homes and became refugees, and in the years following, during which the Arab citizens of Israel lived under the restrictions of military government (restrictions that were lifted only in the 1960s). Neither Maha nor Hasan refer to these events, perhaps because they want to paint an optimistic picture for their daughters who are starting out in their careers, perhaps because they know their narratives will be read by a professor who is Jewish. Still, Hasan's story describes a paradise lost, whereas Maha's story is one of continuity: She has kept her childhood games and brings them out when her grandchildren visit. These basic attitudes play out in the stories of other Palestinian Arab teachers. Men teachers seem more likely to voice criticisms of inequality, inadequate salaries, and the fact that respect for teachers in the community is less than in the past; they comment about the scarcity of options other than teaching for Arab citizens in the Israeli workplace. In this connection Al-Haj (1995) comments, "The concentration of Arab graduates in teaching stems from this lack of alternatives. In many cases, prospective engineers and architects who fail to find a suitable job in the Jewish sector find their way, involuntarily, into the education system" (p. 204). It is thus perhaps not surprising that some men teachers seem to experience their place in the profession as restricted and confining. Women teachers, on the other hand, while no less aware of the difficulties and problems in the school system, seem less confined by their lives in school; rather, as we saw earlier, school can be storied as a place that offers opportunities for personal development, cooperation, and social relationships. Thus Maha comments, "As for the teachers, we feel like sisters, we share happy and sad times. With the other teachers of Arabic, we help one another, organize many joint activities like Arabic Language Day or Mothers' Day." As we see in the next section, the stories of men teachers (and of some women as well) are more likely to be stories of struggle for place, as they confront difficult physical and interpersonal conditions in their workplace.

Classroom as a Site of Struggle

A teacher in the Arab sector, Feisal tells a story that illustrates the vicissitudes of a teacher's sense of place over the span of his career. During the first few years of his career, Feisal had been sent to teach far from home, and the new place was a site of adventure: "The first two years, there was high motivation and we loved the place, we were young fellows." Later moves from one school to another, however, were simply a nuisance for him, and the return to his present school near his hometown is clearly storied as a homecoming. When he was first transferred close to his hometown after a long wait, however, the move he had waited for proved a disappointment:

> We were teaching in rented rooms, the situation was very bad. I felt that I was in a period before the Middle Ages—there was no water, no teachers' room, goats wandered around outside the classrooms, there was no school building, and I had no desire to come to school. I felt that we were like municipal workers, punching a clock and going home.

Al-Haj (1995) explains that since 1984 the government has "allotted some 16–18% of its annual building budget to Arab schools" (p. 107), a percentage that is proportional to the relative size of the population. However, these allocations are inadequate to make up for the discriminatory budgets of previous years; the shortage of classrooms was placed at 20% in 1989. Elementary schools solved the problem by means of rented rooms that were "usually located on the first floor of private houses and, naturally, not built for educational purposes. Many were formerly shops, chicken coops, or stables turned into classrooms for the lack of alternatives" (p. 107). The situation Feisal describes dates to the late 1980s and conditions have improved significantly in the meantime, but gaps still exist. At the high school level, the situation is less problematic because most high schools are relatively new, and local municipal authorities have channeled a substantial part of their budgets to educational services (1995, pp. 106–107).

Because of the fluctuations of supply and demand, Feisal had taught in six different schools in his first few years. Now in his late 30s, with 17 years of experience, Feisal tells how 6 years ago he attended an in-service program that resulted in a major change in his work. He became involved in a new approach to the teaching of English and was instrumental in setting up an English room in his school. Even though he was a relative newcomer to the school at that time, the principal supported him and helped to get financial assistance from the local council and the parents' committee. Feisal for his part "visited English rooms in several schools, especially in the Jewish sector...(and) learned from the field how to build the English room and organize it in a way that would be appropriate for our school." He also took the role of advisor to the other teachers and "built the project from beginning to end." The story stresses Feisal's sense of responsibility for a project which eventually had an impact on the whole school:

> With the success of the project, excellent teamwork developed among the English teachers. This teamwork was talked about in teachers' meetings, and this influenced the other subject coordinators to start to look for projects that would interest the pupils. The principal adopted teamwork also, he began consulting the teachers about critical topics, and overall this had a positive influence on the atmosphere and way of working in the school.

Feisal goes on to tell that the principal of the school left for a higher position a couple of years ago, and the new principal, who was a "political appointment," had an authoritarian approach that was very different from that of the previous principal. Feisal comments that in the past when he encountered such difficulties with a principal, his motivation fell and he would try to be transferred to another school, but this time he decided to stay and fight against the changes, to preserve what he had accomplished. Other teachers and parents joined in and after 2 years the new principal left. "I felt that I was the winner this time, I stayed and the principal left and the atmosphere I loved and the feeling of belonging were restored." Feisal's account illustrates how the sense of place interacts with other factors in the development of his career, and the challenge of establishing a place for himself in the profession has been instrumental in making him the teacher he is today.

A story that dates from a somewhat earlier period (the mid-1970s) is told by Haled, a teacher who was sent, with only 2 years of teaching experience, to be the principal of a small school in a Bedouin community. On his arrival, the picture that greeted him was similar to that portrayed by Feisal: a makeshift building, no water, animals wandering outside. For Haled, this school became his life's work, as he set about to improve the facilities and grounds as well as to build the educational program. He described carrying water in buckets for the trees and plants that he and the pupils planted together. For 22 years Haled worked to develop the school, enjoying cooperation with a nearby kibbutz. Then a

Ministry decision closed the school along with other small schools that were deemed to be an economic burden. Haled's initial response was to nurse his disappointment and loss; he was sent to be a teacher in another school where he described himself as spending most of his time smoking and drinking coffee. After some months, however, Haled's attention was caught by the large number of disaffected youth who did not seem to be engaged in learning. He started to work with these students, and got them involved in gardening on the school grounds, just as he had done in the Bedouin school. Haled knew that he was beginning to make a difference one afternoon when a soccer game was in progress near the flowers that his students had planted, and he saw them standing and using their bodies to protect the plants from the ball and the soccer players. "This year taught me that despite all the pain it was possible to help the pupils." Haled later became a principal of a junior high, and continued to develop the same educational philosophy that had sustained his early years: "My concern is to integrate students into society, everyone is involved in building the school, there is a feeling that everyone can help and contribute." But it is not difficult to see how that philosophy is grounded in a very concrete way in the place and the conditions that were given to him over his career.

Samira is a Moslem woman who participated in a study of teacher-leaders in the Arab sector, conducted by Shapira (1999). In an account of the study by Hertz-Lazarowitz and Shapira (2005), Samira tells of her struggle to further her career and make an independent life for herself in between the traditional space of her home village and the modern space of the university where she studied. Samira recounts:

> From an early age I have believed…that a woman is no different than a man.… As far as her abilities and strengths are concerned, I think a woman is entirely like a man. My father…it doesn't matter to him whether we're boys or girls.… He really treats us all equally…he encouraged us…to go on learning, to go on studying. My mother is closer to tradition, more closely tied to the earlier Arab mentality.… Mother says I don't fit into our sector, and that with my head and style of life, I should live among the Jews. (p. 57)

Samira goes on to tell of a time when she returned home from work at 1:30 in the morning. Her father was waiting for her and greeted her angrily, worried that her behavior would cause the community to talk about her. For Samira, the only important question was whether her father trusted her, and he told her that he did. To this she responded:

I've stayed here not for my own sake but for yours and mother's. I don't want people to say that you didn't succeed in bringing up your daughter properly so that in the end she left you and went to live with the Jews, abandoning the life and customs of the Arabs. I came back so that people wouldn't point a finger at your honor and the honor of my mother and that of my sisters. But if you push me too hard, I won't hesitate to get my things and go back to Haifa. (p. 57)

As Samira tells this story, one sees her struggling to live in two places at once, to remain close to her family and the traditions of her community, yet at the same time to find her place in the larger world. After telling about the many different jobs she worked at while studying, jobs which gave her financial independence and brought her into contact with many different people, Samira adds that through this work:

My mind also became independent; I was thinking differently. I wasn't a/the type of girl who returns every evening to the village. I simply became independent in every aspect. When I finished studying, I felt there was a huge gap between the way I lived my life and the life in the village. Eventually, I decided I'm going back, but each year I feel I must take a university course in order not to lose touch with things. (p. 60)

Samira performs an unusual and difficult juggling act, managing to stay in contact with both places, her native village and her city life; both places contribute to shaping her identity as someone who lives a life "in-between" two very different places (He, 2005).

The stories of Feisal, Haled, and Samira all tell of teachers' struggles to find a place for themselves in teaching, in their communities, and in the wider society. Each of them has confronted difficulties and experienced hard times as a result of their professional choices and commitments. Two features are particularly striking in each of these stories: one is the great creativity they have displayed, and the second is the fact that each of them, while primarily committed to developing their own school and community, has also been very involved in working and interacting with Jewish colleagues, learning from them (as well as no doubt teaching their Jewish partners) and changing, finding ways to adapt new knowledge to their local circumstances while maintaining their own cultural identity. Their stories would not be the same without this interaction, which challenges them but also spurs them to develop what is unique and valuable in their own setting. Their stories are shaped by moving back and forth from their place to the place of the other. In the final section, I examine stories in which meetings with the "other" are central, and what comes into view is the way that such stories themselves serve as meeting places.

STORIES AS MEETING PLACES

Sarah is a teacher and teacher-educator in the Jewish sector, who took part in an in-service program that involved encounters among teachers from the diverse communities in the country (Elbaz-Luwisch & Kalekin-Fishman, 2004). Huria, a participant in the same program, is a Moslem woman teaching the Arabic language in a junior high school in a small Arab town. The program, aimed at fostering dialogue among teachers from the different communities and encouraging the development by teachers of multicultural curricula in the schools, included a number of activities around the theme of "place." In one of the exercises, participants were asked to bring an object that represented the place they come from. They were organized at random into small groups, told one another the stories of their objects, and then searched for commonalities and differences that allowed them to put together a joint product—a poster, picture, or story—that brought all the objects together in a single narrative. In another exercise, the teachers were led through a visualization exercise in which they reconstructed from memory a significant place from their childhood that they then drew and told about in small groups. In this exercise, Sarah recalled and drew a picture of the area around her house and of the old Muslim cemetery that she passed through every day, stopping to play or sit there on her way to school.

These exercises generated a lot of conversation and connection among the participants. Sarah and Huria were drawn together during the program, and their dialogue occasioned reflections on the sense of place for both women, as well as for Kalekin-Fishman, one of the organizers and facilitators of the program who later participated in a three-way conversation with them (Kalekin-Fishman, 2005). As narrated by Kalekin-Fishman, Sarah found:

> that the program of encounters has facilitated dialoguing with people she had always taken for granted. Because of having met Huria, she now looks back on her childhood and thinks differently about the house she lived in—"abandoned property." Only through the "dialoguing" with Huria did she realize concretely

that the property had belonged to an Arab family that had fled or been banished in the course of the 1948 war. This was before Sarah and her father arrived in Israel. "We didn't have a choice, you know," she reminds me. "We came with nothing and were grateful that the government rented us a place to live. Only now have I begun to think of these things again. I also remember other things. You know, we went to school on the hill, stepping over and around tombstones—a ruined Muslim cemetery." She feels steeped in guilt at finally beginning to understand the plight of the "other," and repeats the painful truth, "We had no choice." (Kalekin-Fishman, 2005)

For Sarah, the place that has come into question is her own childhood home, a place where she had grown up not seeing the evidence of other lives lived there before her arrival, evidence of upheaval. Huria tends to focus rather on her own place in the wider society and to question how it has changed as a result of the violent struggle of recent years. Because of her husband's work in a large "mixed" town, they have many good friends there; yet

since the outbreak of the second Intifada (Palestinian uprising) in the occupied territories, she refrains from visiting friends in the Jewish town. One of the friends called her, and reminded her that a long time had elapsed since they had last met. But she put off the invitation. "The atmosphere is not right. I don't want our friends to feel embarrassed in front of their Jewish neighbors. A Muslim woman in religious dress coming to visit them in these times.... The truth is," she adds, "I never felt this way before." (Kalekin-Fishman, 2005)

For Kalekin-Fishman, participation in the encounter with these two women occasions a reflection on identity and how it is elaborated by all three of them. She finds that despite challenges to their understandings of the past and to their sense of place in the present, none of the women invokes nostalgia; all three women "work with students today and aspire to think in contemporary terms." As a result, in her view, their identities do not appear to show the complexity, fragmentation, or

...the presumed disorder that is postulated as characteristic of post-modernity.... Their identifications as teachers, as women in their families of orientation are all of a piece.... As professional teachers, as women who care very much about family living, they demonstrate identities that are coherent and consistent. (Kalekin-Fishman, 2005)

Kalekin-Fishman goes on to emphasize the constructivist approach that Sarah and Huria take in their work and in their lives. It is this approach that gives rise to an interest in "others," a willingness to learn about them and even to identify with their situations. Huria puts herself in the shoes of her Jewish friends, and Sarah ponders over and over the experiences of her childhood living in the space vacated by Arabs whose lives were put in turmoil when the state was established. Perhaps it is this openness to others that enables all three women to deal with the challenges to identity that are provided by the place in which they live and by their own multiple identifications within that place.

In the in-service program, the place of meeting was an artificial one, engineered by program organizers to bring together teachers who have in common their professional identification as teachers. Although the participants in the course all live in the northern part of Israel, everyday life is organized such that for the most part, members of the Jewish and Palestinian communities within Israel do not often meet in meaningful ways. It was in the course of their dialogue and by telling their stories that Sarah and Huria discovered the place that they have in common, in which they live out parallel lives with many similar features.

Sometimes the story itself can provide a place of meeting. In a course for prospective teachers on the topic of multiculturalism in curriculum, I ask students to write the life story of a person who has influenced them. The students are then organized in small groups that read one another's stories, analyze, and learn from them; they then examine the possibilities of learning about cultural difference through the medium of life stories. Although the stories written by student teachers are typically quite diverse, and I allocate them to small groups in a fairly random fashion, it seems that certain themes typically come to be emphasized in the groups. Many of the stories are written about people who have confronted difficulties in their lives and have been able to overcome them, a theme that unites people from all the different communities in Israel, as do the themes of love and caring, family, and sacrifice. The recognition of this common human experience has enabled some Arab students to connect and be moved by the story of a Jewish student's grandparent who survived the Holocaust; one student commented that although she had learned about the Holocaust, reading the life story of the grandmother of a fellow student had had a particular impact for her. As the majority of teacher education students are women, it is not surprising that their stories often tell about female role models, women who have challenged the limitations imposed by gender stereotyping.

The emphasis on themes such as these—identified by the students themselves—allows them to realize that although the stories carry the distinctive sights, sounds, and flavors of different places, giving rise to unique attachments to those places and indelibly shaping the lives lived in them, there are also underlying commonalities that make it possible to connect. It's important to note that there is a risk of stereotyping and reductive thinking in these connections: The students may share a romantic belief that love conquers all, or an admiration for people from different walks of life who overcame hardships, but this will not necessarily help them to confront competing claims or deal with interests that clash.

In a recent section of this course, a small group of Jewish and Palestinian students were examining the stories they had written. One Jewish student, Lia, wrote about her mother who had immigrated to Israel from Argentina, leaving behind a pampered lifestyle for a life of physical labor on a kibbutz. A Palestinian student, Rim, wrote about her grandfather, a farmer who had struggled to provide for his family. Ella, another Jewish student, wrote about a relative, a man who had been a pioneer in the early years of the last century. The hero of Ella's story mentioned conflicts with the "Arab gangs" in the northern part of the country. This term was offensive to Rim and after speaking with me about it, she decided to challenge the members of her group, telling them that the term was insulting to her. (I joined the group, ready to facilitate the discussion if needed, but was in fact a silent observer.) The students reread Ella's story and discussed the phrase "Arab gangs" (a term in use at the time, referring to what might be described as a paramilitary organization); they found that the events in Ella's story had taken place in 1908. This discovery gave rise to a spontaneous burst of laughter in the group, which seemed to release the tension of the earlier discussion. For me, the laughter was about the absurdity of taking offense (and giving offense) around an event that took place almost 100 years ago. As they reflected on what had just happened, Latifa, another Palestinian student in the group, commented, "All the stories have something in common: Rim's grandfather, Lia's mother, and Ella's relative, all of them love this place so much, all of them feel they belong, they care about the place."

This incident moved me very deeply and it has remained with me. Both the laughter that rippled through the group and Latifa's heartfelt statement were genuine. In looking back, however, I find the laughter even more useful than the statement. The statement, with its hopeful invoking of a common human position, seems to risk the closing off of possibilities: it asks us to feel hopeful all the time, not to despair or come to hate the place where we experience grief, not to entertain the feeling of not belonging. The laughter, however, remains open: We may laugh because the situation is absurd (as I did), and given that it is so, we can be generous and admit any kind of human failing that might arise, and still continue laughing. Equally, we may laugh for a variety of other reasons: I did not ask the students, but I imagine that each of them might have given a quite different explanation of what was funny. Carlsen (2005), in a discussion of laughter in interviews, distinguishes three kinds of laughter that came up in dialogue with his research participants: positioning laughter, resonating laughter, and liberating laughter. For me, the laughter in this instance seemed to be liberating, but other readings of the event are possible as well. Perhaps for Rim, whose challenge to the group brought about the discussion, the laughter was "positioning laughter," which "applauds the specific positions taken by the informants in their accounts" (Carlsen, 2005, p. 249), whereas for Latifa the laughter might have been "resonating laughter," which, according to Carlsen, "amounts to the tuning-in to an unutterable 'we'...marks and celebrates this emerging understanding" (p. 249). This multiplicity of meaning, and the overall function of laughter in maintaining openness, is in line with the words of Bakhtin (1984, pp. 122–123), as quoted by Carlsen:

> True ambivalent and universal laughter does not deny seriousness, but purifies and completes it. Laughter purifies from dogmatism, from the intolerant and the petrified; it liberates from fanaticism and pedantry, from fear and intimidation, from didacticism, naïveté and illusion, from single meaning, the single level, from sentimentality. Laughter does not permit seriousness to atrophy and to be torn away from the one being, forever incomplete. It restores this ambivalent wholeness. (Carlsen, 2005, p. 239)

CONCLUDING WORDS

Like the episode of laughter just described, the stories gathered here do not lead to any simple or one-sided conclusions. Rather, they serve to give expression to the diversity of voices that are raised as the members of diverse communities strive to lay claim to a sense of home and belonging in a rather confined place of conflict and struggle. The stories told here could only be imagined in the particular place of Israel at the current time; yet, they may well have significance for teachers and teacher educators in other places around the world. The situation of Israel is unique, but conflict, fear of violence, and hope for a better future are common to all today. As a teacher educator, I have found that there is a strong resonance between my stories and those of colleagues in very diverse places (Canada, Finland, India, just to choose some recent examples from my own experience).

Listening across cultures has its particular challenges, but at the same time offers unique possibilities for enlarging our understanding. Some of the stories express the struggle over identity and belonging between the Jewish and Arab cultures; other stories are more confident, or perhaps less adventurous, illustrating ways of creating a sense of home and of belonging even in the face of uncertainty. I suggest that both kinds of stories contribute something important to the larger dialogue by giving expression to the wide range of concerns that arise in this, as in any, complex human situation. From the examples of Feisal, Haled and Samira, Sarah and Huria, as well as the participants in my course for preservice teachers, I wonder if the willingness to step out of one's place momentarily, to learn about the other and his or her place, to admit diversity, is precisely what enables some of the teachers to narrate an identity that seems coherent. It is rarely a univocal or a simple identity, but it is a workable identity: Living in a difficult and paradoxical place, it is apparent that some of these teachers have been able to forge a sense of belonging that is open to the presence of others. To some degree, participating in the process of telling and listening to personal stories in a multicultural context contributes to the ongoing process by which identity is constructed.

Perhaps the meetings of stories that come about through these encounters, fleeting and partial though they may be, prefigure more concrete forms of meeting that may be possible in the future. Attention to the complex, changing, and overlapping understandings of place seems to be one of the conditions for such meeting.

REFERENCES

Al-Haj, M. (1995). *Education, empowerment and control: The case of the Arabs in Israel.* Albany: State University of New York Press.

Bakhtin, M. (1984). *Rabelais and his world.* (Helene Iswolsky, Trans.). Bloomington: Indiana University Press.

Benvenisti, M. (1986). *Conflicts and contradictions.* New York: Villard.

Berlak, A. (1996). Viewing a cultural diversity course through the lens of narrative. *Theory into Practice, 35*(2), 93–101.

Butt, R., & Raymond, D. (1989). Studying the nature and development of teachers' knowledge using collaborative autobiography. *International Journal of Educational Research, 13*(4), 403–419.

Carlsen, A. (2005). Only when I laugh? Notes on the becoming interview. *Teachers and Teaching, Theory and Practice, 11*(3), 239–255.

Casey, E. (1993). *Getting back into place: Toward a renewed understanding of the place-world.* Bloomington: Indiana University Press.

Chaitin, J., Obeidi, F., Adwan, S., & Bar-On, D. (2002). Environmental work and peace work: The Palestinian–Israeli Case. *Peace and Conflict Studies, 9*(2), 64–94.

Clandinin, D. J. (1985). Personal practical knowledge: A study of teachers' classroom images. *Curriculum Inquiry, 15*(4), 361–385.

Clandinin, D. J., & Connelly, F. M. (1996). Teachers' professional knowledge landscapes: Teacher stories—stories of teachers—school stories—stories of school. *Educational Researcher, 19*(5), 2–14.

Clandinin, D. J., & Connelly, F. M. (2000). *Narrative inquiry: Experience and story in qualitative research.* San Francisco: Jossey-Bass.

Conle, C. (1996). Resonance in preservice teacher inquiry. *American Educational Research Journal, 33*(2), 297–325.

Elbaz-Luwisch, F. (2001). Understanding what goes on in the heart and the mind: Learning about diversity and co-existence through storytelling. *Teaching and Teacher Education, 17*(2), 133–146.

Elbaz-Luwisch, F. (2004). Immigrant teachers: Stories of self and place. *Qualitative Studies in Education, 17,* 3.

Elbaz-Luwisch, F. (2005). *Teachers' voices: Storytelling and possibility.* Greenwich, CT: Information Age.

Elbaz-Luwisch, F., & Kalekin-Fishman, D. (2004). Professional development in community: Fostering multicultural dialogue among Israeli teachers. *British Journal of In-service Education, 30*(2), 245–264.

Erkkila, R. (2001). Identity of northern teachers and experiences of place. Paper presented at the 7th Circumpolar University Cooperation Conference, Tromso, Norway.

Feuerverger, G. (2001). *Oasis of dreams: Teaching and learning peace in a Jewish-Palestinian village in Israel.* New York & London: Routledge Falmer.

Giddens, A. (1991). *Modernity and self-identity: Self and society in the late modern age.* Cambridge: Polity Press.

Goodson, I. F. (1997). The life and work of teachers. In B. J. Biddle, T. K. Good, & I. F. Goodson (Eds.), *International handbook of teachers and teaching* (pp. 135–152). Dordrecht: Kluwer.

Gruenewald, D. A. (2004). A Foucaldian analysis of environmental education: Toward the socioecological challenge of the Earth Charter. *Curriculum Inquiry, 34*(1), 71–107.

Gudmundsdottir, S. (1991). Story-maker, story-teller: Narrative structures in curriculum. *Journal of Curriculum Studies, 23*(3), 207–218.

Gur-Zeev, I., (2001). The production of the self and the destruction of the other's memory and identity: Israeli/Palestinian education on the Holocaust/Nakbah. Studies, *Philosophy and Education, 20*(3), 255–266.

He, M. F. (2005). In-Between China and North America. Presentation in an interactive symposium on Chinese Immigrants' Language, Culture, and Identity Development in International Contexts, AERA annual meeting, Montreal.

Hertz-Lazarowitz, R. (2003). Arab and Jewish youth in Israel: Voicing national injustice on campus. *Journal of Social Issues, 59*(1), 51–66. Special issue on Youth Perspectives on Injustice and Violence.

Hertz-Lazarowitz, R., & Shapira, T. (2005). Muslim women's life stories: Building leadership. *Anthropology and Education Quarterly, 36*(2), 51–67.

Kalekin-Fishman, D. (2004). *Ideology, policy and practice: Education for immigrants and minorities in Israel today*. New York: Kluwer Academic.

Kalekin-Fishman, D. (2005). Trio: Three (auto)biographical voices and issues in curriculum. *Language, Culture & Curriculum, 18*(1), 3–26.

Keinan, A. (1998). *The Rose of Jericho: The land of Israel, environment, identity, culture*. Tel Aviv: Zmora Bitan Publishers (in Hebrew).

Phelan, A. M. (2001). Power and place in teaching and teacher education. *Teaching and Teacher Education, 17*(5), 583–597.

Phillion, J., He, M. F., & Connelly, F. M. (2005). *Multicultural education: Narrative and experiential approaches*. Thousand Oaks, CA: Sage.

Shapira, T. (1999). *Women as innovators in Arab schools*. Unpublished thesis, University of Haifa, Department of Education (in Hebrew).

Silberstein, L. (1999). *The postzionism debates: Knowledge and power in Israeli culture*. New York & London: Routledge.

Yogev, A. (1989). From school reform to ethnic integration in Israeli schools: Social myths and educational policy. In A. Yogev & S. Tomlinson (Eds.), *Affirmative action and positive policies in the education of ethnic minorities. International Perspectives on Education and Society* (Vol. 1, pp. 65–81). London: GAI Press.

CHAPTER 13

Learning Country
A Case Study of Australian Place-Responsive Education

John I. Cameron

AN EVOLVING STORY OF PLACE-BASED TEACHING

Since 1993, I have been teaching "Sense of Place" university subjects at the undergraduate and postgraduate level. The content and the manner of teaching have changed substantially over the years, and have coevolved with my own "practices of place" and the emergence over the past decade of a collaborative network, The Sense of Place Colloquium. Yet the word "coevolution" glosses over many tensions, personal challenges, and difficulties of working within a modern university structure.

Initially, I designed these subjects in response to my earlier experience of full-time researching and lobbying for a major Australian environmental group. I had observed how expressions of strong affiliation with particular places tended to disappear from the discourse as the debate moved from the local to the national level. I encountered people such as community foresters, small-scale farmers, suburban women, and indigenous people involved in conflicts over forestry, urban development, and agriculture whose voices of place attachment were marginalized because they didn't fully accord with the positions of the main protagonists. Disheartened by ritualized public combat over the environment, I left my position with the conservation movement to explore these matters more deeply in a university setting. What lay behind these expressions of love of a place? Could there be a greater role for them in the environmental debate?

During my first years of teaching, I emphasized the theme of "relationship with place," and took students on a 3-day field trip into remote bushland in the Blue Mountains. They were required to write essays on the theme that related their readings in the literature of place to their own experiences. The early essays tended to be either conceptually strong, discussing theories of place or the politics of place, but only loosely linked to actual experience, or they were strong narratives of personal discoveries on the field trip that were conceptually weak. I soon recognized that I needed to deepen the experiential and conceptual bases of the subject and find ways to better integrate them.

In 1994, my partner, Vicki, and I moved to our current home in Faulconbridge, complete with a large European garden, on the edge of the Blue Mountains National Park. It was the first time I had lived in a place that had a garden of any size. As a longtime conservationist and bushwalker, I initially found my gaze moving to the long view across into the bushland of the National Park. The "real country" started out there, beyond the last obvious sign of human intervention. The bush, from my experience of decades of bushwalking, was a place of healing and nurture and provided time for regeneration away from the life-sapping demands of active work in the human-made world.

In the beginning, when I showed some of my conservationist friends around the garden, I felt apologetic about the well-established azaleas, camellias, magnolias, and roses, and proudly pointed to the natives we had planted. Slowly, working with Vicki, who had many years of gardening experience, I came to include the soil, the weeds, and the exotic plants. I began to regard the surrounding bushland in a different way, as something more complex and varied than undifferentiated "bush" that served as a vehicle for my nurture and inspiration. I was beginning the process of inhabiting our place in the Blue Mountains, rather than merely residing as I had done previously. Orr (1992, p. 130) distinguishes between the *resident* who lives in the indoor world of house, office, car, and television, and the *inhabitant* who knows their place, cares deeply about it, and has a mutually sustaining relationship with it. Perhaps ironically, but not coincidentally, I was less concerned with my local environment when I worked as a full-time environmentalist, spending my time on forestry and agriculture research projects and campaigns in remote and rural Australia, than when I left and began teaching at the university.

At the same time as I began gardening, bush regenerating, and exploring the bushland adjacent to our new home, I realized that the way to strengthen the experiential element of my teaching was to base it on regular visits to a place in the students' own locality. Soon after I began to experience the power of inhabitation, I redesigned the subject. I required students to choose a place within half an hour's walk of their home and commit to visit it for several hours a week for each week of the semester.

This new element transformed the class. The process of selecting their place at the outset meant they had to look more closely at their purpose and interest in taking "Sense of Place" to determine the sorts of places in their local area that would be most appropriate to their purpose. It demanded that students face the extent of their knowledge, or ignorance, of their local areas. It meant that the place experiences on which they were drawing for the semester were primarily tied to their locality, rather than to a field trip site in remote bushland (although the field trip was retained for the purpose of deepening students' capacity to relate to place). It also raised for many the vexing question of "What do we do in our place each week?" which provoked in-class discussions of how one actually gets to know a place.

The students chose a wide variety of places to visit for many different purposes. Some researched the connection between personal healing and the "healing" of degraded, neglected, or unloved land, such as the land on either side of major power lines, waste dumps, or polluted sites. Others spent each week in a National Park seeking out the stories of the place, developing their ecological literacy, and discovering how few of the Aboriginal stories remain in most places. A number were interested in marginal or border lands, exploring the sense of place in a paddock and adjacent forest, or a beach and an estuary, or a garden and the surrounding bushland. Others were motivated by the spiritual dimensions of place and chose the most wild and remote locations they could find.

My interest in place as a subject of teaching and inquiry at university grew. Most of the texts that I used at the time were North American (advocates of place or place phenomenologists such as Seamon, 1993; Relph, 1976; Tuan, 1974; Thomashow, 1996; Snyder, 1995; Hiss, 1991), or European phenomenologists such as Merleau-Ponty (1962) and Heidegger (1962), or critics of place advocacy such as Massey (1994). Were there Australian place scholars, and was there a distinctive Australian place scholarship? Through discussion with colleagues, I compiled a list of three dozen place scholars, writers, and educators from universities and organizations around Australia and invited them to attend a gathering. I wanted to create an event that combined the elements of a small conference and a retreat: preparation and dissemination of papers beforehand; experience of place in a retreat-like setting over 4 to 6 days; invited participants with the emphasis on dialogue rather than presentation. I wanted it to be large enough to have a diversity of voices and interests, yet small enough that the mass of people did not obscure the presence of the land.

The first colloquium was held in a place in the upper Blue Mountains not dissimilar from the bushland around Faulconbridge, but more spectacular—heath-covered plateaus with pagoda-like rock formations intersected by deep canyons with temperate rain forest species such as sassafras and coachwood trees. Some of these canyons contain surprisingly spacious sandstone overhangs that can easily accommodate 50 or more people, which was just as well because most of the 4 days were spent in these "caves" overlooking misty, rain-filled forest. The participants rose to the occasion, responding with poetry and passionate enthusiasm to the ideas of others—why place matters, loving a place and grieving its destruction, what a politics of place might be, the role of the university in promoting awareness of place. Softly falling rain on the tree ferns at the cave mouth created a strong sense of enclosure and intimacy. When the piercing cry of the yellow-tailed black cockatoo resounded through the canyon, people stopped and listened in an appreciative silence to this country of mists and sandstone. They welcomed the opportunity to interact with peers who were not simply like-minded, but had a similar feeling for place and a willingness to be outside all day in all weathers. Most of them regarded themselves as lonely voices in academic departments such as philosophy, environmental studies, geography, literature, or psychology, where a concern for place was considered outmoded or reactionary. We agreed to meet again the following year in the heart of the country, the Central Desert, to discuss the interaction between Aboriginal and Western senses of place. The Sense of Place Colloquium was born.

Immediately there were practical and inspirational effects on my teaching practice. I began to read the words of poets and nature writers out loud to students in the bush and in class to inspire them. Once I began looking, I discovered Australian place writing in the works of Eric Rolls (1984), David Tacey (1995), Pete Hay (2002), Tom Griffiths (1996), and many others that I included in the course reader, along with some of the Colloquium papers. I felt I was working with my students to develop a local vernacular inspired by Australian authors as well as those overseas. We were participating in a larger process in Australia—

bringing the appreciation of place more fully into academia and into public discourse. Now I had a way to work with the marginalization of place in the environmental debate that I had previously observed.

I felt encouraged at the colloquium by the descriptions of fieldwork by ecopsychologists and deep ecologists who explored psychological dimensions of place. My students responded quizzically at first. One of them wrote in an essay: "Relationship with a place? Are these people for real? How can I have a relationship with a place when I can barely hold down relationships with other human beings?" The turning point came when I invited them to consider how they related to places they frequented as a child.[1] They began to make connections between their childhood special places and the type of place they selected as an adult. They could see that place had been, and was again, important to their understanding of their sense of self and path through life.

The paper I had written for the first colloquium explored the story of my coming to inhabit Faulconbridge with Vicki in terms of the phenomenological ideas of "dwelling in place."[2] The effect of writing about this process and discussing it with participants was to bring a new consciousness to being in the bush and garden. It required me to acknowledge the previous lack of congruence between home life and work life, not just when I was working as an environmentalist but even more dramatically when I worked in the mining industry as a young man.[3] The new awareness wasn't always comfortable. It was one thing to write a story about my changing perceptions and activities in my home territory, and quite another to live it day by day, to subject my own actions to the same critical reflection that I asked of my students.

In the second colloquium, 30 participants arrived in Alice Springs in Central Australia and were driven to a remote location on the northern fringes of the Macdonnell Ranges.[4] Over a day and a half, we were introduced to the country by local Aboriginal custodians who explained why it is not culturally appropriate or realistic to tell more than the outer layer of a story to visiting "whitefellas" at the outset. We also heard stories of local knowledge by Landcare workers, teachers, artists, and guides for tourist groups who had worked with Aboriginal people. Many of the colloquium group were powerfully moved and understood that they were in country where traditional Aboriginal law based on a deep relationship with the land still is a primary influence on daily life.

By the end of the 6 days, many had experienced the power of place mediated by Aboriginal custodianship that manifested itself through dreams, numinous events, and a different sense of belonging in Central

Australia. The combination of the raw power of the place, the skill of our guides, and the creation of a psychologically safe and conducive space generated the conditions for this to occur. It was as though there was an active nonhuman partner in the colloquium proceedings—the place itself that acted directly on a deeper level of human consciousness than the normal waking state.

I returned to the classroom convinced of the centrality of Aboriginal understandings of "country" for all Australians interested in place, and remodeled the "Sense of Place" class. In the course reader, I added writings by and about Aboriginal people and the way in which they were intimately interconnected with the living beings and landforms of their country. In my presentations to class, I discussed the fact that Australia was home to the oldest intact land-based culture in the world with at least 60,000 years of continuous custodianship. I put forward the view that any attempt to understand sense of place in contemporary Australia had to come to terms with this unique feature, just as it had to deal with the fact that this is the driest continent on Earth (other than Antarctica) with the poorest and most fragile soils. I encouraged students to investigate the Aboriginal history of the areas in which their chosen places were situated, to visit local Aboriginal sites of interest, and to contact the local Aboriginal Land Council. Many who did so found it very difficult to find Dreaming stories[5] for their local places, and the recognition that this previously rich indigenous knowledge was either lost or inaccessible caused some sorrow and reflection among the students. A few were privileged to be able to visit their places in the company of local Aboriginal people, and benefitted greatly from the experience. During this time, Vicki and I were also fortunate to be told stories of our place at an Aboriginal rock art site within a kilometer of our home by a Dharug custodian.[6]

My research became immersed in a debate between two leading Australian scholars that brought out many of the complexities of the relationship between Aboriginal and non-Aboriginal senses of place. A place responsive society is one in which its institutions and customs nurture and support a rich, deep connection with land and place (Cameron, 2001; Plumwood, 2000). Mainstream Australian society, in common with many Western cultures, does not meet this definition at all. In fact, Plumwood argues that modern Australia is the antithesis—a country that has one of the worst records of land and water degradation and loss of biodiversity, and an economic system that treats place in terms of development potential and private property rights. Read (2000) brings evidence from the arts and the lives of particular individuals that some non-Aboriginals do have a strong sense of place, but Plumwood argues that this is despite social institutions and customs, not because of them, and chastises Read for individualizing a structural problem. My contribution, in addition to coining the term *place responsive*, was to examine how learning focused on the experience of place could contribute to place responsiveness at both the individual and collective levels (Cameron, 2003c). As a result, my reflections on the place-based teaching I was doing became part of a larger debate and in turn were fed back to my current students to provide a richer critical and intercultural context for their work.

Meanwhile, on one of my sabbatical trips, Vicki had made contact with a group of Central Australian Aboriginal women artists from the community of Utopia, northeast of Alice Springs. She was invited to record their personal and Dreaming stories, and was able to spend several months with them on their land (King, 2003). She encountered a complex of entangled issues: The stunning representations of country were done by Aboriginal women who were still carrying out traditional ceremonies for that country, working in third-world conditions of poverty, disease, and inadequate services, and who were represented by voracious art dealers who established international markets for their work. When we discussed this situation, the outcomes of the second colloquium, and the debates that we had become part of, we decided to design a new subject, "Place, Art, and Culture in Central Australia," that would involve our taking students on a 3-week field trip to the "Red Centre" to enable them to experience the intercultural richness and complexities of place and art for themselves.

It was an exhausting and extraordinarily intense learning experience for the 26 students who accompanied us. We camped for half the time on Aboriginal outstations, visiting sites and discussing the work being done to combat high rates of alcoholism and petrol sniffing among young Indigenous people. The experience of that land is particularly potent when one is camping and walking. Sitting in the sands of a dry creek bed underneath a eucalypt ghost gum and dwarfed by canyon cliffs or the monoliths of Uluru or Kata Tjuta,[7] the students were emotionally open to the depths of place responsiveness we were trying to convey. The daily practice of drawing and painting in place that Vicki introduced them to became a centrally important way of connecting with the places we encountered. It turned out to be a skillful means of developing students' capacity for observation and reflective silence—far more effective than asking them directly to sit quietly and observe.

After spending time on land still maintained by traditional Aboriginal custodians, some of our group found that the land became a more palpable, active force than seemed imaginable back in Sydney. In this heightened state, students encountered ancient rock paintings and carvings, understood the connection between ceremony, song lines, and modern art, and at the same time saw the drunkenness, desperation, and appalling conditions in which many Aboriginal people live. The interconnections between place, perception, art, and culture came alive for the students. Many of them wrote passionate and thoughtful accounts of what they had witnessed, and produced paintings and drawings that spoke powerfully of their experience of being in this country. Several of them subsequently moved to Central Australia to work with Aboriginal people.

The third colloquium was held in a rural community north of Melbourne and explored issues of place at the rural–urban interface. People in the colloquium began to recognize that although it was wonderful to connect with amazing wild and remote places, we had to realize that most Australians lived in cities. What was the implication of our work for an urban Australian sense of place? For this colloquium, participants wrote about the importance of bringing care and attention to our most neglected and abandoned urban areas (Mathews, 2003), looking for the interplay of the wild and human-made in the urban (Murphy, 2003), and considering the multicultural complexity of urban Australian sense of place in which many recent immigrants carry their home places with them (Stewart, 2003).

I realized that I had to bring the students' experience of urban places more centrally into the semester, regardless of the type of place that they chose to visit. I needed an experience at the other end of the spectrum from the camping trip into wild nature. After several years of trial and error and strong feedback from the students, I came up with a design that took account of the fact that the postgraduate students lived in different cities, often far from the university. I required them to spend a day in the most urban place that was within an hour's travel of their home. They were to prepare by reading material on sensing and understanding urban places (Hiss, 1991; Massey, 1994). To deal with the strong preconceptions many of them had about urbanized places, I asked them to spend several hours in the location that they felt most drawn to, then in the location that they felt repelled by, and to carry out the practices of urban place suggested in the readings.

The exercise had a salutary effect on quite a few of the students. Some had their expectations confounded by finding the central railway station more interesting than they could have imagined, or by discovering hidden "secrets" in the location that they were originally repelled by. One student was so taken by his "urban day" in Sydney that he ventured into the literature of the city and interwove his field notes with reflections on how James Joyce encountered Dublin. Another described the single swooping glide of a currawong bird into one side of a multilevel carpark and out the other side in the language of a numinous event. Even those students who had their negative preconceptions of the city reinforced were moved out of their comfort zone by experiencing it up close, and some went on to consider the social and environmental implications of a highly urbanized society.

As Vicki pursued her research into Aboriginal art and place relations, the more deeply she understood how embedded traditional Aboriginal people were in their traditional country, the more she became saddened by the fact that most of them had been forcibly removed from their land. This led her to confront the displacements in her own life, and conversations between us turned to an acknowledgment of grief and loss of place, placelessness as well as sense of place. Because I had always felt so at home in the bush and had had so many positive experiences there, I realized that my focus had not been on the losses that have occurred in our home place. Archaeologists have found abundant evidence of Aboriginal occupation at dozens of sites around Faulconbridge. Less than a kilometer away is a major Aboriginal site with an emu-hunting sequence long ago carved by local Dharug people. This place was once cared for and known in a way it no longer is, which is a huge loss.

I am also becoming more keenly aware of the physical degradation of the local bushland. I wrote 10 years ago of sitting by the water gliding over the sandstone scarp into Linden Creek. That waterfall is silent now. The stream, increasingly clogged with sediment from road and housing construction and gardens, has gone underground. Many of the deep pools at the base of waterfalls throughout the Blue Mountains are now largely silted up. The nutrient-laden water that inevitably escapes from gardens overlooking the valley flows into Linden Creek, changing its capacity to support life, and eventually making its contribution to the severe nutrient overload in the Hawkesbury River. Weeds, too, cascade down and choke out the native flora.

There are also accounts of what used to be here. Reports from early explorers and settlers mention the abundance of wildlife they encountered: bandicoots, bettongs, quolls, emus, wombats, swamp wallabies, and a vast array of birds. Many of the bird species remain, but the combined onslaught of hunting and feral and domestic animal predation has meant that the emu, Eastern Quoll, and Rufous Bettong disappeared from the Blue Mountains, while many of the other species survive in greatly reduced numbers (Smith & Smith, 1990, p. 14).

As a result, the next time that Vicki and I cotaught the undergraduate "Sense of Place" course, we devoted a class to issues of placelessness and displacement. The response from the students was immediate. They talked in class about feeling alienated from where they lived, of having no sense of place, and being previously ashamed to speak about it, as if not having a sense of place was a personal failure. Others had loved places they had spent their childhood in and were able for the first time to express the grief they felt at having to move. Many of them elected to write essays on the topic with a passion that had often been lacking in previous undergraduate reports. It seemed that the freedom to acknowledge alienation and loss allowed the students to approach their chosen places more honestly and realistically.

My capacity to accept the grief as well as the joy associated with our place at Faulconbridge was deepened as I began to do my meditation practice outside more regularly. At daybreak several times a week, I now make my way down into the bush to one of the intimate and protected "person-sized" sandstone overhangs of dark, lichen-covered exteriors and intricate honey-colored wind-carved interiors. Part of the power of the experience is the sensory awakening that occurs when I step outside; sleepily dark silhouettes in the misty rain in winter, a full blast of birdsong and dawn radiance in summer. As well as learning to simply sit receptively without expectation, I have come to appreciate the importance of compassion as deeply felt openness to loss and the suffering of individuals and the more-than-human-world, to use Abram's (1996) term for "nonhuman" or "Nature."

In 2002, while overseas on sabbatical, I was introduced to a way of responding to place that combined elements of meditative attention and phenomenology—Goethe's way of science. In Goethean science, natural phenomena reveal themselves to the sensitive observer through the trained intuition. Participation between the observer and the phenomenon commences with active looking followed by visualizing what has been observed in as much detail as possible entirely in the imagination (Bortoft, 1996, p. 42). Goethe called this pivotal stage "exact sensorial imagination" (ESI). With discipline and practice, moving back and forth between sensory contact and ESI, Goethean scientists develop a sufficiently receptive and intuitive space within themselves to allow the phenomenon to reveal its distinctive "gesture" and essential nature.

The potentialities and the difficulties of using Goethe's way of science in my place-based teaching became apparent at the same time. What if I could get students to the point where they saw themselves as the means by which their chosen place discloses itself? That they were participating in the further coevolution of the life of the place and of themselves? These possibilities took place responsiveness into another realm of experience and understanding. First I needed to learn these abilities myself.

I undertook an intensive week to trial the Goethean methods in a stretch of wild coastline in Cornwall and became convinced of the power of this process.[8] On my return to Australia, I introduced a lecture and a field trip based on Goethean science, and received a wide range of responses. Some people clearly didn't get it, found it "too weird for words," or produced "gestures" that were obviously preconceived. Others came up with novel and surprising images, and others were so moved that they could barely speak. Many of my students have integrated this process into their understanding of the potential of place relationships.

My "Sense of Place" classes have evolved markedly over the past 12 years through a complex interplay between places of growing importance to me, conversations with Vicki, student feedback, interactions with peers at colloquia and on sabbatical, and developing my own "practices of place." These practices—bush regeneration, exploratory walks, learning place history and ecology, Goethean intuiting, quietly sitting, meditation and compassion practices—all seem to me now to be intertwined expressions of the same fundamental intention.

The students express their enthusiasm for the subjects, and their gratitude to Vicki and me, but I often wonder about the longer term effects. Both undergraduate and mature-age students clearly derive great personal benefit from the subject, but what about my original intention to explore love of place as an abiding motivation for environmental conservation? Occasionally, former students will surprise me with an e-mail or call describing how they have begun working with place issues with farmers, in the workplace, in workshops, and with social workers. There are now local "mini-colloquia" occurring between each national colloquium. It seems that sense of place can become contagious in the right circumstances, but does it bring greater conservation effort and social justice with it?

LOCALISM AND EDUCATION FOR PLACE-RESPONSIVENESS

The continuing redesign of my place-based teaching arises from some of the same sources as the "new localism" that the editors of this book identify—resistance against the destructive forces of globalization and the need for re-inhabitory processes to overcome a growing sense of placelessness. In my case, the resistance took the form of active involvement in campaigns opposing the destructive effects of massive export-oriented forestry and agricultural developments on Australia's fragile soil, water, and vegetation. The impetus for re-inhabitation came partly through my reflections and writing about inhabiting our place at Faulconbridge and partly through my interaction with students who voiced feelings of displacement or placelessness when Vicki and I provided the opportunity.

At the same time, invoking the new localism has required coming to terms with the "old localism." Valuing the local is not necessarily a force for ecological or social justice. Local area advocates can be parochial, narrow-minded, inward-looking, intolerant of outsiders, prone to entrenching traditional power relations, and only concerned with environmental quality in their immediate neighborhood. Massey wrote *Space, Place, and Gender* (1994) as an attempt to find a role for "place" in a socially progressive view of the world because so much of place politics, and equally place theory, seemed reactionary and sexist.

I introduce my students to these ideas through my lectures and readings by Massey and others. The debate between Plumwood and Read over the place responsive society is, in part, a question about the extent to which one can have a truly sustaining relationship with a place while one is a member of a society that perpetuates ecological and social injustice. Although the critique of place advocacy on the grounds of gender and noninclusiveness strikes a chord with many of them, Massey's solution of proposing a "global sense of place," in which place is the ever-changing nexus of social relationships, is less satisfying to them. In the Australian context, relations with the more-than-human world are at least as important as the social world. This raises the interesting question of how to reconcile the progressive demand for a fluid, outward-looking sense of place with the expanded time horizon and experience of changelessness in nonurban Australia, a place often described as "the timeless land."

More subtle influences of the old localism frequently occur in the comments and writings of my students. Because I require them to select a place within a short distance from their home, they are connecting more deeply with a local place. Many are unfamiliar with the process of opening themselves consciously to their sensed, felt experience and to attending to a place in its different aspects for a significant period of time each week. They are naturally protective of themselves and of their places, especially in the initial stages. I have learned to introduce the critical, progressive perspective of writers such as Massey later in the semester to allow time for this period of open engagement. Even so, there are varied responses to the critical material among the students. Some recoil from the larger social ecological picture as being "too much" and maintain a narrow focus on their inner experience, resisting the idea of greater access by others or the prospect of change in their "special place." Others didn't consider the implications of the privileged position they were in as university students being able to engage in such a process, or didn't take up opportunities to involve members of the community in their investigations.

On the other hand, some students followed their growing awareness of the environmental threats to their places into wider ecological consciousness. For one student, a plastic bag that washed up on "her" patch of seashore that she gazed on so lovingly heralded an investigation of sources of marine pollution. Another student found himself the focus of increasing attention by local teenagers every week he visited a spot in a neighborhood park in an underprivileged area. Initially scornful of his attempts to write and sketch, they ended up asking him to help them draw and paint. Their parents, who were suspicious of these activities at first, started talking with him and he became the catalyst of neighborhood get-togethers of people from different ethnic backgrounds that continued well after the end of semester.

In an earlier article (Cameron, 2003d), I identified that one of the key questions for me as an educator was how to bring depth experience and critical thinking together. Using the tenets of adult learning theory (Brookfield, 1986), I have relied on the power of critical reflection on experiences of place, aided by the readings, to foster critical social and ecological consciousness, and the results have been mixed. The tension between encouraging a phenomenological open engagement with what presents itself in a place and stimulating the awareness of critical theory is a delicate matter of timing and emphasis. Gruenewald (2003) casts further light on both the need and the difficulty of working with this terrain. His "critical pedagogy of place" proposes the convergence of the primarily ecological and rural forms of place-based education with the urban multicultural focus of critical pedagogy. In these terms, I have started with the former and have steadily tried to embrace the latter.

Recognizing that people need to develop a mutually enhancing relationship with Nature before they act politically, Gruenewald cautions that "the call to transform oppressive conditions that is so important to critical pedagogy must be balanced with experiencing an empathetic connection to others, human and nonhuman" (p. 8). In work that is strongly in accord with Plumwood's (2000) perspective, Gruenewald's way forward is to proceed with two processes hand-in-hand, re-inhabitation (learning to live well in our places by recovering and renewing Indigenous thought and practices) and decolonization (liberation from colonizing thought that exploits other people and places). He suggests that the two processes can be brought together by asking two questions about our local places: "What needs to be conserved?" and "What needs to be transformed?"

These are potentially powerful questions that I will be asking students to consider in the future: questions about what should and shouldn't change about their place, and why. This is a way of confronting them with the issues of change, who has agency, who benefits, what is valued, and what is lost. I am reluctant to be critical of those students whose responses seem to come from the old localism, that are class-blind or gender-blind, or come from within the person's comfort zone. Sometimes as much as 10 years later I have been surprised by former students contacting me and saying that they had finally understood what I had been suggesting to them about place; they hadn't been ready to hear it at the time, but somehow "the experience had just stayed with me." So although I can only claim mixed results in fostering critical social and ecological consciousness during the class, individual time frames differ greatly, and perhaps there are longer-term effects.

These individual factors interact with the particularities of each place to further complicate the situation for an educator. As Gruenewald notes: "Perhaps the most revolutionary characteristic of place-based education is that it emerges from the particular attributes of [a] place" (2003, p. 7). It defeats the efforts of those who would standardize education experience through curriculum or other means. In the examples of the two students I previously mentioned, the one who visited the seashore developed greater ecological awareness, whereas the one who visited the park developed greater sociocultural awareness, particularly related to his own agency. It could reasonably be argued that they learned these things in part because of the particular attributes of "their" places that could not be predicted or designed in, together with circumstantial and individual factors. The combination of all three means that the critical place-based educator is faced with a more limited and a more challenging role than a conventional educator. The role is more limited because we do not provide the content—that is provided by what presents itself in the place from its particular characteristics as mediated by the individual student's response. It is more challenging because the opportunities to stimulate the student's critical ecological and social consciousness (while holding the tension of wanting them to deepen their engagement with place) are highly specific and variable.

NARRATIVES OF PLACE AND PLACE-BASED EDUCATION

As I think back over my teaching experience in the light of recent place theories, I return to my use of the word *responsiveness*. One of the leading place philosophers on whom I draw is Malpas (1999). I have noted the tendency in some place literature for the places themselves, in their particularity, physicality, and otherness, to disappear behind a generalized discussion of human responsiveness. Malpas comments that in books such as Tuan's Topophilia (1974), "...it is not place as such that is important, but just the idea of human responsiveness—a responsiveness that need not itself be grounded in any concept of place or locality at all" (p. 30). This raises the question of whether I, too, have been so concerned with enhancing students' capacity to respond, to quiet down and pay close attention, to observe and listen well, to open their hearts—that the places themselves, in their particularity, physicality, and otherness tend to disappear. To what extent am I using place as a vehicle for developing human responsiveness in general, rather than being concerned for the qualities and well-being of the place itself? In other words, is the form of place-based education I teach more anthropocentric or ecocentric?

This is a difficult question to ask of oneself as an educator. Of course I am concerned about my students as human beings, and I nudge them toward more fully functioning humanness. I am also deeply interested in the places the students choose, and concerned that the qualities of these places are brought forth and respected. It's not an either/or question. In the early weeks of the semester, the practices of responsiveness need to be discussed and modeled out in the bush. At the same time, what they are responding to, the places in which the field trips are occurring, is also in focus. I am blessed by having relatively wild country with remarkable natural features within a short drive of campus, so that exercises are less in danger of becoming too human-centered. Nonetheless, each semester, a significant proportion of the students write essays that center on their own processes of thinking and feeling rather than the attributes and history of the places they chose to visit, so Malpas's criticism is fair warning to students and teachers alike. I suspect that, like the matter of critical consciousness, it is a question of timing. For some students, the skills of human responsiveness, which receive insufficient attention in many schools and homes, are so underdeveloped that they spend the entire semester learning to listen, to care, and to pay attention to their own felt senses—and that is progress enough.

Malpas, who draws primarily on the works of Heidegger (1962) and Davidson (1984), shows how place has a central role in the theory of human experience, identity, and action. He does this by drawing out how interrelated the structuring of our inner world is with the world "out there." For example, our memories are nested within each other the way places are nested within other places with multiple and overlapping connections. Childhood memories of place are not to be dismissed as nostalgia. They are critical to self-identity, to the narratives we develop about our lives, and to our capacity for self-reflection (Malpas, 1999, pp. 182–183). He also notes that psychological studies of autobiographical memory suggest that as we age, such places and memories become increasingly important to us.

This is significant because it suggests that place-based education needs to be age-sensitive. Most proponents, such as Thomashow (1996), include "mapping" of childhood place experiences as important parts of revitalizing place relationships, but perhaps its importance is only fully realized by students later in life. I have found that my postgraduate students, who are often in their 40s and 50s, are more receptive to the workshop on re-inhabiting our childhood places of significance than undergraduate students, who are primarily in their 20s. It is no coincidence that in my early 50s, I began writing about the significance of early childhood contact with the hill country around Canberra (Cameron, 2003b) for my subsequent environmental and educational work.

Narrative is given a vital role by Malpas in structuring thoughts, feelings, and experiences, a sense of self, taking action in the world, and place itself. For him, it is not simply a matter of place containing and being structured by stories; our very sense of who we are as individuals is a narrative connected intimately with place, and the possibility of our being able to take action is structured by narrative and place. These stories are not just given, a simple stringing together of events; they are an act of creation themselves. He writes of "the inseparability of a sense of place from the capacity for linguistic and narrative articulation" (1999, p. 153). I am especially interested in how this articulation occurs in writing.

These ideas illuminate some key features of the evolving story with which I began this chapter. On the one hand, the narrative I told of the evolution of my teaching is structured by the qualities of places in Faulconbridge and the Blue Mountains. For example, the moist rain forest and protective sandstone outcrops surrounded by heathland encouraged a feeling of protection and an attitude of receptivity that would have been very different in slate country. The occurrence of person-sized caves on our land in Faulconbridge predisposed me to talking with my students about the more meditative and reflective place responses these places engendered. On the other hand, the land here also carries the traces of narratives written on it: the geological and biological evolution, the subtle marks of Aboriginal occupation, the less subtle stages of European settlement and subsequent environmental degradation.

My own sense of place and my capacity to engender place responsiveness in my students has come out of the reciprocity of place and narrative. My ongoing attempts to articulate in writing the power and mystery of what has been happening for Vicki and me in our place, and for our students in their places, has strengthened this reciprocal relationship. Yet I have also been made aware of some of the dangers of narratives if this structure is imposed. In occasional conversations with David Seamon, who has taught me much about the phenomenology of place, I have become more sensitive to the pitfalls of narrative and naïve enthusiasm. He has commented that stories of place, and particularly stories of encounter with place, conceal as much as they reveal. They impose a narrative structure of character, development, and continuity that might not actually be there, he says, if one paid closer attention to what actually happened in the process of getting to know a place, and was less concerned with finding a story in it. Perhaps the discontinuities, the abrupt shifting from one fleeting impression to another, give a more revealing account of how we come into a place than a story. Most place writing, he suggests, reveals more about a writer's enthusiasm for a place or for being a nature writer than it does about the place itself.

I am mindful of this tension when working with students as they encounter their places week-by-week, and I encourage them to keep an ongoing account of what is happening in their journals. I caution them to pay attention to what actually presents itself each week, and to be aware of their expectations of what should be there, memories of what was there last week, and the stories that are running in their heads. I ask them whether the story is in the service of the place, or whether the place is only in the service of the story they are constructing.

Many more of the students have experienced the other side of the reciprocal relationship between narrative and place—how places become the poorer for the loss of the stories that once sustained them. This has usually occurred when students in semiurban eastern Australia have attempted to discover the Aboriginal "Dreaming stories" pertinent to their area, and have felt keenly the loss of these stories. It is also a loss of the stories of early settlers—many parts of rural Australia have been depopulated in the last century. Farm buildings and mountain huts are disintegrating into the scrub, taking stories of the inhabitants with them, and we are the poorer for it.

It is often the case that not all has been lost, however. The process of recovering and retelling those stories of country, of restorying the land, is an important collective act. The dominant Western cultural narrative of place in recent centuries may have been one of despoliation, but it is not the only story. As students and colloquium participants gather tales from local Aboriginal people and longtime residents, and weave larger stories, marginalized people find that they have something worth saying that is respected by a section of the community, at least. As some of the stories are told to others and published, another Western cultural narrative is being retold, a narrative of human responsiveness to the more-than-human world that has continued to survive in the margins of the dominant culture. If it is true to the place itself, if it is told with critical social and ecological awareness, such a story contains at least an implicit condemnation of place being viewed as a resource or a commodity in a globalized economy. It might not seem like much in the face of widespread land clearing or urban, coastal, and industrial development, but I have discovered how contagious, and potentially subversive, stories of love of place can be.

EDUCATIONAL, ENVIRONMENTAL, AND INTERCULTURAL POSSIBILITIES

What role can a place-based university course such as "Sense of Place" play in the new localism? On its own, as one subject in an undergraduate or postgraduate degree within an institution that is continually adjusting to the government's neoconservative agenda, perhaps not much can be achieved. However, as part of a broader reawakening of place-consciousness as manifested in the colloquia and the resurgence of place writing in Australia, some contributions can be made.

The subjects I teach have many of the hallmarks of the "place-conscious education" described by the editors of this book. The narrative of globalization is indeed questioned in my classes, not simply in my lectures on ecological sustainability and bioregionalism, but in the design of the subject that emphasizes the value of the local and particular. It is not only children who can be the beneficiaries of reconnecting education, enculturation, and human development. Adult learners in university can reflect on the role of place in their own development, and to reconnect what has been severed—the value of places that were so important to them as children, their sense of identity and place in the world. Some of my students have also contributed to the well-being of the community during the semester through being an unintended focus of attention for local residents, or drawing out the stories of older residents or Aboriginal people and stimulating local interest in them.

Many students, though, were primarily focused on their individual learning during the semester, and so were able to do little in the way of building the collaborative support structures between community and educational institutions, that were suggested by the editors. Having a sequence of place-based subjects that start with individual place experiences and subsequently move out to work with the community on social and environmental projects in these places would be a wonderful possibility. There is as much potential for community involvement in universities as in schools, and indeed the Social Ecology program within which my subjects are situated is oriented toward socially responsive learning and research in the local community.

At its best, a university subject like this could provide graduates with a more critical place consciousness to guard against the new localism slipping back into the habits of the "old localism." There will always be tendencies in communities to fall into complacency, self-interest, and mistrust of outsiders, and it is the traditional role of universities to foster critical awareness in students of the broader historical and social forces at work. Unfortunately, traditional university study has tended to do this at the expense of careful attention to, and engagement in, local community issues. Universities could make a valuable contribution to the new localism by putting a "critical pedagogy of place" into practice with students and local communities so that re-inhabitation and resistance to globalization do not become inward-looking and oppressive.

If the new localism is to make any headway in contending with corporate globalism, it must come to terms with the issue of how to achieve an ecologically sustainable society. Milbrath (1989) creates a strong case that the best way forward is for communities and organizations to ask, "How can we learn our way towards sustainability?" This emphasis on adult learning brings into play the experience of university educators in fostering the environment that is most conducive for a group of adults to learn collectively. Many communities are quite divided on environmental issues, with entrenched conflict between conservationists and industry proponents often putting forward apparently inflexible policies and position statements—not a situation favorable for group learning!

There is also environmental value in fostering the development of more place-conscious and reflective environmental advocates. Dozens of environmentalists have taken "Sense of Place" over the years, often starting, like myself, from a position of feeling burnt-out and recognizing that they have neglected the relationships with the places and people closest to them because of their involvement in large environmental campaigns. They discover the personally sustaining qualities of developing an ongoing "practice of place," and re-experience the connection between local places and global issues. When the process really works, they become more grounded activists, capable of sustaining action over the long haul and less susceptible to burnout. They are also much more amenable to entering a place-oriented collective learning process, and some of my former students have initiated this themselves.

Stories of place can also be the meeting-ground between cultures. The small examples I have encountered in my work point the way toward intercultural dialogue and learning when many other avenues have been blocked by current government policies. I have had enough instances of students and colloquium participants gaining immeasurably from exploring their places with local Aboriginal people, who have in turn appreciated receptive listeners, to recommend the involvement of local Indigenous people and their organizations in place-based intercultural learning as an important aspect of the new localism.

The learning has not always been one way. One Aboriginal woman student of mine was able to contact her elders, sit down, and listen to stories of their tribal land and the ceremonies that used to be held on it. She was able to reconnect physically with the mangrove swamps and coastal woodlands of her people's country. She also gained sufficient detailed information from her elders to be able to document it in a Land Rights claim that was under way and gain access for her people to a wider tract of land than was previously being considered. Other Aboriginal students, although not gaining such immediately tangible benefit, have been able to deepen their connection to kin and country. They have all demonstrated that it is not just "whitefellas" who need to reinvigorate their place relationships. Two centuries of dispossession has meant that many Aboriginal people have been separated from their country, and often their families, and the "Sense of Place" course has been the catalyst for reconnection.

Along with colleagues and former students, I was recently able to investigate the local consequences of place-responsive education in my own region (Cameron, Mulligan, & Wheatley, 2004), and found that intercultural education emerged as the strongest theme. The suggestion that sparked most interest was made by a local Dharug woman who recommended that schools and other community organizations should seriously look at the way that Aboriginal people took responsibility for the welfare of other living things through totemic relationships with plants and animals. Taking responsibility for an adopted totemic species would mean advocating for the needs and rights of that species and therefore learning about habitats and ecosystems, and developing an empathetic relationship with nonhuman life. After the forum, a proposal for funding was prepared that involved local schools, local Aboriginal elders, and the local government council.

The potential impact of taking our place relationships more seriously is clearly substantial. The consequences of the fundamental realignment of our thinking that place philosophers such as Malpas (1999) and Casey (1993, 1997) are calling for are still being explored. As Malpas (1999) says, "The complex structure of place...suggest[s] that the idea of place does not so much bring a certain politics with it, as define the very frame within which the political itself must be located" (p. 198). If place is restored to its central importance for all human experiencing, then it is not only politics that needs to be reframed. By implication, education, environmental sustainability, and intercultural dialogue should not just take place into account, but they should be deeply grounded in place. The new localism could be thought of as the local expression of the need for this fundamental realignment.

THE CHALLENGES AHEAD

Any potential this large also brings with it very great challenges. My "Sense of Place" subjects are being placed under increasing budgetary and administrative constraints and only continue because we are willing to keep resisting the pressures from above. The possibility of a whole sequence of place-based subjects involving the community in an ongoing way appears increasingly distant. The colloquia are also becoming harder to run, not through lack of interest and demand, but because they operate "outside the system," and there is less and less tolerance for such noninstitutional, non-income-generating activities. Yet place-based research and scholarship is on the rise in Australia, as evidenced by the formation of the first national Place Research Network through the University of Tasmania in 2003. But the task of applying this scholarly work in the service of the new localism will be difficult in the current university climate.

I have found that teaching place-based subjects in the way I have also offers personal challenges. If experience is the best teacher, then one must bring one's own place-based experience into the classroom. I have learned a great deal about place responsiveness in the past 14 years, and much of that learning has involved recognizing the limitations in my previous attitudes and mistakes in past actions. It is not easy to acknowledge to students, and in my writing, the limited views I had on native species, for example, or urban sense of place, or the extent and effect of placelessness and displacement. It is even harder to keep subjecting my own "practices of place" to the same critical reflection that I ask of my students, and acknowledging the shortcomings. My "evolving story" illustrates, however, that the personal costs and risks have been more than offset by the heartfelt response from students and the deepening relationship with the place that Vicki and I inhabit.

The place-based educator in the Western world, at least, must also contend with the changes in relationship with the more-than-human world that are occurring in society more broadly. I have noticed that my current students are a little less willing to venture out in the bush, and have had less direct experience of the world of Nature than those 10 or 15 years ago. My generation spent countless hours playing in backyards, creeks, and culverts, collecting tadpoles in ponds, and building hideaways in trees. Now, many of those areas have been leveled for urban development and children are too busy with organized activities and homework, or are spending time in front of a television or computer screen. My older students who are parents say they are also increasingly aware of the dangers of children being abused and abducted, so they are reluctant to let them play on their own "in the wild."

The work of place-conscious education is thus more difficult and more important. It is more difficult because the educator is not drawing on a base of experience of the more-than-human world that the students bring with them. If Nature largely comes to the child through television and limited monitored contact with the outside world, then the teacher has first to dismantle the assumptions and prejudices that come through these means. It is more important because knowledge of the natural world that might come from television and classroom teaching must be accompanied by direct experience in order to develop a real feeling for the species that we share our world with and motivation to protect them and their (our) habitat. If place-based education is providing a larger proportion of the necessary sorts of experiences, reflections, and guidance, then it becomes key to ecological sustainability.

There is clearly a great impetus for the new localism coming from concern about the effects of global corporate capitalism and desire to reconnect with the local. There are also factors in our economy and society that act to deny and obstruct meaningful place relationships. These contending forces are at work in the university. On the one hand, there is renewed scholarly interest in and understanding of the fundamental significance of place, and students are very responsive to place-based subjects. On the other hand, the university sector is succumbing to the forces of neoconservatism and is becoming a less conducive environment in which to foster place responsiveness. Proponents of the new localism need to forge new alliances with a whole range of community-based organizations and educational institutions if the work of place-based education in the university is to flourish.

ENDNOTES

[1] Thomashow (1996, p. 12) notes that "...from the perspective of human development, the period of middle childhood (the ages 9 to 12 years) is a time of place-making in which children expand their sense of self. Their perceptions of the immediate environment undergo a remarkable transformation."

[2] Published in a revised version as Cameron (2003a).

[3] For an account of my ill-fated venture into mineral exploration in the Rocky Mountains, see Cameron (2003b).

[4] For a detailed discussion of the design and results of the second colloquium, see Cameron & San Roque (2003).

[5] Dreaming stories are multilayered stories of the Dreamtime, when mythical ancestor spirits traveled by specific routes (sometimes colloquially called "song lines") creating the forms of the land and the species of life. The Dreamtime is not just the past, it is also the eternal present.

[6] The Dharug people are the traditional Aboriginal custodians of the Hawkesbury and Lower Blue Mountains areas west of Sydney.

[7] These are the Aboriginal names for Ayers Rock and the Olgas, respectively. They are huge sedimentary rock formations southwest of Alice Springs that are sacred to Aboriginal people.

[8] For an account of these experiences of Goethean science, see Cameron (2005).

REFERENCES

Abram, D. (1996). *The spell of the sensuous.* New York: Pantheon Books.

Bortoft, H. (1996). *The wholeness of nature: Goethe's way towards a science of conscious participation in nature.* New York: Lindisfarne Press.

Brookfield, S. (1986). *Understanding and facilitating adult learning*. San Francisco: Jossey-Bass.

Cameron, J. (2001). Place, belonging, and ecopolitics: Learning our way towards the place-responsive society. *Ecopolitics: Thought+Action, 1*(2), 18–34.

Cameron, J. (2003a). Dwelling in place, dwelling on earth. In J. Cameron (Ed.), *Changing places: Re-imagining Australia* (pp. 29–38). Double Bay, Australia: Longueville Books.

Cameron, J. (2003b). Beneath Capital Hill: The unconformities of place and self. In M. Tredinnick (Ed.), *A place on Earth: An anthology of nature writing from Australia and North America* (pp. 55–64). Sydney: University of New South Wales Press.

Cameron, J. (2003c). Responding to place in a post-colonial era: An Australian perspective. In W. Adams & M. Mulligan (Eds.), *Decolonizing nature: Strategies for conservation in a post-colonial era* (pp. 172–196). London: Earthscan.

Cameron, J. (2003d). Educating for place responsiveness: An Australian perspective on ethical practice. *Ethics, Place and Environment, 6*(2), 99–116.

Cameron, J. (2005). Place, Goethe, and phenomenology: A theoretic journey. Paper accepted for publication in special issue of Janus Head, 8(1), 174–198.

Cameron, J., Mulligan, M., & Wheatley, V. (2004). Building a place responsive society through inclusive local projects and networks. *Local Environment, 9*(2), 147–162.

Cameron, J., & San Roque, C. (2003). Coming into country: Catalysing a social ecology. *Philosophy, Activism, Nature, 2*, 76–88.

Casey, E. (1993). *Getting back into place*. Bloomington: Indiana University Press.

Casey, E. (1997). *The fate of place*. Berkeley: University of California Press.

Davidson, D. (1984). *Inquiries into truth and interpretation*. Oxford: Clarendon Press.

Griffiths, T. (1996). *Hunters and collectors: The antiquarian imagination in Australia*. New York: Cambridge University Press.

Gruenewald, D. (2003). The best of both worlds: A critical pedagogy of place. *Educational Researcher, 32*(4), 3–12.

Hay, P. (2002). *Vandiemonian essays*. Hobart: Walleah Press.

Heidegger, M. (1962). *Being and time*. New York: Harper & Row.

Hiss, T. (1991). *The experience of place*. New York: Vintage Books, Random House.

King, V. (2003). Embodied perceptions: Aboriginal expressions of place. In J. Cameron (Ed.), *Changing places: Re-imagining Australia* (pp. 286–295). Double Bay, Australia: Longueville Books.

Malpas, J. (1999). *Place and experience: A philosophical topography*. Cambridge: Cambridge University Press.

Massey, D. (1994). *Space, place, and gender*. Cambridge: Polity Press.

Mathews, F. (2003). Becoming native to the city. In J. Cameron (Ed.), *Changing places: Re-imagining Australia* (pp. 197–205). Double Bay, Australia: Longueville Books.

Merleau-Ponty, M. (1962). *Phenomenology of perception*. London: Routledge.

Milbrath, L. (1989). *Envisioning a sustainable society: Learning our way out*. Albany: State University of New York Press.

Murphy, S. (2003). The practice of stories and places. In J. Cameron (Ed.), *Changing places: Re-imagining Australia* (pp. 221–233). Double Bay, Australia: Longueville Books.

Orr, D. (1992). *Ecological literacy*. Albany: State University of New York Press.

Plumwood, V. (2000). Belonging, naming and decolonisation, *Ecopolitics: Thought+action, 1*(1), 90–106.

Read, P. (2000). *Australians, place and Aboriginal ownership*. Cambridge: Cambridge University Press.

Relph, E. (1976). *Place and placelessness*. London: Pion.

Rolls, E. (1984). *A million wild acres*. Melbourne: Penguin.

Seamon, D. (1993). *Dwelling, seeing and designing: Toward a phenomenological ecology*. Albany: State University of New York Press.

Smith, J., & Smith, P. (1990). *Fauna of the Blue Mountains*. Kenthurst, Australia: Kangaroo Press.

Snyder, G. (1995). *A place in space: Ethics, aesthetics, and watersheds*. Washington, DC: Counterpoint.

Stewart, B. (2003). The blue hour. In J. Cameron (Ed.), *Changing places: Re-imagining Australia* (pp. 116–127). Double Bay, Australia: Longueville Books.

Tacey, D. (1995). *Edge of the sacred: Transformation in Australia*. Melbourne: HarperCollins.

Thomashow, M. (1996). *Ecological identity*. Cambridge, MA: MIT Press.

Tuan, Y.-F. (1974). *Topophilia: A study of environmental perception, attitudes and values*. Englewood Cliffs, NJ: Prentice-Hall.

CHAPTER 14

Place-Based Teacher Education

Matt Dubel
David Sobel

ONE TEACHER'S STORY

First day of school. Whether it's third grade or middle school science or teacher education at the graduate level, the tone of the pedagogy is set that day. The cultural norms are launched, the core values exposed. In my classes on the first day with teachers-in-training, I want to tune them to the particularities of the local community and natural environment. Third of September in southwestern New Hampshire—what's salient? First, it's almost always uncomfortably hot for school. It still feels like summer. The feeling is often, "Do we really have to be inside on such a beautiful day?" Second, the swamp maples have started to turn. Although most everything else is still velvety green, the swamp maples are harbingers of the autumnal blush. Third, from slime mold and stinkhorns in the bark-mulched parking lot islands to golden fly agarics on the edge of school playgrounds, fungi are cropping up everywhere. My challenge is to tune the curriculum to the particularities of this time and this place.

I'm up early to collect mushrooms. Down through the dew-soaked field behind my neighbor's house to the trail along Eliza Adams Gorge, a hemlock-shrouded stream with steep, schisty banks. Under the thick, light-sponging canopy of the hemlocks, no shrubs grow in the understory. Instead, the undisturbed soil provides the perfect matrix for a variety of mushrooms—Lactarius, corals, Russulas, and Amanitas. At the end of last week, I had cruised the trail to make sure there was an ample supply of *Amanita virosa*, destroying angels, for my first class. I'll need a dozen, one for each pair of people in my class to do a focused drawing and observation. I love the way the stark whiteness of their stalks and caps makes them seem to glow in the tree shadows. But a lot changes in five days, and most of the destroying angels are gone; I can find only six or seven.

Frustrated, I seek farther afield and find myself in another grove of hemlocks, farther down the stream, where I'd never gone. It's thrilling to find a new place almost right in my backyard, and this hideaway turns up a number of *Amanita citrina*. These are slightly lemony, not as statuesque as the virosas, but very similar to the untrained eye. My class today will focus on differentiating between the two species rather than focusing on just one. Place-based education, just like vernacular cuisine, means working with what's fresh, cooking with what the garden provides on that day.

I drive to work, stash my shoulder bag and basket of fungi in my office, and dash outside to gather leaves—40 each of sugar maple, red (or swamp) maple, silver maple, Norway maple, and box elder, sometimes called ash-leaved maple. They all grow around the fringes of our small six-acre campus. To the west, we butt up against the K-Mart and Walgreen's shopping plaza, to the north there's a Greased Lightning and a convenience store, to the east a residential neighborhood, to the south, a bike path, and beyond that a little patch of undeveloped floodplain forest. We're in the middle of the city, but there's a verge of forest, a one-quarter-acre Ecopark and a little corner of aspens, grey birch, and sumacs along the bike path. It's not much, but then again, it's similar to what most public elementary school teachers and children have access to. So I use what's available right outside the door to model using the accessible schoolyard.

Off to my first class, the Professional Seminar. The first semester ProSem serves a number of purposes. Primarily, it's the context for the internship choice process. At Antioch New England Graduate School, we require students to visit three to six potential internship sites, mostly classrooms and environmental learning centers, to do observations and then find the most suitable setting for their internships. We manage the process here, over lunch on Fridays. But we also solve problems, deal with emergent issues, and get to know the local environment. After all, most of the 20-, 30-, and 40-something-year-old students are new to Keene, New Hampshire, and the Monadnock Region. Just like it's a good idea to do a field trip around the school on the first day of kindergarten, it's good to get adult learners out in their new community. And inasmuch as it's hot and sunny, we're going swimming. We make quick carpool arrangements and drive north about 15 minutes to a swimming hole on the Ashuelot River.

We park in a little gravel lot and then head across recently hayed meadows toward the river at the base of Surry Mountain. I've chosen this spot because I know not everyone will want to swim and the walk is as sweet as the swimming. Swallows swoop, the mountain looms invitingly, the grass glistens. Is this really school? A shelving ledge slips into the river; there's a gravely little beach. The water is bracing but not too cold, and you can ride a big eddy up to the top of a bit of swiftwater, move out into the current, ride down, and slip back into the eddy for another circuit. As we dry off, I place us geographically in the watershed—the Ashuelot rises in ponds about 25 miles north, passes down through here to the Surry Mountain Dam built for flood-control protection of Keene, then through the center of Keene where it was the economic lifeblood of the city for most of the 19th century, and then on another 30 miles through other industrial towns into the Connecticut River in Hinsdale. Although many of my seminar students don't live here in Keene, and most won't teach here, for the time being they are going to school here, and I want to model appreciation and enjoyment of place, as well as watershed consciousness, as important components of good education at any level.

I lay out the purposes of the Professional Seminar as well. There's something wonderful about meeting on a sun-warmed slab of granite, clothed in bathing suits with towels draped around our necks, for our first formal seminar. It's an example of how venturing out to a special place can be the kind of hook that good teachers use to engage their students, to create an anticipation of exciting learning adventures, a sense of the unexpected. For us, it is a ledge by the Ashuelot River, but for elementary students it could just as well be a copse of trees behind the school, a garden, or a park nearby. We all wish we could spend the rest of the afternoon by the river, but the afternoon offers other opportunities.

My second class is Place-Based Education, a required course for the 12 new students in the Science and Environmental Education concentration in the Integrated Learning program. It's also an optional course for students in the Arts and Humanities concentration, so there's a total of 21 students. My goals in this course are to teach some natural and cultural history content, while at the same time teaching the pedagogy, processes, and politics of education grounded in place. Instead of me telling them why we've created this new term of *place-based education,* I have them read a teacher-written article from the *Community Works*

Journal and have them identify the core elements of this teacher's practice that are unique. I'm trying to model definitions coming up and out of primary source material rather than descending from on high. Then, because our first unit of study is on learning local trees and figuring out why leaves change color, we head outside for leaf identification.

The first long assignment is to do a 6-week observation of a sugar maple tree as it changes color. I ask the students to chart the color change, do a series of whole tree and single twig and leaf drawings, and develop an investigation related to the tree's preparation for winter. Against this backdrop, we'll also learn to identify 20 local trees, create service learning projects in the local Ecopark, work with a downtown historical museum to develop artifact-based programs for the fourth-grade history and geography curriculum, learn about community treasure hunts, school audits, green buildings, and how to connect elementary students with homelessness issues.

For their first homework assignment, each student has to find a sugar maple to observe near home, so I need to be sure that everyone can identify a sugar maple. Last year, I found that when I assumed everyone could figure this out on their own, too many people observed Norway maples, which are often planted in urban settings because of their hardiness and tolerance for salt. And since Norway maples are boring from a color-change perspective, I'm focusing on learning maples today.

Each group of four students gets 50 or 60 leaves. The challenge is to sort them into leaves that are alike. I've given them five different species, but I don't tell them that. And I've chosen a range of leaves within each species—large and small, from the interior and exterior of the tree, some with insect damage, some in perfect shape. The students have to develop an understanding of the species distinctions in the leaf shapes and separate these attributes from the individual variations. Once they've created five groups, then they have to name each species on the basis of some distinctive characteristics—pointy deep valleys leaf, red stem jagged leaf, long stem soft U's leaf —and then create a list of these characteristics. Together we then bestow their formal names and focus on being iron-clad sure that everyone can tell the difference between sugar and Norway maples. (The little bit of latex that leaks from the stem when you pick a Norway maple leaf is a diagnostic feature.) Finally, we all sketch a sugar maple, creating a silhouette drawing of the whole tree. They will all do this on their own for their home tree, create copies of it, and use it to record color changes from week to week.

What are the underlying values in this class? I've tried to model a constructivist approach in both creating a definition of place-based education and in learning diagnostic attributes of different maples. I've used materials right outside the door of the school as the focal point for curriculum. I've tried to balance a focus on content (knowing tree species) and process (close observation, solving problems). I've tried to pair more knowledgeable students with students who have less knowledge about today's topic. And I've put an emphasis on beauty—my syllabus is graphically attractive, the leaves are presented in wicker baskets, the outdoor seating is arranged for coziness and to facilitate focus. I want students to feel comfortable, challenged, and refreshed. I want my practice to embody what I preach.

My last class of the day is Problem-Solving Science. Whereas the Place-Based Education class is for first semester students, the science class is for last semester students in our four semester (fall, spring, summer, fall) program. These students are in their second full semester-long internship, and they're chomping at the bit to be done and have their own classrooms. My class is the last of the week at the end of Friday afternoon (from 4:30 to 6:30) at the end of their program. Therefore, it has to be both fun and relevant, and though I try hard, I sometimes miss the mark.

Only about half of these students have taken the Place-Based Education course, so we start with a similar natural science approach but then go off in different directions. This year I start with a study of mushrooms. Trees are conventional, friendly, recognizable—an easy place to start. Mushrooms, on the other hand, are weird, smelly, hallucinogenic, and poisonous, and not normally part of the elementary curriculum. But mushrooms and all fungi are decomposers; they complete the nutrient recycling that the trees and other photosynthesizers started. They wrap things up and give things a new start, so they're poised at the same point in the ecological cycle as the finishing students in my program.

Because most of my students don't have much knowledge about mushrooms, they're put in the same role as elementary students. And their oddness makes them an interesting curriculum development challenge. In the end, though, I'm not really trying to get my students to teach about mushrooms. Instead, I want them to understand that our study of mushrooms is a prototype for how to approach any natural science topic—insects, rocks, butterflies, salamanders, gerbils. The rules of engagement are roughly the same. I want them to develop an affinity for using what's right outside in the schoolyard as materials for natural science investigations. Mushrooms make a good choice for the beginning of the fall semester because they're prolific then, and it gives us all a good excuse to be outside in the woods before the tough sledding of November through March. When the weather turns, we head inside and focus on physical science—clay boats to teach weight, volume, and density; simple machines; light and sound; paper towel testing to teach the scientific method; and sometimes paper airplanes. I'm modeling a curriculum that follows the seasons here in New England, taking advantage of the warmer months to do natural science based on field experience and, when that becomes prohibitive, doing physical science indoors using classroom materials.

We start by talking about cool science curriculum that will happen in their classrooms in the next couple of months. We'll be doing a lot of curriculum planning, addressing the standards, and creating assessments, so the first thing I try to make clear is that the course is designed to serve their science planning needs. The course is a laboratory for their elementary classroom teaching. Matt describes the plan in his sixth-grade class to have the mandated study of geology focus on the slate quarrying history in his town of Guilford, Vermont. We consider the possibility of having his students make their final presentation to our graduate class. Cara enthuses that she's going to get to teach the oceans curriculum that she designed in the Integrated Learning class as part of her fourth-grade internship in New Castle, New Hampshire. The rocky intertidal shore is just a stone's throw from the edge of the playground at her school. Although I'll be modeling science investigations that use materials and field experiences from Antioch New England's backyard, I also want to get students thinking about the types of science learning experiences that are made uniquely possible in the school and community that they're teaching in. When you've got slate quarries, you use them to study geology; when you've got a shoreline, you use it to study ecology. With that in mind, I hand out a survey that asks students to describe any required science topics in their internship classroom and to inventory any resources for connecting those science units to the school's natural and cultural setting.

With the context set, we launch into mushrooms. Blank charts for mushroom terminology and mushroom questions are posted on the front wall. I delicately distribute beautiful white mushrooms in all stages of maturation to pairs of students in the class, along with an observation sheet taken from Doris's wonderful book, *Doing What Scientists Do* (1991). Their task is to complete an accurate pencil sketch of their mushroom, notice distinctive features, and record questions they have about their mushroom or fungi in general. A sedate quiet settles over the room as they become immersed in drawing, but questions start to spill out as their drawings take shape. What are these funny rough spots of the cap? There's a slug in mine; is it eating the mushroom? Is this mushroom poisonous? Should I be concerned about touching it? What's the difference between a mushroom and a fungus?

Drawings completed, we discuss the observations as a group, and we start to collect a list of mushroom terminology—the volva is the sac at the base of the mushroom, the veil is the skirt of tissue on the shaft of the mushroom below the cap, the cap is convex on some but flat on others, the rough bits of tissue on the cap are called warts. Slowly, we enter into this new world.

Then I lay out all the *Amanita virosa* on one table and all the *Amanita citrina* on another table and ask a couple of students to put each group in order from youngest to oldest. (No names have been attached to any of the mushrooms at this point.) It's an interesting task because it's not a function of size. Rather, you have to look at the shape of the cap, the character of the flesh, the shape and integrity of the veil. Without my telling them how to figure this out, a consensus emerges, and we have started to create a visual representation of the fruiting and spore-producing phase of the mushroom life cycle.

By this point, everyone is eager to know what we've been looking at. I read an excerpt from an elegantly illustrated version of *Snow White*. It's the section where the wicked Queen thinks she has disposed of Snow White and goes to the mirror to get confirmation that she is now the fairest in the land. The mirror chastens:

Over the hills,
Where the seven dwarves dwell,
Snow White is alive and well,
And she is still the fairest in all the land.

Enraged, the Queen retires to her secret laboratory in the dark recesses of the castle and concocts a poison apple that will kill Snow White even if she just takes one bite. At this point, I circulate around the room to show everyone the illustration of the witch's lair. There on the workbench are deadly nightshade, a mandrake root, and the white mushroom we have been looking at—the destroying angel.

Everyone is a bit shocked that we have been working with a deadly poisonous mushroom. But I have chosen to work with destroying angels to create a bit of intrigue and to ensure that I have everyone's attention. I clarify that mushroom toxins are not absorbable through the skin. Nonetheless, with children I suggest driving home the seriousness of mushrooms by having them wash their hands after handling mushrooms. Of course, now there's lots of interest from the class on how to determine the edibility and toxicity of the mushrooms we find.

By 7:00 p.m. I am mostly alone in the building as I collect the mushroom detritus for appropriate disposal, clean the classroom, and make notes for next week. It's been a long but rich day of immersion in the rivers, leaves, fungal flora, classrooms, and educational issues of the Monadnock region. From these starting points, the mycelial threads of place-based education start to spread out from the Integrated Learning program into rural and urban schools across New England.

JUST THE FACTS, MA'AM

Enough with the evocative niceties, let's get down to brass tacks. In the Education Department at Antioch New England Graduate School, we've been training Master's level elementary school teachers for the past 30 years or so in our Integrated Learning program. The orientation has always been toward maintaining the traditions of progressive education that have developed over the past four centuries and have been articulated by luminaries such as Comenius, Rousseau, Froebel, Steiner, Pestalozzi, Montessori, Dewey, and Piaget. Our program is designed for 24 new graduate students each year. Their average age is about 30, and we get a mix of recent college graduates coming back to school after 3 to 5 years of Peace Corps, environmental education, Outward Bound, or private school teaching experiences, as well as older folks and parents transitioning from other professions or returning to school now that their children are out of early childhood.

The faculty draw inspiration from the British Primary School movement of the 1960s and 1970s, the progressive school movement started by Dewey in the early 20th century, the child-centered education orientation of Quaker schools, the social curriculum/responsive classroom structures of the Greenfield Center School, and the arts orientation of the early childhood Reggio Emelia schools in Italy. We believe in multi-age teaching, developmentally appropriate practice, and the preservation of childhood. At the same time, we are committed to improving public education, raising academic standards, and developing teachers and students who will take an active role in shaping a democratic society.

As Antioch New England also has a prominent Environmental Studies program, we enjoy an unusual collaborative relationship between the two departments and attract lots of students with an interest in both teaching and environmental studies. About 10 years ago, we created the Science and Environmental Education concentration in the Integrated Learning program to address the growing numbers of students interested in elementary teaching certification and environmental education. These students are getting trained as elementary school teachers but are also developing an expertise in how to put science and environmental themes at the core of their teaching. They're also developing skills in helping their teaching colleagues connect the curriculum to local places and the community. These teachers-in-training are in the vanguard; they're being prepared to bring the place-based education movement into rural hamlets and inner-city neighborhoods alike.

So are we really doing anything all that different? Basically, I think we're taking the essential truths of Progressive education and melding them with the insights and understandings of ecological science and systems thinking that have emerged in the past 30 years. It's important to recognize that place-based education is inherent in much of progressive education philosophy. Comenius, a 17th-century educator, advocated that, "Knowledge of the nearest things should be acquired first, then that of those farther and farther off." This is essentially the same message as articulated in Mitchell's *Young Geographers* (1934/1971) in the 1930s and in my *Mapmaking With Children* (Sobel, 1998) at the turn of the 21st century. But electronic media have changed the experience of childhood in the past 50 years, and our global consciousness has made us aware of the strain on the earth's ecological systems. These new realities require a pedagogical orientation that reconnects children with the natural world and their local communities. As we come to understand the interplay between the quality of education, the economic life of the community, and the integrity of the environment, we need to train educators who can connect the life of the school with community sustainability. So we strive to develop place-based educators for the sake of children, for the sake of communities, and for the sake of the biosphere.

How do we do it? Over the past 10 years, we've introduced a variety of changes to make our teacher training program more place-based. We've changed the orientation of many courses and added a variety of new courses. We've developed a set of new internships. We've created new opportunities for service learning, getting students involved as consultants in community problem solving. Through our CO-SEED

(Community-Based School Environmental Education) program, we've developed a network of schools and communities striving toward place-based education, and we use these sites to enhance the research and training opportunities for graduate students. Gradually, the pieces are falling in place.

CHANGING COURSES

Because we're a teacher certification program approved by the state of New Hampshire, we have to require students to take a variety of courses that fulfill state mandates. Our core requirements include theory courses like Human Development and Philosophy of Education, curriculum courses in all the major disciplines, and social policy courses like School Law. Then we have a wide range of elective courses such as Building School Leadership Teams, Assessment, Drama in the Classroom, and Storytelling. Within this range of electives, we offer a set of courses focused on place-based education targeted for the science and environmental education students, but available to all students. Our course evolution strategy has been to tinker with our core courses to introduce more place-based elements where appropriate and to recruit our favorite local practicing teachers to teach electives that illustrate how to teach language arts, math, social studies, and science using the local places and community as an integrating context.

Core Courses

Let me illustrate how we enhance the place-based elements in a variety of our core courses. I have chosen to focus on just two or three of the nine core requirements, but the process is emblematic of what is happening in most courses.

Human Development

Human Development is a first semester required course for all students, and it reflects our deep commitment to developmental theory as the underpinning for appropriate curriculum. We put major emphasis on building bridges between autobiographical reflection and stage theory. By engaging students' memories of their own childhoods, we seek to create an empathic understanding of the children they'll be teaching and uncover a fountainhead for good curriculum ideas. When someone has to teach geology to their third graders, I say, "Try to remember what it was about rocks that fascinated you when you were 8 years old, and use that as a curriculum starting point." (For me, I was fascinated with collecting mica at that age, so in one of my courses I've developed a social studies curriculum challenge that focuses on understanding the mica processing industry in Keene between the First and Second World Wars.)

For students, this kind of emphasis on reflective autobiography is a bit unnerving at first. Justin McClellan '96 recalls:

> One of my first writing assignments was not of the argumentative type, nor was it scientific/factual, the opinionated, or my favorite, the narrative. It was a reflection paper. Coming from a typical grade conscious university, I did not understand how I could get credit for writing a two- to three-page paper based on how I "felt" about a particular subject. No research? No argument?

As adults, we may find that we have left the realm of experience of a child. We try to return there by reading texts and immersing ourselves in the lives of children today. Although it's important to be up-to-date with this generation, let us not forget that we were once children, too, with similar school and personal experiences.

The childhood reflection papers take many forms—remembering a doing-nothing summer when you were 13, the experience of getting your first bra, snow days, the death of a grandparent. We direct some of these recollections to be about relationships to place so as to provide the raw material for designing initiatives with children. Sarah Fiarman '95 recalls her suburban neighborhood:

> I walked past 910 California Avenue to the other end of the block, where my neighborhood best friend lived. Two years older than me, my best friend Lorena had long brown hair, which, unlike mine, was always neatly parted and braided. During the week, we went to two different schools and different dance classes, but on the weekends we were each other's entertainment. Despite the fact that we both had backyards, our favorite place to play was across the street in the industrial park.
>
> There was a long, low, grey building which emanated a sense of authority and we knew it must be a HEADQUARTERS for something. A sign which said CERES or SYSTEX or some similarly efficient, robotic sounding name was on the edge of a circular plot of grass. It was a lawn so meticulously trimmed, it had the air of a formal furniture. Lorena and I walked down the service driveway. This led us towards the side of the building to an entrance below ground level. Set back into the building, a side door and four

or five steps leading down to it created a small concrete cave. This was where we loved to play make-believe.

This kind of recollection leads to the understanding that children desire small, enclosed private play spaces, and they'll find them even in processed business landscapes. Imagine how this insight can lead to new ideas for field trips and geography curriculum in suburban neighborhoods.

On the other end of the geographical spectrum, Judith Gibson '03 remembered summering on an island off the coast of Scotland in her childhood:

> As a child, I spent hours wandering around our island. I came to know intimately every gully and outlook, where the streams started and ended, where to pick wild mushrooms or gather mussels. I relished the freedom, the solitude and the thrills of exploration.

Based on her recollection of island exploring, Judith got intrigued with the motif of "islandness" as inherently compelling for children, and she used it for curriculum development purposes:

> The island theme provides a wonderful opportunity to be in control of a miniature world or paracosm. I had my first powerful experience of this when I was with a home-schooling group of six- to twelve-year-olds with my son. Some parents and older children wanted to do a children's version of Shakespeare's *The Tempest*. I thought that since all the action took place on an island, it would be useful to make a model of the island so the younger children could visualize the plot. The younger children loved seeing the papier-maché island take form beneath their hands and soon the older kids drifted over and the model became the focus of our Shakespeare work. One boy was making a rocky inlet for a boat to wait out a storm and was for all intents and purposes there in the cove sitting in his boat. The older kids identified points that fitted with the story and with tiny figures played out some of the scenes.

Judith followed a sequence that we try to cultivate broadly—from recollection of childhood experiences in place, to understanding developmental truths about child/place relationships, to creating curriculum that capitalizes on and cultivates these relationships.

Integrated Learning: Theory Into Practice

Integrated Learning is another required first semester course. Although all our students take at least one course in each major discipline of Language

Arts, Math, Social Studies, and Science, this course models how to integrate curriculum through themes and projects. Themes and projects can emerge from long-standing fascinations of the teacher-in-training or from the curriculum standards of the school district where the intern will be working —from Boatbuilding to Japan to Symmetry to The Forest. But we also encourage students to develop themes and projects based on what's close at hand, following Comenius' directive that, "Knowledge of the nearest things should be acquired first."

Rachel Malamud '03 describes a theme she developed in this class and then introduced in her multiage first- through fourth-grade classroom internship in Marlboro, Vermont:

> Each child in the Primary Room chose a mammal found in Vermont to work on. With help from teachers and the librarian, the students were able to find books and articles that contained information about their mammal. It was wonderful to watch the younger students learning how to read while also learning the basics of research.... The research and writing process made up most of the two and a half month unit. The rest of it included artistic endeavors like dioramas for the younger students and puppets for the older students. To see a thematic curriculum work so well, and cover so many aspects of a student's education—as well as state requirements—was inspiring. Even more amazing was watching the children take so much pride in their work.

Jen Chapin '03 describes a similar social studies initiative with third and fourth graders at The Common School in Amherst, Massachusetts. With Jen's assistance, the classroom teacher implemented a semester-long theme on whaling. A core component was a 6-week simulation of an 1849 whaling expedition on *The Lagoda*, a whaler from New Bedford, Massachusetts—nearby history. Each student had to become one of the crew of the ship and keep a journal documenting their experiences on the voyage. Jen reflects:

> Now, I wouldn't say that I was a skeptic, but I honestly wasn't sure how this writing exercise would go. It was a huge success. I have never seen a group of students so excited and enthusiastic about writing. I watched students who had struggled with research writing blossom and flourish during this creative writing process. Each child wrote something beautiful, eloquent and imaginative.

Other Core Classes

The same principle operates in the other core classes. In Math Methods, we emphasize creating real problems that students can solve in the school or on the playground. In Methods of Teaching Reading & Language Arts, we encourage our teachers-in-training to get students to bring their local experiences into their writing. As an extension of her Reading and Language Arts class, Jennifer McKnight '98 edited the student newspaper in the third-/fourth-grade class at the Oak Grove School in Brattleboro, Vermont. One students' article read,

Secrets of an Ice Fisherman

The best spot for ice fishing is in the Connecticut River. I have caught sixteen bass there. The best time to go ice fishing is between the hours of 8:30 am and 5:30 pm. I like to go ice fishing because you can walk on the ice. I think suckers are the best bait to use. Ice fishing is a great way to walk on water and catch more fish.

One of our goals here is to expand the traditional conception of resources. Resources aren't just the books in the library, the Internet, or the teacher's guide. Childhood memories, the neighborhood park, students' out-of-school experiences, the Historical Society, a grandparent, and the store owner are all resources we want our teachers-in-training to draw on. By encouraging the use of these resources in our core courses, we lay the groundwork for all of our teacher education students, not just the science and environmental concentration students, to connect the life of their classrooms to their surrounding communities.

Place-Based Education Electives

Over the past 5 years, we've created a palette of specialized courses focused on using the environment and the community in the elementary classroom. In the beginning, core faculty taught these courses. Recently, we've started to recruit the best and the brightest classroom teachers and naturalists who work with children to bring their work into the graduate school. Many of these are weekend or half-semester one-credit elective courses. Students might take a total of six to eight of these throughout the whole program. They're presented roughly in the order that most students would take them.

Place-Based Education

This is the seedbed for all the other courses. We explore the evolution of the concept of place-based education, the national context, and pedagogical techniques. Topics and projects include redesigning schoolyards, school energy audits, a simulation case study of implementing place-based reform in a school district, a study of the air quality impact of different carpooling options, and research on the relationship between place-based education and academic achievement.

New England Mammals

It's easy to do place-based education in September in New England, but how about in January when it's 10 below? In conjunction with the Harris Center for Conservation Education, we offer this field course with a focus on tracking and scat identification as a way of understanding local mammal behavior and populations.

Star Search: Exploring the Night Sky

Another good midwinter engagement. This course helps students brush up on their understanding of the solar system and the universe (to infinity and beyond!) as a way of preparing them to teach about why we have seasons, phases of the moon, and why, all of a sudden, there's a 10th planet. Each student has to create a brochure about one of the prominent constellations and explore its mythical and cultural heritage.

Integrating Math and Science Through Mapmaking

This developmental geography course explores mapmaking techniques through the elementary grades, from classroom maps in first grade to neighborhood maps in third grade to solar system maps in sixth grade. A central premise of the course is that mapmaking in the community helps to develop a sense of place.

Food in Schools

An exploration of school lunch programs and innovations in how school lunch programs operate. Students learn about school systems that are building connections with local farms and regional food networks to provide organic, locally grown, healthy meals for students. The relationship between good food and academic achievement is considered.

Vernal Pools

Come the end of March, teachers and students are itching to get outside and breathe some fresh air. The study of vernal pools provides a wonderful link between science, art, and language arts, and vernal pool documentation can also contribute to citizen science initiatives to map and preserve these nurseries for amphibians. Teachers-in-training pose questions and then do field research to answer their questions, in order to prepare them to conduct the same kind of investigations with their own students.

Nature Journaling

Noted artist and field naturalist Clare Walker Leslie teaches this workshop on field sketching and how to use the nature journal in the classroom. Students learn how to draw flowers, birds, and landscapes, and explore how nature journals can enhance the language arts and science curriculum.

Sheep to Shawl

This course centers around a hands-on investigation of the transformation of wool from raw fleece to handcrafted clothing. In so doing, it integrates the history of farming in New England with the arts, from shearing to carding to spinning to dyeing to weaving.

Place-Based Social Studies

The study of regional and national history is made accessible and lively when it's locally grounded. This course is taught by a sixth-grade teacher with in-depth connections to the historical society in her town. Most recently, this course followed a project in which sixth-grade students came to understand the Civil War by examining the historical records of local Vermonters who served in the war. As part of the course, the Antioch New England students attended a formal presentation by the sixth-grade students of brochures they created for the historical society. The presentation was attended by community members and was conducted at the Town Grange.

Life Down Under: Invertebrates in the Classroom

It's easy to find bugs in rural and urban settings on the playground. And creepy-crawlies make for compelling curriculum. The elementary teacher who instructs this class both challenges students to learn insect taxonomy and collection techniques, as well as to understand how to use bug investigations to enhance language arts and math curricula.

Cemetery Quest

The study of the local cemetery is one of the best ways to understand history. Through demographic studies, historical society research, exploration of the symbology of gravestone graphics, and the creation of a curriculum-based treasure hunt, students in this course learn the history of the community and how to engage children in graveyard curriculum.

Service Learning

Solving real community problems provides a compelling rationale for classroom curriculum, from designing a field guide for a local park to developing a composting system for the high school cafeteria to creating banners for a downtown historical celebration. In this course, students identify community needs and then create projects that meet the curriculum standards by making the community a better place.

The Ecology of Imagination in Childhood

This course investigates the developmental underpinnings of place-based education and the significance of the middle childhood years in creating a relationship with the natural world. We examine play motifs in children's engagement with nature and how to develop curriculum design principles based on these motifs, with an emphasis on enhancing the writing process through fantasy, small-world play, and finding special places. These courses abound with examples of exemplary local teachers meeting state standards using local resources. In fact, whenever possible we like the graduate courses to intersect with the real work of local classrooms—by following a project students are working on, by incorporating a presentation from students, or by having the local teacher conduct the graduate course. In this way, these electives unfold not from the instructions of some mass-market curriculum guide, but from the real studies of students in local schools. Just as the study of history or math or literature can come alive when made concrete by local field experiences or local relevance, the study of teaching methods comes alive for our students when made concrete by these inspiring models drawn from the teachers and classrooms in our region.

Each teacher-in-training takes some, but not all of these electives. And many of the science and environmental education concentration students take other elective courses in the Environmental Studies Department. These courses tend to have less of a focus on pedagogy (although we've developed a new course on Urban Environmental Education) and more of a focus on field natural history and ecological science—courses like Conservation Biology, New England Flora, Marine Biology.

In the beginning, we started with natural science courses, but we're now expanding to focus more on literature, history, art, and math from a place-based perspective. As our CO-SEED program (a 3-year school/community improvement initiative) is now working with a number of inner-city Boston schools, we're finding the need to develop more course work in social equity, environmental justice, and multicultural issues. Then there are the other skills place-based educators have to develop: how to serve as an effective professional development facilitator with colleagues; how to conduct program documentation and evaluation; how to make the case that place-based education meets and exceeds the NCLB testing requirements; how to articulate that place-based education is not an add-on to school curricula, but rather a framework for how you do everything. These components are woven into some existing courses, and eventually we'll develop courses that focus more on them. But the best opportunities to develop these skills reside in internships.

REAL-WORLD LEARNING: INTERNSHIPS

One of the unique attributes of our program is the close integration of internships and course work. Instead of having the internship at the end of the program when courses are mostly done, as in many undergraduate preparation programs, internships occur in conjunction with courses in our program. During the first fall semester, students visit a number of settings to do observations and select appropriate internships. They also do a one-on-one tutorial with a student as part of their Reading or Math Methods courses. The first internship occurs during the winter/spring in conjunction with courses—students work at their internship from Monday through Wednesday or Thursday, then attend courses on Thursday afternoon/evening, Friday, and some weekends. In the summer, students take intensive courses. Then in the second fall, students work at their internship from Monday through Thursday, and attend courses on Friday and some weekends.

This commingling of internships and courses means that course assignments often get carried out in classrooms and classroom issues can get worked on in courses. It closes the gap in the scientific method—students can hypothesize and design investigations in graduate courses, conduct the research in their internship classroom, then examine the results and redesign the experiment in courses. The cycle mitigates against ivory-towerism and fulfills Thoreau's suggestion that it's important both to see castles in the air and to build foundations underneath them.

Students in the science and environmental education concentration complete two internships—one in a self-contained elementary classroom, the other with a focus on place-based education. This second internship can involve working with an upper elementary or middle school science teacher, acting as a place-based educator for a whole elementary school, interning in CO-SEED schools in rural or urban settings, teaching with environmental or agricultural education centers that work with a diversity of public schools, or designing professional development workshops for teachers. The students complete the program with elementary teacher certification and a concentration in science and environmental education. Many of them go on to be elementary teachers with a place-based focus, whereas some work in specialized science or environmental settings.

The following case studies describe three self-contained classroom internships and two place-based education internships, each highlighting a different skill we're trying to develop in our graduates. In keeping with the theme of honoring the indigenous and the local, I'll let the graduate students' voices carry the narrative as much as possible.

Focus: Classroom/School as Community

Intern: Patrick Keegan, fourth grade, Chesterfield, New Hampshire
Intern: Jana Sandin, fourth/fifth grade, Boston, Massachusetts

In keeping with Dewey's conviction that the classroom should be a laboratory for democracy, we attempt to place interns in classrooms where the teacher consciously works on modeling the dynamics of a healthy community. It's even better when environmental caretaking is conceived of as an integral part of community maintenance. We believe that children learn to take care of the environment and take an active role in the community by first practicing these skills in small, visible ways in the classroom. The following two accounts illustrate implementing this concept in both rural and urban schools. Patrick articulates well the mechanics of making this work at the classroom level:

> I have participated in a wonderful way of building community this semester during my fourth grade internship. At the beginning of the year each student in the class "applies" for a job. Instead of changing jobs every week, in our class students become "experts in their field" and perform their duties for the entire year. Students may become the wildlife manager (the person everyone turns to when an unwanted bee flies through the window), time keeper (responsible for letting the class know when it is time to end a work

period), and sports manager (who keeps track of balls and jump ropes used during recess), to just name a few.

In order to meaningfully integrate social and academic learning, students campaigned for their jobs as they learned about the election process in the fall. The class studied election laws and procedures. We even paraded around the room with campaign posters, and some students made campaign speeches.

Having been a member of the class for almost three months, it is wonderful to see the evolution of students' ownership of the classroom. Many children are learning that the smooth functioning of the classroom depends on their efforts, and have begun to take responsibility for their environment and learning.

At the Mission Hill School, a diverse inner-city school in a socioeconomically challenged neighborhood, the same principle was manifest in Jana Sandin's approach to having her students try to solve a schoolwide problem:

I chose to create this unit because it fit within the school theme of politics and the fall elections. My cooperating teacher and I decided that we wanted to incorporate a science unit that touched on some sort of environmental political issue. Garbage and recycling was the perfect fit because it provided a topic that was accessible to our fourth- and fifth-grade students, and it was an issue that connects with the larger world. Midway through the unit, I presented the students with this challenge:

Greetings Hawks!

Our investigation into garbage at Mission Hill is underway, and we have already learned a lot of valuable information.

1. Ten pounds of classroom garbage is produced each day by students at Mission Hill. Most of the garbage we produce is paper.

2. Of the 10 pounds of garbage that is thrown away daily, nine pounds of it is recyclable.

3. If students continue to throw away garbage at the present rate, 2,000 pounds (one ton) of garbage will be thrown away each school year. If students recycled, the amount thrown away per year would be only 200 pounds.

Your Challenge:

Now that you have learned about the importance of recycling, it's time for your challenge! Your challenge is to reduce the amount of garbage that Mission Hill produces in its classrooms by 50%. So, instead of producing 10 pounds of garbage each day, your task is to convince students to recycle so that the amount of garbage produced is reduced to five pounds of garbage or less each day.

In order to accomplish this task, you will first need to learn more facts about garbage and recycling to convince other students that they should recycle. You will also need to learn about ways to reduce, reuse, and recycle at school.

Jana's unit involved Internet research, extensive data collection, the writing and practicing of persuasive speeches, conversations about how environmental problems are more heavily born by poor communities, collaboration with the building services staff, and a field trip to an industrial recycling center where some of the students' parents worked. The plan implemented by the students actually led to the 50% reduction targeted in the challenge. Reflecting on this curriculum, Jana commented:

> This unit was successful in providing a science-based school issue that students could investigate and act on. Because the activities were closely connected to the lives of the students, many of them were engaged and invested. Many teachers in the school commented to me how apparent it was that the students in my class were enjoying the science unit because of the work they were doing to promote recycling around the school.

Many of the place-based education programs I work with aspire to the goal of developing a sense of agency, a "locus of control" in students. They want students to feel that they can make a difference, that their participation contributes to the quality of life in the community. Through developing this disposition in the classroom, students will then go out and practice it in their local places. Our challenge is thus to train teachers to create the classroom structures that make this possible.

Focus: Using the Outdoors to Teach Core Curriculum

Intern: Orly Hasbani, second grade, Hancock, New Hampshire

We talk about place-based education rather than environmental education because we're not talking about adding in another subject.

Instead, as Lieberman and Hoody (1998) have said, we are talking about education in the environment, not about the environment. Of course, sometimes it's both, but teachers are under pressure to teach the core curriculum, and we believe that you teach the core curriculum best by grounding it in the real world. We also believe in the virtue of fresh air, sunlight, and quietness in helping to create strong minds and bodies. Orly describes one way to make this happen:

> For the last month and a half, my second-grade class in Hancock has been spending a lot of time in the woods. We've taken hikes in the forest behind the school. We've talked about evergreens and deciduous trees. We even did a plot survey of an area in the forest, counting the numbers of different kinds of trees and then wondering why red oaks and beeches are so much more common than birches and maples. An important part of our study has been Nature Journals and Magic Spots.
>
> Magic Spots is a time for each student and each teacher to sit at a special spot in the forest and observe, think, write, draw, and wonder. Each child has her own spot that she returns to each session. We tried to do Magic Spots twice a week so that children would have a sense of stability and continuity and start to notice things change as autumn progressed. Sometimes we gave a specific assignment, such as drawing a sound map or picking up a leaf, drawing it, and recording some words to describe it. With second graders, 10 minutes the first time is plenty. Towards the end of the tree unit, we were spending 20 minutes working quietly at our spots.
>
> What do students gain from Magic Spots and journaling? The school day is such a busy time for many students with lots of people talking all the time. Magic Spots is a time to exhale. To breathe in. To relax. At Magic Spots students are allowed to draw or write in an environment that is comfortable and safe while learning to take notice of the things around them. They gain a sense of ownership of their journals and create beautiful work. They are inspired by others' sharing of their work and by being close to nature.

Orly articulates well the academic and emotional values of writing in the out-of-doors. Additionally, our research in the CO-SEED schools we've been working with indicates that the quality of children's writing improves measurably when children are writing about local places and experiences they have in them. In one school, third-grade students in two classrooms where the teachers did extensive place-based work scored higher on standardized tests of language arts skills than students in two other third-grade classrooms where the teachers utilized the outdoors less. And teachers from rural Vermont to urban Massachusetts report that students are more motivated to write when they write about community projects. It appears that engaging students in their environment may be valuable not only in nurturing their sense of place, but also in helping them to develop the basic skills that are the cornerstone of all academic achievement. Our challenge is to train teachers who feel comfortable grounding the curriculum in the community and who can articulate the research and pedagogy that support this practice.

Focus: Involving Students in Real Work

Intern: Josh Traeger, Grades 5–8, The Farm School, Athol, Massachusetts

Many of our students complete internships at environmental or community learning centers whose work involves programming for public school teachers and students. Whenever possible, we love to steer interns toward curriculum projects that engage students in real work. The Farm School provides residential school year and summer programs for over 1,500 young people and their teachers each year, a yearlong apprentice program to train adults in modern sustainable agriculture, and an on-site, one-room middle school. Young people work the land and take home the cultural history, vital experience, and personal identity that farms nurture. Teachers work alongside their students and leave with new insights into their craft and into the children they teach. It's a model of engaging students in work that makes a difference, and seeing this in action is a valuable experience for interns. Josh Traeger describes the process of involving students in real work:

> The program I was involved with was only two days long, although two days of farm life works out to be about 30 hours of community time. The students arrive on Monday morning and leave Wednesday. Each week, as a new group of students arrived, I would ask how it was possible for these kids to get anything substantial in such a short time. Remarkably, by Wednesday morning they were excited and eager to be up at sunrise, greeting a new day on the farm, running from the bunkhouse out to be with the cows. The farm school is 100% experiential; without the help of the students the farm would not run. The students quickly realize this as their stay begins. And because the work matters, the students seem even

more eager to help out. The real learning happens when we were farming side by side.

The main gift that I walk away with from the Farm School is the simple idea of doing meaningful work with students, and the compassion that children have for animals.

Real work comes in all shapes and sizes. Writing and editing the community newsletter, creating a trail guide for land owned by the conservation commission, designing the public education brochure on storm-water management for the city, building a neighborhood skating rink, running the school recycling program—all projects our interns have helped to conduct. Research suggests that an effective way to develop stewardship behavior in learners is to start with small, manageable projects with young students and gradually increase the scope and complexity of projects as children mature—from taking care of the guinea pig in kindergarten to running the healthy snacks program for the basketball games in middle school to serving on the Cities for Climate Control committee in high school.

By enabling students to witness these tangible accomplishments and celebrating their ability to make a difference, these experiences help students discover their personal and collective efficacy. Real work fosters not just the skills for stewardship and citizenship, but a proclivity for further involvement. When interns see these projects in action, and see the learning potential of real work, they develop the capability to bring real work into their own classrooms.

Focus: Cultivating Professional Development Skills

Intern: Janelle Shafer, K–12 Place-Based Service Learning Teacher Institute, Rachel Marshall Outdoor Learning Lab, Keene, New Hampshire

I've heard that one of the guidelines for surgeons in training is, "See one, do one, teach one." Although as a potential patient, this makes me a little nervous, as a teacher educator, I sometimes advocate for the same learning process. There's no better way to learn something than to have to teach others how to do it. For emergent place-based educators, this is often a good practice. We challenge interns with a good combination of classroom chutzpah and environmental education background to become one of our team. We put them in internships where they're the experts helping other teachers use the community effectively. Janelle's task was to develop a summer institute on place-based service learning for teachers in the two large school districts in southwestern New

Hampshire. The institute was to be one of the professional development opportunities related to a large federal grant initiative implementing one of the few school choice programs in a rural area.

With support, Janelle had to design the institute, engage the presenters, draft the budget, write and produce the brochure, do recruitment at school faculty meetings, and then teach much of the weeklong program. It was an ungainly task.

> Prior to this internship, I have had very little experience with teacher workshops. I was not familiar with strategies used to help teachers plan a unit during a workshop. My hope was to identify professional development strategies that would scaffold teachers' ideas into a solid service learning unit plan.

> Facilitating the workshop helped me identify ways in which I can make teachers feel more confident in their ability to develop and implement a service learning project. These strategies included:

> a. encouraging them to be realistic, start small and build on project ideas from year to year,

> b. identifying content areas that they already cover in their classroom and helping them to plan a service learning project that would integrate that content area with state standards and frameworks met by their units,

> c. allowing adequate discussion and planning time so teachers could narrow down their ideas and shape a project that was both comprehensive and realistic, and

> d. offering support for their projects by providing curricular resources, funding ideas, and opportunities for reflection.

> I spent a great deal of time helping teachers see the connection between service learning projects and meeting the state standards. For example, the ninth-grade earth science teacher at Monadnock Middle School expressed concern for having to teach soil ecology and was not sure how to integrate a service-learning project. Through brainstorming sessions, she realized her school was considering a compost system for the cafeteria, and she discovered that a composting project could easily integrate soil ecology. As a result, I provided her with curricular resources on composting and soil ecology. By the end of the four days, she not only had an outline for her unit, but she also

felt that the project would help her teach subject matter she already planned to teach and did not perceive the project as an "add-on."

Words cannot describe how I feel walking away from this internship. I feel empowered, excited, thankful, and most of all confident in my ability to work with teachers. I realize I still have a great deal to learn and I look forward to working with teachers in the future to bridge the gap between formal and nonformal education.

In addition to her newfound confidence, Janelle also developed essential skills for a place-based educator: teacher outreach, curriculum consulting, grant writing, evaluation, and overall communications skills. Simultaneous with this experience, I challenged Janelle to write a professional article for publication as part of my Conceptual Development and Learning Theory class. Janelle has a particular concern about attuning environmental education to the needs of urban, multicultural communities, so I encouraged her to do her final paper for my class on this topic. She interviewed African- and Asian-American place-based educators working in our CO-SEED schools in Boston and then drafted an article entitled "The Whiteness of Environmental Education." I made editorial comments; she redrafted it, and submitted it for publication in *Community Works Journal*.

By encouraging our students to use their course requirements to write for a broader audience, rather than just writing for the faculty, we help them to develop the communications skills they need to articulate their pedagogical values and practices to fellow educators, as well as to the community at large. Coupled with an internship focused on building professional development skills, such experiences equip future teacher-leaders, such as Janelle, with the capacity to coach other educators in using the community as the context for learning.

Compare Janelle's and Josh's descriptions of their internships with Patrick's, Jana's, and Orly's and you get a good sense of the value of two different kinds of internships in creating a skill set for new teachers. The self-contained classroom internship gives students the opportunity to refine classroom management skills, address curricular requirements, and understand how to shape the culture of a minisociety. Then, with these foundational skills in hand, the student moves out into the more challenging context of working with other educators and community members to encourage place-based education on a larger scale. We're training our students to be both good classroom teachers with an eye on academic achievement, and good stewards of the community with an eye on the big vision of cultivating a sense of place and building social capital.

In the best of situations, a mutually beneficial relationship between interns and their cooperating teachers emerges that enhances the practice of place-based education. By linking teachers who have a place-based orientation with our students, we supply classrooms with the creativity, energy, and insight that our interns bring. With an intern, teachers gain an assistant to do background research and planning, as well as a collaborator to bounce ideas around with, enabling teachers to innovate more. The internships not only serve our students' professional development, but also serve the mentor teachers as well, and ultimately improve the quality of education for the students involved. Moreover, they frequently produce great curricular models for other teachers to draw on. In this sense, our internships often act as incubators for innovative practices in place-based education. Matt Dubel's internship in Jen Kramer's sixth-grade classroom in Guilford, Vermont, is a good example of this kind of collaborative internship, pairing one of our students with an exemplary place-oriented teacher, and producing some inspiring curricular results. Matt describes his experience in the following section.

ONE INTERN'S STORY

The sun's just breaking over Wantastiquet Mountain as I head south along the Connecticut River valley to Guilford, Vermont. It's the last day of school before winter break and, sadly, the last day of my internship. Turning off the highway to follow the twisting route that leads to Guilford Central School, my eye catches the outcropping of slate that abuts the exit ramp. After spending the past month investigating slate with the sixth-grade class that I'm interning with, I see slate everywhere now. It's part of that phenomenon where newfound knowledge actually enables you to see what was there all the while. Think of the experience of learning to identify something—a white pine, a red-tailed hawk, an eastern swallowtail, anything—and then feeling as if you see it everywhere, like you've stumbled into some great abundance that can only be accessed by your ability to recognize that it's there.

Stegner (1993) writes that "No place is a place until things that have happened in it are remembered in history, ballads, yarns, legends, or monuments." What was once just another pretty Vermont landscape to me is now a place I see through the history of my time working with 15 sixth-graders and one exemplary teacher. As I drive through Guilford this morning, the sights out the window retrace the path of my internship. The white clapboard church evokes the memory of the time we brought the students here to check out its magnificent 19th-century slate roof and to seek out the gravesite of a prominent quarry owner in its cemetery. This landscape abounds with our stories, the product of a season spent engaging students in learning language arts, social studies, science, and mathematics by using the raw materials of the community around them.

Guilford, Vermont, is a town of just over 2,000 people in the southeast corner of the state, just north of the Massachusetts border and just west of the Connecticut River. Don't picture the classic Vermont town green with a steepled church on one end. Instead, imagine several smaller villages, each little more than a crossroads today, though in the 19th century they were distinct communities with unique economies and demographics. Following Route 5, I enter into one of these—the village of Algiers—that lies just north of a string of slate quarries reputed to be the oldest in the nation. It was here, in these quarries, that our study of geology came alive this fall.

Walk into any school and the odds are good that you'll find a class studying geology. But so much of what passes as geology study is bookishly abstract, mystifyingly disconnected from the earth beneath the students' feet. We decided to use the landscape of Guilford to illuminate our study of geology. And what a story we found: volcanism, ancient oceans, continental collision, intense glaciation, and a rock that was a vital part of the human history in the area. This intersection of the natural and cultural history of Guilford through the quarrying of slate became our hook, and a natural link that connected all the core curricula.

Accompanied by geologist John Warren, we ventured out to what was once the largest slate quarry in Guilford. After so much talk of this metamorphic rock, it was a thrill to approach the old quarry and see the hills of scrap slate, then enter the quarry itself through the corridor cut into the rocky hillsides. On either side, the walls were sheer slate: some sheets vertical, some horizontal, some at odd angles. John explained how the metamorphism caused by continental collision over 200 million years ago might have caused the rock to form at such angles. As the quarry walls extended at least 40 feet above where we were standing, we tried to imagine how the slaters worked the quarry. Before long, students were quarrying their own samples to take back to the classroom.

Later, local quarry owner Pete Crossman took us out into his working slate quarry to show us how people really work with slate. After pointing out which veins of slate were good for shingles, which were good for flagging, and which were useless, Pete demonstrated how to split a big sheet and then let our students try. Wes and Kevin jumped in first, and with Mitch's help they managed to split a large slab, over three feet long. It was a triumphant moment.

Pete also showed us the fields where the shanties once stood that housed the slaters, mostly immigrants from Wales. So back in the classroom we set out to learn more about the people who worked in the slate quarries. Students learned how to conduct research using census records and compiled lists of the actual Guilford residents who were slaters in 1860 and 1870. As we were studying statistics at the time in mathematics, using the census records to create the profile of a typical slater became a perfect culminating project to apply and assess students' data analysis skills. They tabulated data from the census reports, separated quantitative from categorical data, determined mean, median, mode, and range for quantitative data, and used their statistics to draw conclusions about the typical slater.

A grand story began to emerge, for us as well as for our students, stretching back over 200 million years to the collision of continental plates and reaching right up to the present in the slate shingles that still cover some of our students' roofs. To help students pull together what they had learned and to assess their skills and understanding, we challenged them to create a PowerPoint slide show that would tell the story of Guilford slate to people in the school, the community, and beyond. Students broke into teams, each charged with gathering the words and images that would answer a key question: How and when was the slate formed? What are the characteristics of slate? Where were the slate quarries and how did people quarry slate? Who worked with the slate? What was and is slate used for?

The process of sifting through all of the accumulated information and identifying the salient points amounted to a massive exercise in summarizing and organizing. Seeing how the students distilled their experiences into the big ideas and supporting details convinced me that grounding learning in place isn't merely an effective strategy for teaching the content of natural or cultural history. It's also a valuable technique for helping students develop the thinking skills that make learning anything more efficient. Because the subject matter was local and relevant, it hooked the students, and they were eager to share what they knew with others. Because it was local, there was an interested community audience, and this awareness motivated the students even more. The students exercised their thinking skills because they had a job to do that they wanted to do well, and summarizing and organizing information was essential to doing it. When students presented their work to a series of community audiences, the scope and quality of what they had achieved was apparent to all.

We hadn't set out purposely to construct a broad, interdisciplinary unit, but that's precisely what evolved. As a science exploration, we began to explore the basic geology, but the human connection to the rock was so pervasive that we were propelled into social studies. The social studies investigation yielded data that told the story quantitatively, so we launched into mathematics. And communicating what we discovered to a broader audience necessitated language arts. To leave out any one discipline not only would have weakened the academic rigor of the project, it would have foreclosed that natural human curiosity to see where the story leads without regard to academic categories. Instead, our students saw the interaction between people and the land they inhabit in full spectrum, and in the process honed skills that cut across the lines of subject areas and disciplines.

Turning off of Route 5, away from the slate quarries, I pick up Guilford Center Road, which follows the contours of the Broad Brook, one of the tributaries of the Connecticut River. The Broad Brook's path, from its sources to its outlet at the Connecticut, takes place almost entirely in Guilford, making it a natural focus for our study of watersheds, streams, and rivers. The Broad Brook flows along the edge of the woods next to the school, so one afternoon we led the students down to the banks of the brook, sat along its waters, and posed the question: Where does this brook start and where does it end? Our students are familiar with the Broad Brook because it flows past many of their homes and most everyone crosses it at least once on the way to school each day. But connecting that casual knowledge of the brook with a more systematic understanding of the movement of water was another thing altogether. Since we were just closing a geography unit, we challenged students to use topographical maps of Guilford to locate possible sources of the brook. From there, we mapped the various paths the tributaries take in forming the brook and the course the brook takes toward the Connecticut.

But the big event was an expedition: a chance to follow the journey of the Broad Brook from source to mouth. Starting in one of the places we had identified as a source, we journeyed along the brook's route by car, making periodic stops to observe the brook and take field notes and sketches (along with splashing a bit in its waters, of course). From steep and narrow to wide and lazy, the brook took on a life of its own.

So the students' task following the expedition was to tell the story of the Broad Brook in the first person, from source to outlet, using their field notes and sketches as raw material. The stories were then illustrated with watercolor and made into accordion books that could be unfolded to reveal the entire course of the brook. The project was conceived by a previous intern, Betsy Carline '04, as an alternative to a prepackaged unit on rivers and streams. Having students transform their observations of a watershed into an illustrated story forges a brilliant connection between science, language arts, and visual arts. There's something about the way a river's course, with its beginning, middle, and end, tension and resolution, models the structure of a good narrative. And just as our geography study flowed seamlessly into the Broad Brook study, the intimate experience students gained of the erosive power of water made for a perfect segue into our study of geology.

If I continued driving on Guilford Center Road, eventually I'd climb to that meadow next to an old farm where we discovered the Broad Brook emerging from a wetland. Instead, I turn on to School Road, not far from one of the old one-room schoolhouses. Until not that long ago, Guilford's children were served by 14 one-room schoolhouses. I know this, and where they are, because Kristen and Elizabeth mapped the locations of all of them. At the beginning of the year, we launched our geography study by having students create thematic maps of their town. Students chose an aspect of the town they'd like to map, and their choices are an indicator of what's prominent in Guilford and relevant to our students: bodies of water, sugarhouses, farms, snowmobile trails, slate quarries, cemeteries, school bus routes, one-room schoolhouses, and students' homes. Using a combination of personal experience, fieldwork, and primary sources, such as the official town history, students created a visual representation of one aspect of their place. Viewed together, the maps produce a remarkable portrait of a rural town. As Madison put it, "A lot of people think Guilford is this little dinky town, but you look at the maps and there's a lot here."

Just before I reach Guilford Central School, I pass by the town office, an essential resource throughout the past months. Much of the primary source material—town maps, town ballots, town annual reports—that our students worked with came from the ever-helpful staff of the town of Guilford. Without those materials, today's big event wouldn't be possible. After studying civics and government for several months, today is the day of our Town Meeting simulation, in which students will deliberate on an issue as townspeople, using the same process that's used to make decisions in Guilford. In fact, Guilford Central School is the site of the annual Town Meeting, and to lend authenticity to our exercise, we'll be using the Town Meeting gavel to call the meeting to order.

The gavel is a small detail, but I think it reminds us all of the connection between what we're doing and the real event that it simulates. The unifying premise throughout our studies this fall has been to use Guilford as the reference point whenever possible to make learning more concrete and more relevant. Walk into our classroom on any given day and you'd see piles of slate on the floor, local GIS maps lining the wall, charts of data copied from the 1860 Guilford census, or stacks of *The Official History of Guilford, VT*. We used authentic artifacts, such as the gavel from Town Meeting; we visited pertinent locations, such as the slate quarries; and we consulted primary sources, such as the town report. We did this because we felt that all of the concrete details and local connections helped students make better sense of bigger concepts, whether the concepts at hand were mean/median/mode, plate tectonics, scale, first-person narrative, or democracy.

So our study of civics and government explored the two forms of democracy used in Guilford: representative and direct. We began during election season, and the authentic way to learn the process of representative democracy was to have the students do as citizens do. Our sixth graders can't vote, but they can do the next best thing: take a copy of the town ballot, a copy of the Vermont Voter's Guide with information on the candidates, make decisions on which candidates to support, and then lobby for their candidates with each other, as well as the actual voters in the room. Interesting, real questions emerged that I suspect don't pop up when teachers use the ubiquitous, prepackaged election materials with students: What is the Patriot Act? Should the government make sure everyone has health care? Do we have a responsibility to support our president during a time of war? What do the political parties stand for? On Election Day, the seventh and eighth grades hosted a mock election, and while waiting in line to vote, the chatter among our students was about candidates: How many people were voting for Bush? Who was Wylie's pick for Auditor of Accounts? Who would the teachers vote for? The ballots for the mock election were simplified (all of the primary grades were participating as well), and our students came out wondering why Michael Badnarik wasn't on the ballot for President, or why the Lieutenant Governor's race was omitted. After you've worked with the real thing, the simplifications designed for kids seem, well, childlike.

To investigate direct democracy, we followed the same principle: have the students do what the adults do to run Guilford. So we started by examining the articles that Town Meeting considered that year, to get a sense of what the community makes decisions about, from the bold (Should the town call on the state to create a universal health insurance system?) to the commonplace (Should the town spend $55,000 on the volunteer fire department?). Then the students suggested articles that they'd like to consider in our own simulated Town Meeting. At last we arrived at a consensus: Our town would decide whether or not to allow the development of a shopping mall in Guilford. The students chose roles, developed their points of view, and honed their arguments. Now this morning they will debate the article as townspeople, using the same procedure for decision-making that towns in Vermont use.

With a bang of the gavel, I bring the Town Meeting to order and introduce the article. Thomas, as the developer of the project, wastes no time in moving the article and steps forward to make the case in favor. For the next 45 minutes, the students engage in a fascinating dialogue. Their comments touch on land use, environmental impact, trail access, community heritage, quality of life, economic development, the survival of small businesses, and the town budget. What I find remarkable is that many of their comments emerge extemporaneously and go beyond what they had prepared to say. As in true dialogue, they seem to listen respectfully to each other, then respond from the point of view of their character. I'm particularly touched by the way Kristen and Elizabeth speak persuasively on behalf of their characters' concern for the rural quality of Guilford. As Kristen's character says, "There are so many busy places in the world, it makes Guilford unique and special and different."

It's wonderful to watch how students employ local knowledge gained in our studies this fall to analyze this particular scenario. Several students bring up their thematic maps to point out the location of the proposed development, and are able to speak with authority about the topography of the area. Just as the thematic maps enhanced our study of the Broad Brook, which in turn enhanced our study of geology, this local knowledge came to bear on Town Meeting. Each project built on the others and added depth to the students' cumulative understanding.

Ultimately, the coalition of interests that support the shopping mall prevail, gaining a majority in a voice vote, and I adjourn the Town Meeting. Then an extraordinary thing happens. Without any prompting, the students get up and start to congratulate each other, allies and opponents alike. Witnessing this, I feel like I've flashed forward 20 years and am seeing these students after a real Town Meeting, acknowledging each other not as fictional characters but as fellow citizens, conducting themselves with civic dignity and mutual respect. Throughout these past months, we've sought to help our students come to know and care for their community at the same time that we've nurtured their intellectual growth, with the conviction that this local knowledge and care was the surest foundation for responsible citizenship. Watching these students today, I see it working.

FROM ABSTRACT TO VIVID

Matt's portrait of how schooling contributes to the life of the town is just one example of how we engage prospective teachers in community service. A commitment to one's place necessarily involves addressing its needs, and in our graduate school we do that through the Antioch New England Institute, our community outreach arm, which includes the Center for Place-Based Education. The Center promotes community-based education through programs such as CO-SEED, which pairs particular schools and their communities in rural and urban settings across New England to collaborate in developing place-based education on a systemic level. On a more intimate scale, there's the Rachel Marshall Outdoor Learning Laboratory, which works with local schools in Keene, New Hampshire, to engage students in service learning projects on public lands.

All of these programs provide opportunities for internships or research, so our community service projects both model the role that we believe schools can play in communities, as well as provide service learning experiences for our graduate students. Throughout our teacher preparation program, we're always trying to find real-world problems to structure the work we ask students to do, and these projects constantly generate real challenges.

In my Place-Based Education class last year, I hitched up my students with Josh Cline, one of the staff members at the Antioch New England Institute. He had a contract with the New Hampshire Fish and Game Department and the Maine Department of Inland Fisheries and Wildlife to write a children's Web magazine about wildlife issues for seventh graders in both states. What a great real problem for aspiring teachers! Josh provided the structure and basic style, then willing students took on the responsibility for writing individual issues. It wasn't easy, and many students complained when they had to do a third or fourth draft, but hey, that's the writing world! And, with the *Wild New England* Web magazine now online, students have great real-world documentation of their research and writing skills, for professional portfolios or potential employers.

Meeting local needs in northern New England's school districts increasingly means addressing the challenge of rural schools struggling to stay open, often as the last cultural and social institution in town. Last spring, faced with shrinking school populations in three elementary schools in towns north of Keene, the Monadnock school district responded by creating a number of first through third and fourth through sixth multiage classrooms. Though the change allowed these small village schools to remain open, local parents were up in arms! How could teachers meet the needs of their children when they had to teach three grade levels in one classroom? Seeing this obstacle as an opportunity, I spoke with the superintendent and offered to find an intern who could work in at least one of the classrooms to provide increased staffing. This would help allay parents' concerns and provide a challenging multiage setting for an Antioch student who had already had a successful single-grade internship experience. It's not hard to imagine building these relationships with village schools in a way that provides great internship opportunities for our graduate students while also helping small rural schools keep their doors open and avoid the pull toward centralization and standardization.

Even though I scoffed when my father wanted me to follow in his footsteps in the travel business after college, I sometimes feel like a travel agent when I advocate for place-based education in schools and in our teacher education program. On the one hand, there are the travelers—the elementary students, teachers, and graduate students yearning for interesting adventures. On the other hand, there's the world of curriculum and the landscapes and communities of New England. My job is to help design the itineraries that connect the desires to the places. Want to learn about percentages? Check out the big sale at K-Mart with 5%, 10%, 20%, and 30% off. Teaching the Revolutionary War? Did you know that Abner Sanger, local citizen and writer, described the march to Concord and Lexington from Keene in his journal that's available at the Cheshire County Historical Society? Have to teach about wetlands? Did you realize there's a beautiful little bog right out behind the playground, about a five-minute walk? For the sake of children, for the sake of communities, and for the sake of the biosphere, we need more teachers who can function like travel agents, connecting students to the places where they live and learn, advancing community well-being and civic engagement alongside academic achievement. Through experiences that engage

Antioch New England's graduate students in the place where they're learning, we hope to cultivate teachers who can do just that.

REFERENCES

Doris, E. (1991). *Doing what scientists do: Children learn to investigate their world*. Portsmouth, NH: Heinemann.

Lieberman, G., & Hoody, L. (1998). *Closing the achievement gap: Using the environment as an integrating context for learning*. San Diego, CA: State Education and Environment Roundtable.

Mitchell, L. C. (1971). *Young geographers: How they explore the world and how they map the world*. New York: Bank Street College of Education. (Original work published 1934.)

Sobel, D. (1998). *Mapmaking with children: Sense-of-place education for the elementary years*. Portsmouth, NH: Heinemann.

Stegner, W. (1993). *Where the bluebird sings to the lemonade springs*. New York: Penguin.

Creating a Movement to Ground Learning in Place

David A. Gruenewald
Gregory A. Smith

Beyond the ideas and programs described in the foregoing chapters, place-based education in our minds is something more than a curricular reform, another means to address the issues of equity and excellence that dominate discourse about American schooling. These issues are without question important, but more important is the issue of human responsiveness and adaptability to the local and global dilemmas that now demand our attention, intelligence, and energy. The collapse of the former Soviet Union and the subsequent globalization of market capitalism have created a set of circumstances that both attract and threaten human populations across the planet. The rapid industrialization of China and India is now demonstrating the transportability of North American, European, and Japanese affluence to other parts of the world (Friedman, 2005). This process will only accelerate as Western corporations and investors seek low-cost but highly motivated and skilled Third World workers previously disregarded during the ideological posturing of the Cold War. And modernizing populations in the Third World will legitimately be only too happy to participate in this distribution of jobs once reserved for the residents of the industrialized North. Poised against the globalization of the Euro-American model of development, however, is the imminent peak of oil production and a global climate increasingly unpredictable because of human-induced warming (Gelbspan, 2004; Heinberg, 2005; Kolbert, 2005). It is only a matter of years or at most decades before planetary limits constrain an economic vision that virtually ignores environmental realities. Given the inability of the centralized political and economic institutions that advance this vision to perceive or respond to its flaws, it seems likely that innovations capable of addressing contemporary challenges will emerge on the margins of power rather than in the center.

It is to people on the margins that this volume is addressed. Those margins include rural communities as well as inner-city neighborhoods largely abandoned by the State and its partners, the transnational corporations. These margins also include the many teachers currently discouraged by the climate of school reform. The inability of the State to respond to catastrophes such as Hurricane Katrina foreshadows the inability of the State to respond to crises that must accompany climate change and the economic disruptions associated with ever-increasing oil prices. People able to join together to address common concerns within the context of their own places will be better able to craft the new solutions required by the changing conditions of human experience. This is what the students at the Greater Egleston Community High School were able to achieve through their decade long struggle to improve the air quality of Roxbury, Massachusetts. This is what the students in coastal Maine are striving to accomplish in their efforts to create viable economic opportunities following the collapse of North Atlantic fisheries. This is what Navajo children schooled in the value of their own traditions and place may in time accomplish as they move into adulthood conscious of their own worth and the potentialities of collective action demonstrated to them by their teachers and families. Young people need an education that affirms their capacity to solve problems and contribute to the welfare of others, an education that speaks to the importance of diversity and adaptation and equity and shared power. When place-based education is implemented in ways that truly conjoin school with community and that provide opportunities for democratic participation and leadership, children are given the chance to partake in the collective process of creating the sustainable and just world that must come to replace the world of discrimination and waste that has begun to unravel around us now.

In an article entitled "The Best of Both Worlds: A Critical Pedagogy of Place," co-editor David Gruenewald (2003) argues that children, youth—and all citizens—must be educated to join in the decolonization and reinhabitation of their places. Decolonization entails grasping the way that the human and natural potentialities of particular communities and places have been diminished or thwarted by patterns of domination and discrimination that benefit one group while exploiting another. Re-inhabitation requires the restoration of relationships to other people and the land characterized by affiliation and responsibility. It will be through a process of re-inhabitation and the recognition that people need to care for one another and their places for the long-term that thoughtful and appropriate adaptations may arise to better meet humanity's economic needs at the same time that they preserve the integrity of the natural systems that support our species. Place-based education is just beginning to demonstrate what this process might look like. Our hope lies in the fact that human beings responding to the possibilities and limits of particular places have for millennia used their intelligence and sensitivity to craft cultures that more often than not have proven their appropriateness and sustainability. What has served our species well in the past could serve us well in the present and future if we only relinquish the modern tendency to impose universal solutions upon the infinite variability of both people and the planet. Local diversity lies at the heart of humanity's biological and cultural success. Place-based education once more taps into this ancient relationship of mind and body with the world.

CHALLENGES AND OPPORTUNITIES

Regardless of our commitment to the promise of place-based education, we are only too cognizant of the challenges faced by educators interested in moving teaching and learning in this direction. The aims of public education from the beginning have been more tied to national than local purposes. In the United States, common schools sought to draw a diverse immigrant population into a single American culture and teach them English. In Europe, state-controlled schools helped to eradicate the languages, dialects, and cultural diversity of the provinces and reorient the attention of peasants and workers away from the periphery to urban centers. For a variety of reasons, state-controlled American schools continue to focus the attention of teachers and learners on standardized and decontextualized learning objectives that often have little direct bearing on the lived experience of diverse people and places. Place-based education endeavors to reverse this trend by asking educators to include more local experience, inquiry, action, and reflection in the practice of teaching and learning. This does not mean that place-based educators necessarily seek to replace standards-based schooling with place-based schooling. Rather, advocates for place-based education aspire to make this powerful approach to learning available at least part of the time to learners in all communities.

However, because there is little in the discourse of high standards and high-stakes testing that asks teachers and learners to know about and participate in the life of local communities, place-based education does involve challenging some of the inadequacies of standards-based schooling. One of these is the common prejudice against the local. Too often, local knowledge and experience are seen as backward and uninformed, even by people who live in rural and inner-city communities. Convincing school administrators, teachers, and community members that examining phenomena close to home and taking action within the community will better prepare young people to participate in modern society will not necessarily be an easy sell. Yet, as several chapters in this volume show, local knowledge and experience can be crucial to the intellectual development of students and to their ability to thrive in their own communities. Indeed, local knowledge has often been the seedbed of fresh ideas and innovation that have fueled urban societies (Morgan, 1984). Local knowledge may also be the best way to guard against the negative consequences of global forces on local communities everywhere (Bowers & Apffel-Marglin, 2005). As noted above, place-based education has the potential to reestablish the value of long-standing relationships between people and their specific locales in ways that mediate the press for individual achievement and opportunity in contemporary "global" societies.

Given the long-standing nature of conventional educational practice, however, few teachers are currently prepared to incorporate outside-of-classroom phenomena into their work with students. In schools where textbooks, standards, and tests tend to drive instruction, many teachers have been transformed into technicians responsible for delivering instructional content developed by others. In contrast, place-based education requires them to become the creators of curriculum as well as collaborators with other community members. Little in their own educational experience or professional training has helped them acquire the skills or the confidence needed to do this work. Some individual educators and occasionally teams of educators have on their own developed programs that link their classrooms to their community and region, but it would be as unrealistic to expect all educators to demonstrate these entrepreneurial and creative talents as it would be to expect them to teach reading or manage student behavior without appropriate support. Professional development activities for experienced teachers and administrators and the incorporation of place-based learning opportunities in teacher and administrator preparation programs will need to become more widespread if place-based education is to become common.

An important impediment to movement in this direction is the degree to which place-based education counters the school experience of most citizens. A school's institutional legitimacy is often based upon the degree to which its structure, activities, and social relations conform to the memories of a community's adults, regardless of whether or not their own school experience was supportive or intellectually meaningful. Schools that violate those memories and norms are often viewed with skepticism. This is especially true if school programs engage students in activities that are not construed as viable educational work. Along with test scores, seat time in a series of academic courses has become a common measure of educational quality. For some, travel to and from learning experiences outside the classroom is seen as wasted time, and activities, including even recess, that are not clearly linked to formal measures of academic achievement, are seen as a waste of tax dollars. Many adults believe that children and youth should be off the streets during school hours. Convincing them that monitoring streams, conducting surveys, collecting information for news articles, or participating in agency or business internships are worthwhile will require persistence and regular public presentations that demonstrate the value of outside-of-classroom student learning. This is not something that is likely to happen overnight. However, when community members and educational leaders become engaged in place-based learning experiences with students and their teachers, attitudes, perceptions, and even trends can begin to change.

Place-based education's emphasis on the completion of real work in communities also calls into question the common belief that high-status knowledge is more theoretical than practical. Because high-status knowledge is associated with social mobility and desirable professions, an education that includes the acquisition of practical skills is often viewed as second-class, another species of vocational education and student tracking. For this reason, educators concerned about equity and social justice often avoid school reform efforts that require students to invest their time and energy in activities that may be more pragmatic than intellectual in nature. Courses that situate the learning of chemistry in the community, for example, tend to be seen as inappropriate for students who plan to attend college. This prejudice against linking learning to real-world problem solving, however, is paradoxical. While it is true that public perception perpetuates a vision of liberal arts education standing above practical affairs, it is also true that application, problem-solving, and cooperative abilities are publicly espoused by the same business leaders who have pushed higher academic standards and more stringent accountability measures during the past two decades. Ironically, these educational aims may be better served by a place-based curriculum than by a standards-based curriculum that promotes high-status and decontextualized knowledge.

Place-based education thus poses many conceptual and practical challenges to schools currently dominated by academic standards and testing. When compared to classroom-based pedagogies aimed at covering standards and preparing for tests, a place-based focus on real work in local communities contrasts starkly. But because the policies and perceptions that perpetuate school-as-usual are unlikely to change quickly, it is vital that advocates for place-based education not create a false dichotomy between an education that focuses on the local and an education that focuses on academic content, or between local decision-making power and the need for accountability. Few movements succeed when their advocates position themselves in total opposition to current structures and processes. Although we may dream of a totally different approach to public education than the one that currently exists, it is necessary to work with, while trying to change, what we have. Support for place-based education does not mean abandoning all of the practices common to schooling; it is not a simple either-or proposition. Support for place-based education means creating space within the current structures and practices of schooling for more relevant and engaging learning that focuses on local situations and experiences; it means challenging and sometimes changing assumptions and policies that make creating this space difficult. Therefore, it is crucial to emphasize that place-based educators care about and deliver on academic content, and that this approach to education produces results that our current systems of accountability fail to promote or measure (Rural School and Community Trust, 2003; Sobel, 2004).

Despite these challenges, changes in the social, economic, and political context of public education may create the space in which the introduction of place-based learning approaches could become more common. None of this will be easy, but it is not as if the institution of public education is stable and impenetrable. We live in a period of flux and uncertainty. Such eras have traditionally held within them the possibility of major shifts in common understandings and institutional practice.

LEADERSHIP ROLES FOR EVERYONE
Our experience as practitioners, scholars, and advocates for place-based education tells us that many people in fact believe it is a good idea. Few actively oppose the goal of connecting the education of young people to

local communities and consciously aiming to ready them through direct experience to participate in democracy at the local level. The problem is that the institution of school, and the assumptions on which it continues to operate, are extraordinarily resistant to change. In this final section we will briefly describe leadership roles for teacher leaders, traditional educational leaders, community leaders, and student leaders interested in furthering the work of place-based education.

Teacher Leaders

Teacher leadership is a relatively new concept in schools that has recently gained momentum with a surge of literature (Lieberman & Miller, 2004; York-Barr & Duke, 2004) and credentialing opportunities such as National Board Certification. This trend to acknowledge teachers as the leaders they are usually assumes and promotes a vision of leadership that is limited to what takes place within the classroom or the school. Without question, these are places where teachers do exercise important leadership roles that impact the lives of children and youth. Place-based education challenges all teachers to rethink the role of teaching beyond the classroom and to consider the relationship of teaching to the places where children, youth, and adults actually live and learn. As the chapters in this book have shown, all communities are places worthy of careful study and learning. All communities are also products of political decision making. If the education of young people is to prepare them as citizens capable of caring for theirs and others' communities and acting on their behalf, then teachers need to see themselves as integral to this process.

Today's teachers, however, are literally under siege. The media constantly portrays teachers and schools as incapable of producing students able to meet high standards or even minimum competencies. The standards and testing movement, epitomized by the increasingly problematic No Child Left Behind Act, has made the study and practice of teaching more prescriptive than ever. It has also significantly constrained conversations about the role of teacher to generic techniques and dispositions that will supposedly increase achievement "for all students." There is very little in the official discourses surrounding teaching that encourages teachers to develop intimate knowledge of their students' communities and to creatively conceive of diverse communities as "texts" for inquiry, reflection, and action.

Teachers who practice place-based approaches to teaching do so in spite of these challenges. Although their motivations are varied, all place-based educators seek to make learning more meaningful and participatory. Many teachers who move toward place-based approaches in their teaching report feeling renewed in their work; a relevant and engaging curriculum is as important to teachers as it is to students. This is especially true in light of recent data showing that half of all new teachers leave the profession within five years (National Commission on Teaching and America's Future, 2003) and that 70 percent of teachers strongly advocate real-world learning (Melaville, Berg, & Blank, 2006). Some teachers, such as Elaine Senechal (Chapter 5), find that teaching in places such as Roxbury, Massachusetts, means that education must be tied more closely to the political realities and lived experience of local communities. For Senechal and many others, the role of teacher is also one of an active citizen who participates sometimes as a change-agent and as a community leader. If schools are to help prepare future generations for democratic participation, it only makes sense that the most important adults in a school—teachers—become models of participation in the democratic process and mentors to the children and youth in their charge.

Traditional Educational Leaders

The field of educational leadership continues to redefine the role of the school administrator from "building supervisor" to "leader" who must be responsive to diverse communities within and outside of schools. Still, principals and superintendents lack experience as instructional leaders capable of making connections between these diverse communities, teacher work, and student learning. As with teachers, school administrators are often under enormous pressure to raise test scores or to respond to demands from vocal interests groups such as parents of children who are gifted, disabled, or non-White. The multiple demands experienced by school leaders often put them in a crisis- or response-mode that leaves little time for the relationship-building necessary to learn about—and from—a place and its people. Given these conditions, calls for "community collaboration," which have steadily increased in the teacher and school leadership literature over the last two decades (Epstein, 2001; Furman, 2002), can result only in superficial relationships that privilege some groups and work to strengthen the structures and processes that make place-based education difficult even to talk about or imagine.

The presence of more school leaders who actively support and participate in place-based education would greatly improve the environment for teachers who are interested in place-based approaches, but who may feel vulnerable in their risk-taking. Some teachers have developed the ability to legitimate and advocate for their place-based practices by showcasing student achievements in portfolios, demonstrations, and community events. Sometimes, these place-based teachers become the "stars" of their school and are seen by their administrators as valuable assets in the work of demonstrating accountability to the public. Other times, teachers interested in developing place-based practices may appear threatening to school leaders who are concerned about issues of liability and control and in maintaining what for them is the more comfortable status quo. In these cases, administrators may actively discourage place-based teacher initiatives.

How might a school leader support the development of place-based education? As with many leadership activities, an essential first step is to take stock of the work currently under way in one's immediate community of practice. Any school leader (teacher or administrator) might ask, who in our school or district is particularly good at connecting classroom learning to the communities that our school or district serves? Such an inquiry would net any number of teachers in most every community, and identify also those non-formal educators and organizations who invite teachers and students into their alternative community-learning spaces. Identifying, mapping, and thus making more visible a community or region's place-based learning activities could be one step toward encouraging such practices and developing a network of support among interested teachers and community members.

Furman and Gruenewald (2004) describe five additional ways that educational leaders, especially principals, can support place-based learning: (1) shaping the cultural politics of the school, (2) negotiating the borders between imposed mandates and place-based teaching, (3) actively supporting place-based initiatives, (4) securing resources, and (5) identifying professional development opportunities. All of these activities, however, require that an educational leader become knowledgeable about the places and communities surrounding the school, and knowledgeable, too, about the power of place-based education and its impact on communities and learners. The best way for a leader to move in these directions, we believe, is through firsthand experience and participation in a place-based project within his or her own school community.

Community Leaders

As Michael Morris demonstrates in his chapter about Albuquerque's Institute for Community and Educational Leadership, if educational leaders are to be of service to communities, they need to learn to listen carefully to what community members and leaders desire for themselves; they need to know the places in which their schools are embedded. Community leaders exist in diverse roles in all communities. Leadership, as Morris describes it, does not always mean official titles and institutional affiliations. Often it means knowledge about and care for a place and its people, as well as the commitment to act in the best interest of communities not represented by institutional leadership.

As we have argued, the institutional environment of schooling currently works against the development of more place-conscious and place-responsive teaching and learning. Members of the community who work outside the formal structure of schooling, however, do not directly experience the pressures common to teachers and administrators. Community members and leaders, those with titles and those without, are not held responsible for the many increasing expectations put on teachers and administrators. Regular taxpaying citizens and community groups are thus in a position to act somewhat more freely than those people who are employed by a school; these voices from outside of schools can be a powerful source of support for legitimating and initiating place-based education.

While the institution of school remains isolated from communities, most school leaders are very receptive to the wishes of communities. Place-based education, as exemplified throughout these pages, suggests a variety of roles for community members. Some teachers are ready to initiate collaborative projects in the local community. Others need to be invited outside of the routine of school to see for themselves how community learning and participation connect with their vision of themselves as teachers. For many teachers whose college education lacked attention to place-based pedagogies, community groups and community-based organizations can become catalysts for new approaches to teaching. The literature on school-community collaboration (e.g., Furman, 2002) increasingly calls on school leaders to develop stronger ties with communities. Community members and groups can take advantage of this collaborative climate by advocating for and initiating projects important to their community with appropriate teachers and groups of students. Because of the insular nature of the institution of school, it is unlikely that school policies will explicitly promote place-based education without this kind of direct community support.

Student Leaders

Young people can be a community's, or a nation's, source of hope and inspiration, or they can be singled out as scapegoats for the failures of the adult community. With all the attention focused nationally on the large numbers of children failing to perform at standard, it is no wonder that many young people tune out from what happens at school (Blum & Libbey, 2004). The situation for students who drop out most frequently and benefit least from schools—Native American, Latino, Black, and poor students—is even worse and has not significantly improved over the last two decades of increased attention to standards and testing (McNeil, 2000). Place-based education has the potential of turning this situation around. A study conducted by the Horatio Alger Association found that 95 percent of students aged 13–19 say real-world learning would improve their school (Melaville, Berg, & Blank, 2006). All of these disenfranchised, alienated, and under-engaged students need all kinds of support so that they can take more control of their own learning. Place-based education, with its emphasis on meaningful experiences, local relevance, and direct participation, can show teachers and students new reasons to care about learning.

Whether the focus is on small rural towns, densely populated urban centers, or schools, we have in the United States a "participation gap" that is just as serious as the "achievement gap." In fact, it can be argued that the obsessive focus on the achievement gap that we have experienced since No Child Left Behind is deepening the participation gap and the sense of alienation many children and youth experience in school. If democratic participation is a valued social goal in this country, then educators and policymakers need to find ways to engage students in the work of participatory democracy in their experience of school. An essential piece of this complicated puzzle is to reclaim local knowledge and the educative value of experiences in local communities. Throughout this book are examples of shared leadership between students, teachers, and community members where young people learn not only about their democratic rights, but also about their responsibilities to act, individually and collectively, on issues and situations that require a community-based response. Community well-being, in its necessarily diverse manifestations, is too important a goal for schools to continue to ignore. In order for students to take on the roles necessary to contribute to the well-being of their communities, they must first be seen by a community's adults as capable contributors and potential leaders. These adults—teachers, administrators, and community members—must then create experiences through which students can begin to take on significant leadership roles.

Ivan Illich once wrote, "People who have been schooled down to size let unmeasured experience slip out of their hands" (Illich, 1971). The educational trends of standardization and businesslike accountability measures have turned school-aged citizens into commodities or "products" whose value must constantly be measured by tests. Schools can do better; many schools, teachers, and leaders are doing better. If there is a "product" associated with schooling that deserves our attention, that product is the future of the places in which people live. We can either begin paying attention to these places in our educational policy and practice, or we can continue to ignore them. If we choose to pay attention, places and the people who inhabit them can become powerful teachers that enrich everyone's experience of learning.

The globalization of free trade, the mobility of capital, and the advent of the Internet are proving to be extraordinarily disruptive to the social and natural communities that support humanity and all life-forms on the planet. These central elements of the 21st century are also contributing to the consolidation of wealth in the hands of fewer and fewer people, exacerbating the circumstances of the truly poor and threatening the middle class throughout the developed world. If people believe Margaret Thatcher's assertion that there is no alternative to a continuation of this process, the outcome for future generations does not seem especially hopeful. Overpopulation, the peaking of oil production, the elimination of human rights that will accompany growing economic disparities, and global climate change could well challenge *Homo sapiens* as much as the conditions that generated the agricultural and industrial revolutions.

Large centralized economic and political institutions are demonstrating less and less interest in the welfare of common people in their pursuit of policies and practices that generate wealth for the few. If the mass of humanity is to preserve or reclaim the resources and social practices necessary to guard their own security and ability to care for the young, diverse actions in many local communities may prove to be more successful than national and international activities that tend to be stymied or co-opted by those in power. This is a lesson to be taken from the movements of indigenous peoples in Mexico and South America where coalitions of local groups have been able to challenge long-standing patterns of exploitation and domination.

Place-based education could prove to be one component of similar efforts in the United States and elsewhere. Young people who have developed a sense of connection to place and community will be more likely to invest their intelligence and energy in efforts to restore and preserve that which is necessary to support their lives. When they have developed skills and understandings that allow them to differentiate between life-enhancing and life-destroying activities and practices, they will be better able to resist those who would exploit and colonize them and to participate in activities that will regenerate the social and natural commons once central to the perpetuation of human communities. As experienced collaborators, they may be able to join with others to form effective organizations able to advance the welfare of the many rather than the few.

Regardless of our enthusiasm for place-based education, we do not see it by any means as a panacea for the economic, environmental, political, and social dilemmas that confront modernity. Vast changes will accompany the consequences of human overpopulation, the peaking of fossil fuel production, global climate change, and environmental degradation. Human communities will need to demonstrate a level of flexibility and adaptability rarely encountered in the historical record. There is no guarantee that people will be able to negotiate these challenges without a serious disruption of the forms of technological and social support that characterize contemporary life. Faith in progress and capitalism's invisible hand has driven and continues to drive the process of economic globalization. These concepts have proven to be a source of extraordinary creativity, but they are only ideas, and they appear to have run their course.

What the experience of learning in place does offer is familiarity with the local—its potentials and its limitations. If taught in ways that involve collaboration and the practice of kindness, this educational approach could also strengthen human ties and encourage the practice of mutuality and democracy. Grounded where possible in ways of being and knowing that have contributed to the sustainability of human communities in the past and present, place-based education might lead to the conservation and transmission of exactly the once common but diversely expressed understandings that must again become widespread if the descendants of today's people are to bequeath to their children cultures that foster a generosity of spirit, respect for others, and a deep and abiding love for this planet.

In contrast to globalization's assertion that there is no alterative to the course of modern development initially embraced by Western Europe and North America and now transported to nearly every country on the globe, we believe that the future of humanity will once more be tied to the emergence of diverse, regional societies grounded in the unique possibilities of their own locales. These societies need not be isolated from one another, but no longer will they be threatened by the imposition of a single economy and a single vision of what it means to live a good life. True diversity involves allowing a multiplicity of cultures to thrive and prosper, not the hypothetical provision of opportunities for diverse people to pursue the blandishments of consumerism and the market. In some small way, learning in place could help support the emergence or re-emergence of such cultures and the promise they hold for future generations.

REFERENCES

Blum, R. W., & Libbey, H. (Editors). (2004). School connectedness—strengthening health and education outcomes for teenagers. *Journal of School Health* 74(7), 229–299.

Bowers, C. A., & Apffel-Marglin, F. (Eds.). (2005). *Rethinking Freire: Globalization and the environmental crisis.* Mahwah, NJ: Lawrence Erlbaum Associates, Inc.

Epstein, J. (2001). *School, family, and community partnerships.* Boulder, CO: Westview Press.

Friedman, T. (2005). *The world is flat: A brief history of the twenty-first century.* New York; Farrar, Straus, and Giroux.

Furman, G. (Ed.). (2002). *School as community.* Albany: State University of New York Press.

Furman, G., & Gruenewald, D. (2004). Expanding the landscape of social justice: A critical ecological analysis. *Educational Administration Quarterly,* 40(1), 49–78.

Gelbspan, R. (2004). *Boiling point: How politicians, big oil and coal, journalists, and activists are fueling the climate crisis—and what we can do to avert disaster.* New York: Basic Books.

Gruenewald, D. (2003). The best of both worlds: A critical pedagogy of place. *Educational Researcher,* 22(4), 3–12.

Heinberg, R. (2005). *The party's over: Oil, war, and the fate of industrial societies.* Gabriola Island, BC: New Society Publishers.

Illich, I. (1971). *Deschooling society.* New York: Harper & Row.

Kolbert, E. (2005). The climate of man: Part I. *New Yorker,* April 25, 56–71.

Lieberman, A., & Miller, L. (2004). *Teacher leadership.* San Francisco: Jossey-Bass.

McNeil, L. (2000). *Contradictions of school reform: Educational costs of standardized testing.* New York: Routledge.

Melaville, A., Berg, A., & Blank, M. (2006). *Community-based learning: Engaging students for success and citizenship.* Washington, DC: Coalition for Community Schools.

Morgan, A. (1984). *The small community: Foundation of democratic life.* Yellow Springs, OH: Community Service.

National Commission on Teaching and America's Future. (2003). *No dream denied.* Washington, DC: NCTAF.

Rural School and Community Trust. (2003). *Place-based learning portfolio.* Washington, D.C.: Rural School and Community Trust.

Sobel, D. (2004). *Place-based education: Connecting classrooms and communities.* Greater Barrington, MA: The Orion Society.

York-Barr, J., & Duke, K. (2004). What do we know about teacher leadership? Findings from two decades of scholarship. *Review of Educational Research,* 74(3), 255–316.

AUTHOR INDEX

A

Abdi, S., 106
Abram, D., 292
Adams, J. Q., 54
Adwan, S., 262
Alaska Native Knowledge Network,
  129, 132, 150
Al-Haj, M., 269, 270
American Psychological Association,
  17–18
Apffel-Marglin, F., 148, 149, 348

B

Bakhtin, M., 278
Ball, E., 148
Banks, J. A., 199
Barnhardt, R., 3, 57, 114, 119, 120
Bar-On, D., 262–263
Bartsh, J., 2
Beaulieu., L. J., 180
Bellow, S., 31–32
Benvenisti, M., 260–261
Berenbaum, M. R., 162
Berg, A., 352, 355
Berlak, K., 256
Berlin, I., 203
Blank, M., 61, 74, 352, 355
Bluehouse, P., 57
Blum, R., 74, 355
Bortoft, H., 292
Bourdieu, P., 177

Bowers, C. A., xiii, xviii, xix, 145,
  148, 149, 150, 197, 348
Boyer, P., 117
Brander, B., 148
Brookfield, S., 295
Bruner, J. S., 214
Bullard, R., 145
Burch, W. R., 169
Butt, R., 266

C

Cahan, S., 214
Cajete, G., 57, 120, 145, 148
Cameron, J., 288, 289, 295, 298,
  303, 305
Campbell, M., 21
Canada, G., 105
Carlsen, A., 278
Carlson, B., 124
Carmona, R., 56
Casey, E., 142, 143, 260, 264, 303
Castells, M., 212
Cavallo, D., 159
Chaitin, J., 262
Clandinin, D. J., 265, 266
Coalition for Community Schools,
  150, 180
Colchado, J., 50
Coleman, J., 177
Comstock, A. B., 155, 163, 165
Conle, C., 256

359

Hatton, S. D., 19
Hay, P., 286
Haymes, S., 150, 212
He, M. F., 265, 273
Heidegger, M., 285, 298
Heinberg, R., 345
Hertz-Lazarowitz., 255, 259–260, 272
Hiss, T., 285, 290
Hobbs, D., 181
Hoody, L. L., 21–22, 330
hooks, b., 150, 212
Hug, J. W., 6
Hynes, M., xv

I

Illich, I., 355
Innovation Center for Community and Youth Development, 67, 81

J

Jackson, W., xvii, 149
Jacobs, J., 210
James, K., 118
Janz, B., 142
Johnson, J., 67
Jordan, W., 61

K

Kahn, P. H., 157
Kalekin-Fishman, D., 259, 274–276
Kawagley, A. O., 57, 119, 120
Keane, D., 161–162
Kehrberg, G. A., 7
Keinan, A., 262
Keith, M., 212
Kellert, S. R., 157
Kelly, P., 203–204
Key, S., 177
Kilpatrick, H., 1
King, M. L., 211
King, L., 126
King, V., 289
Knapp, C., 1, 5, 6, 7, 13, 15, 19
Kocur, Z., 214

Kolbert, E., 345
Korten, D., xi
Kretzman, J., 69, 78, 177
Kymlicka, W., 208, 210

L

Ladson-Billings, G., 139–140
Lai, A., 148
Laria, A., 107
Lasch, C., 207
Lawrence, B., 180
Libbey, H., 74, 355
Lieberman, A., 351
Lieberman, G. A., 21–22, 330
Liebowitz, M., 21
Lippard, L., 47
Louv, R., 158, 169–170
Luke, T., 145
Lyson, T. A., 180–181

M

Mabey, R., 169
MacIntyre, A., 208
Maine Commission on Secondary Education, 73
Malcolm, S. B., 162
Malpas, J., 297, 298, 303
Mander, J., xi, 217
Marsh, G. J., 159
Martinez, H., 104, 107
Massey, D., 142, 285, 290, 294
Mathews, F., 290
McDonough, M. H., 169
McGinty, M., 158
McKenna, D. D., 162
McKenna, K. M., 162
McLaren, P., 214
McLaughlin, M., 61, 74
McNight, J., 69, 78, 177
McPortland, J., 61
McTighe, J., 76
Mednick, A., 21
Melaville, A., 352, 355
Mergen. B., 157
Merleau-Ponty, M., 285
Milbrath, L., 301

Miller, L., 351
Mitchell, L. C., 317
Monbiot, G., 169
Morales-Vasquez, R., 197
Morgan, A., 348
Mulkey, D., 180
Mulligan, M., 303
Murphy, S., 290

N

Nabhan, G. P., 157
Nachtigal, P., 212
National Commission on Excellence
    in Education, xiii
National Commission on Teaching
    and America's Future, 352
Neperud, R. W., 214
Newmann, F. M., 6–7
Nieto, S., 103–104, 107
Noddings, N., 197, 199
Null, E., 184

O

Obiakor, F. E., 107
Obeidi, F., 262
Oliver, D. W., 6–7
Orr, D., xiv, 6, 146, 214, 284
Osborn, N. A., 12

P

Palmer, P. J., 31
Peel, J. D. Y., 206
Phelan, A. M., 266
Phillion, J., 265
Pile, S., 212
Plumwood, V., 288, 296
Powers, A. L., 6, 19
Prakash, M., xvii, 148
Prawat, R. S., 215
Preskill, S., 206
Proudman, B., 13
Putman, R., 68–69, 177
Pyle, R. M., 155, 157, 158, 161, 162,
    163, 168, 170

R

Raymond, D., 266
Read, P., 288
Reisberg, M., 148
Reiss, H., 217
Relph, E., 285
Robinson, M. W., 161
Rodriguez, L., 104
Rolls, E., 286
Rosenberg, M., 52
Ross, C., 98
Rugen, L., 21
Rural School and Community Trust,
    150, 348

S

Sage, S., 22
Sandel, M. J., 208
San Roque, C., 305
Savaria-Shore, M., 104, 107
Schiermann, S., 125
Schlesinger, A. M., 199
Schmidt, F., 178
Scollon, R., 125
Seamon, D., 285
Sears, S., 23
Seif, E., 76
Selznick, P., 208
Senechal, E., xvi, 3
Shapira, T., 272
Shapiro, E., 107
Shuman, M., xii
Silberstein, L., 265
Skelton, J., 105
Sleeter, C. M., 199
Smith, G., 6, 50, 148, 197
Smith, J., 292
Smith, P., 292
Snyder, G., 142, 285
Sobel, D., 6, 7, 148, 157, 317, 348
Soja, E., 146
Solnit, R., 36
Sorensen, M., 2
South Carolina Rural Education
    Grassroots Committee,
    188–189

INDEX

Political ecology, 146

Poverty, 145, 176

　Albuquerque, New Mexico, 235

Pre-industrial societies, achievements, xviii

Preservation of childhood, 316

Primary source material, 339

Privilege, 295

Problem-Based Learning (PBL), 22–23, 74

Problem-solving science, see Inquiry-based science

Program Evaluation and Education Research (PEER) Associates, 19

Project Change, 237, 248, see also Institute for Education and Community Leadership

Q

Quaker schools, 316

R

Rachel Marshall Outdoor Learning Lab, 332, 342

Racism, 51, 139, 145, 234–237, 247

Radical multiculturalists, 212

Rural Entrepreneurship through Action Learning (REAL) Enterprises, 186, see also Entrepreneurship

Real work, 331–332, 350

Real world learning, 355

Recycling, 328–329

Reflection, 25

Reflective autobiography, 319–320

Reggio Emilia schools, 316

Reinhabitation, vii, 135, 149–150, 346

　processes, 294

　requirements, 347

Relationship, 146–147

Republican political theory, 203, 204, 205, see also Jefferson; Liberal political theory

Resource-based industries

　decline, 66, see also Extraction-based economies

Roxbury Community College, 92, 93

　Environmental Studies Department, 101

Roxbury Environmental Empowerment Project (REEP), 86, 88–89, 91, 101, 107, 109, see also Grassroots organizations; Greater Egleston Community High School

Roxbury, Massachusetts, xvi, 85, 346, 352

Rural development strategies, 174, 176, see also Community development

Rural School and Community Trust, 2, 49, 150, 173-194, see also Annenberg Rural Challenge

　community revitalization, 69

　linking schools to community, 70, 79

　training tools, 81

S

Saami culture (Finland), 266

Sacred places, 33, 35, 36

Save the Children/USA, 245

Scholastic Art Awards, 46

Schooling

　grammar of, 141–142

　homogeneous, 140–141

Schools

　budgets, 72, 95

　consolidation, 180, 188

　disregard of place, 144

　factory-like, 33

　isolation from community, xviii, 179–180

　role in community development, 56, 180–182

School leaders

　collaboration with diverse communities, 352

377

9 780805 858648